palgrave advances in
irish history

Palgrave Advances
Series Standing Order ISBN 1-4039-3512-2 (Hardback) 1-4039-3513-0
(Paperback)
(*outside North America only*)

You can receive future titles in this series as they are published by placing a standing order. Please contact your bookseller or, in case of difficulty, write to us at the address below with your name and address, the title of the series and the ISBN quoted above.

Customer Services Department, Macmillan Distribution Ltd, Houndmills, Basingstoke, Hampshire RG21 6XS, England

palgrave advances in irish history

edited by

mary mcauliffe, katherine o'donnell
and leeann lane

palgrave
macmillan

First published 2009 by
PALGRAVE MACMILLAN

Palgrave Macmillan in the UK is an imprint of Macmillan Publishers Limited, registered in
England, company number 785998, of Houndmills, Basingstoke, Hampshire RG21 6XS.

Palgrave Macmillan in the US is a division of St Martin's Press LLC,
175 Fifth Avenue, New York, NY 10010.

Palgrave Macmillan is the global academic imprint of the above companies
and has companies and representatives throughout the world.

Palgrave® and Macmillan® are registered trademarks in the United States,
the United Kingdom, Europe and other countries

ISBN-13: 978-1-4039-3215-0 hardback
ISBN-10: 1-4039-3215-8 hardback
ISBN-13: 978-1-4039-3216-7 paperback
ISBN-10: 1-4039-3216-6 paperback

This book is printed on paper suitable for recycling and made from fully managed and
sustained forest sources. Logging, pulping and manufacturing processes are expected to
conform to the environmental regulations of the country of origin.

A catalogue record for this book is available from the British Library.

A catalog record for this book is available from the Library of Congress.

10 9 8 7 6 5 4 3 2 1
18 17 16 15 14 13 12 11 10 09

Printed and bound in Great Britain by
CPI Antony Rowe, Chippenham and Eastbourne

contents

editors' foreword

mary mcauliffe, katherine o'donnell and leeann lane

The *Palgrave Advances in Irish History* gives a much-needed historio-graphical and interpretative overview of Irish history from 1601 to the present. The chapters are thematic, focusing on established subdivisions of the field. The authors consider those histories that focus on the dec-ades and centuries after 1601 and the defeat of the Gaelic Earls at the Battle of Kinsale. Aimed at advanced undergraduate and postgraduate students, scholars and general readers it outlines the contours and key debates and methodologies in the field and offers frameworks for future developments.

While there has always been a large amount of history written in and about Ireland much of it has focused on the (putative) nation state and relations with Britain. It has only been in very recent decades that substantial work has been written by social and cultural historians, involving methods and archives not traditionally employed by political historians. The book consists of ten chapters with a preface by Professor Nancy J. Curtin that introduces the book and situates the work within the contexts of the discipline of Irish history and the current interna-tional development of Irish Studies.

The chapters are thematic rather than chronological as this enables a study of the connections, contradictions, interactions and disruptions that might be lost in a chronological survey. Each chapter gives a critical appraisal of the findings, themes, debates and methodologies of a par-ticular aspect of Irish history-writing. Contemporary political crises and their ensuing cultural debates have informed, energised and polarised the writing of Irish history. The delineation of how political agendas have impacted on both the writing and reception of Irish history is the central theme for all of our authors.

An interesting aspect of this volume is that besides its focus on politi-cal histories it offers a comprehensive account of Irish history in its manifold aspects, such as identity, labour, local, institutional and wom-en's history and history of the Irish population and diasporas, sexuality and culture, language and traditions. This work is a welcome introduc-tion to the wide-ranging and dynamic writings of a younger generation of historians.

preface

nancy j. curtin

We might date the beginning of modern Irish historiography in 1936 with the founding of the journal *Irish Historical Studies*. The challenge then was to nurture a scientifically based history, to cleanse the historical record of its mythological clutter, to engage in what one of its eminent founders, T. W. Moody, later called 'the mental war of liberation from servitude to the myth' of Irish nationalist history, by applying value-neutral methods to the evidence, separating fact from destructive and divisive fictions.[1] With the confidence of positivist science behind them, generations of historians trained by the deliverers T. W. Moody, R. Dudley Edwards and D. B. Quinn proceeded to scratch beneath the surface of the received past, producing a history that was technically impressive, but that had become disassociated from popular collective memories, depriving the Irish people of the 'beneficent legacy' of a national history. At least this was the charge of the Rev. Brendan Bradshaw in a provocative article in 1989 that launched the so-called revisionist controversy.[2] The good news is that it is all over. The Irish state has heeded the call for a more 'usable past' by its assertive sponsorship of the commemorations of the great milestones of the Irish past, such as the Great Famine, the United Irishmen's rebellion of 1798, and more recently the Rising of 1916. Such efforts have employed and encouraged the work of professional historians, making it accessible for the Irish at home and abroad. There are many reasons for these commemorations, not the least being the ending of conflict in Northern Ireland and with it the fear that the past was too contentious and politically threatening.

The impact of the revisionist debate on the history produced in the academy, however, is rather difficult to trace. Most of the chapters in this volume refer to the controversy but less as a point of departure to situate the newer work in Irish history and more as a simple chronological or developmental marker. While at times the revisionist debate was characterised by bitterness and distortion, ultimately it led to a close examination of the practice of Irish history and a growing awareness among those practitioners that the history they were writing needed to transcend the nationalist preoccupations of many anti-revisionists and the excessively empirical tendencies of the revisionists. What was tedious about the controversy was a tendency to situate it in a simple

Irish–British polarity. What followed though, and indeed, was certainly in progress under the radar of the adversaries' scrutiny, was a flowering of Irish history in multiple varieties, as fully displayed in this refreshing and useful collection of essays.

One of the reasons for the growing irrelevance of the revisionist/ anti-revisionist debate has been the recent tendency to challenge the nation as the basic and ascendant unit of analysis for historians across the profession. History has always been one of the more secure disciplines in the academy, and the assumption that its practice was best undertaken and understood in an exclusive national framework had long gone unquestioned. So British, American or Irish historians could wallow in their exceptionalism and empiricism while other disciplines, some equally entrenched in the academy, and others battering at the gates, began to focus on transnational and cross-disciplinary questions. Literary studies and anthropology, for example, appropriated history, and attempted, to the outrage of so many historians, to inject it with some theoretical authority and utility. Structural changes in the academy, like the relative decline of history faculty positions in relation to rising student populations, induced employers, demanding more bang for their buck, to hire in regional or global fields, or at least to expect that their national historians would spread out. Innovative interdisciplinary programmes – American Studies, European Studies, Medieval Studies and even Irish Studies – contended with established traditional disciplines for students and college resources. This is not to say that national history has lost its high position. It just has to make room at the top for competing approaches, and inject itself with a little theoretical or methodological relevance. These essays demonstrate that Irish historians have responded with alacrity to this challenge as a constructive opportunity. This response has had to address two basic questions. Firstly, how, spatially and theoretically, should the Irish historian situate his/her national unit of analysis? And secondly, how has the Irish subject been constructed through that space as well as through time?

If Irish history is to be seen as having relevance to other histories and disciplines it must shed its limiting parochialism and so-called exceptionalism. The Irish experience is too particular, so it is assumed, to conform to general patterns and can, therefore, safely be ignored by British, European or colonial historians.[3] It is to address this marginalisation that historians have been widening the spatial arena in which Irish history would be situated. One time-honoured but hardly uncontested approach has been to see Ireland as a colony in the Atlantic World. This has been countered by those who see the structures and dynamics of Ireland as more akin to European society. And most recently, others still will argue that Ireland must be seen as part of an Anglo-Celtic archipelago – the New British history. Constitutionally, Ireland has been everything – a colony, a kingdom, a province and a republic, but each status has been complicated by the presence of another. Thus, as a colony Ireland was a little too proximate and shared many of the characteristics of a frontier borderland, as a kingdom it was less than sovereign, as a province it was less than integrated and as a republic it was a little too colonial.[4] Of course all national histories are particular in their way, but by casting Ireland in a larger spatial unit of analysis, what might appear as anomalous might be both typical and illuminating.[5]

Connecting things Irish to more ubiquitous global processes involves not only looking outwards but also looking inwards, to the construction of the Irish subject. History is about nations but it is also about people, how they see themselves in relation to their families, their communities, their churches, their states, how they experience quotidian life through generations, through opportunities and setbacks, how their expectations and aspirations are nourished or limited. A truly usable past should be, as E. P. Thompson has enjoined, one that 'helps us to know who we are, why we are here, what human possibilities have been disclosed, and as much as we can know of the logic and forms of social process'.[6] And this challenge, of necessity, is interdisciplinary.

History, one of the oldest and most complacent of academic disciplines, is, ironically, a hotbed of disciplinary hybridity. The denizens of history departments engage in political history, economic history, social history and one could go on. Interdisciplinarity is hardly new. But the challenge coming from the interlopers in literary and cultural studies or anthropology who have questioned the practice of history as too empiricist and transparent in its treatment of the sources, has been regarded by some historians as an irritant.[7] But even when the challenge has been perceived as hostile, it has stimulated engagement. And much of the historiography highlighted in these essays, shows considerable receptivity to the theoretical and new methodological possibilities staked out by such identity-interrogating approaches as postcolonialism and feminist theory. Postmodernist theory in general has significantly questioned the possibility of simply recovering the past, the essence of the traditional historian's *métier*. The empirical enterprise of narration is no straightforward method, complicated as it is by the subjectivity and context of the historian and the limits of the remnant historical record.

And yet, what the editors and contributors to this volume have done is not only to engage with new approaches, but also to validate and reinvigorate the scientifically based methods lauded by modern Irish history's founders. In addressing contested questions of whether Ireland was or was not a colony, whether the default position in Anglo-Irish relations is conflict or integration, whether the Act of Union was catastrophic or beneficial to Ireland, Irish historians are responding to the old injunction to think globally and act locally. Historians apply their empirical training, scour the archives, reclaim new sources and ask new questions, questions specific to Irish history but also those that resonate with other disciplines, national histories and general processes.

Palgrave Advances in Irish History carries tremendous expectations and potentially hazardous burdens. Such a guide should mark the contours and key methodological and substantive debates and developments in the field as well as point to the most fruitful avenues of future research. It should be an introduction into the field for students and interested amateurs, while at the same time offering the professionals, the Irish historians, but also those scholars in other fields and disciplines, a more sophisticated engagement. By charting the course of Irish history-writing over the last several decades this book does all that, but is perhaps more remarkable for what it does not do. It offers no new orthodoxy about how Irish history should be practised, but rather a methodological and theoretical pluralism with a purpose. These chapters focus on the full range of subfields within Irish history, not only the standard political, social and economic histories, but also the histories of gender and sexuality, institutions, the diaspora, identity construction and the arts. Even that is not an exhaustive list, and readers may well quibble about what is excluded or included. Readers may also question the conclusions drawn by the various contributors on the state of their art. But a purposive pluralism relishes dialogue rather than imposing boundaries or limits. And where the tendency of the new approaches has been to challenge disciplinary and national boundaries, they have also, as these chapters reveal, challenged internal boundaries. Methodological and archival innovations in one subfield may inspire adaptive and fruitful responses within another subfield. This volume is organised in separate chapters, but they are also contiguous. And so this volume showcases the full range of Irish histories.

As an American-born historian of Ireland, working in a North American university, and directing an interdisciplinary Irish Studies programme, I fully welcome this extraordinarily useful, thoughtful and nearly comprehensive collection. Its pedagogical uses are obvious and abundant, but I also learnt a lot about the practice of my craft in subfields different from my own. But mostly I felt a pride in and enthusiasm for the variety of Irish histories being written. In conversation with my colleagues in other fields or disciplines, I can refer them to this volume for the interesting ways in which Irish historians have been interrogating the concept of the diaspora. Or I can recommend as a model of interdisciplinarity the chapter on art and culture. Mostly I can say anything you are doing, we are doing too, and in ways that may inspire you. Come take a look.

notes

1. T. W. Moody, 'Irish History and Irish Mythology', *Hermathena*, cxxiv (Summer 1978), p. 8.
2. Brendan Bradshaw, 'Nationalism and Historical Scholarship in Modern Ireland', *Irish Historical Studies*, xxvi, no. 104 (November 1989), pp. 335–6. The most important contributions to the controversy have been reprinted, Ciaran Brady (ed.), *Interpreting Irish History: The Debate on Historical Revisionism, 1938–1944* (Dublin, 1994). Also see D. George Boyce and Alan O'Day (eds), *The Making of Modern Irish History: Revisionism and the Revisionist Controversy* (London, 1996). For my own contribution, see Nancy J. Curtin, '"Varieties of Irishness": Historical Revisionism, Irish Style', *The Journal of British Studies*, vol. 35, no. 2, (April 1996), pp. 195–219.
3. The most stunning example of such omission may be Linda Colley, *Britons: Forging the Nation, 1707–1837* (New Haven, Conn., 1992).
4. See, e.g. Andrew Murphy, 'Reviewing the Paradigm: A New Look at Early Modern Ireland', *Éire-Ireland*, vol. 31, nos. 3–4 (Fall/Winter 1996), pp. 13–40; S. J. Connolly, *Religion, Law, and Power: The Making of Protestant Ireland 1660–1760* (Oxford, 1992); Jane Ohlmeyer, 'Seventeenth-Century Ireland and the New British and Atlantic Histories', *The American Historical Review*, 104, no. 2 (April, 1999): pp. 446–62.
5. See, for example, the comparisons that have been forged by Irish and Indian historians: C. A. Bayly, 'Ireland, India and the Empire: 1780–1914', *Transactions of the Royal Historical Society*, 6th Ser., vol. 10 (2000), pp. 377–97, and Michael Silvestri, '"The Sinn Féin of India": Irish Nationalism and the Policing of Revolutionary Terrorism in Bengal', *The Journal of British Studies*, vol. 39, no. 4 (October, 2000), pp. 454–86.
6. Dorothy Thompson (ed.), *The Essential E. P. Thompson* (New York, 2001), p. 455.
7. See, for example, Stephen Howe, *Ireland and Empire: Colonial Legacies in Irish History and Culture* (Oxford, 2000).

1

irish political history: guidelines and reflections

patrick maume

introduction

The political history of modern Ireland has been dominated by the challenge of how to achieve a stable political order whose legitimacy would be generally accepted. For most of the last three centuries it was believed that the struggle for control of the state, and the actions of those who actually controlled it, were the central determinants of the Irish experience. Historians and politicians debated whether the story of the Kingdom of Ireland revolved around the extension of the authority of Crown jurisdiction over the whole island, or whether it was the assertion of legislative independence culminating, for what became the dominant Irish political tradition, in the Republic? For conservatives, Irish problems stemmed from barbaric anarchic resistance to law as such, thereby promoting violence and ignorance and paralysing commerce; if this resistance were ever to prevail, anarchy and tyranny would ensue. Liberals and nationalists, who were overlapping but not identical in their thinking, asked *whose* law was being resisted and whether the 'barbarians' opposed civilisation as such or rather the arbitrary rule of a self-aggrandising elite.[1] For Whigs or nationalists Ireland's religious development was explicable in terms of the effects of state decisions. The Establishment of the Anglican Protestant Church and the accompanying Penal Laws, which impinged on the economic, political and educational freedoms of Catholics from the late seventeenth into the nineteenth century, and official favouritism persisting when formal disabilities had been removed. Economic problems were similarly attributable to past trade restrictions, and their solution (for many) lay in protectionism and histories of the land question were written in terms of land legislation. In the recent past, popular perceptions of

1

Irish history have been dominated by a 'nationalist-Whig' narrative, which sees Ireland as a single entity pursuing an inexorable struggle to shake off colonial domination, with differences over whether this necessarily required full separation from Britain. The Unionist counter-narrative derived from the conservative view, combining elements of the defence of Protestant ascendancy, a view of Britishness as more conducive to liberal-universalism than Irish nationalism, and Ulster particularism defined in Protestant–Unionist terms. These histories were disseminated through official and unofficial educational systems, the latter operating through a mass print culture and the associational networks which disseminated it, which can be seen as voicing the aspirations of popular audiences, or trying to reshape that audience in respectable terms.

In recent literature it is also possible to distinguish a modernist narrative, which sees the central theme of Irish history as the struggle for economic and social modernisation, a view with roots in both nationalist and liberal unionist historiography, and disintegrationist tendencies which aim to unsettle one or more dominant narratives by recuperating groups or individuals excluded from dominant self-images: feminists, immigrant groups, agricultural and urban labourers, etc. These cannot be separated from the influence of nationalism and unionism; hence, for example, the appearance of rival pro-union and anti-union traditions of socialist history.[2] Any form of popular history is expressed through a genealogy of political movements with whom the protagonist selectively identifies, finding their experience relevant, and aiming to carry them on to victory. The discipline of Irish history has, since the mid- twentieth century, been marked by a debate on what has become known as 'revisionism'.[3] Irish historical revisionism began by challenging the 'Irish-Ireland' tradition of history, which claimed the Irish people are a unified Celtic nation viciously oppressed throughout their history by English/British imperialism.[4] In understanding the heated nature of discussions of 'revisionist' history, it should be understood that many people in Ireland retain a strong sense of their received version of history as a personal possession, and react angrily to what they experience as attempted dispossession. This derives from such factors as the use of history in ongoing political debates (not least over Northern Ireland), a sense of local identity which remains strong, albeit declining with increased urbanisation and mobility and, especially when dealing with relatively recent events, oral tradition and personal knowledge. An example of these factors is Meda Ryan's defence of the West Cork Irish Republican Army (IRA) leader Tom Barry against Peter Hart's claim that he killed prisoners after the Kilmichael ambush in the War of

Independence.[5] Ryan also argued that certain killings committed by the West Cork IRA in the same period were not sectarian murders of civilians, as argued by Hart and accepted by many nationalist leaders at the time, but reprisals against spies and informers.[6] Although Ryan's book contains useful material it assumes Barry and the War of Independence IRA should not be treated as historical figures whose actions can be discussed and criticised; the only legitimate response to their actions during the War of Independence is unqualified identification and uncritical regurgitation of their self-representations into an Ireland changed beyond recognition since they acted or wrote.[7]

Critics of revisionist history, such as Brendan Bradshaw,[8] complain that it reflects an unrealistic attempt at producing a 'value-free' history, which attempts to be purely factual and morally neutral. In doing so, revisionists evade the violence and suffering which punctuate the Irish experience and the role of human agency in these traumas. This is often extended into accusations of a positivism that assumes everything that happened was inevitable, thereby colluding with power-holders past and present. It is arguable, however, that the historical approach associated with the pioneers of Irish revisionism, T. W. Moody, R. D. Edwards and the journal they founded, *Irish Historical Studies*, is not in fact 'value-free'. On the contrary it could be argued that it reflects an ethical commitment to civic peace through mutual understanding and recognition of the Other based on a common ground of scholarly technique, as opposed to the view that the Other is fundamentally illegitimate and must disappear through assimilation or expulsion. Anyone who has read the urbane sneers of J. P. Mahaffy,[9] before the foundation of Trinity College, as he insinuated that Ireland was inhabited only by naked savages, or the paranoid rants of Fr. Timothy Corcoran[10] (in the *Catholic Bulletin* and similar publications) maintaining that every Protestant and Unionist must have been in conscious bad faith and that it can never be admitted that a Catholic historian might have been wrong or a Protestant right about anything, will recognise the attractions of such a revisionist commitment in 1938.[11]

Defences of revisionism should bear in mind that it is misleading to present the historical process as a conflict between unthinking 'tradition' and critical history.[12] There are polemicists who maintain that 'traditional' views must be maintained, even if false, because of the, allegedly, beneficial overall effect of the national narrative[13] or who see Irish history in terms of a conflict where to admit any correctness on one side denies all legitimacy to the other,[14] but these positions do not exhaust the issue. 'Traditional' views of particular historical events

often arose for concrete reasons, even if they were and are occasion-
ally distorted by being preserved in memory after the circumstances
against which they were defined have vanished and been forgotten.
For example, mid-Victorian landlordism may not have been as ruthlessly exploitative and tyrannical as generally believed, but anyone who
reads the pro-landlord *Dublin Evening Mail* of the 1880s with its sneers
at 'a mud-hut franchise' will understand much about why landlordism
attracted such hatred. The ironic mode of narration favoured by many
revisionist historians is not necessarily morally superior to the tragic
or reverential tone of much 'traditional' history; the problem arises
when reverence or irony appears not as the outcome of critical thought,
but is used to preclude it.

This chapter primarily deals with the modern period of Irish history.
It should be borne in mind, however, that until the end of the Union
between Britain and Ireland which came into effect on 1 January 1801,[15]
Irish political debates often referred back to the mediaeval period, a
reflection of the fact that until post-1960s' expansion of higher education and the decline of the institutional churches and of classical
education a much higher proportion of the Irish historical profession
were mediaevalists than nowadays. James Lydon's *The Making of Ireland*
(1998) is an original survey by a mediaevalist which emphasises how
issues about the constitutional relationship between Britain and Ireland
in the modern period had clear mediaeval precedents, an interesting
'primordialist' corrective to views of Irish history drawing on Ernest
Gellner[16] and other modernisation theorists, which depict present-day
national identities as by-products of modernity.[17] Other survey works,
which are essential to the study of early modern and modern Irish history, include Alvin Jackson's *Ireland 1798–1998: Politics and War* (1999).
Jackson places his work in the contested territories of Irish history,
within a framework that is chronological and integrates, unusually, a
comparative view of Ulster-Scots, Protestants, Unionist traditions and
the Nationalist, Irish, Catholic traditions. Paul Bew's *Ireland: The Politics
of Enmity 1783–2006* (2007) is another useful account structured around
successive attempts to find a political framework for the reconciliation
of the rival communities, with particular emphasis on the use and misuse of the legacy of Edmund Burke. Its treatment of the violence and
disasters of Irish history in the period and of the persistent attempts to
resolve them lays particular stress on the vast amount of underexam-
ined material on the political histories of the nineteenth and twentieth
centuries and the continuing capacity of original research to complicate
received narratives.

eighteenth-century ireland and the patriot tradition

While the history of eighteenth-century Ireland is still dominated by the political upheavals of its previous decades, a major scholarly gain of the later twentieth century has been the ability to see beyond the retrospective knowledge of the ultimate fate of its governing elite, beyond later attitudes to corruption and religious intolerance, to come to an understanding of how the system worked and appeared to those who ran it.[18] Even the terminology used to describe the eighteenth-century élite is affected by hindsight. The terms 'Anglo-Irish' and 'Protestant Ascendancy' are often used to refer to the Anglican aristocracy alone, whereas 'Protestant Ascendancy' (which W. J. McCormack has shown to have been coined by conservatives in the 1780s) actually referred to the legal supremacy of the whole Anglican community over the Catholics. The position of non-Anglican Protestants was left ambiguous as circumstances dictated; in eighteenth-century usage 'Protestant' often referred to Anglicans alone, hence Wolfe Tone's ambition to unite 'Catholic, Protestant and Dissenter'. Edmund Burke criticised this form of supremacism as unsustainable precisely on the grounds that while Catholic plebeians might be persuaded to defer to a Protestant-dominated aristocracy as their natural superiors, they would hardly extend such deference to their Protestant equals or inferiors. 'Anglo-Irish', an older term could refer to any person of settler descent, and, from the late nineteenth century, was also sometimes used to refer to any Irish speaker of English. The Protestant elite was often referred to (or referred to itself) as 'the Irish nation' – that is, the political nation, those who participated in government and enjoyed civic rights. The Anglican Archbishop John George Beresford, who died in 1862, recalled shortly before his death that when he was a boy the expression 'the Irish nation' had usually been taken to mean the Protestants, whereas now it was usually assumed to mean the Roman Catholics. Many nineteenth-century nationalists (such as Thomas Davis) as well as Unionists such as Thomas MacKnight argued that Ireland could not call itself a nation until the term was used unselfconsciously to include the members of all Ireland's religious communities.

Debate continues about how far eighteenth-century Ireland was either a relatively 'normal' European *ancien regime* society[19] or a dysfunctional colony with a minority ruling by force over an alien majority. Its crimes and vices, however, are increasingly seen in their contemporary context rather than as they appeared in the retrospective gaze of nineteenth-century reformers.[20] One of the best introductions to eighteenth-century

Ireland is David Dickson, *Ireland: New Foundations, 1660–1800* (2nd edition, 2000) which provides a welcome synthesis of the ongoing reinterpretation by academics of Early Modern Ireland. One major criticism of a history focussing on the Irish Parliament of the eighteenth century has been that it overlooks the political identity of the Catholic majority and often underplays the appetite for radicalism during this period, particularly in the 1790s. The image of a native people reduced to universal immiseration, found in Daniel Corkery's *Hidden Ireland* (1924) itself reproducing what were seen as the commonplaces of social history, has been challenged by the recognition of the survival of an 'underground gentry' of large tenant farmers.[21] After years of neglect Irish Jacobitism has been rehabilitated into an exciting avenue of research by authors such as Breandan Ó Buachalla[22] and Eamonn Ó Ciardha in his *Ireland and the Jacobite cause, 1685–1766: A Fatal Attachment (2002)*. Jacobitism with its ideology of allegiance to the deposed and exiled Stuart kings, is now seen as a serious political project commanding widespread allegiance well into the eighteenth century throughout Ireland, while the existence of agrarian secret societies has been rescued from conservative denunciations and later nationalist/liberal denial, co-option or condescension.[23]

The eighteenth-century Patriot tradition, seen by admirers as encapsulated in the relatively autonomous settlement of 1782 known as 'Grattan's Parliament',[24] has been debunked so often that it is hard for twenty-first-century readers to realise the nature and extent of its attractions for earlier commentators. Liberal unionists and radical nationalists rapidly pointed out that the eighteenth-century Irish Parliament, dominated by government appointees and representatives of an 'Irish [political] nation' which was predominantly aristocratic and exclusively Protestant, are problematic ancestors for the populist nationalism of the nineteenth century.[25] The view that Grattan's Parliament would have repealed all anti-Catholic legislation but for malign English pressure is now recognised as retrospective fabrication. There was significant pressure from Westminster to relax these Penal Laws; the major repeal measures in the 1790s reflected a tactical 'race for the Catholics' with patriots and Westminster competing for Catholic support.[26] Jacqueline Hill's study of the Dublin guilds under the unreformed corporation of the eighteenth and early nineteenth centuries shows how their Patriot politics, based on corporate privilege, metamorphosed into support for the Union with Britain as a bulwark of Protestant ascendancy.[27]

Recent scholars such as Gerard O'Brien emphasise that 'patriotism' was less a coherent position than a rhetoric used by political 'Outs' to harass political 'Ins' and make themselves worth buying off.[28] The representative figure of the tradition may not be Grattan, with his recognition that 'the Irish Protestant cannot be free so long as the Irish Catholic is a slave' but the ruthlessly job-seeking and anti-Catholic arriviste John Foster (1740–1828).[29] Modern social and economic historians (notably L. M. Cullen) add that the image of a country raised by Grattan's Parliament to prosperity within a few years, by legislation promoting tillage and encouraging Irish industries and still invoked to support Fianna Fáil's (FFs)[30] policies of encouraging tillage and industrial protectionism in the 1930s, underestimates earlier economic development and ignores the influence of demand from an industrialising Britain.[31] Where then did the glowing image of Grattan's Parliament originate? In the sense of political betrayal and economic decay after the failure of the Union to produce political stability and British-style growth; in the decaying physical relics of eighteenth-century grandeur conspicuous in Dublin; in the fact that eighteenth-century Patriots, unlike United Irishmen, could be presented as respectable models for Irish nationalism within the British system; in the personal cult of Grattan, appealing to constitutional nationalists and liberal unionists cataloguing lost opportunities for an Irish patriotism encompassing (or led by) the landed gentry.[32] The image of Grattan as eminently constitutionalist has recently been challenged by Daniel Mansergh, who presents him as pioneering mass mobilisation to bring pressure to bear on administration, and as a half-willing initiator of a radicalisation which escalated into the violence of 1798.[33]

the united irishmen

The United Irish Society, founded as a reformist movement and which developed into the secret society behind the great Rising of 1798 was, for a long time, too sensitive a topic for direct discussion after its defeat. Loyalists fitted the rebellion to the template of accounts of seventeenth-century conflicts which depicted Irish Protestants as victims and Catholics as perennial persecutors, while liberals (and many surviving rebels) attributed it to official provocation. A countervailing tendency towards romanticising the rebels as selfless heroes developed with Young Ireland[34] and the belated gathering of oral testimony by figures such as R. R. Madden and Luke Cullen.[35] This became dominant in the later nineteenth century, encouraged by celebrations of the 1898 centenary as a nationalist counterblast to Queen Victoria's 1897 Diamond Jubilee. The Wexford-born Franciscan friar P. F. Kavanagh produced a *People's History of 1798* combining criticism of the United Irishmen as a secret society with exaltation of those Wexford priests (a small minority condemned by their bishop) who participated in the Rising. This 'priests and people' interpretation dominated commemorations in 1898 and 1948.[36] The first major post-independence narrative history of 1798, *The Year of Liberty* (1969) by Thomas Pakenham, is shaped by the Northern Troubles and emphasises violence and bloodshed.

The run-up to the bicentenary in 1998 produced a wide range of new publications.[37] One of the dominant interpretative frames was supplied by Kevin Whelan. Whelan argued that accounts such as Pakenham's were distorted by reliance on loyalist propaganda, apologetics emanating from liberals and defeated rebels and retrospective accounts by Catholic populists, all of whom had a vested interest in downplaying popular politicisation and portraying the rebellion as a spontaneous uprising by ignorant and bigoted (or peaceful until provoked) masses. Instead, Whelan argues, the Wexford Rising was a planned mobilisation by a pre-existing organisation. Whelan's villains are the Dublin Castle administration, presented as manipulating if not actually creating Orangeism, as well as the Catholic hierarchy and Daniel O'Connell, for propagating a specifically Catholic version of Irishness which Whelan sees as displacing the Enlightenment views disseminated by the United Irishmen and – it is implied – only recovered again in the 1990s.[38] Another of Whelan's contributions to the ongoing and unresolved 1798 debate, the *Fellowship of Freedom: The United Irishmen and 1798* (1998) reflect the changes in historiography around United Irishmen research and writing. He includes and expands on work by academics such as Nancy J. Curtin,[39] allowing for the appreciation of the success of United Irishmen propaganda and other aspects such as the role of women in Irish radicalism, the influence of freemasonry and the influence of the United Irishmen on social and cultural thought. Curtin's work is seen as one of the most sustained and comprehensive reassessments of the subject in her detailed analysis of the United Irishmen and their success in enlisting mass, popular support.

Another pupil of L. M. Cullen, Tom Dunne, argues that the Whelan interpretation is unrealistic in assuming that the Catholic peasantry either had no political culture of their own or were entirely transformed by a few years of United Irish propaganda. He states that considerable evidence exists of more atavistic, and perfectly understandable, popular attitudes based on memories of conquest, dispossession and religious persecution, and that the good intentions of the United Irishmen and the atrocities and propaganda of the loyalists cannot obliterate the consequences of invoking widespread popular violence.[40] Much of the scholarship on 1798 concentrates on why the Rebellion took the course it did. While works by Whelan, Cullen, O'Flanagan and others[41] are invaluable the most detailed account of the Rebellion in Wexford can be found in Daniel Gahan, *The People's Rising: Wexford in 1798* (1995). A. T. Q. Stewart, *The Summer Soldiers: The 1798 Rebellion in Antrim and Down* (1995), deals with Ulster while Kildare and Wicklow are the focus of Liam Chambers' *Rebellion in Kildare, 1790–1803* (1998) and *The Rebellion in Wicklow, 1798* (1998) by Ruan O'Donnell respectively. Ian McBride's *Scripture Politics: Ulster Presbyterians and Irish Radicalism in the Late Eighteenth Century* (1998) discusses how far the particular form which the United Irish movement took in Ulster was influenced by specifically Presbyterian beliefs.

the union and o'connellism

Moving on from the historiography of the 1798 Rebellion, two interpretative frameworks are discernable in discussions of Irish politics under the Union, recuperating debates that took place throughout the Union's existence. Liberal unionists such as William Cooke Taylor argued that the Union had been unavoidable and it could be saved by constructive unionist politics.[42] Nationalist accounts emphasised the corruption which smoothed its ratification and argued that its co-option by Ascendancy, post-Union resistance to Catholic Emancipation and the general tardiness of reform were inevitable, not only because of anti-Irish and anti-Catholic prejudice in Britain, but because the sheer difference between Ireland and Britain made their political cultures incompatible. The debate, about the extent to which the corruption used to secure the Union exceeded contemporary standards of political manoeuvre, is continued by G. C. Bolton, Patrick Geoghegan and David Wilkinson.[43] A useful summary of the Act and its historiography is Michael Brown, Patrick Geoghegan and James Kelly's (eds) *The Irish Act of Union, 1800: Bicentennial Essays* (2003). The London-Irish Liberal journalist, Richard Barry O'Brien, is now chiefly remembered as the official biographer of Charles Stewart Parnell (1846–1891), but his contemporary political significance rested on his voluminous compilations, which documented the repeated blocking of reforms within the Union by landlord interests and which argued that Liberal principles logically entailed granting the desire of the Irish majority for autonomy.[44] Liberal Unionists such as Thomas MacKnight put forward a rival narrative which listed reforms undertaken by Liberal governments under the Union and arguing that only by its continuation could Ireland be preserved as a viable polity, since the alternative was sectarian civil war and economic ruin.[45] The central problem with these arguments was that the inability of Unionists to secure mass political support outside Ulster after the extension of the franchise in 1885 meant that such 'constructive Unionism' implied a form of 'enlightened despotism' hard to square with liberal principles. For an intensive meditation on the workings and long-term consequences of the Union the most comprehensive works are Oliver MacDonagh, *Ireland: The Union and its Aftermath* (1977) and *States of Mind* (1985). For a view which emphasises the limitations and hypocrisies of British Liberalism as applied to Ireland, see the writings of J. J. Lee, such as *The Modernisation of Irish Society 1848–1918* (1973).

The campaign for Catholic emancipation is often personified in Daniel O'Connell (1775–1847), obscuring his numerous allies. One of the key works which allows a comprehensive overview of O'Connell and Catholic Emancipation is Fergus O'Ferrall's *Catholic Emancipation: Daniel O'Connell and the Birth of Irish Democracy* (1985). The starting point for any modern study of O'Connell is the eight volumes of O'Connell's correspondence edited by Maurice O'Connell (1973–80) and also his *Daniel O'Connell: The Man and his Politics* (Dublin, 1990). This provides the basis for Oliver MacDonagh's classic biography *O'Connell* (1991).[46] O'Connell's parliamentary career is generally regarded as more anti-climactic; though he allied with the Whig Party (especially after 1836) and secured legislation on tithe and local government, the value of these concessions was limited by conservative resistance and the Whigs themselves, who generally viewed O'Connell with contempt. Later separatists argued that while O'Connell advocated non-violence he might not have obtained those concessions without the peasant resistance, and noted that while refusing office himself he secured it for others. This reveals a tension in the interpretation of Emancipation; from a primarily nationalist standpoint, office-taking under the Union represented corruption, but it could also be seen as breaking traditional Tory-Orange dominance of administration and fulfilling Catholic Emancipation. Angus D. MacIntyre's *The Liberator: Daniel O'Connell and the Irish Party, 1830–1847* (1965) deals specifically with O'Connell as a parliamentarian. Desmond Keenan's *Ireland 1800–1850* (2001) and *The Grail of Catholic Emancipation* (2002) are more sceptical studies, which draw heavily on the Whig-liberal unionist newspaper the *Dublin Evening Post*.

Irene Whelan has shown that the decisive factor in driving Catholic bishops to supporting O'Connell's populist agitation for Catholic emancipation was the fear that resurgent Evangelical Protestantism might gain sufficient influence to put the power of the state behind Protestant proselytism.[47] Thereafter a significant theme of episcopal politics was the desire to improve Catholic representation within the administrative apparatus and create a Catholic professional class responsive to the wishes of the hierarchy. Secondary schools such as Clongowes[48] aimed to create such an élite, even if their products tended to move across Europe and the Empire rather than remain in Ireland. The attendant struggle for a Catholic University was an attempt to supervise all stages of the professional formation of such a class; and the unwillingness of any British government to recognise such an institution reflected the limitations of any attempt to underpin the Union by co-opting the Catholic clergy. This is extensively detailed in Donal Kerr's *Peel, Priests and Politics: Sir Robert Peel's Administration and the Roman Catholic Church in Ireland, 1841–46* (1984) and also in his work *Nation of Beggars? Priests, People, and Politics in Famine Ireland, 1846–1852* (1998).[49] This administration-centred 'Catholic Whiggery' existed throughout the Union, in shifting an unstable combination with various shades of nationalism and liberal unionism; the bishops were unable to provide stable mass support for such an elite, while nationalists such as Charles Gavan Duffy (1816–1903) and A.M. Sullivan (1829–84) argued that 'faith and fatherland' were better served by the nationalism of a predominantly Catholic people than by a self-serving elite, who would inevitably ingratiate themselves with existing power structures and betray clerical patrons once these were of no further use to them.[50] The result of these tensions and compromises, as well as the Catholic faith of the majority and the commitment of Catholic religious, was a major Catholic clerical role in the administration of Irish social policy that survived for most of the twentieth century.

The nineteenth-century historiography of O'Connell tended to be based on the image of O'Connell as a specifically Catholic and clericalist hero-figure or on the Young Ireland critique of him as a great man corrupted by autocratic leadership, a desire to make deals with Whig administrations to obtain jobs for relatives, and a 'morbid' fear of bloodshed. The critical view was strengthened by the defeat of the Home Rule party by Sinn Féin, who presented themselves as heirs to Young Ireland and cast their constitutionalist opponents as neo-O'Connellite job-hunters. An extreme expression of this interpretation is the view that O'Connell's campaign for Catholic Emancipation merely benefited West-British Catholic jobbers whereas national independence would have automatically brought religious equality.[51] The 1905 publication of O'Connell's youthful journal, which revealed that he had been

alienated from Catholic orthodoxy for a period, began a renewed interest in O'Connell as reforming radical and democrat in Sean Ó Faolain's
popular biography *King of the Beggars: A Life of Daniel O'Connell* (1938);
its highpoint is Maurice O'Connell's edition of the Liberator's correspondence and Oliver MacDonagh's standard biography.

The possibility should be considered, however, that this version of
O'Connell is oversanitised, in regarding the Liberator primarily as a liberal, glossing over his verbal violence and in presenting O'Connellism
as an extension of O'Connell. While much research needs to be done
on O'Connell and his politics, one of the best recent assessments of
these is Oliver MacDonagh, in his 'O'Connell's ideology' in Laurence
Brockliss and David Eastwood (eds) *The Union of Multiple Identities:
The British Isles, c. 1750–1850* (1997).[52] Relatively little work has been
done on the relationship between O'Connellism and the 'tithe war' of
the 1830s, and how this fed conservative-Protestant narratives which
looked to the return of a Conservative government, expectations
which were disappointed by the unwillingness of the Peel government
of 1841–6 to embrace Protestant exclusivism.[53] Also of real interest to
researchers are the social networks that drove O'Connellite mobilisation, which is part of the more recent approach to O'Connellism
emphasising popular mobilisation and political symbolism being
developed by Gary Owens.[54]

the young ireland tradition and the famine

The Young Ireland movement of the 1840s[55] is of interest for its impact
on later generations through its didactic mass nationalist literature. The
contrast drawn by Young Irelanders such as Thomas Davis between their
role as educators (through *The Nation*[56] newspaper) and O'Connellite
reliance on a single arbitrary leader also highlights the political role of
newspapers in nineteenth- and twentieth-century Ireland. For most of
the Union period (and to some extent beyond it) conservative newspapers enjoyed disproportionate success because of their attractiveness to
advertisers. The tension between newspapers as political vehicles and
commercial entities is an abiding theme of Irish media history, with
recurring rivalries between journals whose primary aims were political, or educational, as their conductors might have it, acquiring both
support and constraints from a political movement (the *Nation, United
Ireland*) and those which enjoyed more commercial success but were
constrained by fear of political hostility; for instance, the *Freeman's
Journal* before its capture by the Irish Party, the *Irish Independent* under

the Murphy dynasty. The growth of literacy led to an expanding newspaper market; Mary-Louise Legg has charted how expansions in local newspaper titles coincided with the major political agitations of the O'Connell era and the 1880s.[57] The last major political newspaper conceived as the vehicle for a movement was FFs *Irish Press* (1931–95), a direct response to the perception that newspaper opposition was a major hindrance to the growth of the party;[58] although party 'house journals' survived at the end of the twentieth century, newer media reduced them to niche operations.

In 1945 the centenary of Davis's death attracted more official attention than the centenary of the Famine, but the Young Ireland cult had already become fossilised through the demise of the Union and land system against which they defined themselves and through the appearance of more recent and prestigious literary and political heroes, even if some of these, such as Pearse, removed certain Young Ireland writers from their context to exalt them as preachers of a timeless 'Gospel of Nationality'. Present-day interest in the Young Ireland movement is stronger among North American and Australian scholars than in Ireland. The major recent study of the movement is by the Tasmanian scholar Richard Davis, and Young Ireland exiles play a central role in Thomas Kenneally's popular account of the post-Famine diaspora in *The Great Shame* (1989).[59] Such accounts along with the biographies of Thomas Davis by the Australian John Molony, *'A Soul Came into Ireland': Thomas Davis 1814–45* (1995); and the American Helen Mulvey *Thomas Davis and Ireland* (2003), do not fully escape patterns laid down by nineteenth-century idealisation. A better approach might involve placing the Young Irelanders in relation to the Irish Whig and Tory intelligentsias of their day. The latter have been intermittently explored, the former almost entirely neglected; researchers would need to assess the options open to these young activists and the context within which they defined themselves.

The overshadowing of the Famine by Young Ireland was partly due to an impulse already visible in such works as John Mitchel's *Last Conquest of Ireland – Perhaps* (facsimile 2006) indicating a sense of the Famine as a humiliation and defeat and an attempt to present the Young Irelanders' 1848 rebellion,[60] however ramshackle and abortive, as a redeeming gesture of defiance. This overshadows the extent to which many Young Irelanders feared popular violence before the uprising and, after its failure, felt disgust that the people had not followed them.[61] Mitchel also attempts to redeem the Famine by attributing it to British malevolence – part of a struggle that is still going on and can therefore still be redeemed by victory.[62] Nationalist (especially separatist) commentators on later near-famines, such as those of 1879 and 1899 in Connacht, both of which provoked major land agitation, often blurred the difference further by assimilating the whole of Ireland to the poorest regions of the West and speaking as if the Famine was still going on; for example, food exports during the First World War were presented by separatists as potentially (and deliberately) producing a new Famine. This trope declined with the recession of the Great Famine into history and with the new Irish state's experiences of administrative responsibility. Traces recur in some material from the 150th anniversary commemorations presenting Ireland and the Irish diaspora as suffering an ongoing psychological trauma traceable specifically to the Famine. Mitchel's conspiracy theory, though almost universally rejected by scholars, starts from a prima facie case also put forward, without the same conclusion, by the Irish Conservative (and subsequent Home Rule leader) Isaac Butt[63] – how could so many have died, in a short period of time, 1845–9, in part of the wealthiest state on earth? How was it also that British policy was based on the concept that Ireland should pay for itself, rather than being a charge on the whole United Kingdom? The Mitchelian view that no reform could be expected from the landlord-dominated British government was challenged by land reform from the 1880s but survived in popular culture and the Republican subculture. Modern Famine scholarship was initially dominated by an administrative perspective, visible in the O'Neill and Edwards volume of 1956 and inspired by the move from published to archival sources;[64] this has been supplemented by studies of political and literary culture analysing the factors which shaped official famine policy and the nature of contemporary responses.

The predominant academic view until the early 1990s was that while the official response to the Famine had often been shortsighted, nevertheless, the Famine was an unavoidable Malthusian catastrophe, a view underlying the contemporary official response. Cormac O Grada, however, argued that Irish society was adapting before the Famine (albeit slowly and painfully); while significant population decline and emigration were unavoidable, the Famine itself was caused by the unpredictable appearance of the blight.[65] This implies government could have made more difference. A principal symbol of the shortcomings of government policy was Treasury Secretary Charles Trevelyan, chief coordinator of official relief schemes and author of the principal government apologia, to which Mitchel's work is a riposte. Trevelyan as chief villain was popularised by Cecil Woodham-Smith's *The Great*

Hunger: Ireland: 1845–1849 (1992) but this has recently been challenged by Robin Haines.[66] The Famine anniversary of the mid-1990s raised public consciousness and produced a great deal of local material. Christine Kinealy's studies of the administration of relief and the sufferings of its recipients were particularly outspoken in condemnation of official attitudes.[67] Peter Gray in *Famine, Land and Politics: British Government and Irish Society 1843–1850* (1999) explored the sources of government policy, arguing that a 'providentialist' blend of loosely evangelical religion and belief in the laws of classical economics as divinely-ordained, restricted government willingness to intervene.

fenianism and the irish republican brotherhood (irb)

Attempts to recreate a constitutional nationalist party based on the tenant right issue broke down through personality disputes, sectarian tensions and the willingness of some leading party members to accept office under a Liberal Government.[68] Some Liberal commentators argued that the 'shock therapy' of the Famine had in fact produced beneficial long-term economic results which were making the political assimilation of Ireland within the Union possible. These predictions were rapidly falsified by the appearance of a new radical nationalist organisation, helped by the growing political and economic clout of the Irish emigrant community in America. Founded in 1858, the underground separatist IRB[69] maintained a continuous existence until 1924. Much of the early literature on the movement consists of participant memoirs placing the organisation in a heroic light; this was echoed by many writers in the mid-twentieth century, encouraged by the role of the early twentieth-century IRB in the independence struggle and its participants' emphasis on continuity with the older rebellion. This was reinforced by well-researched biographies, such as Marcus Bourke's *John O'Leary, Recollections of Fenians and Fenianism*, (1969) in the years around the 1967 centenary of the Fenian Rising. A rival tradition treating Fenianism with pity or derision derived from loyalist and constitutional nationalist writers; already visible in the late Victorian and Edwardian period it was forced into occlusion by events after 1916 but revived in recent decades, partly because of the use of police files – which display considerable contempt for their subjects – as a major source. Leon O Broin, who produced the first full narrative history of the IRB, uses administrative sources but is generally reverential.[70]

A sharp dose of demythologisation was administered in the 1980s by R.V. Comerford, much of whose work explores the full range of

mid-century Irish political activity obscured by later theories of nationalist 'apostolic succession'. Comerford argues in *The Fenians in Context:
Irish Politics and Society, 1848–82* (1985) that the IRB of the 1860s is
best viewed as the product of that particular time and place. He writes
that most activists were primarily interested in recreation and social
self-assertion, and that much sympathy for Fenianism arose after it
was safely defeated and available for co-option.[71] Comerford has been
challenged by John Newsinger and other critics, often from leftist or
republican perspectives, who argue that the personal risk and sacrifice
involved, at least on the part of core activists, indicate serious ideological commitment.[72] The combination of high membership turnover with
a highly committed core is common among radical groups, so the two
views are not necessarily contradictory. Owen McGee's recent history of
the IRB reflects extensive knowledge of the source material and desire
to rehabilitate the 'forgotten generation' of Irish-based IRB activists who
emerged after 1867 and who were sidelined by Parnellism and displaced
by younger separatists before the 1916 Rising. McGee, to some extent,
applies the Whelan thesis to the late-Victorian IRB, presenting the participants as genuinely secular republicans, outmanoeuvred and written
out of history by Catholic-constitutionalist politicians whose sensibility
influenced even the following generation of republican-separatists.[73] As
with Whelan, this can be criticised as projecting contemporary secular-
ist attitudes onto the past.

the land question and home rule

The alliance between Parnellite parliamentarians, the IRB and land agitation after the agricultural downturn of the late 1870s produced the
almost uniquely effective nationalist political machine of the 1880s.
Earlier nineteenth century grassroots agitation was driven by separatists who believed, as did the conservatives of the *Evening Mail*, that
the British parliament would never undercut the rights of property.[74]
However, the unexpected willingness of Gladstone to make concessions
to tenants and his subsequent embrace of Home Rule gave constitutional
nationalism a degree of credibility never anticipated by radical separatists. This led some later commentators to see the post-1886 Home Rule
alliance as 'natural'; the attempts of the 1880–5 Gladstone government
to contain agitation by force as well as concessions, and the opportunistic nature of the embrace of Home Rule by most of Gladstone's lieutenants are relatively under-emphasised by scholars, yet provide much of
the explanation for the willingness of the Parnellite minority to resist

Gladstone and the anti-Parnellite majority in the 1890 split. Much academic history from the mid-twentieth century focussed on the Irish Parliamentary Party (IPP)[75] led by Charles Stewart Parnell[76] and subsequently by John Redmond. This reflected, among other things, the literary impact of the 'Parnell myth' deriving from contemporary Parnellite propaganda and taken up by Yeats and Joyce and the importance of the Irish Question in late Victorian and Edwardian British politics. This led to an extensive literature surrounding the upheavals it produced in the British political system. Much of this literature reflected the tendency of British liberal historians – such as J. L. Hammond[77] – and some Irish historians who regretted the violence of 1916–23 and the limitations of the successor states to suggest a Home Rule parliament might have allowed gradual and peaceful transition to independence and a society more receptive to outside influences and less defensive.

The 'lost opportunity' historiography had two principal foci – the defeat of Gladstonian Home Rule and the later career of John Redmond. The first major study of the IPP as a whole was Conor Cruise O'Brien's *Parnell and His Party* (1957), covering the years 1880–90.[78] The great pioneer of the academic study of the IPP was F. S. L. Lyons, whose works included the first full-scale biography of Parnell since Barry O'Brien (there had been several shorter lives), a biography of John Dillon, *The Fall of Parnell* (1960) and a survey *Ireland Since the Famine* (1971) which became a widely used school and college textbook.[79] His works, like Cruise O'Brien's study and the studies of ecclesiastical high politics by Emmet Larkin,[80] reacted against the supporters of the 'Parnell myth' who viewed the anti-Parnellites as cravenly subservient to Gladstone and the Catholic bishops. Instead these works emphasise the rational motivations of anti-Parnellism and the extent to which Parnell's refusal to accept majority rule can be seen as undermining his own achievements and anti-democratic. The Parnellite view that the anti-Parnellites were not a majority of Irish nationalists because they had ceased to be nationalists strikingly recalls later claims by hardline Republicans. Lyons' *The IPP 1890–1910* (1951) was the first account of a period traditionally overshadowed by the intense activity of the late 1880s and the years before the First World War.[81] Margaret O'Callaghan's *British High Politics and a Nationalist Ireland: Criminality, Land and the Law under Forster and Balfour* (1994) is an interesting critique of the 'lost opportunity' view of the Parnell movement which argues that even before the split created by the divorce case, British Unionism had successfully countered the Gladstone–Parnell alliance by presenting the land agitation and its parliamentary allies as essentially criminal rather than political. McGee's IRB history takes a similar view, though his revival of the contemporary separatist claim that even the Gladstonians never intended to implement Home Rule and supported it merely to divert Irish nationalist opinion from more radical options has not found general acceptance.

In many respects Lyons' works have not stood up well to subsequent research; he takes a Westminster-centred approach which downgrades such phenomena as the 'Ranch War',[82] and his memoir-based framework draws less deeply on archival material than appears at first sight. These deficiencies have been addressed by younger scholars. Alan O'Day, for instance, also takes a Westminster-centric approach but in a variety of authored and edited volumes explores his material more deeply and widely than Lyons.[83] Paul Bew's major contributions have been to conceptualise the nature and limitations of the relationship between the Irish Party and agrarian politics throughout its existence, and the limitations of its attitudes to the Unionist minority; his view of Parnell as a fundamentally conservative figure trying to retain some role in Irish life for his class by detaching it from the unsustainable land system remains dominant.[84] There were numerous publications on Parnell around the 1991 centenary of his death. The major recent contributions to the Parnell literature have been Frank Callanan's study of the Parnell Split and a biography of T. M. Healy.[85] Callanan's strongly researched rehabilitation of the Parnellite perspective emphasises the vitriolic Catholic-populist invective deployed by the anti-Parnellite Healy, whose verbal savagery tends to be overshadowed by the high-politics approach of Lyons and Larkin, but which was central to the Parnellite image of martyrdom, and the irresponsibility and incompetence displayed by most of Parnell's lieutenants-turned opponents. It is debatable (and probably unknowable) how far Callanan's view of Parnell as engaged in a visionary attempt to coalesce disadvantaged groups against the dominance of the conservative Catholic-farmer and professional ethos represented by Healy represents a projection of later concerns; a more cynical reading of Parnell in an opportunistic struggle for personal power cannot be excluded. David Lawlor's *Divine Right? The Parnell Split in County Meath* (2007) is a useful local study of the most notorious example of anti-Parnellite clerical electoral intimidation, though greater contextualisation would be needed to sustain its claim that Meath was typical of the country as a whole. Dermot Meleady's *Redmond: The Parnellite* (2008) which covers its subject's career to 1900 in the first volume of a projected two-volume study, provides (among other valuable material) the first detailed history of the Parnellite party between Parnell's death and party reunion in 1900.

Discussions of John Redmond produced before Meleady's ongoing reassessment echo the pattern established by his early apologetic biographers, Stephen Gwynn and Denis Gwynn, son of Stephen and author of the official life of Redmond.[86] Even pro-republican accounts of the period generally accept the Gwynn view of Redmond as a sincere patriot let down by British politicians and by extension present the IPP as ineffective rather than actively corrupt, as contemporary Republicans claimed. A focus on the self-consciously statesmanlike-Redmond also emphasises the 'dignified' aspect of the IPP, playing down the role of the sectarian Ancient Order of Hibernians within the IPP organisation and the continuing role of land agitation in keeping party organisations alive at local level. It is arguable that much treatment of the later Home Rule party involves seeing the more self-consciously conservative and constitutionalist commentators who called themselves Redmondites after 1918 as characteristic of the larger conglomerate IPP under Redmond; this is now being counterbalanced by local studies.[87] This can be developed further by asking how far has the distinction between constitutional and physical-force nationalism under the Union been retrospectively clarified and exaggerated in reaction against post-Union political violence and the revolutionary dictatorships of the twentieth-century world.[88] There is also a tendency, arising from Liberal nostalgia and the treating of the Third Home Rule Bill period as characteristic of the whole post-Parnell era, to play down the deep tensions between the Irish Party and post-Gladstonian Liberalism. It is acknowledged, for example, that suspicions of Liberals being lukewarm on Home Rule contributed to the weakening of the Irish party's hold on nationalist opinion from 1914. It is unfortunate in this context that Lyons' biography of Dillon, *John Dillon: A Biography* (1968), the leader most associated with the Liberal Alliance, is so under-theorised. Eugenio Biagini's *Irish Nationalism and British Democracy 1876–1906* (2007) is, however, an extensive survey of the nature and implications of the Liberal-IPP alignment for both parties, which argues that the Gladstonian home rule project did create a genuine affinity between the IPP and significant sections of British public opinion. David Fitzpatrick's *Politics and Irish Life 1913–21: Provincial Experiences of War and Revolution* (1998) centred on Co. Clare, was a pioneering study of the displacement of the IPP by Sinn Féin and maintains that there was considerable continuity of personnel between the two movements at local level. Other local studies question how far Fitzpatrick's model is applicable to all localities.

Another of Parnell's lieutenants, William O'Brien, has provoked much recent debate over the Home Rule era. O'Brien came to prominence as the editor of Parnell's weekly paper *United Ireland*, and during the land agitation of the late 1880s his repeated imprisonments brought popularity almost equal to Parnell's own. O'Brien's maladroit manoeuvres during the 'Parnell' split permanently damaged his reputation, but from 1899 he emerged as the driving force of the United Irish League, which used a land agitation based in impoverished Connacht to unite the parliamentary nationalist factions in 1900. After the 1903 Land Conference agreement between landlords and tenants, O'Brien embraced the idea of gradual Home Rule through compromise with moderate Unionists, something he had previously opposed. O'Brien's political bungles led to marginalisation within the Home Rule movement; he founded a Cork-based dissident group, the All-for-Ireland League, but on retirement in 1918 endorsed Sinn Féin. O'Brien published four voluminous memoirs[89] but a life of O'Brien on the same scale as Callanan's *Healy* (1996) will probably be required to sort out the mixture of insight, fantasy, wishful thinking, semi-cryptic gossip and self-serving mendacity in his vast published and unpublished archive. There are two modern biographies.[90] Philip Bull in his *Politics and Nationalism: A Study of the Irish Land Question* (1998) sees O'Brien as incarnating lost possibilities for the IPP. He attributes the Party's long-term failure to the MPs' success in forestalling a grassroots-led renewal spearheaded by the United Irish League.[91] Paul Bew's *Conflict and Conciliation* (1987) argues that the All-for-Ireland League represented a serious attempt to reconcile the Unionist minority. Callanan's treatment of O'Brien in his biography of Healy, who entered an opportunistic alliance with O'Brien in later years, is much more sceptical.

unionism under the union

The defeat of Southern Unionism (especially the hardline variety defined through defence of aristocratic rule and Protestant supremacy, which for obvious reasons lacks present-day exponents) distorts understanding of Irish politics under the Union, since contemporary nationalists and liberals defined themselves in reference to the existing regime and its defenders and cannot be fully understood apart from them. Only recently has significant work been carried out on the conservative resistance to Catholic Emancipation and the political response of landlords and other Southern Irish conservatives (as distinct from the British government) to the Land War and the Home Rule movement.[92] The intermediate period has recently been addressed by Andrew Shields's *The Irish Conservative Party 1852–1868: Land, Politics and Religion* (2007). An exception is the 'constructive unionism' of the 1880s and 1890s, seen as an attempt to defuse the demand for Home Rule by sponsoring land purchase and economic development, which inspired some 'lost opportunity' works. This is often seen as incarnated in Sir Horace Plunkett's private and official work for Irish agriculture (its genuine importance is enhanced by Plunkett's ability to attract the services of able and articulate publicists).[93] Andrew Gailey's *The Death of Kindness* (1987), a dissection of Unionist policy under the chief secretaryships of Gerald Balfour and George Wyndham, argues convincingly that their reform measures were opportunistic stopgaps rather than a worked-out strategy of 'killing Home Rule by kindness': it was privately criticised for opportunism by Plunkett and produced a backlash by a variety of hardline unionists.[94] The last years of Southern Unionism have been covered by Patrick Buckland and, in more personal and elegiac terms, R. B. MacDowell.[95] A recent tendency to present Southern Unionists as helpless victims of a bigoted majority has some validity, but requires the following qualifications: (1) the biggest losers among Southern Protestants/unionists were often least articulate; Southern Unionists from the business and professional classes were protected to some extent by their economic importance to the new state (2) Southern Unionism contained a strong anti-democratic element based on the view that those who knew best (in their own opinion) how to run the country should not be hindered by uncouth and ignorant majorities. Traces of this may be seen in ex-Unionist participation in the Blueshirt movement, this facet of the Blueshirts is under-explored by comparison with the movement's notorious reliance on Catholic corporatist ideology.[96]

The role of Ulster Liberalism in post-1886 Unionism, though emphasised in such contemporary works as MacKnight's *Ulster As It Is* (1896) and giving rise to occasional tenant-farmer and Presbyterian protest movements even after 1886, has tended to lose out in accounts of Unionism because of its electoral weakness compared to Conservative Unionism, the decay of the Liberal-Nonconformist subculture in post-1914 Britain and the imagery, popular strength and institutional continuity of Orangeism.[97] Recent work, which highlights the strength of the Ulster Liberal Unionist tradition, includes Brian Walker's *Ulster Politics*

1868–86 (1989), which even suggests Liberalism might have bridged the Orange–Green divide in Ulster – a view widely questioned by other historians, and Paul Bew's discussion of liberal Unionist responses to the Third Home Rule Bill in *Ideology and the Irish Question* (1998).[98] There are several useful studies of the politics of Victorian and Edwardian Belfast, then Ireland's only industrial city, which produced both a nascent labour movement and a working-class Orange protest tradition (e.g. Ian Budge and Cornelius O'Leary, *Belfast* [1973]; Austen Morgan, *Labour and Partition* [1991]; Terence Bowman, *People's Champion: The Life of Alexander Bowman* [1997]).

Ulster Unionist historiography tended to focus on the great rallies of the Ulster Crisis (1910–14) and the heroic image of Edward Carson as symbol of Ulster determination. This emphasis, reproduced in such works as *Ulster's Stand for Union* (1922) by Ronald MacNeill and the official life of Carson by Marjoribanks and Colvin, was carried over into A. T. Q Stewart's Buchanesque *The Ulster Crisis* (1967) and maintained by popular Unionist writers during the Troubles. Buckland's *Ulster Unionism* (1972) places greater emphasis on Unionist organisation but still focusses primarily on the 1910–14 period.[99] The major reassessment of Unionist historiography has been carried out by Alvin Jackson, who has produced pioneering studies of the first Ulster Unionist leader, the Cavan landlord Edward Saunderson, a monograph on the late Victorian and Edwardian Irish Unionist parliamentary party and a short study of Carson as well as a survey history of modern Ireland and a book on the concept and politics of Home Rule.[100] Jackson highlights the shift in Ulster Unionist leadership at the beginning of the twentieth century from a predominantly Anglican landed elite in the 'shatterzones' of South Ulster to a more Presbyterian business class based in Belfast and the northeastern counties and more inclined to see itself in Ulster-particularist terms (since its main electoral base lay in the new elected local councils of north-east Ulster). He also details the ambivalence behind Unionist leaders' threats of violence (contemporary nationalist and liberal accusations of 'bluff' were thus exaggerated but not entirely unfounded) and the Carson campaign's reliance on significant British support (painfully relevant to post-1969 Unionist attempts at Carson-style mass mobilisation).

the irish revolution

Much of the significant work done on post-Parnellian Irish politics before the First World War has appeared in studies of the cultural movement and of groups outside the Irish Party, such as the labour movement, the suffragettes and the cultural renaissance.[101] These studies, however, often tend to be written from the viewpoint of advocates who show little interest in the motives of those who opposed or criticised their subjects; the literary movement also produced its mythologisations, which obscure as much as they offer insights. A wider synthesis is needed, incorporating these movements within its narrative rather than treating them as add-ons; Roy Foster's work (notably his Yeats biography) reflects such an approach.[102] In some respects the best study of pre-1914 Sinn Féin is still Richard Davis' *Arthur Griffith and Non-Violent Sinn Féin* (1974).[103] There is no substantial account of the sizable faction within Sinn Féin that advocated republicanism rather than Griffith's Hungarian dual monarchy idea'.[104] Despite the widespread identification of Sinn Féin with Griffith, even biographies of him tend to focus on his post-1914 activities,[105] when he was largely a figurehead, rather than his earlier, more important role in the survival of a separatist movement. The primary focus of Padraic Colum's official biography is on the post-1916 period and Treaty.[106] Brian Maye's work is a bulky defence against criticisms rather than a fully conceptualised biography.[107] The present writer believes Griffith was the last Young Irelander as well as the forerunner of the post-independence Irish state, and that his 'Hungarian policy' was primarily a tactically motivated attempt to win over Irish Party supporters by reinventing Parnellism.[108] Sheila Carden in *The Alderman: A Life of Tom Kelly (1868–1842)* (2008) gives some useful insight into the role of municipal reform politics in pre-1914 Sinn Féin.

Padraic Pearse,[109] long seen as the iconic figure of the Easter Rising, has been downgraded in recent decades in reaction against the 'lay priest' image cultivated by his use of the language of Catholic martyrology and echoed by some early biographers.[110] Despite the subsequent publication of documentary collections and some specialised studies, Pearse's historical image is still dominated by the Ruth Dudley Edwards biography, a conscious though not wholly unsympathetic demythologisation.[111] Pearse's image has also been affected by the historical rehabilitation of Eoin MacNeill, associated with FX Martin and with MacNeill's son-in-law, Michael Tierney. This research, groundbreaking in its time, is now ripe for reconsideration. The Tierney interpretation accepts MacNeill's perspective on such issues as Ulster Unionism without discussing how MacNeill's views may have been shaped, or distorted, by his Antrim background; the Catholic political and cultural conservatism shared by MacNeill and Tierney requires a more detached assessment.[112] From the immediate post-Rising period an extensive literature grew up around James Connolly, building on Connolly's own writings which revise the nationalist canon, to argue that the natural consequence of the nationalist quest for equal citizenship is an Irish socialist republic imposing national control on the economy.[113] Another minority view emphasises the role of the IRB and sees Tom Clarke as the iconic figure[114] though this approach is limited by scarcity of material because of the secret nature of the IRB.

Because of its geographically diffuse nature the War of Independence has chiefly been seen either as a series of discrete local incidents viewed through contemporary memoirs, or as an extension of Michael Collins' Dublin campaign, viewed through a series of laudatory Collins[115] biographies by Beaslai, O'Connor and Coogan among others.[116] Recent academic work and the opening of new sources, such as the memoirs collected by the Bureau of Military History, are giving a clearer picture of the struggle, beginning with Charles Townshend's classic overview of *The British Military Campaign in Ireland* (1978).[117] Michael Laffan's *The Resurrection of Ireland* (1999) analyses the development of the post-1916 Sinn Féin party as a mass movement, and its decay as the military struggle developed.[118] Arthur Mitchell's *Revolutionary Government in Ireland* (1994) reconstructs the Dáil administrative system, although it can be questioned how much purchase these had at ground level.[119] Mary Ellen Kotsonouris's *Retreat from Revolution: The Dáil courts 1920–24* (1996) and David Foxton's *Revolutionary Lawyers: Sinn Féin and the British Courts, 1916–1923* (2008) are also relevant. Scholars associated with David Fitzpatrick's Trinity College seminar in the 1980s, notably Peter Hart and Joost Augusteijn, have produced local studies of the IRA's military campaign, replacing the lazy images of universal popular mobilisation against an alien enemy and the emphases on the exploits of flying columns with studies of how mass support for the campaign developed, of the networks on which the flying columns relied, and the processes whereby a relatively small proportion of total IRA membership came to engage Crown forces in direct combat.[120] Michael Hopkinson in *The Irish War of Independence* (2002) has produced the first survey of the War of Independence to cover the whole country.[121]

ireland from 1922

The post-independence state can be seen both as a success story, symbolised by two peaceful changes of government within 25 years of a civil war and the preservation of parliamentary democracy while most of Europe succumbed to dictators, and also a story of economic failure and social authoritarianism not finally dissipated until the 1990s. A further paradox is that the accommodation of powerful vested interests within the political system can be seen both as responsible for democratic success and as the cause of socio-economic failure. One of the major British legacies to the southern state was inserted almost casually in the 1920 Government of Ireland Act; the single transferable vote system of proportional representation in multiseat constituencies. This encouraged small parties and competition between candidates within parties. It has been the subject of intermittent debate throughout the state's existence. The dominant criticism levelled in the state's early decades was that it encouraged political fragmentation and could potentially lead to instability.[122] In fact this was restrained by the emergence of a bipolar 'FF versus the rest' system. This view was predictably associated with the largest party, FF, which made two attempts to introduce a 'first past the post' system; it was also held by some Fine Gael sympathisers. The most notable of these sympathisers was James Hogan, whose *Election and Representation* (1945), perhaps the most intelligent work of conservative political thought in twentieth-century Ireland, recalls how in the late 1920s FF used the Cosgrave government's dependence on independents to deny its legitimacy and argues that a strictly proportional system, producing lengthy minority government, might have plunged Ireland into 'Mexican politics'.[123]

It should also be borne in mind that some expectations of supporters of the system, such as Swiss-style coalition governments containing all major parties, have not been realised and there has been a tendency to reduce proportionality by reducing the size of constituencies. More recent criticisms of the system come from an administration-centred perspective which argues that the absence of safe seats and strength of intraparty competition encourage representatives to focus on constituency issues, and suggest a nationwide list system might produce higher-calibre legislators. This reflects an ongoing discussion about whether the tendency of the post-independence state towards centralisation, visible in such measures as the appointment of city and county managers to oversee the functions of elected councils, disempowered local communities through remote and unaccountable government, or whether a decentralised administration would have been dominated by corrupt and self-serving local vested interests.[124]

the civil war and treatyite politics

In terms of professional historiography the pro-Treaty side benefited
from greater articulacy and desire to state their case to overseas audiences.[125] The most forceful recent statement of the view that the defeat
of the Republicans was vital in preserving Irish democracy is Tom
Garvin's *1922: The Birth of Irish Democracy* (1996). Garvin emphasises
how republican rhetoric denied legitimacy to anyone who disagreed
with them and the considerable potential for localised anarchy and
misrule stifled by the imposition of central authority.[126] Bill Kissane's
The Origins of Irish Democracy (2002) questions this approach, emphasising that Irish nationalist politics were already permeated by democratic
assumptions. He notes that there was a long history of electoral competition, especially at local government level, and nationalists had long
based their claim to autonomy on an electoral mandate.[127] This, however, is not necessarily incompatible with the view that the Civil War
represented a vital conjuncture at which a different outcome could have
disrupted democratic development. For example, pre-independence
nationalist politics also favoured belief in a single dominant party.

  Kissane's *The Politics of the Irish Civil War* (2005), while rightly pointing out that Free State authorities resorted to or tolerated such measures
as death squads and executions by courts-martial during the Civil War,
flinches from, rather than refuting the argument that such measures
might have been necessary to preserve the new state.[128] John Regan,
The Irish Counter-Revolution 1922–36 (1999) serves as a valuable corrective to accounts that play down repressive and authoritarian elements
within pro-Treaty politics.[129] It is marred, however, by a contemptuous
attitude towards its subjects, and an unargued assumption that counter-
revolution is generally bad and revolution good without ever defining
revolution. Regan assumes that a Redmondite Catholic professional
class were the pre-war establishment, and the increasing dominance of
Catholic professionals within Cumann na nGaedheal[130] at the expense
of populist ex-Sinn Féiners represented a return to the status quo. It
is arguable that the conservative wing of Cumann na nGaedheal saw
themselves as upholding the independence project against criticisms
from Britain and Unionists, the latter disproportionately represented
in the commercial sector. Regan also underestimates how far they were
motivated by desire to rebut Unionist predictions that a Catholic-
nationalist state would break down through sheer infantile lawlessness
and incompetence. This argument is reinforced by the government's
attempts to legitimise itself through bureaucratic managerialism,

symbolised by its well-publicised Shannon Scheme, which supplied hydroelectric power of a volume far greater than the country's immediate needs but allowing the later development of a national electricity supply grid.

The debate over pro-Treaty politics links up with an older argument about the Blueshirts.[131] Critics of the movement have argued that it represented a serious fascist threat to Irish democracy; defenders claim its fascist trappings were superficial and its driving force was legitimate fear of a FF or IRA dictatorship, encouraged by systematic republican disruption of opposition meetings with their 'no free speech for traitors' calls, and reaction against the ruinous impact of the Economic War[132] on the cattle trade. The first modern study, *The Blueshirts* (1971) by Maurice Manning, argues this defence case on the basis of interviews as well as published sources.[133] Mike Cronin emphasises the Economic War and the movement's role as sponsor of social gatherings, as suggested for the Fenians by Comerford.[134] Both play down its use of fascist symbolism and rhetoric, which were highlighted by Regan, who sees these as developing from authoritarian tendencies visible in the later years of the Cosgrave government. It might be noted, however, that some of de Valera's contemporary supporters praised his autarkic and pro-tillage policies as Mussoliniesque while denouncing the Blueshirts as pseudo-fascist West Britons. Fearghal McGarry, also the author of a book on Irish politics and the Spanish Civil War, has produced a biography of the Blueshirt leader Eoin O'Duffy that emphasises his political extremism and increasing personal instability.[135]

the age of de valera

The contemporary Republican case over the Treaty has enjoyed less intellectual respectability, being associated with hardline republicanism or a FF propaganda noted for its rationalisations and elisions of awkward material. In the popular mind, Eamon de Valera dominates the first decades of the new state.[136] Despite the immense electoral success of FFs founding leader and the admiration his abilities engendered in a wide range of people who actually met him, the combination of his tortuous rationalisations, his view of executive power which regarded parliamentary oversight as undue interference with the authority of the government and reduced the Dáil to an electoral college; and the exhaustion of his governments and their original policies after 1945, contributed to the growth of a 'black legend' which overshadows his contemporary defenders. The most notable of these is the official biography by T. P. O'Neill and Lord Longford, so extensively supervised by its subject that it has been called a disguised autobiography.[137] The most extreme statement of hostility is Tim Pat Coogan's *Eamon de Valera* (1995), which presents its subject as a self-glorifying neurotic secretly aware of his own fraudulence and attributes his electoral success to public ignorance and backwardness.[138] Diarmuid Ferriter's *Judging Dev: A Reassessment of the Life and Legacy of Eamon de Valera* (2007) draws on its subject's archive to attempt a more balanced view, while Deirdre MacMahon is at work on a major biography.

The rest of the FF leadership élite have been neglected in comparison with de Valera, even the numerous studies of Sean Lemass[139] are more concerned with his career as Taoiseach than his earlier role as de Valera's right-hand man. Dick Walsh's *The Party: Inside Fianna Fáil* (1986) is a journalistic account of the rank-and-file FF mindset, seen in retrospect by a journalist whose mature sympathies lay further to the left.[140] The indispensable academic analysis of FFs achievement and consolidation of political hegemony is Richard Dunphy's *The Making of Fianna Fáil Power in Ireland* (1995).[141] Dunphy's work is particularly impressive in its analysis of how aspects of early FF, now recalled with distaste, were political assets in the 1920s and 1930s. Protectionism, now remembered chiefly for producing economic stagnation, had a long nationalist pedigree and enabled FF to appeal to both workers and employers, while the Cosgrave government's slowly eroding adherence to free trade, whatever its abstract merits, offered only remote and dubious hope.[142] Similarly, the 1937 constitution, criticised by liberals at the time, and in recent decades, for its Catholic and familialist ethos, did reflect contemporary opinion and achieved a degree of consensus which escaped its Free State predecessor.

The early historiography of the Second World War period, known in the state as 'the Emergency', is marked by a defensive tone, seen as a reaction to contemporary British perceptions of Irish neutrality as implicitly pro-German. Such accounts emphasise the extent to which the Irish government in practice assisted the Allies, writing neutrality as a final assertion of Irish sovereignty, and asserting the extent to which it assisted in healing the divisions of the interwar period. Robert Fisk's *In Time of War* (1985), the first major archivally based study of Irish neutrality, implicitly justifies the desire of the southern government to assert its independence, at the same time downplaying the contribution of Northern Ireland to the Allied war effort and emphasising the abject incompetence of the Stormont government in preparing for air attack and the sufferings of civilians in the 1941 Belfast blitz.[143] Some recent accounts are more critical of the operation of neutrality. Donal O'Drisceoil emphasises how wartime censorship assumed that the interests of the state and FF government were identical, treated legitimate debate as subversive and distorted public awareness by presenting the combatants as morally equivalent.[144] Brian Girvin is unusual in explicitly arguing that the Irish state would have done better to enter the war on the Allied side. Girvin's conclusion that Irish neutrality reinforced the tendencies towards self-righteousness, insularity and cultural and economic protectionism which contributed to the disastrous post-war performance of the state echoes Lyons' famous comparison of neutral Ireland to the inhabitants of Plato's cave blinking amazedly when they emerged into an utterly transformed post-war world.[145] This view is reinforced by the notorious tendency of both FF and Inter-Party governments in the immediate post-war period to exaggerate Ireland's importance on the world stage, consequently overestimating their leverage in seeking an end to partition. Their 'sore thumb' policy of raising partition at every international forum merely provoked impatience among delegates attempting to rebuild a devastated post-war Europe.[146]

ireland since 1945: lemass and after

The period between 1945–59, which saw Ireland fall behind comparable nations in Western Europe, is recalled as a 'dark age' and has attracted less detailed attention than the period up to 1945, though this has changed as the long-term effects of the opening of the archives in the late 1980s and 1990s feed through into publications. Much of what has been written was driven by an understandable anger at national underperformance and its human consequences, especially when that underperformance seemed to be repeating itself in the 1980's. A classic example is J. J. Lee's pioneering survey, *Ireland 1912–85: Politics and Society*, written in 1986.[147] Tom Garvin argues that Ireland's pre-war performance was not particularly out of line with Western Europe, and that the post-war hiatus can be traced to decisions consciously not taken for ideological reasons and because of the opposition of vested interests. This is reminiscent of Lee's indictment of 'the possessor classes', or socialist advocacy of state planning as the answer to Ireland's problems, but Garvin's progressive views are much more those of a secular anti-Burkean right-winger who sees the function of government as the creation of a social, economic and intellectual infrastructure which allows the unleashing of individual potential. Such an infrastructure, in this view, requires a class of experts and a population sufficiently well-educated to value expertise above the seductive slogans of irresponsible populists.[148]

The obstructions to systematic change were epitomised by the first Inter-Party Government (1948–51) that tried to project an image of can-do modernity in reaction against de Valera's insistence that the government knew best and the people had no right to ask the government to explain itself. This, as much as the internal rivalries of a multi-party coalition, lay behind the self-projection of such ministers as Noel Browne and James Dillon as dynamos of action.[149] It also lay behind the government's implosion when Browne's colleagues refused to back his plans for a state-controlled maternity health service against the medical profession and the Catholic hierarchy, and helps to explain why it is chiefly remembered for this fiasco. It was also the government which finally declared the Irish Republic in 1949, and is remembered for establishing that an alternative government to FF was possible. However, that government has attracted at least one monograph[150] and there have been several studies of its most distinctive component, the short-lived social-republican party Clann na Poblachta.[151] Another product of this period was the All-Party Anti-Partition Campaign, launched in response to the British guarantee of the constitutional status of Northern Ireland after the Republic's departure from the commonwealth. This rapidly came to be seen as a monumental hypocrisy by those southern politicians who were anxious not to be outdistanced on the issue by their political rivals. Grassroots members found the Irish government kept a tight control on the organisation and its propaganda, while the IRA border campaign of 1956–62, repressed by internment and other measures, produced an uneasy feeling that official anti-partition propaganda led enthusiasts into subversive organisations. This encouraged some individuals to argue that partition should be accepted de facto, a reaction more usually associated with the revulsion following the outbreak of the post-1969 Troubles and the possibility that Northern violence might destabilise the southern state.

Most accounts of Sean Lemass as Taoiseach are overwhelmingly favourable. The economic boom of the 1960s which followed his concerted drive to abandon protectionism and attract foreign investment, and which accompanied a wider move towards cultural openness was generally attributed to him. The economic slowdown of the 1970s and 1980s underpinned Lemass's image as maker of 'the best of decades', and most early accounts hail him as a uniquely visionary figure, the maker of modern Ireland. A partial exception is Bew and Patterson's

Lemass and the Making of Modern Ireland (1982), which emphasises the political constraints he faced and the extent to which his policies were influenced by the need to hold together the FF support coalition when the policies of the 1930s had clearly exhausted themselves.[152] Although more recent accounts, reflecting the wider social and economic transformations of the 1990s, see Lemass as a transitional figure,[153] and while emphasising the social conservatism of the period, highlighted in the recently re-released 1968 documentary *Rocky Road to Dublin*, it remains the case that the earlier changes did prepare the way for later developments. The extension of the education system, the movement from economic protectionism to active encouragement of foreign investment and to eventual membership of the European community (privately regarded with suspicion by the aged de Valera as compromising traditional views of sovereignty), the dismantling of much of the apparatus of formal cultural protectionism: these were political decisions taken in the 1960s whose implications worked themselves out over time.

From the late 1970s an increasing body of 'instant history' has made its appearance, ranging from journalistic commentary on current affairs to studies of different aspects of public administration to the increasing body of historical publications made possible by cheaper publication techniques, the growth of higher education and the growing fluidity of party allegiances in a less static society. The period between Lemass and the early 1990s is now seen as a discrete interval which has passed from current politics into history and which marks the deliquescence and final displacement of the social, administrative and cultural arrangements and assumptions formed in the last decades of the Union and the early years of the new state. In mid-twentieth-century Ireland, the era of the landlords, the time of Parnell and Davitt, even O'Connell could be seen as recent history, and Catholic and nationalist popular culture emphasised the concept of an unchanging national tradition. Now as a body of formal historiography extends to cover the twentieth century, a generation grows up for whom even the period before the boom of the 1990s seems remote.

the northern ireland state

The central issue involved in the history of Northern Ireland is how far it can be said to have a distinct identity. Much nationalist historiography treated it simply as an ancien régime relic. The local élite of businessmen and landowners who dominated Stormont cabinets

were treated as an aristocracy whipping up bigotry and fear among
the Protestant population and throwing them a few crumbs of patronage gained by discrimination against the Catholic minority. It was
asserted that if Britain withdrew support and the regime collapsed,
most Protestants would quickly realise that their fears were unfounded.
The drawbacks of this interpretation and its disregard for the actually
expressed views and self-definition of the Unionist population and
its dismissal of the possibility that Unionists might have legitimate
reasons for not wishing to join the southern state have led later commentators to underestimate the amount of truth it contained and
downplay this contemporary plausibility. As with the history of the
southern state, the history of interwar Northern Ireland and of the
decades of the Troubles (with their vast bulk of 'instant history') over-
shadow the period between 1945 and the 1960s. Until the recent work
of Henry Patterson[154] there was no overview of the post-war Stormont
machine comparable to Patrick Buckland's *Factory of Grievances* (1979),
and Brian Barton's biography of Lord Brookeborough breaks off at its
subject's accession to the premiership in 1943. Recent years have, however, seen useful studies of the Nationalist Party of Northern Ireland
by Eamon Phoenix, covering the formative years of the statelet, and
Brendan Lynn.[155] As in the south, this is partly due to restrictions on
archive access, and partly because the atmosphere of the immediate
post-war decades, with its sense that the state had stabilised and that
social and economic improvement driven by the expansion of the welfare state would slowly percolate society, is difficult to recapture when
the sources of the Troubles are all too obvious in retrospect. A major
step forward has been taken by Henry Patterson's use of the recently
released Stormont records to show that the tension between hardcore
reactionaries and semi-liberal modernisers pre-dated the premiership
of Terence O'Neill, with whom this conflict is often associated. The
hopes and fears associated with O'Neillism and the limitations and
breakdown of the modernising project when faced with the civil rights
movement's demand for 'British rights for British citizens', a demand
less easily dismissed than the anti-partition campaign of the 1950s,
which actually emphasised some of the same statistics about anti-
Catholic discrimination, is best treated in Bob Purdie's classic *Politics
in the Streets* (1990).[156]

In the vast literature on the Troubles, the extremes are better
documented than the centre ground. Apart from an early history by
McAllister,[157] the moderate nationalist Social Democratic and Labour
Party (SDLP) is under-explored and much of what has been written about

it revolves around, or echoes, its dominant leader, John Hume.[158] Other perspectives are provided by the memoirs of Austin Currie and Paddy Devlin and the recent Chris Ryder biography of Gerry Fitt, drawing on Fitt's own recollections.[159] For a more critical view of Fitt see Michael Murphy *Gerry Fitt – A Political Chameleon* (2007). David Hume's study of the post-Stormont Ulster Unionist Party provides many insights into its problems.[160] The party never recovered from the loss of Stormont's administrative resources and the defection of its traditional governing stratum into political quiescence after O'Neill and Faulkner. Although it maintained numerical superiority over the Democratic Unionist Party (DUP), partly because of renewed trust from the mid-1970s in British commitment to the Union, it was held together by a passivity reflecting a fear of disrupting the 'Unionist family'. The failure of this approach to assert any effective control over affairs was shown by the 1986 Anglo-Irish Agreement.[161] The danger's to party unity involved in taking a proactive approach, are illustrated by the career of David Trimble, who has been the subject of two biographies[162] as well as appearing in much material on the peace process. Graham Walker has recently provided the first narrative history of Ulster Unionism from the 1905 foundation of the UUC (Ulster Unionist Council) to the post-2004 ascendancy of the DUP.[163] The major studies of the DUP by Steve Bruce and Pollak and Moloney date from the 1980s and, like the party itself, are overshadowed by the figure of Ian Paisley and the role of Evangelical Protestantism in underpinning the 'no surrender' ethos.[164] Less has been written on the party in the late 1990s and early 2000s, perhaps because of the distaste of most observers for the combination of bigotry and opportunism culminating in that party's arrangement with Sinn Féin in the 2006 St. Andrews Agreement.[165] This gap has been filled to some extent by Ed Moloney, *Paisley: From Demagogue to Democrat?* (2008) with its discussion of the role of Peter Robinson in creating an effective party machine from an initially unsophisticated fundamentalist and populist membership, and its startling conclusion that in displacing the Ulster Unionists the DUP has come to resemble them. The study of post-Civil War Sinn Féin and the IRA was pioneered by J. Bowyer Bell in the 1960s and his publications remain a valuable resource.[166] The recent history of these organisations remains less accessible despite extensive post-cease-fire revelations; much relevant literature derives from adherents following a party line or angry dissidents with axes to grind. These texts are drawn on in such works as those of Ed Moloney and Rogelio Alonso.[167] Loyalist paramilitarism, though the subject of some academic works, such as those of Sarah Nelson and Steve Bruce,[168] has attracted less attention, possibly because its reactive and semi-criminal nature makes it less rewarding as a subject. Students can benefit by such competent journalistic accounts as the histories of the Ulster Volunteer Force (UVF) and Ulster Defence Association (UDA) by Cusack and MacDonald.[169]

the death of irish history?

Ireland in the twenty-first century is remarkably different from the traditional image of the island. The Northern Ireland Troubles have ended and a devolutionary structure has stabilised through a pact of extremes. The Northern parties increasingly seem disconnected from a wider public, and in the south, as late as the socio-economic crises of the 1980s, parliamentary politics were highly polarised between Charles Haughey's FF and Garrett Fitzgerald's Fine Gael-Labour alliance, each seen by its supporters as representing Ireland's salvation and by its opponents as a threat to all that was best in the nation. Now the populist catch-all parties which dominate the state engage in Continental-style coalition politics increasingly focussed on administrative competence, having adapted their ethos to an extent which their founders would scarcely recognise. The small and highly denominationalised professional and managerial classes of the late nineteenth and earlier twentieth centuries have become much more numerous, more professionalised and predominantly secular. Hidden traumas have come to light as the struggle of cultural protectionists against Anglo-American popular culture and its attendant attitudes ends in defeat, itself part of a wider global phenomenon of the breakdown of cultural deference. Rural Ireland is a shrinking minority; the suburban belt of a badly planned Dublin reaches towards the Shannon, the Slaney and Carlingford Lough. From being a nation of emigrants, the recurrence of emigration in the 1980s after its cessation in the 1960s was a major trauma of that decade, Ireland now attracts an increasing flow of immigrants who raise further questions about the Irish experience.[170]

Alvin Jackson ends his survey of modern Irish history by asking whether the secularisation and economic takeoff of the southern state and the conclusion of the Northern Troubles mark the end of Irish history as commonly understood.[171] Tom Garvin argues that while vestigial political violence may continue, the basic issues that drove the national conflict are solved and Irish politics have assimilated to the developed world as a whole.[172] Brian Girvin has presented Irish history as a progression from failed Union with Britain to a European Union that has overseen the politico-economic settlement its precursors sought in vain.[173] Others point to the problems of affluence, the growth of relative inequality, the strains on social services and the persistence of paramilitary and criminal underworlds as proof that Ireland remains a contested site. New departures in history writing, as evidenced by Diarmuid Ferriter's *The Transformation of Ireland 1900–2000* (2005), show that other areas of Irish history, families, social justice, women and children, previously neglected by scholars, are now ripe for investigation and the development of a fresh, more inclusive historical methodology. It may be premature to suggest that Irish political history has come to an end and been replaced by administration, or that Irish exceptionalism has been dissolved in global and worldwide trends, but it will always be possible to learn much about politics, governance and social life from studying the conflicts and dilemmas of the Irish past.

notes

1. Seamus Deane, *Civilians and Barbarians* (Derry, Field Day, 1983).
2. John Whyte, *Interpreting Northern Ireland* (Oxford, Oxford University Press, 1991).
3. The word 'revisionism' first gained currency as a term of abuse by orthodox Marxists from about 1885 to denigrate the work of Marxist writer Edward Bernstein who extensively used the writings of Marx and Engels to argue for change through evolution rather than revolution.
4. For a critical overview see Kevin Whelan, 'The Revisionist Debate in Ireland', *Boundary 2*, 31.1 (New York, Duke University Press, 2004), pp. 179–205.
5. The Kilmichael Ambush occured on November 28, 1920 at Kilmichael Co. Cork, when 36 local IRA men, under the command of Tom Barry, ambushed and killed 17 members of the Auxiliary Division of the Royal Irish Constabulary (RIC).
6. Peter Hart, *The IRA and its Enemies: Violence and Community in Cork, 1916–23* (Oxford, Clarendon Press, 1999); Meda Ryan, *Tom Barry: IRA Freedom Fighter* (Cork, Mercier Press, 2003).
7. For a more sophisticated critique of Hart see John Borgonovo, *Spies, Informers and the 'Anti-Sinn Féin Society': The Intelligence War in Cork City, 1920–21* (Dublin, Irish Academic Press, 2007); John Borgonovo (ed.) *Florence and Josephine O'Donoghue's War of Independence: A Destiny that Shapes our Ends* (Dublin, Irish Academic Press, 2006).
8. Brendan Bradshaw, 'Nationalism and Historical Scholarship in Ireland', *Irish Historical Scholarship*, vol. 26, no. 104 (November 1989), pp. 329–51. For the wider debate sparked off by this essay, see Ciaran Brady (ed.) *Interpreting Irish History: the Debate on Irish Revisionism 1938–94* (Dublin, Irish Academic Press, 1994); D. G. Boyce and Alan O'Day (eds) *The Making of Modern Irish History: Revisionism and the Revisionist Controversy* (London, Routledge, 1996).
9. Irish classicist and polymathic scholar, he was Professor of Ancient History and later Provost of Trinity College, Dublin. Among his works were *History of Classical Greek Literature* (4th edn, 1903 seq.); *Social Life in Greece from*

Homer to Menander (4th edn, 1903); *The Silver Age of the Greek World* (1906); *The Empire of the Ptolemies* (1896); *Greek Life and Thought from Alexander to the Roman Conquest* (2nd edn, 1896); *The Greek World under Roman Sway from Polybius to Plutarch* (1890).

10. Born in North Tipperary in 1871 into a farming family with strong nationalist political involvement, he was first Professor of Education at University College Dublin and argued that state action could restore the Irish language as the national vernacular despite his own ignorance of the language. His authoritarian views on education and society reflected Irish Catholic attitudes of the period.

11. W. B. Stanford, *Mahaffy: Biography of an Anglo-Irishman* (London, Routledge and Keegan Paul, 1971); E. Brian Titley, *Church, State and the Control of Education in Ireland 1900–1944* (Dublin & Toronto, McGill-Queen's University Press, 1983).

12. Evi Gkotzaridis, *Trials of Irish History: Genesis and Evaluation of a Reappraisal* (London, Taylor & Francis Group, 2006).

13. Cf. Desmond Fennell, *The Revision of Irish Nationalism* (Dublin, Open Air, 1989).

14. Brian P. Murphy, *Patrick Pearse and the Lost Republican Ideal* (Dublin, J. Duffy & Co., 1991), *The Origins and Organisation of British Propaganda in Ireland* (Millstreet, *Aubane Historical Society*, Co. Cork, 2006).

15. There were two complementary Acts that brought this union into effect – one passed though the parliament at Westminster, and the other was passed by the Dublin parliament. The phrase 'the Act of Union 1800' refers to this process, sometimes it is referred to as the Act of Union 1801 as it came into effect at the start of that year.

16. Ernest Gellner, 1925–95, British philosopher, anthropologist and sociologist and self-described Enlightenment rationalist fundamentalist. His works include *Words and Things* (1959), *Thought and Change* (1964), *Saints of the Atlas* (1969) and *Plough, Sword and Book* (1988).

17. James Lydon, *The Making of Ireland: From Ancient Times to the Present* (London, Routledge, 1998); for a statement of the 'modernist' view see Richard English, *Irish Freedom: A History of Nationalism in Ireland* (London, Macmillan, 2007). D. G. Boyce's *Nationalism in Ireland* (London, Routledge, 1982) is an older, less theoretically driven survey.

18. Toby Barnard, *The Kingdom of Ireland 1641–1760* (Basingstoke, Palgrave Macmillan, 2004); *A New Anatomy of Ireland: The Irish Protestants, 1649–1771* (Yale, Yale University Press, 2004); David Dickson, *Old World Colony: Cork and South Munster 1660–1840* (Cork, Cork University Press, 2005).

19. Sean Connolly, *Religion, Law and Power: The Making of Protestant Ireland 1660–1760* (Oxford, Clarendon, 1992).

20. A. P. W. Malcolmson, *Archbishop Charles Agar: Churchmanship and Politics in Ireland, 1760–1810* (Dublin, Four Courts Press, 2002); *Nathaniel Clements: Government and the Governing Elite in Ireland, 1725–75* (Dublin, Four Courts Press, 2005).

21. L. M. Cullen, *The Hidden Ireland: Reassessment of a Concept* (Dublin, Lilliput Press, 1989)

22. Breandan Ó Buachalla, *Aisling Ghear: na Stiobhartaigh agus an t-Aois Leinn, 1603–1788* (Dublin, An Clóchomhar, 1996).

23. Samuel Clark and James S. Donnelly Jr., *Irish Peasants: Violence and Political Unrest, 1780–1914* (Manchester, Manchester University Press, 1988).

24. 'Grattan's parliament' was named after Henry Grattan (1746–1820) who with the support of the popular militia, the Irish Volunteers, declared the independence of the Irish Parliament on 16 April 1782. Detailed outlines of the Patriot tradition can be can be found in such works as Francis Godwin James's *Ireland in the Empire, 1688–1770: A History of Ireland from the Williamite Wars to the Eve of the American Revolution* (Cambridge, Harvard University Press, 1973); and the structure of eighteenth century politics is concisely described by J. L. McCracken in his reliable overview, *The Irish Parliament in the Eighteenth Century* (Dundalk, Dundalgan Press, 1971).

25. W. M. Thackeray, *Barry Lyndon* (London: Futura Publications, 1974); D. P. Moran, *The Philosophy of Irish Ireland* (Dublin, 1905; University College Dublin Press edition, with introduction by Patrick Maume, 2006); J. J. Lee in Brian Farrell (ed.) *The Irish Parliamentary Tradition* (New York, Barnes and Noble, 1973).

26. Tom Bartlett, *The Fall and Rise of the Irish Nation* (Dublin, Gill and Macmillan, 1992).

27. Jacqueline Hill, *From Patriots to Unionists: Dublin Civic Politics and Irish Protestant Patriotism, 1660–1840* (Oxford, Clarendon Press, 1997).

28. Gerard O'Brien, *Anglo-Irish Politics in the Age of Grattan and Pitt* (Dublin, Irish Academic Press, 1988).

29. A. P. W. Malcolmson, *John Foster: the Politics of the Anglo-Irish Ascendancy* (Oxford, Oxford University Press, 1978).

30. Fianna Fáil was constituted in May 1926, and led by Eamon de Valera. Members of Fianna Fáil at first refused to be seated in the Dáil but finally entered in 1927. In 1932 Fianna Fáil gained 48 per cent of the seats in the Dáil, and de Valera became President of the Executive Council of the Irish Free State and Minister for External Affairs. Since then the party has remained the largest party in Ireland and is rarely out of office.

31. L. M. Cullen, *The Emergence of Modern Ireland, 1600–1900* (London, Batsford Academic, 1981). This last point was anticipated by James Connolly.

32. W. E. H. Lecky, *History of Ireland in the Eighteenth Century* (London, University of Chicago Press, 1972, first published (1878–90); for Grattan's importance as role model for Lecky see Donal McCartney, *W.E.H. Lecky: Historian and Politician* (Dublin, Lilliput Press, 1999). The most recent example of the tradition of Grattan biography deriving through Lecky from the official life by Henry Grattan Jr. is R. B. MacDowell's *Grattan* (Dublin, Lilliput Press, 2001).

33. Daniel Mansergh, *Grattan's Failure: Parliamentary Opposition and the People in Ireland, 1779–1800* (Dublin, Irish Academic Press, 2005).

34. Young Ireland was a mid-nineteenth-century political, cultural and social movement, which was to revolutionise the use of Irish nationalism as a political force in Irish society. In 1848 its leader William Smith O'Brien led a shambolic rebellion which failed to have any real impact – however, the writings of many of the Young Irelanders had far reaching effects on nineteenth and twentieth century Irish thinkers and revolutionaries.

35. Luke Cullen, a Carmelite based at Clondalkin in Dublin, along with R. R. Madden, collected the reminiscences of old rebels in Wexford and Wicklow in the early nineteenth century.

36. Thomas Bartlett, David Dickson, Daire Keogh, and Kevin Whelan (eds) *1798: A Bicentennial Perspective* (Dublin, Four Courts, 2003) contains (among much else) a survey of the historiography.

37. Much of the argument and more recent thinking on the 1798 Rebellion can be found in the collection of essays by Kevin Whelan, L. M Cullen, Thomas Graham, Anne Kinsella, Thomas Bartlett and Daniel Gahan in Daire Keogh and N. Nicholas Furlong (eds), *The Mighty Wave: The 1798 Rebellion in Wexford* (Dublin, Four Courts Press, 1996).

38. Kevin Whelan, *The Tree of Liberty* (Cork University Press, 1996).

39. Nancy J. Curtin, *The United Irishmen; Popular Politics in Ulster and Dublin 1791–98* (Oxford, Clarendon, 1994).

40. Tom Dunne, *Rebellions: Memoir, Memory and 1798* (Dublin, Lilliput Press, 2004).

41. L .M. Cullen, *The Emergence of Modern Ireland* (New York, Holmes & Meier Publishers, 1981); various chapters in David Dickson and Hugh Gough (eds) *Ireland and the French Revolution* (Dublin, Irish Academic Press, 1990) and in Whelan (ed.) *Wexford: History and Society* (Dublin, Geography Publications, 1987).

42. William Cooke Taylor, *History of the Civil Wars of Ireland* (London, 1832); ibid. *Memoir of Daniel O'Connell* (University College Dublin, Press reprint, ed. Patrick Maume, 2004).

43. G. C. Bolton, *The Passing of the Irish Act of Union: A Study in Parliamentary Politics* (Oxford, Oxford University Press, 1966); Patrick Geoghegan, *The Act of Union: A Study in High Politics 1798–1801* (Dublin, Gill and Macmillan, 2001); David Wilkinson, *The Duke of Portland: Politics and Party in the Age of George III* (London, Palgrave Macmillan, 2003).

44. *Oxford DNB* entry 'R. Barry O'Brien', by Patrick Maume.

45. Thomas MacKnight *Ulster as it is* (2 vols, London, 1896).

46. Other worthwhile biographical studies of O'Connell, include, most notably Fergus O'Ferrall's *Daniel O'Connell* (Dublin, Gill and Macmillan, 1981.); C. Chenevix Trench, *The Great Dan: a Biography of Daniel O'Connell* (London : Cape, 1984).

47. Irene Whelan, *The Bible War in Ireland: The 'Second Reformation' and the Polarisation of Protestant-Catholic Relations, 1800–1840* (Dublin, Lilliput Press, 2005).

48. Clongowes Wood College is a private secondary boarding school for boys in Co. Kildare run by the Society of Jesus (The Jesuits) since 1814.

49. Some reflections on later manifestations of the phenomenon may be found in Patrick Maume, *The Long Gestation: Nationalist Political Life 1891–1918* (Dublin, Gill and Macmillan, 1999); Lawrence MacBride, *The Greening of Dublin Castle: The Transformation of Bureaucratic and Judicial Personnel in Ireland 1892–1922* (Dublin/Washington, Catholic University of America Press, 1991).

50. Charles Gavan Duffy, *My Life in Two Hemispheres* (London, 1898); A. M. Sullivan, *New Ireland* (London, 1877).

51. 'Seacranaidhe' [Frank Ryan] *Irish Emancipation* (Dublin, 1929).

52. MacDonagh had previously published this biography in two volumes, *The Hereditary Bondsman: Daniel O'Connell 1775–1829* (London, Weidenfeld and

Nicolson, 1988) and *The Emancipist: Daniel O'Connell 1830–47* (London, Weidenfeld and Nicolson, 1989).

53. Stewart Brown, *The National Churches of England, Ireland and Scotland 1801–46* (Oxford, Oxford University Press, 2002); Wayne E. Hall, *Dialogues in the Margin: A Study of the Dublin University Magazine* (Washington, Colin Smythe Ltd., 2000). For an example of this discourse see the speeches of Rev. Henry Cooke in William McComb, *The Repealer Repulsed* (1841; 2003 University of Dublin Press reprint, ed. Patrick Maume).

54. Gary Owens in Peter Jupp and Eoin Magennis (eds) *Crowds in Ireland c. 1720–1920* (London, Macmillan Press, 2000).

55. The Young Ireland Movement grew out of Daniel O'Connell's Repeal movement and was heavily influenced by the ideas expressed by Thomas Davis, Charles Gavan Duffy and others writing in the *Nation* newspaper – which advocated the Repeal of the Act of Union. The Young Ireland group split with the Repeal Association in 1845 due to tensions over O'Connell's attempt to promote his son John O'Connell as his successor and Young Ireland's refusal to renounce threats of physical force in principle as well as in practice. In 1848 a group of Young Irelanders launched an ill-prepared and unsuccessful rising. Most of the leaders were arrested, tried, and transported to Australia.

56. 'The Nation' was first published on 15 October 1842. The founders were Charles Gavan Duffy, Thomas Osborne Davis and John Blake Dillon.

57. Marie-Louise Legg, *Newspapers and Nationalism: The Irish Provincial Press, 1850–92* (Dublin, Four Courts Press, 1999).

58. Mark O'Brien, *De Valera, Fianna Fáil, and the Irish Press: The Truth in the News?* (Dublin, Irish Academic Press, 2002).

59. Richard Davis, *The Young Ireland Movement* (Dublin, Gill and Macmillan, 1987); Thomas Kenneally, *The Great Shame* (New York, Vintage, 1998).

60. The 1848 Rebellion, which lasted a week, was led by Young Irelander, William Smith O'Brien. All of the action took place in Co. Tipperary. The failure to capture a party of police barricaded in widow McCormack's house near Ballingarry marked the effective end of the revolt. O'Brien and three leading colleagues were arrested. Their death sentences were commuted to transportation to Australia.

61. Melissa Fegan, *Literature and the Irish Famine 1845–1919* (Oxford, Clarendon Press, 2002).

62. John Mitchel, *The Last Conquest of Ireland – Perhaps* (University of Dublin Press reprint, 2005); Christopher Morash, *Writing the Irish Famine* (Oxford, Clarendon Press, 1995). (For a similar view of the Land War in East Galway as a continuation of the Battle of Aughrim, which has never ended and can still therefore be won, see Bishop Duggan of Clonfert recorded in W. S. Blunt, *The Land War in Ireland* [London, 1912].)

63. Isaac Butt (1813–79), born in Donegal, son of a Protestant Rector. He trained as a barrister and became a member of both the Irish and English bar. By 1873 Butt turned the Home Government Association, which he founded, into a political party calling it the Irish Home Rule Party. However by 1877 his influence on the party was waning and he had effectively been replaced as leader by Charles Stewart Parnell. He died in 1879.

64. R. Dudley Edwards and T. Desmond Williams, *The Great Famine: Studies in Irish History 1845–52* (reprinted Dublin, Lilliput Press, 1999 with a historiographical introduction by Cormac O Grada.)

65. Cormac O Grada, *Black '47 and Beyond: The Great Irish Famine in History, Economy, and Memory* (Princeton, Princeton University Press, 2000).

66. Robin Haines, *Charles Trevelyan and the Great Irish Famine* (Dublin, Four Courts Press, 2004).

67. Christine Kinealy, *This Great Calamity: The Irish Famine 1845–52* (Dublin, Gill and Macmillan, 1994); *The Great Irish Famine; Impact, Ideology and Rebellion* (London, Palgrave Macmillan, 2001).

68. J. H. Whyte *The Independent Irish Party 1850–9* (Oxford, Oxford University Press, 1958).

69. The Irish Republican Brotherhood (IRB) grew out of the Fenian movement which was founded in the 1850s, in New York, by James Stephens in Ireland and John O'Mahony. Their aim was to overthrow British rule in Ireland and to create an Irish Republic.

70. Leon O Broin, *Revolutionary Underground* (Dublin, Gill and Macmillan, 1976).

71. R. V. Comerford, *The Fenians in Context: Irish Politics and Society, 1848–82* (Dublin, Wolfhound, 1985).

72. John Newsinger, *Fenianism in Mid-Victorian Britain* (London, Pluto Press, 1994).

73. Owen McGee, *The Irish Republican Brotherhood: From the Land League to Sinn Féin* (Dublin, Four Courts Press, 2006).

74. Paul Bew, *Land and the National Question* (Dublin, Gill and Macmillan, 1978). The nexus behind the early Land League is best reflected in the career of Michael Davitt – T. W. Moody, *Davitt and Irish Revolution 1846–1882* (Oxford, Clarendon Press, 1984). Laurence Marley, *Michael Davitt: Freelance Radical and Frondeur* (Dublin, Four Courts Press, 2007).

75. The Irish Parliamentary Party (IPP) was formed in 1882. It had originated in the Home Government Association which was established in 1870 by Isaac Butt. In the 1880s, the IPP developed into a powerful and successful party under Parnell's leadership. He created a highly popularist, centralised, disciplined and modern party. In 1890–1, the IPP split after Parnell's fall, and never fully recovered its unity or prestige. The end came when the IPP was all but obliterated by Sinn Féin in the 1918 election.

76. Charles Stewart Parnell, born in Avondale, Co. Wicklow in 1846 into a Protestant, landowning aristocratic family. In 1875 he was elected MP for Co. Meath. By 1979 he was leader of the IPP at Westminster. He was elected the first President of the Land League at a meeting in the Imperial Hotel, Dublin, on 21 October 1879. In 1890 he was cited in a divorce between Katherine O'Shea and her husband – he later married Katherine. After this, many took the view that he was no longer a fit person to lead the IPP and in December 1890 the IPP split into 'Parnellite' and 'anti-Parnellite' factions. Parnell was hurt politically and personally; the fight to survive in politics took its toll and he died in October 1891. His funeral to Glasnevin Cemetery, Dublin, 11 October, was attended by nearly 250,000 people.

77. J. L. Hammond, *Gladstone and the Irish Nation* (London, Cass, 1938); for a rebuttal which emphasises short-term political calculation see A. B. Cooke

& John Vincent, *The Governing Passion: Cabinet Government and Party Politics in Britain, 1885–86* (Brighton, Harvester Press, 1974).

78. Conor Cruise O'Brien, *Parnell and his party, 1880–90* (London, Clarendon Press, 1957).

79. F. S. L. Lyons, *The Fall of Parnell* (London, Routledge & Kegan Paul, 1960); *John Dillon* (London, Routledge & Kegan Paul, 1968), *Ireland Since the Famine* (London, Weidenfeld and Nicolson, 1971), *Charles Stewart Parnell* (London, Gill & Macmillan, 1977); Alan O'Day, 'F. S. L. Lyons: Historian of Modern Ireland', in Walter L. Arnstein (ed.) *Recent Historians of Great Britain* (Iowa State University Press, 1990), pp. 173–92.

80. Although Larkin's work expanded to cover the whole nineteenth century, it began with the Land League and Parnellite era; *The Roman Catholic Church and the Creation of the Modern Irish State 1878–1886* (Dublin, Gill and Macmillan, 1975); *The Roman Catholic Church and the Plan of Campaign in Ireland 1886–1888* (Cork, Cork University Press, 1978); *The Roman Catholic Church in Ireland and the Fall of Parnell 1888–91* (Liverpool, Liverpool University Press, 1979).

81. F. S. L. Lyons, *The Irish Parliamentary Party 1890–1910* (London, Faber, 1951).

82. The 'Ranch War' 1904–9 witnessed particularly high rates of agrarian conflict in the Irish countryside.

83. Alan O'Day, *The English Face of Irish Nationalism: Parnellite Involvement in British Politics 1880–86* (Dublin, Gill and Macmillan, 1977); *Parnell and the first Home Rule Episode* (Dublin, Gill and Macmillan, 1986); *Irish Home Rule 1867–1921* (Manchester, Manchester University Press, 1998); Alan O'Day and George Boyce (eds) *Parnell in Perspective* (London, Routledge, 1991); *Irish Nationalism 1867–1922* (London, Routledge, 1999); *Ireland in Transition 1879–1922* (London, Routledge, 2004); *The Ulster Crisis 1885–1922* (London, Palgrave Macmillan, 2006).

84. Paul Bew, *Conflict and Conciliation: Parnellites and Radical Agrarians, 1890–1910* (Oxford, Clarendon, 1987); *Ideology and the Irish Question* (Oxford, Clarendon Press, 1997); *Parnell* (Dublin, Gill and Macmillan, 1980).

85. Frank Callanan, *The Parnell Split* (Cork, Cork University Press, 1993); *T. M. Healy* (Cork, Cork University Press, 1996).

86. Stephen Gwynn, *John Redmond's Last Years* (1919, reissued London, Hard Press, 2006); Denis Gwynn, *John Redmond* (London, Harrap, 1932). See also Paul Bew, *John Redmond* (Dundalk, Dundalgan Press, 1996) and John Finan, *John Redmond and Irish Unity* (Syracuse, Syracuse University Press, 2004). Dermot Meleady, *Redmond: The Parnelite* (Cork, Cork University Press, 2007).

87. David Wheatley, *Nationalism and the Irish Party: Provincial Ireland 1910–1916* (Oxford, Oxford University Press, 2005); Fergus Campbell, *Land and Revolution: Nationalist Politics in the West of Ireland 1891–1921* (Oxford, Oxford University Press, 2005).

88. Brian Farrell (ed.) *The Irish Parliamentary tradition* (Dublin, Gill and Macmillan, 1973); Alan J. Ward, *The Irish Constitutional Tradition: Responsible Government and Modern Ireland, 1782–1992* (Dublin, Irish Academic Press, 1994).

89. *Recollections* (London, 1905); *Evening Memories* (Dublin, 1920); *An Olive Branch in Ireland and its History* (London, 1910); and *The Irish Revolution and How it Came About* (Dublin, 1923).

90. J. V. O'Brien, *William O'Brien and the Course of Irish Politics* (Berkeley, University of California Press, 1976); Sally Warwick-Haller, *William O'Brien and the Irish Land War* (Dublin, Irish Academic Press, 1990).

91. Philip Bull, *Land, Politics and Nationalism: A Study of the Irish Land Question* (Dublin, Gill and Macmillan, 1998).

92. Alan Blackstock, *Loyalism in Ireland 1789–1829* (London, Boydell & Brewer, 2007); Andrew Shields, *The Irish Conservative Party 1852–1868* (Dublin, Irish Academic Press, 2007).

93. Sir Horace Plunkett (1854–1932), son of Lord Dunsany, of Dunsany Castle, Dunshaughlin, County Meath. In 1891, he was appointed a member of the Congested Districts Board and in 1892 was elected the Unionist MP for South County Dublin. He was a pioneer of agricultural co-operation. He developed agricultural policy in Ireland in his role as the first President of the Irish Agricultural Organisation Society (1894). He helped establishIreland's first co-operative at Doneraile, Cork and opened the first creamery in Drumcollogher, Limerick. He was involved with the Home Rule movement, and later founded the Irish Dominion League, whose aim was to have Ireland united and within the commonwealth. In 1922 he was made a Senator of the new Irish Free State. In 1923 his house was burned down during the Civil War and he subsequently moved to England, where he died in 1932.

94. Andrew Gailey, *Ireland and the Death of Kindness: The Experience of Constructive Unionism 1890–1905* (Cork, Cork University Press, 1987).

95. Patrick Buckland, *Irish Unionism: The Anglo-Irish and the New Ireland* (Dublin Gill and Macmillan, 1972); R. B. McDowell, *Crisis and Decline: The Fate of the Southern Unionists* (Dublin, Lilliput Press, 1997).

96. Conor Cruise O'Brien, *Passion and Cunning; Essays on Nationalism, Terrorism & Revolution* (New York, Simon & Schuster, 1988).

97. James Loughlin, *Gladstone, Home Rule and the Ulster Question 1882–93* (Dublin, Humanities Press International, 1987), *Ulster Unionism and British national Identity since 1885* (London, Pinter, 1995).

98. Brian Walker *Ulster Politics: The Formative Years* (Belfast, Ulster Historical Foundation, 1989), Paul Bew *Ideology and the Irish Question: Ulster Unionism and Irish Nationalism 1912–16* (Oxford, Clarendon Press, 1998).

99. Edward Marjoribanks and Ian Colvin, *The Life of Lord Carson* (London, Victor Gollancz, 1932–6); A. T. Q. Stewart, *The Ulster Crisis* (London, Faber and Faber, 1969), Patrick Buckland, *Ulster Unionism and the Origins of Northern Ireland* (London, Barnes and Noble, 1972).

100. Alvin Jackson, *The Ulster Party* (Oxford, Oxford Historical Monographs, 1989); *Sir Edward Carson* (Dundalk, Dundalgan Press (W. Tempest) Ltd, 1993); *Colonel Edward Saunderson: Land and Loyalty in Victorian Ireland* (Oxford, Clarendon Press, 1995); *Ireland 1798–1998* (London, Blackwell, 1999); *Home Rule: An Irish History* (London, Weidenfeld, 2003).

101. Cliona Murphy, *The Women's Suffrage Movement and Irish Society in the Early Twentieth Century* (Philadelphia, Temple University Press, 1989); Margaret Ward, *Hanna Sheehy Skeffington: Suffragette and Sinn Féiner* (Cork, Attic Press, 1996).

102. R. F. Foster, *W. B. Yeats, A Life: Vol. 1, The Apprentice Mage* (Oxford, Oxford University Press, 1997); *Vol. 2, The Archpoet* (Oxford, Oxford University Press, 2003).

103. Richard P. Davis, *Arthur Griffith and Non-Violent Sinn Féin* (Dublin, Anvil Books, 1974). See also Virginia Glandon, *Arthur Griffith and the Advanced Nationalist Press 1900–22* (New York, Lang, 1985) which incorporates Griffith within an useful overview of the political journalism of the period.

104. Arthur Griffith (1872–1922), journalist and politician; He was a founding member of the Celtic Literary Society in 1893 and was a member of the IRB, Gaelic League, and a founder of Cumann na nGaedheal, a cultural and educational association. In 1904 he published a pamphlet on the 1848 Hungarian Revolution entitled *The Resurrection of Hungary: A Parallel for Ireland* in which he set out his ideas on Irish independence under a dual monarchy, like that of Austria–Hungary. In 1905 he founded Sinn Féin.

105. Griffith was elected as Sinn Féin MP for East Cavan in the 1918 general election, but, following his own recommended policy of abstentionism, he joined other Sinn Féin MP's who assembled as Dáil Eireann in Dublin in 1919, proclaimed themselves the parliament of Ireland. Eamon de Valera was elected president of the new republic and Griffith was vice-president. Griffith led the Irish delegation in London that negotiated the Anglo-Irish Treaty of 6 December 1921 which established the Irish Free State as a self-governing dominion within the British Commonwealth. Following de Valera's rejection of the treaty and his resignation from Dáil Eireann, Griffith was elected President of the Dáil. He died in 1922.

106. Padraic Colum, *Arthur Griffith* (Dublin, Browne & Nolan, 1959).

107. Brian Maye, *Arthur Griffith* (Dublin, Griffith College Publications, 1997).

108. Patrick Maume, 'Young Ireland, Arthur Griffith and Republican Ideology: The Question of Continuity', *Éire-Ireland*, XXXIV: 2, Summer 1999, pp. 155–74.

109. Patrick Pearse was born in Dublin in 1879. He joined the Gaelic League in 1895 and became editor of its paper, *An Claidheamh Soluis* ('sword of light'). He founded a bilingual school for boys, St. Enda's, Rathfarrnham in 1908. He was a supporter of physical force republicanism; he joined the Irish Volunteers in 1913 and was elected Director of Organisation. In 1915 he joined the IRB and led the breakaway Volunteers who resisted conscription to the British Army on the outbreak of World War I. He played an active role in planning the Rising of 1916 and was appointed Commandant-General of the Army of the Irish Republic and President of the Provisional Government. During Easter Week 1916 he served in the General Post Office (GPO) Dublin. On 29 April 1916 he surrendered unconditionally on behalf of the Volunteers to Brigadier-General W. H. M. Lowe in Parnell Street. He was tried by court martial and was executed by firing squad in Kilmainham Jail on the 3 May 1916.

110. Louis Le Roux, *Patrick Pearse* (Dublin, Talbot Press, 1932). The writings of Desmond Ryan, Pearse's ex-pupil, though unreferenced are somewhat more detached and draw on personal knowledge.

111. Ruth Dudley Edwards, *Patrick Pearse: The Triumph of Failure* (London, Gollancz, 1977). Pearse's letters and educational writings have been edited by Seamus Ó Buachalla: other recent treatments include Sean Farrell Moran *Patrick Pearse and the Politics of Redemption* (Washington, Catholic University of America Press, 1996) and Elaine Sisson, *Pearse's Patriots* (Cork, 2005).

112. F. J. Byrne and F. X. Martin (eds) *The Scholar Revolutionary: Eoin MacNeill (1867–1945) and the Making of the New Ireland* (Shannon, Irish university Press, 1973); Michael Tierney, *Eoin MacNeil: Scholar and Man of Action*, ed. F. X. Martin (Oxford, Clarendon Press, 1981). For a hostile republican view of Tierney's promotion of a MacNeill cult, see Padraig O Snodaigh, *Two Godfathers of Revisionism: 1916 in the revisionist canon* (Dublin, Fulcrum Press, 1991).

113. The literature on Connolly is too extensive to detail here, and there is no standard edition of his works; for some introductory titles see the discussion in the section on Labour later in this essay.

114. Kathleen Clarke, *Revolutionary Woman: Kathleen Clarke 1878–1972, an autobiography* (Dublin, O'Brien, 1991).

115. Michael Collins, (1890–1922) took part in the Rising of 1916, was Director of Intelligence for the IRA during the War of Independence, Minister for Finance in the First Dáil of 1919 and member of the Irish delegation during the Anglo-Irish Treaty negotiations, both as Chairman of the Provisional Government and Commander-in-Chief of the National Army. He was shot and killed in August 1922, during the Civil War.

116. Piaras Beaslai, *Michael Collins and the Making of the New Ireland* (Dublin, G. G. Harrap & Co. Ltd, 1926); Frank O'Connor, *The Big Fellow; A Life of Michael Collins* (London, Nelson, 1937); Tim Pat Coogan, *Michael Collins: A Biography* (London, Hutchinson, 1990). For an account of Collins that focuses on his administrative activities and emphasises documentation over oral accounts – an approach which can be questioned in dealing with a clandestine revolutionary movement – see Peter Hart, *Mick: The Making of Michael Collins* (London, Picador, 2005). This is complemented – indeed, outclassed – by David Fitzpatrick's *Harry Boland's Irish Revolution 1887–1922* (Cork, Cork University Press, 2002) which describes how its subject sustained the IRA campaign through a network of personal and organisational contacts.

117. Charles Townshend, *The British Military Campaign in Ireland* (Oxford, Oxford University Press, 1978). Townshend's *Political Violence in Ireland: Government and Resistance since 1848* (Oxford, Clarendon, 1984) is also indispensable for any student of the subject.

118. Michael Laffan, *The Resurrection of Ireland: The Sinn Féin Party 1916–23* (Cambridge, Cambridge University Press, 1999).

119. Arthur Mitchell, *Revolutionary Government in Ireland: Dáil Eireann 1919–21* (Dublin, Gill & Macmillan, 1994).

120. Peter Hart, *The IRA and its Enemies*; Joost Augusteijn, *From Public Defiance to Guerrilla Warfare: The Experience of Ordinary Volunteers in the Irish War of Independence, 1916–1921* (Dublin, Irish Academic Press, 1996).

121. Michael Hopkinson, *The Irish War of Independence* (Dublin, Gill & Macmillan, 2002). This is modelled on the author's classic *Green against Green: The Irish Civil War* (Dublin, Gill & Macmillan, 1988).

122. Cornelius O'Leary, *Irish Elections 1918–77: Parties, Voters and Proportional Representation* (Dublin, Gill & Macmillan, 1979).

123. James Hogan, *Election and Representation* (Oxford, Blackwell, 1945); for Hogan see Donncha O Corrain (ed.) *James Hogan (1898–1963) Revolutionary, Historian and Political Scientist* (Dublin, Four Courts Press, 2000).

124. Mary Daly, *The Buffer State: The Historical Roots of the Department of Local Government* (Dublin, Institute of Public Administration, 1997).

125. Donal O'Sullivan, *The Irish Free State and its Senate: A Study in Contemporary Politics* (London, Faber, 1940); Terence de Vere White, *Kevin O'Higgins* (London, Methuen, 1948).

126. Tom Garvin, *1922: The Birth of Irish Democracy* (Dublin, Gill & Macmillan, 1996).

127. Bill Kissane, *Explaining Irish Democracy* (Dublin: University College Dublin Press 2002).

128. Bill Kissane, *The Politics of the Irish Civil War* (Oxford, Oxford University Press, 2005).

129. John M. Regan, *The Irish Counter-Revolution 1921–36: Treatyite Politics and Settlement in Independent Ireland* (Dublin, Gill & Macmillan, 1999).

130. Founded in 1923, Cumann na nGaedheal was formed from the pro-Treaty wing of Sinn Féin and formed the government of the new Irish Free State. It continued in power until 1932 when it was defeated at a general election by Fianna Fáil. It merged with the Centre Party and the National Guard to form Fine Gael in 1933.

131. The Irish Army Comrades' Association (for ex members of the Irish Free State Army) was established in 1932, and became popularly [known] as the Blueshirts. In 1933 General Eoin O'Duffy became their leader; he remodeled the organisation along lines influenced by fascist organisation in Italy and Germany. The members adopted a uniform of blue shirts and were renamed the National Guard. They had a specifically Catholic ideology based on papal social teaching, though there were some Protestant Blueshirts; anti-Semitism was present in the movement though its extent is debated. Later in 1933, the National Guard joined with Cumann Na nGaedheal and the National Centre Patry to form Fine Gael.

132. This was a trade war between the Irish Free State and Britian, which lasted from 1933 until 1938. It involved the refusal of the Irish state to pay 'land annuities' to Britain; this led to retaliatory imposition by the UK of 20 per cent import duty on Irish agricultural products. The Anglo-Irish Trade Agreement of 1938 finally settled the land annuities question, but the Economic war had damaged the Irish economy.

133. Maurice Manning, *The Blueshirts* (Dublin, Gill & Macmillan, 1971).

134. Michael Cronin, *The Blueshirts and Irish Politics* (Dublin, Four Courts Press, 1997).

135. Fearghal McGarry, *Eoin O'Duffy: A Self-Made Hero* (Oxford, Oxford University Press, 2005); *Irish Politics and the Spanish Civil War* (Cork, Cork University Press, 1999).

136. Eamon de Valera (1882–1985), born in New York but brought up in Limerick. In 1908 he joined the Gaelic League, and in 1913 he was in the Irish Volunteers. During the Rising of 1916 commanded the 3rd Battalion at Boland's Mill. In 1917 he was elected MP for East Clare and became president of both Sinn Féin and the Irish Volunteers. He rejected the Anglo-Irish treaty and was on the Republican side during the Irish Civil War. He founded Fianna Fáil in 1926, and in 1932 was President of the Irish Free State when FF came to power. He remained as leader of Fianna Fáil until 1959. He then served two terms as President of the Irish Republic, 1959–73. He died in 1975.

137. T. P. O'Neill and Lord Longford, *Eamon de Valera* (London, Hutchinson, 1971). This line was anticipated by several official biographies of de Valera published during their subject's career and by Dorothy Macardle, *The Irish Republic: A Documented Chronicle of the Anglo-Irish Conflict and the Partitioning of Ireland, with a Detailed Account of the Period 1916–1923* (London, V. Gollancz, 1937) which has been described as the ur-text of 'the Stalinist school of Fianna Fáil historiography'. A late example of this reverential treatment is Terry de Valera, *A Memoir* (Dublin, Currach Press, 2004).

138. T. P. Coogan, *Eamon de Valera: Long Fellow, Long Shadow* (London, Arrow Books Ltd; new edition, 1995). Coogan takes over and expands suggestions about de Valera's psychological makeup deriving from Owen Dudley Edwards, *Eamon de Valera* (Cardiff, University of Wales Press, 1987).

139. Sean Lemass (1899–1971) was appointed Minster for Industry and Commerce when Fianna Fáil entered government in 1932. In 1945, de Valera nominated him as Tánaiste, and he succeeded him as Taoiseach in 1959. He has been regarded as the economic architect of the modern Irish state.

140. Dick Walsh, *The Party: Inside Fianna Fáil* (Dublin, Gill & Macmillan, 1986).

141. Richard Dunphy, *The Making of Fianna Fáil Power in Ireland 1923–48* (Oxford, Clarendon Press, 1995).

142. Brian Girvin, *Between Two Worlds: Politics and Economy in Independent Ireland* (Dublin, Gill & Macmillan, 1998); the author subsequently reassessed the mildly favourable reassessment of 'infant industry' protectionism offered here; Mary Daly, *Industrial Development and Irish National Identity 1922–39* (Dublin, Gill & Macmillan, 1992); Patrick Maume, *D. P. Moran* (Dundalk, Historical Association of Ireland, 1995) discusses the waverings of a protectionist pro-treatyite between Fianna Fáil and Cumann na nGaedheal.

143. Robert Fisk, *In Time of War: Ulster and the Price of Neutrality, 1939–45* (London, André Deutsch, 1985).

144. Donal O'Drisceoil, *Censorship in Ireland: Neutrality, Politics and Society 1939–45* (Cork, Cork University Press, 1996). Clair Wills, *That Neutral Island: A Cultural History of Ireland During the Second World War* (London, Harvard University Press, 2007) develops these themes while ultimately maintaining that neutrality was inevitable.

145. Brian Girvin, *The Emergency: Neutral Ireland 1939–45* (London, Macmillan, 2006).

146. T. F. O'Higgins, *A Double Life* (Dublin, Townhouse, 1996).

147. J. J. Lee, *Ireland 1912–85: Politics and Society* (Cambridge, Cambridge University Press, 1986).

148. Tom Garvin, *Preventing the Future: Why Was Ireland so Poor for so Long?* (Dublin, Gill & Macmillan, 2004). Mary Daly, *The Slow Failure: Population Decline and Independent Ireland* (Madison, University of Wisconsin Press, 2006) takes a similar approach in describing how policymakers were constrained in recognising new social trends by ideological commitment to Catholic social theory and ruralism.

149. Noel Browne, *Against the Tide* (Dublin, Gill & Macmillan, 1986); John Horgan, *Noel Browne: Passionate Outsider* (Dublin, Gill & Macmillan, 2000); Maurice Manning, *James Dillon: A Biography* (Dublin, Wolfhound Press, 1999).

150. David McCullagh, *A Makeshift Majority: The First Inter-Party Government* (Dublin, Institute of Public Administration, 1998).

151. Kevin Rafter, *The Clann: The Story of Clann na Poblachta* (Cork, Mercier Press, 1996); Eithne MacDermott *Clann na Poblachta* (Cork, Cork University Press, 1998).

152. J. J. Lee, *Ireland 1912–85: Politics and Society*; Paul Bew and Henry Patterson, *Lemass and the Making of Modern Ireland, 1945–66* (Dublin, & and Macmillan, 1982).

153. John Horgan, *Sean Lemass: the Enigmatic Patriot* (Dublin, Gill & Macmillan, 1999); Brian Girvin and Gary Murphy (eds) *The Lemass Era: Politics and Society in the Ireland of Seán Lemass* (Dublin, University College Dublin Press, 2005).

154. Henry Patterson, *Ireland since 1939: The Persistence of Conflict* (Dublin, Penguin, 2006); Eric Kaufman and Henry Patterson *Unionism and Orangeism in Northern Ireland Since 1945: The Decline of the Loyal Family* (Manchester, Manchester University Press, 2007).

155. Eamon Phoenix, *Northern Nationalism: Nationalist Politics, Partition and the Catholic Minority in Northern Ireland, 1890–1940* (Belfast, Ulster Historical Foundation, 1994); Brendan Lynn *Holding the Ground: The Nationalist Party in Northern Ireland* (Aldershot, Ashgate Publishing Company, 1997).

156. Bob Purdie, *Politics in the Streets: Origins of the Civil Rights Movement in Northern Ireland* (Belfast, The Blackstaff Press, 1990).

157. Ian McAllister, *The Northern Ireland Social Democratic and Labour Party* (London, Macmillan Press, 1977).

158. Barry White, *John Hume: Statesman of the Troubles* (Belfast, Blackstaff Press, 1985); G. M. F. Drower, *John Hume: Peacemaker* (London, Gollancz, 1996); Paul Routledge, *John Hume: A Biography* (London, Harper-Collins, 1997); Gerard Murray, *John Hume and the SDLP* (Dublin, Irish Academic Press, 1998).

159. Paddy Devlin, *Straight Left: An Autobiography* (Belfast, Blackstaff, 1993); Austin Currie *All Hell Will Break Loose* (Dublin, O'Brien Press, 2004); Chris Ryder, *Fighting Fitt*: The Gerry Fitt Story (Belfast, Brehon Press Ltd, 2006). Michael Murphy, *Gerry Fitt: A Political Chameleon* (Cork, The Mercier Press Ltd, 2007) is a less reverential treatment.

160. David Hume, *The Ulster Unionist Party 1972–1992* (Lurgan, Ulster Society, 1996).

161. Fergal Cochrane, *Unionist Politics and the Politics of Unionism since the Anglo-Irish Agreement* (Cork, Cork University Press, 1997).

162. Henry MacDonald, *Trimble* (London, Bloomsbury Publishing PLC, 2000); Dean Godson, *Himself Alone: David Trimble and the Ordeal of Unionism* (London, HarperCollins, 2004).

163. Graham Walker, *A History of the Ulster Unionist Party: Protest, Pragmatism and Pessimism* (Manchester, Manchester University Press, 2004).

164. Edward Moloney and Andy Pollak, *Paisley* (Dublin, Poolbeg Press Ltd, 1986); Steve Bruce, *God Save Ulster: The Religion and Politics of Paisleyism* (Oxford, Clarendon Press, 1987); Clifford Smyth, *Ian Paisley: Voice of Protestant Ulster* (Edinburgh, Scottish Academic, 1988); Dennis Cooke, *Persecuting Zeal: A Portrait of Ian Paisley* (Dingle, Brandon Books, 1997).

165. This is addressed sympathetically by Steve Bruce's *Paisley: Religion and Politics in Northern Ireland* (Oxford, Oxford University Press, 2007).

166. J. Bowyer Bell, *The Secret Army: The IRA* (3rd rev. edn, Transaction Publishers; 1997), *The Irish Troubles: A Generation of Violence, 1967–92* (Dublin, Gill &

Macmillan Ltd, 1993), *The IRA 1968–2000: An Analysis of a Secret Army* (London, Routledge, 2000).

167. Ed Moloney, *A Secret History of the IRA* (London, Allan Lane Publishers, 2002); Rogelio Alonso, *The IRA and Armed Struggle* (London, Routledge, 2006).

168. Sarah Nelson, *Ulster's Uncertain Defenders: Protestant Political, Paramilitary, and Community Groups, and The Northern Ireland Conflict* (Belfast, Apple Tree Press, 1984); Steve Bruce *The Red Hand: Protestant Paramilitaries in Northern Ireland* (Oxford, Oxford Paperbacks, 1992), *The Edge of the Union: The Ulster Loyalist Political Vision* (Oxford, Oxford University Press, 1994).

169. Jim Cusack and Henry MacDonald, *UVF* (Dublin, Poolbeg, 1997); idem., *The UDA: Inside the Heart of Loyalist Terror* (Dublin, Penguin Ireland, 2004).

170. Roy Foster, *Luck and the Irish: A Brief History of Change 1970–2000* (London, Allen Lane, 2007) is a useful discussion of these developments.

171. Alvin Jackson, *Ireland 1798–1998: Politics and War* (London, Blackwell, 1999).

172. Tom Garvin, *Nationalist Revolutionaries in Ireland, 1858–1928* (Oxford, Clarendon Press, 1987); *Preventing the Future: Why Was Ireland so Poor for so Long?*

173. Brian Girvin, *From Union to Union: Nationalism, Democracy and Religion in Ireland – Act of Union to EU* (Dublin, Gill & Macmillan, 2002).

2
ireland 1600–1780: new approaches

michelle o'riordan

introduction

The writing of the history of Ireland in the seventeenth and eighteenth centuries has traditionally involved deep immersion in the administrative and economic documentation of the period. Soldierly colonists and those adventurers who were involved in the English wars in Ireland amassed a great deal of land in Ireland and evolved into a formidable political layer in their own right. Their creation of a political state that eventually challenged the authority of the Crown administration in Ireland is a fascinating and worthwhile historical study. The economic profile of the country, likewise, developed in ways directed by and tuned to the necessities, tastes and preoccupations of this political class. Source material concerned with these matters has been well used and interpreted by historians who produced cogent and recognisable images of Ireland. This sense of Ireland so created has, for many generations, formed the foundation of what is now understood to be the immediate background of the Ireland of the twentieth and the early twenty-first centuries. The passage of time, centuries in this case, creates a sense of dissatisfaction with long-held notions of historical causality, concepts of 'progress', and 'development'. New disciplines in social and economic studies, ethnic studies, gender studies and the realignment of identities and goals and ethnicities brought about by changes in economic fortunes, world-changing wars and more gradual changes in mass education, transport, communications and technology, create a sense of dissatisfaction with some, hitherto seemingly canonic understandings of past events and the political and economic personality of the state.

In the final decades of the twentieth century, many Irish historians became increasingly impatient with the prevailing historical images of seventeenth- and eighteenth-century Ireland, having, themselves, lived through changes in the country from the beginning of the twentieth century. It may be that they found their own experiences contradicted commonly understood ideas about the seventeenth and eighteenth centuries in Ireland and did not account, in any comprehensive way, for that country in which they lived and worked and wrote. Irish language sources have frequently been exploited to varying extents in the writing of Irish history concerning the two centuries following the death, in 1603, of Elizabeth I of England. Being a principally literary and subliterary source, this material has always lent itself to a less vigorous historical analysis; literary analysis has been quite thorough in many instances, but there is a looser sense of historical causality and discipline than is the case with other kinds of more familiarly 'historical' documents. Nevertheless, the images of the catechising priests and authors from Louvain and the beguiling notion of the Jacobite poet hopelessly devoted to a lost Stuart cause, have formed part of the sense of Irish identity in the two centuries before the Act of Union in 1801. A comprehensive re-evaluation of these almost burlesque images has not yet been formulated, but many individual studies challenge the marginalised existence of Irish and Irish-speaking peoples, which these images imply.

the median identity

Sources in the Irish language, though almost overwhelmingly literary, or subliterary in nature, have always underpinned the sense of the missing voice in works on Irish history that concentrated on the development of an Irish state created by a British government. Nicholas Canny's comprehensive account *Making Ireland British, 1580–1650* (2001) describes the creation of this state of affairs, and the tensions and political evolutions and revolutions which marked its emergence. Among the elements which forged the dual nature of the nation that emerged were those continental seminarians who saw, according to Canny, a role for themselves as intermediaries between the exiled Irish and those who remained in Ireland, whether of Old English[1] or of Irish ethnicity.[2] The writings in Irish, in Latin and in English of the Counter-Reformation clergy in Ireland or from their places of refuge on the Continent have been noted and analysed, most recently, by Bernadette Cunningham (2000), and Nicholas Canny (2001).[3] Their effort, it is argued, was aimed at placing Roman Catholicism at the unifying centre of an identity that could withstand the pressures of Calvinist British anti-monarchical developments. The efforts of the exiles in Europe and the Irish at home, of whatever ethnicity, to secure internal unity and external support for their political and social ambitions has, heretofore, been the story of the seventeenth century. Their failure, in raw political, military and economic terms, and the emergence of the Irish British state has constituted the main story of the eighteenth century. More recent historical work has reintroduced elements to both these narratives which nuance and shade the binary tales of Irish versus English and Catholic versus Protestant, to produce a more recognisable, ambivalent, variegated account of cultural conflict and exchange, religious strife and coexistence and economic injustice and cooperation.

scholarly life

Subdivisions between Irish-speaking and English-speaking populations and those who spoke or wrote or understood both have sometimes become attached to a sense of confessional political identity. Recent work on the triliguality of seventeenth-century Ireland, recognising the centrality of Latin writing, if not spoken Latin, has added a further incentive to re-examine some of the overlooked areas of interchange, such as that between the historian Dubhaltach Mac Fhirbhisigh (c.1600–71)[4] and Sir James Ware[5] (1594–1666). Nollaig Ó Muraíle's *The Celebrated Antiquary Dubhaltach Mac Fhirbhisigh (c. 1600–1671): His Lineage, Life and Learning* (1996)[6] studies the academic and other contacts of Dubhaltach Mac Fhirbhisigh. This examination of Mac Fhirbhisigh's work and connections indicates that a life in letters similar to that lived in contemporary Britain or Europe was possible also in Ireland, in spite of the political, economic and military upheavals of the time. A sense of continuity, and even of banality in the everyday existence of those whose lives and fortunes were not of interest to the chroniclers of the times, and of those whose affairs did not come into the notice of state papers and other such documents, is provided by modern work on smaller areas of interest. Not all Irish emigrants were noble pensioners. The majority was made up of students, soldiers, merchants, clergymen, adventurers, beggars, chancers and the partners and dependants of all these. The major syncretic or synthetic work, which will reknit the narrative into a new story eventually, has not yet been created, but matters are tending in that direction.

stimulus and 'response'

Some Irish language sources, mainly published materials, have, recently, been examined by Tony Crowley in *The Politics of Language in Ireland 1366–1922: A Sourcebook* (2000). The book is a collection of texts in and about the Irish language from the first colonial administrative legislation about the Irish (Statutes of Kilkenny 1366), to articles concerning the language in the constitution of the Free State in 1922. A 'politics of language' emerges from this study of a half a millennium of history. Crowley writes that 'the story of relations between the two main languages of Ireland over the past 600 years is quite as complicated as the history of the political relations between Ireland and England (and later between Ireland and the United Kingdom)'.[7] Plotting these relations through the tabulation of texts as various as legal documents, devotional works, religious tracts, works on grammar, dictionaries, political pamphlets, newspaper articles, journals and occasional poems, Crowley creates a framework of texts against which the structure of Irish–British political relations over 500 years can be understood. The sections 'covering' the period 1607–90 and 1690–1800 are punctuated by, successively, the so-called Flight of the Earls (1607),[8] the 1641 Rebellion[9] and the Williamite Wars (1689–91).[10] The eighteenth century is periodised in the implementation of the Penal Laws (c. 1704–40s), reforms in the Irish parliament (1782) and the 1798 Rebellion, concluding with the Act of Union in 1800. Both centuries were rich in writings in Irish. Comprehending the Irish Catholic population that spoke and read the Irish language under the locution 'Catholic Gaeldom',[11] Crowley outlines its 'response' to 'wholesale defeat' as being an 'allegiance to the European Counter-Reformation, and cultural attacks on the new order, coupled to the lament for the lost cultural formation of Gaelic Ireland'.[12]

The contribution of the Irish colleges in Europe was the production of devotional works in Irish, 'prompted by' the publication of the *New Testament* by the Established Church in Ireland.[13] These 'prompted' works include Bonaventura Ó hEoghusa's *An Teagasg Críosdaidhe* (Antwerp 1611), F. O'Maolchonaire's *Sgáthán Shacramuinte na hAithridhe* (Louvain 1618) and Theobald Stapleton's *Catechismus* (in Irish and in Latin, Brussels 1639). 'Other responses to the wrecking of Gaelic culture were made in the forms of histories and poetry',[14] among them, Seathrún Céitinn's *Foras Feasa ar Éirinn* (c. 1618–34) and Mícheál Ó Cléirigh's *Annála Ríoghhachta Éireann* (1632–36) and *Focloir no Sanasan Nua* (1643). Among the poets and prose writers mentioned are the anonymous author of the comic/satirical *Pairlement Chloinne Tomáis* (c. 1616, 1626), and the poet Dáibhidh Ó Bruadair. A poem by Diarmaid Mac Muireadhaigh from the end of the century is cited in full[15] (23 quatrains). The period 1690–1800 was poor in published works in Irish, but rich in manuscript literature, details of which must be sought elsewhere.[16] Tony Crowley's historiographical sourcebook, with its contextualising commentary, reinforces a certain reading of Irish material in the binary relation familiar to all.

Ultimately, the work contributes to a discussion of Irish political nationalism refracted through the concept of who was 'for' and who was 'against' the Irish language in all its forms, uses and expressions and 'the history presented in this text, with all its shifting trends and manifestations, shows language often to be the vehicle for debates concerned with cultural identity and therefore political legitimacy'.[17] Understandably, within this particular framework, the focus is almost entirely on Irish–British relations. The relationship is articulated in a stimulus-response mode, a sense of historical causality which pervades some writing on this period. Materials that illustrate aspects of that binary relationship are presented in an engaging and informative context.

a clash of ethnicities

Introducing a more nuanced reading of the enterprise of governing Ireland without its consent during the seventeenth century, Nicholas Canny's book *Making Ireland British 1580—1650* (2001), with its self-explanatory focus, examines forensically the state apparatus, principally through the policies of 'plantation', that combined with the disparate nature of what he terms the Irish 'response' to create a British Ireland in the 70 years between 1580 and 1650. Canny identifies the Irish political élites on the Continent as having as much influence on matters in Ireland as those who lived in Ireland. The 1641 insurgency and its immediate aftermath is the culmination of this particular study. 'Decoding cultural conversations' is Canny's apt description of the interaction between the innovators from Britain and the innovators in Ireland whose agendas clashed with not entirely foreseen consequences for either group in his chosen period. He masterfully outlines the dilemma, of being Irish-born and Catholic, in which the Old English found themselves, as they tried to maintain a privileged position in respect of their loyalty to the English Crown, while having grave reservations about Crown policy, and finding themselves disadvantaged with each new plantation.[18]

The ultimate ambition of the Old English was to secure separate kingdom status for Ireland, subject to the Crown but not subject to the English parliament. Their putative constitutional bias was undermined by their disinclination to accept decisions of Irish parliaments which became increasingly dominated by new planter interests. The speeches by Patrick Darcy (an English-trained lawyer from Galway)[19] urging parliamentary sovereignty in Ireland were used in the later eighteenth century by members of the Protestant political élites in Ireland. The arguments put forward by Darcy were used in a context which concealed his essential dependence on the Crown in Ireland. This later use of Darcy speeches also concealed his sense that an Irish Parliament independent of that of England could secure a like-minded majority in favour of putting a stop to the parliamentarian, Calvinist and increasingly anti-monarchical inclinations of an Irish parliament that contained a burgeoning planter class whose strength came from English parliamentary support. In short, Darcy and his confrères 'considered royal rule to be their ultimate shield against the hostility towards Catholic worship and proprietorship which was displayed consistently by the government administration in Ireland, by a stridently Protestant group within the House of Commons in England, and also by the subscribers to the National Convention in Scotland'.[20] This dependence on the monarchy would be at variance with the political goals of those later independents who made use of certain of Darcy's arguments. Canny's brief sketch of the career of the somewhat maverick views of John Cusacke[21] (an Old English author and lawyer of the 1630s) highlights the uneasy politically median position of the Old English, whose political identity showed the influence of the monarchically –authoritarian-inclined Catholic 'nations' of Europe where many of them had been educated.

The same continental influence is credited with the increasing sense among the Catholic Irish that royal rule under a British (or other agreed) monarch was the natural form of government for the Irish. Canny, agreeing with Breandán Ó Buachalla's thesis in *Aisling Ghéar: na Stíobhartaigh agus an tAos Léinn* (1996), suggests that Irishmen educated abroad imported into Ireland the sense of absolutism growing in the Catholic monarchies of Europe, and that this sense of the fitness of political matters was disseminated in Irish literature by poets such as Eochaidh Ó hEoghusa (c. 1560–1616) and Fearghal Óg Mac an Bhaird (fl. 1600). Following this trend, Canny identifies other sources of influence (cultural, political and religious) on Irish political leaders, namely the Old English continentally trained Catholic clergy and the Old English wives of Irish lords. Ethnic allegiances were thus 'rapidly' eroded with the result that the terms 'Catholic' and 'Irish' came to replace 'Gaelic' and 'Old English' as identifiers of certain strands of political allegiance within Ireland and increasingly outside Ireland in Continental Europe where, it seemed, the fortunes of both would be determined. Irish support for Stuart monarchs was, according to Canny,

'always tentative and qualified'.[22] Seeking always to secure the identity
of Irish political culture with the Catholic monarchs of Europe and to
maintain a relationship of loyalty with the Pope, Irish Catholic exiles
whose opinions we are aware of from their writings, such as those of
Flaithrí O'Maolchonaire (nominated Catholic Archbishop of Tuam),[23]
deviated from the Stuart loyalty in favour of Spanish and French roy-
als whose support might be cultivated if not always counted on. As far
back as 1971, Tómas Ó Fiach's article 'Republicanism and Separatism
in the Seventeenth Century'[24] noted how the interests of the Tyrone
and Tyrconnell families proposed to govern Ireland without a prince,
as a republic, modelled on the newly emergent tiny republics on the
Continent.

It seems clear in Canny's *Making Ireland British* that where the use
of Irish literature and subliterary material is concerned, the discussion
still circles around the more-or-less literal readings of contemporary
published material (such as the Louvain devotional works) and in reference to extant literary works (such as bardic poems). Material that falls
into the catechetical category seems still to be ranked, along with the
literary, polemical and historical, as providing positive or negative evidence for the emergence of a sense of the Irish Catholic state in the late
sixteenth and early seventeenth centuries.[25] Such material still awaits a
literary and historical hermeneutic that would enable its exploitation
by both literary scholars and historians to the benefit of both disciplines
and to the greater advantage of material itself, which in the current
configuration exists either in a culturally impenetrable bubble or is
read as the articulated élite 'Gaelic Response'. Canny's valuable concept
embodied in the title *Making Ireland British* gives cogency and coherence
to the thesis presented in his work and provides a framework through
which to view certain developments in Irish history.

creating the 'irish catholic'

Foremost among those who seemed, in their writings, according to
Bernadette Cunningham in The *World of Geoffrey Keating: History, Myth
and Religion in Seventeenth-Century Ireland* (2001), to urge the subsum-
ing of the older ethnic community under the political and cultural
domination of the later one, was the priest, poet, historian and author
Geoffrey Keating (c. 1569–1644). He urged the absorption of Gaelic
Irish identity under the political hegemony of the Old English, while
maintaining the 'best' of the literary culture of the one, and discard-
ing an established religious and political culture in favour of the more

attractive Old English style. The sense of his role in guiding the theoretical and even theological basis for an Irish identity, built upon a Catholic allegiance and with a certain ambivalence towards the English/Scottish monarch, is predicated upon the median role outlined by Canny for the Old English of the seventeenth century. The sense of 'responding' to developments rather than the less exceptional volitional behaviour of civilised societies and people seems to be the pervading tone of the latest work on this towering literary figure of the seventeenth century. Bernadette Cunningham's work on Keating provides a rounded biographical, bibliographical and historical study of this single individual and his writings (in Irish and in Latin). Cunningham's explication of Keating's works, devotional and literary, in their contemporary context, with an eye to tracing the evolution of the Old English and later Irish identity, opens a seam in Irish history that has only begun to be explored. An earlier study by T. Ó Dúshláine, *An Eoraip agus litríocht na Gaeilge, 1600—1650: gnéithe den Bharócachas Eorpach i litríocht na Gaeilge.* (1987), outlined some of the literary, theological and polemical continental sources of many baroque themes, tropes and flourishes in Irish seventeenth-century literature, including the devotional literature. Individual studies by Bernadette Cunningham and others have repeatedly referred to this element in Irish literature, that perceived the influence of European Catholic thought and writings, which, it is argued, exercised a considerable influence on the creation of the Irish Catholic as identified in later historiography.

Political Thought in Seventeenth-Century Ireland: Kingdom or Colony (2000), the collection of essays edited by Jane Ohlmeyer, addresses aspects of what it meant to be Irish in the seventeenth century.[26] The collected essays consider many aspects of political theory and writings in seventeenth-century Ireland. The failure of the unifying power of a shared Roman Catholic identity is outlined most comprehensibly, given the minute and tortuous variations on the subject of loyalty to Rome and loyalty to the monarch, in Tadhg Ó hAnnracháin, '"Though Hereticks and Politicians should misinterpret their good zeale": political ideology and Catholicism in early modern Ireland'.[27] The pamphlet and publications war involved truly serious-minded commentators such as Peter Lombard, Philip O'Sullivan Beare, Richard O'Ferrall and John Lynch,[28] who wrote in Latin (Irish, English and Spanish were the other languages of, at least, O'Sullivan Beare). Richard O'Ferrall, and the others were probably fluent in Irish and English and some other continental language(s); John Lynch, for instance, settled in France and was, more than likely, fluent in French. Biblical echoes in the articulation of protonationalistic sensibilities surrounding the military efforts of Owen Roe O'Neill[29] and his supporters during the 1641 rebellion, are discussed in the Jerrold Casway article 'Gaelic Maccabeanism: The Politics of Reconciliation'.[30]

Does the intellectual content of the politics of the seventeenth century lie behind the questions concerning the nature of Ireland's relationship with England, kingdom or colony? This theme, on which Jane Ohlmeyer has done much work, is addressed in the studies presented in the volume through the writings of known individuals of the period.[31] The task of explaining, rationalising and surviving the civil wars in England and Scotland and the related wars in Ireland, created an intellectual ferment among literate and literary contemporaries which led to widespread reformulations of both traditional and emerging allegiances and loyalties. As Ohlmeyer remarks, in respect of the writers whose works come under attention in collected studies of the volume, 'Many of the writers who feature in this volume could be more accurately labelled propagandists rather than political theorists; yet their works critically shaped ideas about politics and political culture in early modern Ireland'.[32] As with all written sources, claims about their power to shape or their quality of having been shaped can become part of a circular argument. The able articulation of arguments, in English for the most part (of the material studied in this volume), seems to have created formulations of sectarian and radical political and religious positions that survived through the two following centuries, and in some instances, beyond. The Irish 'historical' writings of Geoffrey Keating (in *Foras Feasa ar Éirinn*), and the contemporary Latin work (*Cambrensis Eversus*), by Keating's contemporary and fellow Roman Catholic priest John Lynch, are addressed by Bernadette Cunningham, in 'Representations of king, parliament and the Irish people in Geoffrey Keating's *Foras Feasa ar Éirinn* and John Lynch's *Cambrensis Eversus* (1662)'.[33] Cunningham suggests that such texts may be read to 'discover mid-seventeenth-century perspectives on kingship, sovereignty, parliament and law in an Irish context'.[34] The intention of the writers themselves, according to Cunningham, was to illuminate the present as much as to describe the past. Keating's work concluded with the coming of the Anglo-Normans to Ireland in the twelfth century. His introduction sets out his intention to contradict accounts that Gerald of Wales gave of twelfth-century Ireland. John Lynch's more contemporary work had the declared intention likewise to defend Ireland's reputation against the calumnies of Cambrensis, which were used, polemically, ever since Gerald of Wales wrote his colourful and politically motivated description, to justify various political and military stratagems by the ethnically non-Irish inhabitants of Ireland. The recycling of Geraldus's work in the service of the claims of successive generations of Irish and Anglo-Irish polemicists is a worthwhile study in itself. The claims to civility of the 'Old English' rested in some measure on the exaggerations and memorable misrepresentations in Geraldus's work. John Lynch's interest in Keating (he translated *Foras Feasa* into Latin), and his use of the work that was widely disseminated as a manuscript only[35] highlights the many ways in which the lives, politically and intellectually, of both men overlapped.

confederated catholics

The 12 years of continuous conflict, that took place in Ireland from 1641–to 1653, ruptured the British state, which Canny's study describes. The median role attributed to Old English Catholics was likewise challenged in the kaleidoscope of loyalties and betrayals that characterised the fraught decade. Contributors to Micheal Ó Siochrú's edition of essays in honour of Donal Cregan (d. 1995), *Kingdoms in Crisis: Ireland in the 1640s: Essays in Honour of Donal Cregan* (2001), examine every aspect of the 1641 Rebellion. As Ó Siochrú points out in his introduction, the Confederate Association of Catholics in Kilkenny[36] in 1642 represented the only sustained self-government by the Irish of Ireland from that time until 1919.[37] The confederated Catholics themselves showed how little progress had been made in the forging of a single political identity among them, whether or not that had been a conscious goal or a realisable one, by those Counter-Reforming Old English prelates of Canny's and Cunningham's works. Their association itself was, in many respects, an effort to take control of an uprising that had many of the characteristics of a popular uprising and therefore presented a risk to all established interests. Covenanters' opposition to Charles I in Scotland and their initial successes gave heart to those in Ireland whose ambitions were not shared by all Catholics, Irish or Old English. The Civil War in England complicated the nature of loyalties and allegiances and made allies of enemies against, respectively, monarchists and parliamentarians. Class interest rather than ethnic identity, suggests Ó Siochrú, was the factor that united socially élite Catholics and divided them from plebeian interests of whatever ethnicity.[38] Agreement across the traditionally cited divide of native Irish and Old English did not necessitate rationalisation on the grounds of ethnic unity in adversity. Moderates controlled the confederation until defeat seemed to prove them wrong and allowed more scope for radicals on both sides of the confederacy. The predominance of lawyers and prelates in the forefront of the confederacy gave its proceedings a scholarly air not borne out in the reality of the wars in which it was involved. Tension was created by its frequent dissatisfaction with the decisions of soldiers in the field and vice versa.

violence and sectarianism

A recent work on the mid-seventeenth century has taken the unfashionable step of identifying victims and perpetrators in a historiography that is vexed with a sense of responsibility to the present. *The Age of Atrocity: Violence and Political Conflict in Early Modern Ireland* (Dublin 2007) is the title of a collection of essays edited by David Edwards, Pádraig Lenihan and Clodagh Tait. An introductory essay by the three editors suggests that Irish history cannot reasonably be studied without acknowledgement of some near genocidal episodes that characterised the efforts of the English state to take full control over Irish land and resources in the period from 1534 to 1691, 'rather than work in cooperation with local elites, therefore, the crown displaced them and drove a radical course of colonisation trying to reshape Irish society, in government, language and culture, as a replica of England.'[39] This statement of affairs, fairly radical in itself, informs the tone of the volume in articles that seek to expose the levels of violence that accompanied, for instance, the confiscation of native landowners to the eventual four-fifths dispossession that took place.[40] In those stark terms it is easy to imagine that much violence accompanied such changes, especially where ownership and possession of land is involved.

In the case of Ireland, from the outset, issues of religious allegiance complicated matters. Altogether, a toxic mix of two kinds of aggression created a very violent two centuries. Different aspects of that violent period are examined. David Edwards[41] argues, in his article 'The Escalation of Violence in Sixteenth-Century Ireland', that the English conquest of Ireland under the Tudor monarchs brought a new level of militarised violence to Irish society. The nature of societal violence changed from that of endemic internecine petty warfare that had its own internalised restrictions, and characterised most early modern European societies, to outright warfare on a scale that expanded over time to create a permanent state of war by the state on the native population. This picture is nuanced to take into account periods of relative peace in different areas, and the effect of shifting alliances in areas that were under the control of lords who were of varying bellicosity. Edwards identifies the precise period 1546–67, the period during which the subjugation of Irish midland lords was accomplished, as the time during which the nature of the violence changed, permanently. Vincent P. Carey, in his 'Atrocity and History: Grey, Spenser and the Slaughter at Smerwick (1580)'[42], suggests that the massacre of the garrison of Spanish and Italian allies of the Irish at Smerwick (Dún an Óir) in Co. Kerry in November 1580 marked a calibrated change in attitudes towards the justified violence of war among English army captains. Carey argues that, for these writers, the Irish 'barbarians' (and their allies) were justly massacred in an enterprise that sought to expand the 'civility' of the English polity. Some of the theories lying behind the violent action of military men are seen by Carey in the literature of the period, particularly in the works of Edmund Spenser and the secondary literature arising from it.

Hiram Morgan, in '*Slán Dé fút go hoíche*: Hugh O'Neill's Murders',[43] reminds historians that Irish lords too, were adept at political murder, and that Hugh O'Neill was certainly guilty of the murder of his rivals and their allies. Morgan, however, makes the salient point that, with the growth of centralised authority and the increasing power of the organs of the state, in this instance a state in the process of conquering Ireland by military force, political and military leaders like O'Neill, had also to conceal their activities in a way that their predecessors had no need to do. So that the formerly, almost accepted, necessity to wipe out rivals within a ruling family, now became matters of judicial oversight of the centralising powers that sought to arrogate all such authority to themselves. This too created another layer of violence outside the controlling effect of might against right; levels of judicial violence escalated with the entry of an alien state apparatus into the admittedly violent world of the Irish warlords, permitting in many cases, the elevation of lords too weak to protect effectively their own people.

The propagandist use of the reports of deaths of those considered to have persecuted others in the early modern period is the subject of Clodagh Tait's '"The Just Vengeance of God": Reporting the Violent Deaths of Persecutors in Early Modern Ireland'.[44] Those who were regarded as having persecuted just men were often said to have suffered a tortured death, howling with remorse and seeing visions of their evil deeds, without achieving the peace of forgiveness. Among those who were reputed to have literally 'died roaring' were persecutors of Irishmen and women; Lord Justice Drury was responsible for the execution in 1579 of the heroes/martyrs Bishop Patrick O'Healy of Mayo and Conn O'Rourke, both Franciscan priests. His burial, delayed possibly for financial reasons, became associated with bad weather and other untoward episodes, blamed by his enemies on his maltreatment of the two priests. A similar set of beliefs grew around the death of Henry Ireton, Oliver Cromwell's nephew and commander of Cromwell's army in Ireland after the Lord Protector's departure. His involvement in the death of Albert O'Brien, Catholic Bishop of Emly, after the surrender of Limerick in 1651 was cited in the lurid reports of his death (possibly from plague) crying out as he died that he had never ordered the prelate's persecution. Ireton's original burial with honours in Westminster Abbey in 1652 was undone during the restoration of the monarchy in England in 1661, when he was disinterred and hanged and beheaded and given a traitor's burial under the gallows at Tyburn in London in vengeance for his involvement in the death of King Charles I. His head was on public display for further punishment. Similar events were the fate of many others, including Sir Charles Coote (d. 1642 in Co. Kildare)[45] and Sir Henry Brouncker who having condemned a priest, died that evening in a frenzy. The final victory of the weaponless against their persecutors, in this scheme of things, was the desecration of the reputation of the persecutor *post mortem*. The violence done to the body of Henry Ireton some ten years after his burial in England merely highlights the centrality of certain kinds of almost ritualised violence in the public sphere during this period.

Brian Mac Cuarta in 'Religious violence against settlers in south Ulster, 1641–2'[46] suggests that the rapid social advancement and enrichment of planted Protestants in South Ulster in the mid-century, and the seemingly uncontrolled avarice of their ministers accounted in some measure for the violence offered to them at the outbreak of the 1641 rebellion. In so far as this rebellion assumed, in some areas of the country, the characteristics of a populist uprising, the reported massacre of these settlers during the first weeks of the rising would indicate that popular prejudice against newcomers, supposedly inflamed by overenthusiastic reforming Catholic priests, led hordes of Catholic tenants to massacre their replacements on religious and economic grounds. In an article aptly titled 'The Other Massacre: English killings of Irish, 1641–2', Kenneth Nicholls attempts to speak from the unmythologised side of the coin of mutual slaughter during that period in Ulster. Catholic Irish were killed in numbers that were at least on a par with, if not exceeding, those of the fabled massacre of Protestant settlers at the beginning of the rebellion. Nicholls's argument has polemical undertones because discussions of the subsequent history of the province of Ulster in all succeeding centuries have been undertaken in the light of Protestant fears and preparedness in the wake of the much documented 'massacres' of 1641 and the lurid depositions surviving from the victims and their spokespersons. Nicholls's attempt to address the losses on the side of those burdened with the blame of the original frenzy makes interesting reading. He takes the pamphlet literature of England in the period when the English army was coming to grips with the rebellion in the province of Leinster as a focal point, noting that massacres mentioned in accounts published in London to the dubious (nowadays) honour of the Protestant army (contemporary term for the state's forces in Ireland), provide some creditable evidence of atrocities against the Catholic population. Growing mutual distrust and the temptation of reprisal killings led to the breakdown of trust between neighbours and others whose former good relations included mutual fostering and marital links. Nicholls argues that the Rising in 1641 and the wars that followed would, today, be termed 'ethno-religious' conflicts and were paralleled by similar conflicts between Russian Orthodox and Polish Catholic peoples in the Ukraine in the mid-seventeenth century.[47]

As with all conflicts, the outbreak of communal hostilities in Ulster in 1641 led to refugee crises elsewhere where the 'shocked, bereaved, despairing, and impoverished' arrived with their fears and their poverty.[48] Their fate is discussed in John R. Young, '"Escaping Massacre": Refugees in Scotland in the Aftermath of the 1641 Ulster Rebellion'. Many settlers, who were expelled from their homes or fled from fear, were linked to Scotland by ties of kinship and by religion (Church of Scotland). They were identified as such in records from the Scottish Privy Council – as

> great nombers of his Majesties good subjects and our own countrey men thair are daylie forced to flee out of Ireland to those parts in the west countrey quhair they find best occasion of landing.[49]

And as fellow Scots, these refugees, while not welcome, especially the destitute among them, were accepted as a duty by the Church of Scotland; those who were not Scots were welcomed on account of their Protestant religion. Church institutions did their best in an organised way to mitigate the destitution of the refugees. The record of their narratives of suffering and deprivation shows another facet of a violent century. The Church of Scotland and Privy Council archive material used by Young to recreate a sense of this period, reveal aspects of social organisation, cohesion and responsibility that provide a consoling foil for the grim matter of their enterprise.

Glancing sidelong at Oliver Cromwell's career as a military officer in the English Civil Wars – before he turned his attention to Ireland – John Morrill contextualises the notorious Cromwellian massacre of civilians in Drogheda. Morrill notes that the disparate wars that made up the English Civil Wars were characterised, for the most part, by fair adherence to the rules of war as they existed at the time. This involved sparing of civilians, fulfilment of terms for surrendered troops and avoidance of cold-blood killings. Exchange of prisoners was common, and their execution, after battle, rare. Exceptions to these conventions existed and Morrill notes the behaviour of Cromwell and his Ironsides in the taking of Basing house in October 1645 as part of the Parliamentarian war against Royalists in England. Cromwell's description of his own conduct and his self-justification in the brutal taking of that fortified dwelling and its subsequent 'slighting' was but a step away, suggests Morrill, from the sack of Drogheda four years later. The difference between killing in hot and cold blood is the crux of the issue for Morrill. Citing statistics on death rates for set battles in the period in Ireland, England and Scotland, Morrill reveals that the 'average death rate in all the set-piece battles in Ireland was roughly three times the rate in England (30 per cent as against 10 per cent)'.[50] Setting Cromwell's perceived anti-Catholicism and anti-Irishness in context, he relies on the available written statements by Cromwell condemning the sin but not the sinner, that is, to be Catholic is to be deluded, but seductive priests and prelates are to blame for their malign influence over their flock; to be Irish is to be disadvantaged in respect of civility and economy, but again, seductive priests and prelates are to blame for deluding their congregations in the continuity of their traditions, religious and ethnic.

The consistency of this policy regarding Ireland with his policy in respect of his fellow-Englishmen is used by Morrill as evidence of Cromwell's even-handedness, and his lack of specific animus towards Irish Catholics. His excesses in Drogheda and Wexford, were by his own admission, *in terrorem* measures, piously undertaken to prevent future bloodshed. (It would appear that the garrisons of Dundalk, Carlingford and Newry were affected as desired and fled or surrendered at once).[51] Following this example, others that were offered terms, took them, and were then spared a massacre, which contrasted, favourably, Morrill tells us, with the behaviour of other Parliamentarian commanders. The atrocities at Wexford were part of an 'unauthorised massacre'.[52] Altogether, the minutiae gleaned from contemporary sources in this article make it clear that the hazards of war in this period meant that captive garrisons and besieged or conquered civilians were at the unpredictable mercy of the victor in any particular episode. In an altogether different vein, Micheál Ó Siochrú in, 'Propaganda, Rumor and Myth: Oliver Cromwell and the Massacre at Drogheda' revisits the contemporary oral and written accounts, propaganda and opinion, that formed the popular cultural background to the behaviour of Cromwell and his troops in Ireland. The frenzied English press exhortations to avenge Protestant blood in Ireland, a land of 'savages' and 'cannibals'[53] equipped those who campaigned in Ireland with the moral incentive to behave in ways that made the Irish campaigns (as noted in Morrill, above) more bloody and unsparing than those in England. The underlying sentiment sponsored by the Parliamentarian administration was that God had marked out the Irish for destruction,[54] and that Godly English (parliamentarian) had been given victory in England (over the royalists) to accomplish that mission. Ó Siochrú emphasises the role of the Duke of Ormond (1610–88)[55] in the dissemination of stories about Drogheda and the Parliamentarian army – bad as they were – in order to gain the support of the King (who was ambivalent about the worth of aiding his loyal Irish subjects), monarchists and royalists in England. On the other hand, Irish prelates and confederates used their control of a printing press and the dissemination of rumour and gossip as well as reports, to create a climate in which their demands might be met by a general population inclined to surrender on terms in order to enjoy some semblance of peace.

All sides in the many-faceted wars could accuse each other of black propaganda that gave their followers little sense of advantageous or disadvantageous conduct. Cromwell's righteous indignation at the hypocritical prelates leading their ignorant flocks to destruction[56] was an accusation levelled on all fronts by the conflicting factions. Indeed, it was the Earl of Ormond that emerged, in the Catholic Irish propaganda, as the bigger demon. His betrayal of his fellow Irishmen, and his denial of Catholic toleration seemed to many to be unforgivable in the light of his kinship with some of the foremost Catholic loyalists in the field. Propaganda on his behalf was as virulently anti-prelate (Catholic) as any statement issued by Cromwell.[57] Ó Siochrú's account of the propaganda wars that accompanied the military wars is hugely engaging – perhaps because the conflicting printed and otherwise disseminated claims of competing factions is such a feature of modern warfare, politics and the public sphere. As a corrective to overzealous apportioning of praise and blame in matters of warfare in a period before internationally agreed rules of engagement, John Childs in, 'The laws of war in seventeenth-century

Europe and their application during the Jacobite War in Ireland, 1688–91' outlines the generally held sense of the laws of war in Europe and their application in Ireland during the wars of 1688–91.[58]

A collection of essays in Alan Ford and John McCafferty's (eds), *The Origins of Sectarianism in Early Modern Ireland* (2005) address from theoretical standpoint, the level at which thinkers and those who articulated learned opinion exercised influence. Behind the well-documented wars, treaties and other political arrangements lay the shift in consciousness of individuals and perhaps of whole population groups. Ford and McCafferty's book addresses the rise of the confessional state and the emergence of the subject/citizen whose religion (the period did not tolerate the option of no religious affiliation) differed from that of the monarch or the administration. Ford's discussion differentiates between sectarianism and the murderous division to which the existence of sectarianism can give rise: social, political and religious divisions provide a ground for the growth of sectarianism, or are the result of sectarianism. Sectarianism of itself is not always a device for division and evil, just that of differentiation.[59] Ford's thesis emphasises the tendency of society to attempt cohesion and that this tendency, in Ireland, at any rate, where religious and ethnic boundaries were fluid in many instances, through intermarriage and other ties, limited the reasonable grounds for intercommunal strife. He identifies the main groups thus:

> The normal bonds of society could thus offset the formal division between Protestant and Catholic. There was, in fact, a tension between custom and pragmatism on the one hand and doctrine and dogma on the other.[60]

The discussion itself tends to avoid noting that the establishment of the Anglican church as a minority dominant state church, with its attendant structures, and the disabling legislation against adherents of other faiths, disadvantaging the majority population for at least 150 years, might have given grounds for the growth of a toxic element that overrode the normal social cohesion that could have made sectarianism the innocent differentiator of the thesis.

Ute Lotz-Heumann, in 'Confessionalisation in Ireland: periodisation and character, 1534–1649' [61] argues for the re-periodisation of sixteenth- and seventeenth-century Irish history and the revisiting of catch-all terms like 'Counter-Reformation' that she regards as both misleading and anachronistic in the context of Irish history of that period. She argues instead for the application of the theory of 'confessionalisation' with its attendant heuristic tools in the Irish case and summarises that its adoption would encourage a wider approach to the analysis of religious and political strife. Its adoption would 'draw attention to the fact that almost all early modern governments strove to enforce the *cuius regio, eius religio* principle'.[62] In consequence, the problem at the root of the religio-political conflicts in early modern Ireland, the English government's continuous insistence on enforcing Protestantism and suppressing Catholicism, can be seen first of all as a normal European phenomenon of the period and does not have to be seen as a colonial or 'unique' characteristic.[63] Her thesis would identify differentiations within Irish Catholicism, 'for Ireland, I suggest differentiating between two movements of Catholic confessionalisation in this transitional period: the movement of Catholic reform, combined with constitutional opposition and upheld by the loyal Old English community, on the one hand, and the militant counter-reformation, upheld by Gaelic Irish and independent Old English nobles, on the other.'[64] This refreshing restatement of affairs would allow a wider angle of interpretation than the binary Irish–English conflict seems to afford.

Just how the Irish episcopacy set about harnessing the considerable amount of loyalty, enthusiasm, confusion, impoverishment and general disorder that characterised their defeated co-religionists and fellow-countrymen in the interests of forging an Irish Catholic identity is the matter addressed by Tadhg Ó hAnnracháin in '"In imitation of that holy patron of prelates the blessed St Charles": episcopal activity in Ireland and the formation of a confessional identity, 1618–1653'.[65] In spite of the turmoil of the times, the Irish Catholic hierarchy sought to implement, to their utmost ability the reforms urged by legendary reformers like Charles Borromeo (1538–84), the Archbishop of Milan. This man, canonised 26 years after his death, was the iconic saint of the Catholic reformers. He urged that prelates seek and receive frank and critical judgement on their behaviour and decisions from their confreres. The contentious tone of much of the surviving correspondence between Irish priests, their bishops and their governors and provincials is due, in some measure, to the influence of the Bishop of Milan's insistence on self-awareness and internal regulation. Ó hAnnracháin sees this tendency as an example of the permeation of Tridentine principles into the practice of the Irish hierarchy. Indeed, provision for Irish bishops was on a par with that in the established church between 1618 and 1630, a situation that compared favourably with contemporary Transylvania where Catholicism was not outlawed, but where it was impossible, nevertheless, to provide a traditional structure and Catholics, though within their legal rights, had to make do with an *ad hoc* provision of pastoral care. Ó hAnnracháin argues that ethnic divisions among the clergy were (after the initial period) not the principal source of confrontation between reformers and traditionalists, but that political allegiances and entrenched interests among regular and secular clergy were more likely to lead to conflict within the Catholic community, among priests and among the laity.

> The fact that the episcopal leadership of the Tridentine movement of reform in Ireland was present in both the principal ethnic communities in the island was arguably a point of cardinal importance in defining the wider Catholic identity which emerged in the first half of the seventeenth century. That it resulted in the new religious culture establishing deeper roots throughout the country seems undeniable. This was of particular significance in Gaelic Ireland as the Old English wing of the hierarchy developed first and there was initial strong opposition on the part of some Old English prelates to the appointment of Gaelic Irish bishops, largely on the grounds that their doubtful loyalty might excite the wrath of the state against all Catholics. The struggle against the development of a Gaelic episcopal branch, even in Ulster where the state's anxieties concerning the possibility of insurrection and/or invasion were most acute, however, was largely lost in the course of the 1620s.[66]

Events subsequent to the 1641 uprising, however, showed fissures within the Catholic community and hierarchy that threatened to split the reforming church between those whose principal loyalty was to the monarchy (in this case the Stuarts) and would settle for toleration under them, and those whose principal loyalty was to religious freedom and sought a monarch who would grant freedom of religion.

Religious freedom, or religious toleration, two conflicting concepts bound up with notions of due loyalty to the deity and to the monarch, dogged every informed political move made by those persons engaged with social, economic and political survival in the fraught century between 1550 and 1650. English Catholics felt that Ireland offered a safe haven against prosecution in their homeland during the Elizabethan period. David Edwards's 'A Haven of Popery: English Catholic Migration to Ireland in the Age of Plantations'[67] examines this rarely mentioned group. His discussion ranges over those English Catholics who were part of the Tudor military campaigns, those who came to Ireland as Protestants but who became Catholic or whose families became Catholic in Ireland, and those who fled to Ireland as a stepping-stone to Continental Europe, along with those who came for a Catholic education. He also mentions English pilgrims to holy sites in Ireland during the 1620s.[68] It is clear from Edwards's essay that the practice of religious prosecution [against Catholics] in Ireland was neither as advanced nor as thorough as that practiced in England. Details provided by Edwards of some of the individuals in these categories throw an interesting light on an image of Ireland seldom discussed – Ireland as a desirable and safe destination.

> To take the Lancashire-born priest and future martyr, John Almond (b. 1567). As a teenager, if not a little earlier, he had had to go to Ireland to receive a Catholic education. Similarly, Ralph Corby, who was destined to be hanged, drawn and quartered at Tyburn in September 1644 for serving as a Jesuit missionary in England. He was born in Dublin in March 1598 'of English parents, natives of the bishopric of Durham'. As 'zealous converts' to Catholicism, in the 1590s they had gone over into Ireland 'for the freer exercise of their religion' and to escape persecution – and the threat of family separation – at home.[69]

Confessional compatibility seemed to dictate marriage alliances to some extent; English Catholics tended to marry Irish Catholics of whatever ethnicity; English Protestants tended to marry Irish Protestants, and vice versa. Nor did religion dampen the zeal of those English adventurers who happened to be Catholic. Catholic planters in Laois/Offaly and elsewhere did not mitigate their massacres for religious reasons. Among them were the energetic and brutal Cosby and Harpole, Thornton (of Limerick), Davell (of Carlow) and others involved in dispossession and execution of local Catholic Irish lords and their followers.[70] Mixed allegiances and mixed ethnicities subsisting throughout Ireland and especially in those areas that had undergone systematic plantation, means that the 1641 conflict cannot be looked upon as an uncomplicated religious or ethnic conflagration. English Catholic names were found among the lists of 'Irish rebels' and Irish rebels sometimes attacked English Catholics among them in spite of shared religious sympathies.

Shared commitment to Catholicism did not mean that harmony prevailed among the Irish Catholics. Brian Jackson in 'Sectarianism: division and dissent in Irish Catholicism'[71] identifies a crippling and divisive disharmony in the documentation surviving from a local dispute between the vicar general of Armagh and ordinary of Drogheda on the one hand, and the Franciscans of Drogheda on the other, during the years 1618–1625. Drogheda town itself straddled two ecclesiastical areas of jurisdiction, a division physically denoted by the river Boyne. To the north of the river the town was in the diocese of Armagh, to the south, in that of Meath. The seven years of dispute between the vicar-general of Armagh and the friars exposed a many-faceted Catholicism. Both sides threatened recourse to secular authority to settle their dispute, both sides claimed that they were under severe government persecution, both declared that the other was not fully trained or legitimate and so forth. This essay, like that of Edwards's, exposes layers of continuity and domestic 'normality' in a period that is, historically, periodised by military and civil crises. Townspeople in Drogheda and neighbouring Dundalk and in the further Armagh, joined church sodalities, undertook related charity work, practiced petty social exclusivism and altogether conducted themselves in a manner that is hard to imagine when focusing on historical crises. This, after all, was the town that was sacked by Cromwell some 25 years later—a real town, with a socially differentiated population who had private lives, professional interests and petty grievances of their own, all very familiar to a modern eye.

volition

Complementing the 'response' concepts so ably set forth in accounts such as that of Canny, noted above, are the less extensive and more intensive studies of individual experiences or tracing of a single theme. *The Irish in Europe, 1580–1815* (2001) edited by Thomas O'Connor gathers together the work of a number of scholars whose focus is narrow but whose combined contributions amount to a new approach to Irish history concerned with the two centuries after the departure of the Northern Earls in 1607.[72] Volitional effort seems to provide the basis for much of the activity and developments outlined in the studies. Exploring Spanish historiographical resources and Spanish administrative records, Ciaran O'Scea, in 'The Devotional World of the Irish Catholic Exile in Early-Modern Galicia, 1598–1666'[73] delves into the personal records of Irish emigrants in Galicia. His discovery of a number of Irish wills has given him the opportunity to make a rare voyage of discovery into the religious mentality of both Gaelic and Old English migrants. This mentality is set firmly in the context of contemporary Galician practice and reveals several distinctive characteristics which mark the Irish off from their Spanish hosts, the Old English from the Gaelic Irish and men from women.[74] The variety of allegiances, loyalties and unexpected variants on these, among the main social and political groupings of Irish who settled in Galicia gives texture and colour and a recognisable ambience to named members of an expatriate Irish community and includes some fine details on the lives and ambitions of women.

The behaviour of Irish migrant communities (mostly from Munster in this instance) documented in Spanish notarial sources such as those examined by O'Scea, indicate, like some other sources,[75] that Irish people abroad conducted themselves in a manner similar to, and familiar to, those whose religious, economic and social configurations they might share abroad. And so, those Irish in Galicia, notably in La Coruña, a major naval and military centre quite close to the important pilgrim centre of Santiago de Compstela, who left documentary evidence such as wills behind, indicate in their final wishes, a fully rounded sense of themselves, their lives here and hereafter, and their social aspirations for those members of the family left behind. The scarcity of similar documentation surviving in Ireland hides the normal pursuits of such people and leaves the field to the more equivocal accounts by antagonistic witnesses, propagandists or by poets whose works are intentionally at a remove from 'documentary' reality. Members of the Munster noble families of O'Sullivan Beare, O'Sulivan Mór, O'Driscoll, McCarthy, along with members of their client families (such as O'Donovan, O'Riordan, McSweeney) settled there, many of the noblemen as Spanish pensioners. Long established trading links with Ireland made it also a likely and familiar destination for members of Waterford merchant families.[76]

Light is cast on the preoccupations of such families concerning property, education and religion through the wishes expressed in their testaments; through their sense of the just or equitable or desirable disposal of their property and in their expressed plans for their children. O'Scea points out that the novelty, in some respects, of the wills he examines lies in their belonging to members of Irish noble families written in the religious freedom (for them) of Counter-Reformation Spain. The reticence that characterised references to religion and so forth is evident in wills from the surviving Irish and Old English wills drawn up in Ireland, seems to be absent from the more forthrightly pious or committed statements contained in these Spanish documents. The Castilian model was that favoured by the testators in those documents examined by O'Scea, which meant that only a portion of the testators property was free to be willed as they wished, the remainder legally devolving on legitimate heirs in varying proportions. It is therefore on the quantum in which the testator enjoyed freedom of disposal that O'Scea focuses his discussion. Following the established practice in Ireland for members of noble families, most noble migrants requested burial in a named convent of the Franciscans or Dominicans. The participation of members of their chosen confraternity, of which the testators proved to have been life-long members, was a feature of 80 per cent of O'Scea's chosen wills.[77] The continuity suggested by these details in the lives of devout or newly-devout Catholics between their lives in Southwest Munster and Northwestern Spain, indicates a level of civil life, social organisation and normal social intercourse, which are not features of Irish life generally referred to or suggested to have obtained in the accounts of Irish life under the conditions of war and plantation. It is to be supposed from O'Scea's work that the substructure at least, of an ordered and socially engaged life, subsisted in the scrappy and prejudicial accounts surviving of life as lived by the warring Irish nobility of the period.

O'Scea notes also, how, though Old English merchant families had access to money and to property, often owning houses and other properties in Galicia, while the members of noble Irish families seemed dependent entirely on their pensions, the weight of nobility seemed heavier in the latter group, and social tensions were predicated on the division between merchant and nobleman even in the straitened circumstances obtaining for many of them at the time.[78] The wills of one Dermot O'Sullivan and his family, indicate that these Irish nobles had been accepted into the higher social levels of their adopted communities through nobility of blood, relative prosperity and through thorough engagement in the religious life of the city. Testators also left money for the support of the Irish students in colleges in Salamanca and in Santiago. Centred on sources in Spain also, Patricia O Connell's chapter entitled, 'The early-modern Irish college network in Iberia, 1590–1800' studies the role of the Irish colleges and looks at an influential subgroup of the Irish Spanish migration. She sees the colleges as elements of the diplomatic, social and commercial networks that joined specific regions of the two countries together from the early seventeenth century. Her work suggests that *ancien régime* Ireland, Spain and France were not descrete 'nations', in the modern sense, but collections of regions with differing levels of economic, social and cultural relations with other European regions'.[79] Best of all, it extends the story of the continental colleges movement into the eighteenth century when, by degrees, political developments involving anti-Catholic feeling (notably the suppression of the Jesuits 1767), the fading of the distinctive Irish colony through naturalisation as well as by decline in new arrivals and other internal tensions in the Catholic countries of Europe made it impossible for Irish students to continue to depend on welcome, education or patronage in these obsolete institutions. The emergence of France with a greater role in the Irish emigrant community lessened the importance of the Spanish connection throughout the eighteenth century.

This emphasis on the 'region' is a feature of much of the latest writing, which explores sources subsisting in underused records in continental Europe. These are somewhat skewed in the direction of Spain and Iberian sources, but that is to be expected at this stage in the move away from tried and tested theories, which one senses is the trend being developed with collections such as this of O'Connor. Staying within the Spanish sphere, Clare Carroll in, 'Custom and law in the philosophy of Suárez and in the histories of O'Sullivan Beare, Céitinn and Ó Cléirigh'[80] specifies the group to which she gives attention. They are those Irish writers in the Irish and Latin languages whose writings seem to show the influence of Spanish 'categories of political thought'.[81] Tadhg Ó Dúshláine's 'Devout Humanism Irish-Style: The Influence of Sir Thomas More on Seathrún Céitinn'[82] complements Carroll's (article, 'Custom and Law') underlining the dual pedigree of 'early-modern devotional literature in Irish, the Catholic humanist tradition, mediated through England and the older medieval tradition which survived the sixteenth century and emerged revitalised in the baroque'.[83]

In Éamon Ó Cíosáin, 'A Hundred Years of Irish Migration to France, 1590–1688',[84] attention is turned, once again, to the elements of independent action that motivated the Irish who emigrated to France. The 'Wild Geese' whose departure to France seems to be *the* definitive migration is modified by Ó Cíosáin to take into account sizeable migrations before that date which were more or less voluntary. This is in contrast to what amounted to the effective banishment of the Irish military men who left with Justin McCarthy at the end of the seventeenth century. The mid-century saw the migration of Munster people exploiting existing trade routes and connections to Brittany. Ó Ciosáin tracks down O'Donovans, O'Sullivans, O'Callaghans, Murphys, O'Learys, McCarthys and others who appear in marriage registers and other documents from the 1630s. Some 1,000 persons listed as Irish Catholics appear in the census rolls of Brittany in 1666; the neighbouring provinces of Anjou and Normandy hosted like numbers. Irish clergy had a continual if sporadically funded presence in France, culminating in the successes of the Irish colleges in Paris and in Nantes in the 1670s and 1680s. Irish migrations to France reflected not only the ebbs and flows of Irish–English relationships but 'answers to events, which affect the continent as a whole: Counter-Reformation, the Thirty Years' War, Bourbon-Habsburg rivalry, epidemics and food-shortages.'[85]

Mary Ann Lyons, in her article 'The Emergence of an Irish Community in San Malo, 1550–1710' complements Ó Cíosáin's work with a focus on one community underlining 'the breadth and depth of Hiberno-French links in the *ancien régime* period'.[86] Irish Jacobites whose military careers wavered as treaties were signed and were broken are examined by David Bracken, in 'Piracy and Poverty: Aspects of the Irish Jacobite Experience in France, 1691–1720'.[87] The lawlessness and rootlessness attendant on periodic demobilisation affected Irish troops and Irish emigrant women as much as any other, and some insights into the more pathetic aspects of this side of the Jacobite career on the continent are outlined by Bracken. Awareness of the lifestyle of Irish mercenaries and other military and clerical emigrants gives a greater context to contemporary and traditional works such as the well-known lament from County Cork, *Caoineadh Airt Uí Laoghaire*, the hero of which had been in the Austrian service. Meidhbhín Ní Úrdail's work on eighteenth- and early nineteenth-century Irish manuscript literature and subliterary survivals may be seen against the surprisingly wide background experience of Irish men and women either at first-hand or vicariously through emigrant family connections.[88]

The ephemeral court at San-Germain-en-Laye (the Irish experience from 1690–1712) is examined by Edward Corp, 'The Irish at the Jacobite Court of San-Germain-en-Laye'. The ambitions, hopes, disappointments and failures of that small community are well analysed in this article. Corp focuses on the 'quality of the relationship between the Stuarts and their Irish dependants ... and the particular challenge posed to the Stuarts by the need to dispense scarce patronage and favors among loyal subjects of three kingdoms'.[89] Individual Stuart efforts to help the indigent Irish who could not return home included James II's personal efforts to persuade Louis XIV not to disband Irish regiments; the successive sales of family jewels and other valuables for their relief; and the distribution of subventions by Pope Innocent XII for the support of his 'poor Catholic' followers. Though individual efforts seem to have been heroic, the sense of deflation and thwart with the failing Stuart enterprise grew throughout the eighteenth century among the Irish abroad even if the expressions of Jacobitism in Ireland seemed to adhere to a Stuart restoration, even if only in its allegorical modes.

Irish clerics educated on the Continent, especially in France, provided the bulk of the parish clergy in Ireland itself during the eighteenth century. Their participation in the intellectual life (many in the faculties of theology and philosophy in the University of Paris) of *ancien régime* France may have contributed to the creation of a climate of opinion in

Ireland open to the radical 'enlightened' sensibilities that led to the formation of non-denominational societies such as the United Irishmen.[90] Liam Chambers, in 'A displaced intelligentsia: aspects of Irish Catholic thought in ancien régime France', examines the intellectual life abroad of Irish clerics who involved themselves in French affairs – such as the conversion of protestants and in the Jansenist controversies – before the foundation of the Royal College of St Patrick at Maynooth in 1795.

The establishment of communities of Irish clerical scholars in Paris (mainly in Collège des Lombards and in Collège des Irlandaises) is examined in Priscilla O'Connor, 'Irish clerics and Jacobites in early eighteenth-century Paris, 1700–30',[91] in its social and political and ethnic make up. Providing some one third of Irish parish clergy, the French-trained priesthood played a formative role in Irish Catholic religious life in Ireland. A more detailed study of the Collège des Irlandaises, its background and its development and its principal personalities in the context of its considerable contribution to the continuation of Irish studies during the eighteenth century is presented in Proinsias Mac Cana, *Collège des Irlandaises Paris and Irish Studies* (2001). The fortunes of second- and third-generation Irish in France, and of the students at the numerous colleges for Irish students in Paris, Bordeaux, Toulouse, Nantes, to name the more important ones, are examined in Liam Swords, 'The Irish in Paris at the End of the ancien régime'.[92] The article examines, briefly, the careers of some of those who, once trained, never returned to Ireland and became involved at all levels in French life, including in the professions of teachers and tutors to members of influential French families.[93] Naturalisation of Irish emigrant families was common when siblings, following each other, married into French families. Those who abandoned the priesthood became, in many instances, doctors and formed a recognisable coterie of Irish doctors in Paris.[94]

The career outlets provided in France and on the continent generally, for those whose education took them into the second and third levels were, in many instances, those, that under better political circumstances, would have been successfully pursued in Ireland. The army, the navy, the law, the church and so forth (legitimate and likely careers for those of their class and education, thwarted in their ambitions at home by laws that sought to exclude them from any influence in public life) gleaned a portion of these émigrés, many of whom had been sent to France as young teenagers with the fees to cover a single term.[95] The émigré community itself set up bursaries and benevolent funds to support students and other indigent Irish. Continual contact with Ireland through the arrival of new students, their siblings, parents, returning

students and professionals, meant that at many levels the Irish community in France and those in Ireland were abreast of developments in
both countries. The network of Irish professional men in Paris, through
the colleges, particularly, saw to it that new Irish emigrants had the
necessary documentation to apply for commissions in the army, and
in other tightly controlled French institutions. They made good the
absence of registered births, marriages and deaths, occasioned by the
lack of a legal establishment for Catholics in Ireland.

Altogether, the Irish in Paris, at least, integrated themselves 'into the
social and financial networks of *ancien régime*-France', forming their
own Masonic lodge *L'Irlandaise du soleil levanat*.[96] Many of these were
at pains to survive the Revolution which overtook them, and especially
those priests among them, in the 1790s. How thoroughly integrated the
Irish had become in their chosen fields in France is, perhaps, best shown
in the incidental facts with which Liam Swords colours this engaging
account of the Irish in Paris before the Revolution: '[w]hen the Bastille
fell on 12 July 1789, one of its two chaplains was a Clonfert priest,
Thomas MacMahon, (a doctoral graduate from the Sorbonne) from
Eyrecourt, Co. Galway. He was pensioned by the revolutionary government with a greater income than he had enjoyed as chaplain.'[97] The
Collège des Irlandaises was turned into a prison by the revolutionary
government and many Irish priests, regulars and seculars, and military
men were imprisoned and many executed.

jacobite and jacobin

The traditional split, between, on the one hand, Jacobite, Catholic,
romantic sensibilities, and on the other, those of enlightened, Protestant,
cosmopolitan feeling, each representing, respectively, the indigenous
populations of Ireland and that of the newer planter populations, is
challenged at all levels in the collection of some 33 essays *1798: A
Bicentenary Perspective* (2003), edited by Thomas Bartlett, David Dickson,
Daire Keogh and Kevin Whelan. As pointed out by Kevin Whelan, in
respect of the orator Edmund Burke, 'An "Irish" Burke has emerged ... in
recent writings, with the recognition that his arguments (conservative
in a British framework) became radical when transposed into Ireland.'[98]
A 'precocious' political consciousness characterised the Irish Catholic
poor in the eighteenth century, imposed in part by their unwilling
participation in the process of colonisation. Jacobitism was a feature
of this political class and it carried and cultivated a messianic charge
in the protonationalistic rhetoric of its songs and poems. Jacobitism

articulated political ambitions that belonged to a people for whom they were, at least temporarily, barely realisable.

The literary nature of much of the overt and covert expression of Jacobitism in Ireland allowed for the entertainment of illegal political thoughts and ambitions on two levels. The allegorisation of all matters to do with the political aspirations of that portion of population of Ireland for whom the status quo was intolerable in the long term, encouraged a community of interest spreading across the social levels and across the physical boundaries to those Irish outside of Ireland upon whom most of the hopes of those awaiting political deliverance devolved. When the military strength of Jacobitism no longer existed, the literary and allegorical narrative of the Ireland depicted in, and envisioned by the popular Jacobite literary and subliterary traditions, provided a base of sorts for elements of it to become Jacobin in the late eighteenth century.[99] This bridging function created the necessary links between the Jacobite efforts in the mid-century with the Jacobin effort of the 1798 rebellion. The preponderance of Munster-men in the armies of Louis XIV and XV and the strength of both the Irish manuscript tradition and the Jacobite literary tradition in Munster, along with the long-standing links between Irish merchants and France, lent an organic continuity to those connections that became relevant militarily, to the United Irishmen at the end of the eighteenth century.[100] The experience, on the other hand, of Irish priests and others during the Terror in France, created a suspicion and fear of republicanism in its more radical forms.

During the course of the eighteenth century, the focus of Irish voluntary emigration was no longer solely on the continent of Europe; the Americas now made themselves felt as a resource, and with the American Revolution, something of an example. Breandán Ó Buachalla's 'From Jacobite to Jacobin',[101] notes the characteristics of the messianic mode of thought that pervades the written sources of, purportedly, verbatim accounts taken after the 1798 rebellion as after the 1641 rebellion. A world turned upside down, or set right after having been set topsy-turvy, is the expressed wish of the 'millennial' mindset. The Jacobite sensibility in Ireland cultivated and expressed dissatisfaction with the displacement of a 'true' noble class with a base herd of newcomers. Graphically depicted (among other things) as a wronged young woman, bound in chains, oppressed by an ugly, unworthy goblin-like creature, awaiting rescue, by a true prince, Irish Jacobite songs and writings provided a recognisable narrative for all levels of thought and participation. The tantalising possibility of the kind of salvation outlined in the

Jacobite dream during the first half of the eighteenth century gave edge and nuance to Jacobites songs. The failure of the military enterprise gave a poignancy and a curiously fertile bitterness to the same tropes and themes in the second half of the eighteenth century. Its power lay in its rhetoric that 'became in the course of the eighteenth century a corrosive radical idiom which undermined the legitimacy of the *status quo* and which foretold its eventual demise; it also became increasingly more strident and blood-curdling'.[102]

Ó Buachalla suggests that the legitimation of the millennial vision of Jacobite poetry was predicated upon the legitimising prophecy.[103] This all-pervading and subversive vision equipped generations of Irish people, whose political aspirations and identity they felt to be thwarted, to imagine political scenarios in which they were victorious and indeed, equipped their imaginations to recognise the circumstances that might achieve their dreamt-of ends. Irish sources commented on the American Revolution in terms that indicated their fully developed awareness of what such a precedent might mean for themselves. Vincent Morley's *Irish Opinion and the American Revolution, 1760–1783,* (2000) shows how much in tune those who read and wrote the Irish language were with the latest information from the American colonies, and how varied opinions of the events could be. The examination of such sources, not usually heretofore taken into account, enlarges the image of Irish life from that of a roiling and revanchist peasantry, addicted to dreams of glorious triumph, to a more credible one of an ambitious, though thwarted, people, alert and aware of those matters that had relevance for them, and doggedly preparing themselves in a rational and recognisable manner for opportunities to improve their circumstances, socially, and politically. Irish Catholic opinion, during the 1770s still championed a Bourbon victory (against Britain). Irish celebration of Washington and John Paul Jones, the American naval commander, ignored the overwhelmingly Protestant/Puritan character of the North American revolutionaries and championed their opposition to the Hanoverian monarch.[104] The Jacobite rhetoric in which Catholic Irish political ambitions were usually articulated (in extant poetic and propagandist sources) can suggest an irrational and impulsive, if not whimsical engagement with political reality on the part of the disenfranchised Irish. The corollary of this is the intimation that any action on their part would be headlong, ruthless, bloody and futile. Violent disorder and ruthlessness certainly characterised the 1798 rebellion, as it did the sporadic and deadly agrarian disturbances, which punctuated the eighteenth century throughout Britain and Europe. None of these events depended on a Jacobite underpinning to display characteristics which were, and continue to be, a feature of activist politics where highly motivated minority groups struggle against, not only, the 'enemy' but also against a quiescent majority in whose interest, they assert, they act.

It might well be argued that the current quasi-unification of Europe has encouraged the sense of regional identity across national boundaries. This re-establishes, in a certain way, and in some respects, the natural areas of shared interest and shared history that transcend national boundaries and come into their own when those boundaries become significant in a way that allows for cross-boundary identities. Recent studies expand the binary relationship between Ireland and Great Britain to include other relationships with other regions/states/peoples. Whatever one's political attitude to the current status quo, the relevance of the sense of the union of European states for writing Irish history is evident in these publications of the twenty-first century.

notes

1. 'Old English' is a term that became a popular self-description for a period in the seventeenth century by those descendants of Anglo-Norman settlers in Ireland, in order, principally, to distinguish themselves from newer Elizabethan adventurers in Ireland.

2. Nicholas Canny, *Making Ireland British, 1580–1650* (Oxford University Press, 2001), p. 417.

3. Bernadette Cunningham, *The World of Geoffrey Keating: History, Myth and Religion in Seventeenth-century Ireland. (Dublin, Four Courts Press, 2001)* and Nicholas Canny, *Making Ireland British, 1580–1650*.

4. Dubhaltach Mac Fhirbhisigh (c. 1600–71) was an Irish genealogist, translator and scribe. His best-known work is the *Leabhar Genealach*.

5. Sir James Ware (c. 1594–1666), Dublin-born historiographer, educated at Trinity College, Dublin. His *History of Ireland* was published in 1633.

6. Nollaig Ó Muraíle, *The Celebrated Antiquary Dubhaltach Mac Fhirbhisigh (c. 1600–1671): His Lineage, Life and Learning* (Maynooth, An Sagart, 1996; reprinted 2003).

7. Tony Crowley, *The Politics of Language in Ireland 1366–1922: A Sourcebook* (London, Routledge, 2000), p. 1.

8. The 'Flight of the Earls' refers to the unlicensed and secret departure from Ireland of the Earl of Tyrone (d. 1616) and the Earl of Tyrconnell (d. 1608) in September 1607. They planned to travel to Spain but political intrigue and diplomatic wrangling kept them away from Spain and they eventually settled in Italy.

9. The 1641 Rebellion is the name given to a 12-year conflict that originated in a pre-emptive strike by Ulster Catholic landowners against the state and spread throughout Ireland. It acquired, in some areas, the characteristics of a populist uprising. In 1642, the disaffected landowners, members of the Catholic

clergy and Catholic lawyers and merchants created a Confederate Association that met in Kilkenny in order to organise a military and civil structure to conduct the war that had become involved with the English civil wars and contemporary Scottish wars.

10. The Williamite wars in Ireland, known also as *Cogadh an Dá Rí*, refer to military conflicts following the deposition of King James II in 1688 when he sought to recover his three kingdoms from his daughter Mary and her husband, a Dutch prince, and James's kinsman, William of Orange. Factions in Ireland, often defined by religious allegiance, supported both sides—Catholics, for the most part, supporting James II and Protestants, for the most part, supporting William and Mary. In many respects the war in Ireland was a proxy war between two major Catholic powers, Louis XIV of France – who supported James II—and the Holy Roman Emperor and the King of Spain who supported William.

11. Crowley, *The Politics of Language*, p. 55.

12. Crowley, *The Politics of Language* p. 55.

13. Crowley, *The Politics of Language*, pp. 55–6.

14. Crowley, *The Politics of Language*, p. 56.

15. Crowley, *The Politics of Language*, pp. 78–80.

16. In this period the manuscript literature to which Breandán Ó Buachalla and Vincent Morley, and Meidhbhín Ní Úrdail, have devoted much attention, was produced; much of what remained of earlier manuscripts was copied; and these provide, in some instances, sole witnesses today.

17. Crowley, *The Politics of Language*, p. 3.

18. Canny, *Making Ireland British*, pp. 403–5.

19. Patrick Darcy (1598–1668) was a Galway-born barrister who was a member of the Middle Temple in London. He was elected to the Irish Parliament in 1634 where he opposed Wentworth. He was an influential member of the Confederation of Kilkenny and was an architect of the peace signed in 1646 with the Marquis of Ormond.

20. Canny, *Making Ireland British*, p. 408.

21. John Cusacke, absolutist thinker and Irishman, educated, like many of his peers on the continent, published a series of pamphlets between 1615 and 1647, which were a re-reading of kingship, law and government. He also argued that the King was the central lawmaker in contrast to the writings of Sir Edward Coke who emphasised the importance of common law and custom.

22. Canny, *Making Ireland British*, p. 419.

23. Flaithrí O'Maolchonaire (c. 1560–1629) was the Roscommon-born Archbishop of Tuam. He was the Papal Legate at Kinsale and was chaplain to Hugh O'Donnell with whom he returned to Spain after the Kinsale defeat. He translated Spanish and Catalan devotional works into Irish and also wrote poetry. In 1606 he became the Provincial of the Irish Franciscans, and in 1606–07 he established, under the patronage of Philip III of Spain, an Irish college at Louvain.

24. In *Léachtaí Cholm Cille* 2 (1971) pp. 74–87.

25. Canny, *Making Ireland British*, pp. 421–30.

26. One of a sequence of studies emerging from an enlightened engagement of the Folger Shakespeare Library in Washington of which Hiram Morgan's

(ed.) *Political Ideology in Ireland 1541–1641* (Dublin, Four Courts Press, 1999) is another.

27. Jane Ohlmeyer (ed.), *Political Thought in Seventeenth-Century Ireland: Kingdom or Colony*. (Cambridge University Press, 2000), pp. 155–75.

28. Peter Lombard (c.1555–1625) was born in Waterford and educated in Oxford and in Louvain. He was made Archbishop of Armagh in 1601. He was the author of *De Hibernia Insula Commentarius Stromaticus* (1600), an account of the Elizabethan wars of the 1590s in Ireland. Philip O'Sullivan Beare (c. 1590–1630), nephew of Donal O'Sullivan Beare, Lord of Dunboy, was educated in Santiago de Compostela in Spain. In 1621 he wrote *Historiae Catholicae Iberniae Compendium*, a history of the Elizabethan wars in South Munster, principally, and focusing especially on the O'Sullivan participation in those conflicts. In 1615, he wrote an account of Irish emigré ecclesiastics and other professional men (*Zoilomastix*) that also included a denunciation of the works of Geraldus Cambrensis and of Richard Stanihurst. John Lynch (c. 1599–1673), Galway-born priest, published in 1662 a refutation of Cambrensis, under the pseudonym Gratianus Lucius. Richard O'Ferrall, OFMCap (d. 1663) and Robert O'Connell OFMCap., (fl. 1650s) completed an account of the wars in Ireland during the 12 years 1641–53 known now as *Commentarius Rinuccinianus*. Conor O'Mahoney, of the Society of Jesus, was a Cork-born controversialist whose *Disputatio Apologetica* (Lisbon 1645), advocated complete independence for Ireland.

29. Owen Roe O'Neill (c. 1590–1649), was a nephew of Hugh O'Neill, Earl of Tyrone. He was commissioned in the Spanish service in 1606 and returned to Ireland to participate in the wars following the 1641 rebellion. He led the notable victory at Benburb in 1646.

30. Ohlmeyer (ed.), *Political Thought in Seventeenth-Century Ireland*, pp. 176–88.

31. Jane Ohlmeyer is editor of *Ireland from Independence to Occupation, 1641–1660* (New York, Cambridge University Press, 1995), a collection of articles that trace the gradual political disqualification of Ireland during the Interregnum.

32. Ohlmeyer, *Ireland from Independence to Occupation*, p. 1.

33. Bernadette Cunningham, 'Representations of king, parliament and the Irish people in Geoffrey Keating's Foras feasa ar Éirinn and John Lynch's Cambrensis eversus (1662)', in Ohlmyer (ed.), *Political Thought in Seventeenth-century Ireland*.

34. Cunningham, *The World of Geoffrey Keating*, p. 131.

35. Cunningham makes the point that Keating was, by far, more popular in Ireland than Lynch, enjoying a hugely vigorous life in the manuscript tradition, and being translated into both Latin and into English within 30 years of its first appearance (*The World of Geoffrey Keating*, p. 132).

36. The Confederation of Kilkenny was so called because its Supreme Council met for the most part in the city of Kilkenny. Its General Assembly, the main organ of government – bound together by an oath of association and representing two thirds of the country – met nine times between August 1642 and January 1649. Its objectives were to form a national government in a time of social and political turmoil; to counter government military measures with an organised military resistance of its own; and to negotiate a peace settlement with the King. These objectives seemed to have been achieved by 1649 after which the Confederation dissolved itself.

37. Micheal Ó Siochrú, *Kingdoms in Crisis: Ireland in the 1640s: Essays in Honour of Donal Cregan* (Dublin, Four Courts Press, 2001), p. 11.
38. Ó Siochrú, *Kingdoms in Crisis*, p. 15.
39. David Edwards, Pádraig Lenihan and Clodagh Tait, *The Age of Atrocity: Violence and Political Conflict in Early Modern Ireland.* (Dublin, Four Courts Press, 2007), p. 9.
40. The introductory essay refers to recent and current academic debates about the validity of such approaches. Edwards, Lenihan and Tait refer to the most active participants in those debates, pp. 16–19.
41. David Edwards, 'The Escalation of Violence in Sixteenth-Century Ireland', in Edwards, Lenihan and Tait, *The Age of Atrocity*, pp. 34–78.
42. Vincent P. Carey, in Edwards, Lenihan and Tait, *The Age of Atrocity*, pp. 79–94.
43. Hiram Morgan, in Edwards, Lenihan and Tait, *The Age of Atrocity*, pp. 95–118.
44. Clodagh Tait, in Edwards, Lenihan and Tait, *The Age of Atrocity*, pp. 130–53.
45. For details of the controversial life and death of this man, see Kevin Forkan, 'The Strange Death of Sir Charles Coote, 1642', in Edwards, Lenihan and Tait, *The Age of Atrocity*, pp. 204–18.
46. Brian Mac Cuarta, in Edwards, Lenihan and Tait, *The Age of Atrocity*, pp. 154–75.
47. Kenneth Nicholls, in Edwards, Lenihan and Tait, *The Age of Atrocity*, pp. 176–91; p. 191.
48. John R. Young, in Edwards, Lenihan and Tait, *The Age of Atrocity*, pp. 219–41.
49. Ibid., p. 220.
50. John Morrill, in Edwards, Lenihan and Tait, *The Age of Atrocity*, pp. 242–65; p. 264.
51. A letter of thanks to Cromwell from the Parliament for his actions at Drogheda noted particularly the effect the massacre would have on others 'who may be warned by it'. See Micheál Ó Siochrú, in Edwards, Lenihan and Tait, *The Age of Atrocity*, p. 273.
52. Micheál Ó Siochrú, in Edwards, Lenihan and Tait, *The Age of Atrocity*, p. 260.
53. Micheál Ó Siochrú, in Edwards, Lenihan and Tait, *The Age of Atrocity*, pp. 266–82; p. 271.
54. See Ó Siochrú, in Edwards, Lenihan and Tait, *The Age of Atrocity*, p. 271.
55. James Butler, 12th Earl of Ormond (1610–88) was the commander of the army in Ireland when the 1641 rising broke out. He led the army against the Parliamentarians but surrendered to Michael Jones in 1647. After regrouping the Royalist opposition he was again defeated by Jones at the Battle of Rathmines in 1649. He escaped to the Continent with the Prince Charles who later became King Charles II. His loyalty was rewarded with a dukedom at the Restoration. He fell out of favour in 1685 and died in 1688.
56. Ó Siochrú in Edwards, Lenihan and Tait, *The Age of Atrocity*, pp. 266–82; p. 276.
57. Ó Siochrú in Edwards, Lenihan and Tait, *The Age of Atrocity*, p. 278.
58. John Childs in Edwards, Lenihan and Tait, *The Age of Atrocity*, pp. 283–300.
59. Alan Ford, 'Living together, living apart: sectarianism in early modern Ireland', in Alan Ford and John McCafferty (eds), *The Origins of Sectarianism in Early Modern Ireland* (Cambridge, Cambridge University Press, 2006), pp. 1–23.

60. Alan Ford in Alan Ford and John McCafferty (eds), *The Origins of Sectarianism in Early Modern Ireland*, p. 23.
61. Ute Lotz-Heumann in Ford and McCafferty (eds), *The Origins of Sectarianism in Early Modern Ireland*, pp. 24–53.
62. Lotz-Heumann in Ford and McCafferty (eds), *The Origins of Sectarianism in Early Modern Ireland*, p. 32.
63. Lotz-Heumann in Ford and McCafferty (eds), *The Origins of Sectarianism in Early Modern Ireland*, p. 29.
64. Lotz-Heumann in Ford and McCafferty (eds), *The Origins of Sectarianism in Early Modern Ireland*, p. 44.
65. Tadhg Ó hAnnracháin in Ford and McCafferty (eds), *The Origins of Sectarianism in Early Modern Ireland*, pp. 73–94.
66. Ó hAnnracháin in Ford and McCafferty (eds) *The Origins of Sectarianism in Early Modern Ireland*, p. 78.
67. Ó hAnnracháin in Ford and McCafferty (eds), *The Origins of Sectarianism in Early Modern Ireland*, pp. 95–126.
68. Ó hAnnracháin in Ford and McCafferty (eds), *The Origins of Sectarianism in Early Modern Ireland*, pp. 108–9.
69. Ó hAnnracháin in Ford and McCafferty (eds), *The Origins of Sectarianism in Early Modern Ireland*, p. 107.
70. Ó hAnnracháin in Ford and McCafferty (eds), *The Origins of Sectarianism in Early Modern Ireland*, pp. 120–2.
71. Brian Jackson in Ford and McCafferty (eds), *The Origins of Sectarianism in Early Modern Ireland*, pp. 203–15.
72. As part of a contribution to migration studies, the editor, Thomas O'Connor, edited and published the fruit of a conference on the Irish in Europe held in Maynooth in December 1999. Thomas O' Connor (ed.), *The Irish in Europe, 1580–1815* (Dublin, Four Courts Press, 2001). The results address, under the rubric of migration studies, areas that fill out the experience of the Irish in Ireland and abroad in the period 'between the Reformation and the French Revolution', p. 9, and address a 'significant dimension of the Irish historical experience … [in] its European context', p. 9.
73. Ciaran O'Scea, 'The Devotional World of the Irish Catholic Exile in Early-Modern Galicia, 1598–1666', in O'Connor (ed.), *The Irish in Europe, 1580–1815* (Dublin, Four Courts Press, 2001), pp. 27–48.
74. O'Scea, 'The Devotional World of the Irish Catholic Exile in Early-Modern Galicia, 1598–1666', p. 21.
75. See, for instance, D. J. O'Doherty, 'Students in the Irish College Salamanca (1595–1619)', in *Archivium Hibernicum*, 2 (1913), pp. 1–36; and idem., 'Students in the Irish College Salamanca (1619–1700)', in *Archivium Hibernicum*, 3 (1914), pp. 87–112, in which the students' 'declaration' held in college archives, are examined for background, social standing, family and other connections of students ranging in age from early teens to late twenties.
76. O'Scea, in O'Connor (ed.), *The Irish in Europe, 1580–1815*, p. 30.
77. O'Scea, in O'Connor (ed.), *The Irish in Europe, 1580–1815*, p. 37.
78. O'Scea, in O'Connor (ed.), *The Irish in Europe, 1580–1815*, p. 41.
79. Patricia O Connell, 'The Early-Modern Irish College Network in Iberia, 1590–1800', in O'Connor (ed.), *The Irish in Europe, 1580–1815*, pp. 49–64.

80. Clare Carroll, 'Custom and law in the philosophy of Suárez and in the histories of O'Sullivan Beare, Céitinn and Ó Cléirigh', in O'Connor (ed.), *The Irish in Europe, 1580–1815*, pp. 65–78.

81. O' Connell in O'Connor (ed.), *The Irish in Europe, 1580–1815*, p. 21.

82. Carroll in O'Connor (ed.), *The Irish in Europe, 1580–1815*, pp. 79–92.

83. O'Connor, *The Irish in Europe 1580–1815*, p. 22. And see, Tadhg Ó Dúshláine's *An Eoraip agus litríocht na Gaeilge, 1600–1650: gnéithe den Bharócachas Eorpach i litríocht na Gaeilge.* (Baile Átha Cliath, 1987) which examines the influence of continental baroque modes on Irish language material in the seventeenth century.

84. Éamon Ó Cíosáin, 'A hundred years of Irish migration to France, 1590–1688', in O'Connor (ed.), *The Irish in Europe, 1580–1815*, pp. 93–106.

85. Ó Cíosáin in O'Connor (ed.), *The Irish in Europe, 1580–1815*, pp. 96, 97; p. 106.

86. Mary Ann Lyons, 'The Emergence of an Irish community in Saint-Malo, 1550–1710', in O'Connor (ed.), *The Irish in Europe, 1580–1815*, pp. 107–26; p. 24.

87. David Bracken, 'Piracy and poverty: aspects of the Irish Jacobite experience in France, 1691–1720', in O'Connor (ed.), *The Irish in Europe, 1580–1815*, pp. 127–42.

88. Meidhbhín Ní Úrdail, 'Máire Bhí Ní Laoghaire: File na "Rilleadh Cainte"', in *Eighteenth-century Ireland: Iris an Dá Chultúr*, 17: 2002 pp. 146–56.

89. Edward Corp, 'The Irish at the Jacobite court of San-Germain-en-Laye', in Thomas O'Connor (ed.), *The Irish in Europe, 1580–1815*, pp. 143–56; p. 24; pp. 152, 154, 166, 168.

90. Liam Chambers, 'A Displaced Intelligentsia: Aspects of Irish Catholic Thought in ancien régime France', in O'Connor (ed.), *The Irish in Europe, 1580–1815*, pp. 157–74; p. 173.

91. Priscilla O'Connor, 'Irish Clerics and Jacobites in Early Eighteenth-Century Paris, 1700–30', in O'Connor (ed.), *The Irish in Europe, 1580–1815*, pp. 175–90.

92. Liam Swords 'The Irish in Paris at the End of the ancien régime', in O'Connor (ed.), *The Irish in Europe, 1580–1815*, pp. 191–205.

93. Swords in O'Connor (ed.), *The Irish in Europe, 1580–1815*, p. 193.

94. Swords in O'Connor (ed.), *The Irish in Europe, 1580–1815*, p.194.

95. Swords in O'Connor (ed.), *The Irish in Europe, 1580–1815*, p. 192, p. 196.

96. Swords in O'Connor (ed.), *The Irish in Europe, 1580–1815*, p. 198.

97. Swords in O'Connor (ed.), *The Irish in Europe, 1580–1815*, p. 203.

98. Thomas Bartlett, David Dickson, Dáire Keogh and Kevin Whelan (eds), *1798: A Bicentenary Perspective* (Dublin, Four Courts Press, 2003), p. 4.

99. Bartlett et al. *1798: A Bicentenary Perspective*, pp. 6–7.

100. Bartlett et al. *1798: A Bicentenary Perspective*, p. 7.

101. Breandán Ó Buachalla, 'From Jacobite to Jacobin' in Bartlett et al., *1798: A Bicentenary Perspective*, pp. 75–96.

102. Ó Buachalla in Bartlett et al., *1798: A Bicentenary Perspective*, pp. 75, 78.

103. Ó Buachalla in Bartlett et al. *1798: A Bicentenary Perspective*, p. 79.

104. See also, Vincent Morley, 'George III, Queen Sadhbh and the Historians', in *Eighteenth-Century Ireland: Iris an Dá Chultúr*, 17: 2002, pp. 112–20.

3

the irish famine: history and representation

margaret kelleher

Turned wrong way round, the relentless unforeseen was what we schoolchildren studied as 'History', harmless history, where everything unexpected in its own time is chronicled on the page as inevitable. The terror of the unforeseen is what the science of history hides, turning a disaster into an epic.

Philip Roth[1]

So the grammar of the past is a two-fold grammar. It is no longer and yet it *has been*. In a sense we are summoned by what was beyond the loss of what is no longer to be faithful to what happened. Here we confront problems of historical representation and reference to the past, but we must never eliminate the truth-claim of what has been.

Paul Ricoeur[2]

what happened? famine demography: a million deaths

Historical estimates of the mortality caused by the Great Famine of 1845–51 have varied widely, from a figure of half a million to that of one and a half million.[3] In recent years, a figure in excess of one million famine deaths, around 1.1 million, has gained general acceptance among historians.[4] The population of Ireland in 1845 was eight and a half million approximately, by 1851 this had declined to six and a half million. 'When estimates of "natural" growth are taken into account, the "missing" total of some 2,400,000, or more than a quarter of the country's population', notes historian Peter Gray, this two and a half

84

million 'missing' a combination of famine mortality and emigration.[5] While the consensus as to the extent of mortality is welcome, and arbitrates between some of the excesses of nationalistic and revisionist famine historiography (to be discussed later), a fundamental challenge remains for all commentators and students of this event. Is historical comprehension, and imaginative apprehension, possible with regard to the nature and scale of this disaster, the deaths of over one million individuals, and the departure, within six years, of one in four people?

Despite its prominence in Irish history and cultural representation, the Great Famine of 1845–51 was far from Ireland's only famine and, in relative terms, may not even have been its deadliest. In 1740 a prolonged spell of cold weather throughout Europe caused famine in Ireland because of destruction to both root and cereal crops.[6] One estimate for the number of crisis victims is between 300,000 and 400,000, from a contemporary population of about 2.4 million, making this in relative terms even more deadly than the 1840s disaster.[7] In the century after 1740, numerous other subsistence crises followed, usually occasioned by bad weather and involving large-scale outbreaks of fever; these include the years 1755, 1766, 1783, 1800–1, 1816–9, 1822, and 1830–1. The seasonal deprivation in the years 1816 and 1822, in particular, risked becoming famine; 'still', as the economic historian Cormac Ó Gráda has observed, 'a combination of private charity and government aid was nearly always enough to stave off the worst before 1846'.[8]

The dating of the beginning of the Great Famine is somewhat contentious; while the year 1845 is generally employed to denote the beginning of the crisis, large-scale famine mortality began a year later. Famines and disasters in other countries, and in more recent times, have shown the fatal significance of naming and dating. For example, in 1943 the delayed official declaration in Bengal of 'famine' caused a vital delay in relief operations,[9] while, in mid-nineteenth-century Ireland, the premature declaration by the administration in autumn 1847 that 'famine' had ceased brought fatal consequences. In autumn 1845, the first appearance of *phytophthora infestans* (potato blight) led to widespread scarcity but not mass starvation. This aversion of a major crisis may be credited both to the partial nature of the potato failure in 1845 and to the relief measures implemented by the government of Sir Robert Peel which included public relief works and state depots of grain for emergency distribution.[10] In August 1846, the potato blight recurred, leading to an almost total failure of the potato crop. Reports of death from starvation began as early as October, and these multiplied in the months that followed.

One of the first deaths to gain public attention, and to be reproduced with powerful effect in later histories, was that of Dennis McKennedy 'from Coolasnahee near Skibbereen', employed on the local public works. The annual report of the Poor Law Commissioners for 1846 recorded the findings of his post mortem, that no food existed in his stomach but 'in the large bowels a portion of undigested raw cabbage mixed with excrement'.[11] Writing from West Clare, on 24 December 1846, to his superior in the Board of Works, District Inspector Captain Wynne reported,

> I ventured through that parish [Clare Abbey] this day, to ascertain the condition of the inhabitants, and although a man not easily moved, I confess myself unmanned by the extent and intensity of suffering I witnessed, more especially amongst the women and little children, crowds of whom were to be seen scattered over the turnip fields, like a flock of famishing crows, devouring the raw turnips, mothers half naked, shivering in the snow and sleet, uttering exclamations of despair, whilst their children were screaming with hunger. I am a match for any thing else I may meet with here, but this I cannot stand.[12]

The following figures and brief chronology may give some idea of the scale of deprivation and hunger. The public works restarted by Lord John Russell's administration in September and October, 1846, employed, by the end of the year, over 440,000 people, mostly men, but also women and children, and by March 1847 some 714,000. A change of government policy to the provision of outdoor relief through soup kitchens, beginning in Spring 1847, led to the distribution, by early July, of more than three million rations nationally, with more than one in three of the population and, in some areas, almost all the inhabitants fed by the state.[13] Viewed by the administration as a temporary measure, however, the soup kitchens were gradually phased out in the following months and all were closed by September, to be replaced by an extension of the poor law whereby local communities were made responsible for the relief of local destitution. The poor law extension act of 1847 also included the infamous Gregory clause, tabled by Sir William Gregory, which denied relief to any tenant holding more than a quarter acre of land. Mass evictions, beginning in early 1847, reached a peak in 1848 and continued in large numbers into the early 1850s; the total number of evictions between 1846 and 1853 is estimated at 70,000, affecting some half a million people, one notorious instance being that of Kilrush

Union in West Clare in which over 12,000 people were evicted between 1847 and 1850.[14]

The estimates of emigration for this period suggest that, by the end of 1847, almost a quarter of a million people had left for North America and Australia, and tens of thousands had gone to Britain. The rate of emigration declined in late 1847 but rose again in the winters of 1848–9 and 1849–50 with the numbers emigrating to America exceeding 200,000 a year in 1849 and 1850 and reaching a peak of just under a quarter of a million in 1851.[15] In summary, well over a million people emigrated from Ireland between the mid-1840s and early 1850s. Although emigration from Ireland was not a new phenomenon, its scale in this decade was unique and its legacy ('push migration with a vengeance')[16] was especially potent in relation to Irish–American political activity in the late nineteenth century and early twentieth century.[17] From a demographic perspective, famine emigration has been seen as a sort of safety valve or form of disaster relief; in its absence, many more deaths would have occurred, though those who could avail of this possibility were not the most vulnerable, more likely small farmers or artisans rather than the landless poor.[18]

In spite of official declarations to the contrary, the famine did not end in 1847. In July 1848 the potato blight returned and caused, according to official figures, the failure of half of the total potato crop; by July 1849, the numbers once again on outdoor relief neared 800,000, one eighth of the entire population. Deaths in workhouses rose sharply between September 1848 and May 1849 and continued to be high as late as 1851. Gray estimates that 'some 2500 deaths per week' occurred nationally in workhouses alone for the early part of 1849 and, by summer 1849, they held a quarter of a million people.[19] This long duration of the Irish famine, at least five years, makes it exceptional in international terms, a year or two years (Bengal 1943–4, Finland 1868, Soviet Union 1932–3) being more typical. Regional variations were large, with mortality at its highest in districts in Clare, Cork, Mayo and Leitrim and at its lightest in areas such as north Down or south Wexford. More generally, along the east coast, famine mortality was light and mainly occurred in the first half of 1847. In areas of the west, northwest, and southwest, one third or more of the population died and considerable deprivation continued into the early 1850s.[20] The conventional view that Dublin remained largely untouched by famine, with expensive balls held in Dublin Castle while thousands starved, has been modified by recent studies which show a considerable impact on the city's lower classes, largely as a result of migration and the spread of infectious disease.[21]

Whom did the famine kill? Recent demographical studies point to significant variations in relation to age, class, and, to some extent, gender, as well as the major regional differences mentioned above. Both children under ten years of age and older people over 60 were over-represented among the famine dead, the young vulnerable to dysentery and the old to typhus; though making up less than one-third of the population, these groups accounted for three-fifths of famine deaths.[22] The available evidence suggests that mortality rates for men were slightly higher than those of women, but the differential is very small; while historians proffer both physiological and cultural explanations, the former, in existing historiography at least, seem the more convincing.[23] The deeply unequal impact of the famine, in terms of class, has at times been crudely represented in notions of 'winners' and 'losers'; alternatively, Ó Gráda's detailed study of occupational change in Ireland, between 1841 and 1851, yields more precise and useful evidence. By 1851, there were some 25 per cent fewer farm labourers in Ireland, with significant decreases also in the numbers of domestic servants, farmers, and small tradesmen such as spinners, weavers, and shoemakers; conversely, marked increases are evident in the numbers of paupers, beggars, bailiffs and rate collectors.[24] Also worth noting are the high rates of excess mortality, linked to fever, among doctors, clergymen of all denominations, and workhouse officials.

theories of causation

The subject of famine's causation and the related issue of government responsibility have proved to be fiercely divisive issues in studies of the Great Famine, and also serve to differentiate the major strands in Irish famine historiography. Central to nationalist interpretations of the famine is the view that, in the famine period, Ireland produced enough food, in grain and livestock, to feed its poor and that mass exports from Ireland to Britain during these years greatly contributed to mortality. This view was disseminated most powerfully by the Young Irelander John Mitchel in writings such as his *Jail Journal* and *The Last Conquest of Ireland (perhaps)*, both of which were first published in installment form in 1850s in American newspapers. The image of ships leaving Ireland, laden with corn, under armed guard, while people starved, recurs throughout literary treatments, and was circulated influentially in the autobiography of An tAthair Peadar Ó Laoghaire (Fr Peter O'Leary), *Mo Scéal Féin* (1915, *My Own Story*), and also in Liam O'Flaherty's best-selling novel *Famine* (1937).

Historian James Donnelly has shown how an indictment of the British government for its failure to prevent mass food exports became a crucial tenet in the public memory of famine that was constructed in Irish America in the late nineteenth century. This belief also became central to the 'genocide thesis' regarding famine's causation, namely that famine deaths were caused by a deliberate government policy not to prevent mass mortality in Ireland. In Mitchel's oft-quoted words, 'The Almighty indeed sent the potato blight, but the English created the famine.'[25] Here Mitchel refutes the view held by some of his contemporaries that the famine was 'God-given', a belief in providentialism that was shared by some influential policymakers and which fuelled the ire of nationalist politicians for many generations.[26] A century or more after the 1840s, the genocide thesis persisted in popular refusal to employ the term 'famine' for the events of the 1840s (the view being that 'famine', as in large-scale food shortage, did not occur), and the use instead of terms such as 'great hunger' or the qualifier 'potato famine'. In Irish, the somewhat euphemistic term 'an drochshaol' (literally the 'bad' or 'hard time') has accompanied 'an gorta mór' ('the great hunger') in popular use.

The belief that Ireland produced enough food to feed its population, and that a prohibition on food exports would have prevented the famine, has been convincingly debunked by later historiography. Economic studies have shown that exports of grain from Ireland during the famine years were significantly reduced in previous years, and that, contrary to popular understanding, grain imports, including Indian corn from America, greatly exceeded exports after 1846. In 1846–7, for example, food imports were more than twice as much as food exports. More crucially, given that the potato met approximately 60 per cent of Irish food needs when the famine began, even a full prohibition of all exports would not have filled the enormous food gap that resulted from potato failure.[27] Debates regarding the issue of government responsibility are more complicated, and continue to dominate current historiography, the nationalist chestnut that a famine in Liverpool or Yorkshire would have produced a different reaction to one in Ireland proving more difficult to dislodge than other shibboleths. In addition to the economic arguments regarding food imports cited above, revisionist historians have emphasised the scale of government relief operations and of its financial contribution, arguing that it is anachronistic to transport back to 1840s Ireland our contemporary expectations of government responsibility and intervention. On the other hand, one can point to many calls made in late 1846 for at least a temporary prohibition of exports and for an escalation in official intervention. One example is that of the novelist William Carleton, whose political views were far from those of John Mitchel. In his novel *Black Prophet*, first published in installments from May to December 1846, he wrote of there being a 'kind of artificial famine' in Ireland and forcefully criticised the British legislature for its 'long course of illiberal legislation and unjustifiable neglect'.[28] Most historians agree that the official decision in autumn 1847 to place the burden for relief on the Irish poor law alone had disastrous consequences, and evoked significant opposition at the time. These latter views are themselves revisionary in many important respects, and show the emergence, from the mid-1990s onwards, of a new generation of famine interpretation that is post-revisionist while continuing to challenge the excesses and simplifications of earlier nationalistic interpretations.

Examples of this third strand may be found in the work of Peter Gray, Cormac Ó Gráda and James Donnelly, from whom my earlier discussion borrows heavily, and who have contributed judicious conclusions to many of the previously divisive famine debates. Regarding the British government response, for example, Gray pays tribute to the 'extraordinary' administrative structures created by the government in its relief programmes of summer of 1847 but sharply criticises its response, from autumn 1847, as 'grossly inadequate'; 'that more was not in fact spent on keeping the people alive', he concludes, 'was due to the triumph of ideological obsession over humanitarianism.'[29] In his definitive study, *Black '47*, Ó Gráda writes that 'if policy failure resulted in deaths, then ... they were largely the by-product of a dogmatic version of political economy, not the deliberate outcome of anti-Irish racism' ;while clearly rejecting the genocide thesis, he cedes 'some truth' to Mitchel's claim that 'Ireland died of political economy'.[30] This new generation of famine historians has replaced earlier sweeping denunciations and evasions with precise and detailed investigations of famine economics and ideological dogma; in the area of famine causation, this now makes possible some disentangling of the comprehensible from the (in)excusable, with continuing relevance for the political economies of our own times.

the representation of famine history and 'memory'; famine commemoration

The year 1995 saw the beginning of the sesquicentenary of the Great Irish Famine. A flood of commemorative activities took place in the ensuing years, a famine 'fever' which brought an element of famine 'fatigue' and also, as will be discussed later, exposed continuing ideological dogmas. Yet, given the condescension with which the act of commemoration, most especially at a popular level, can be greeted by academics, it is important to acknowledge from the outset the rich achievements of this period. At a local level, these included school essay projects, reminiscent in a way of the large folklore project of the late 1930s, many famine talks and lecture series, and, most visibly, the public honouring of 'sites of memory' such as previously unmarked famine burial grounds, the simple stone marker erected in 1997 on the site of a killeen, or grave for unbaptised children, at 'Trá na bPáistí' ('The Children's Strand') in Carraroe, Co. Galway, being one of the most moving.[31] In national terms, commemorative activities ranged from the dedication of famine monuments (for example, John Behan's 'Famine Ship' at Murrisk, Co. Mayo, unveiled on 20 July 1997 by President Mary Robinson as the Irish National Famine Memorial) to the controversial famine concert held in the Summer of 1997 in Millstreet Co. Cork, made even more notorious by its being the setting for the reading of British Prime Minister Tony Blair's 'apology'.[32]

Government spending on the commemoration was considerable, yet the decision, in July 1997, to end the commemorative period, a decision heavy in irony given the events of 150 years before, led to a regrettable and premature scaling back of activities and of reflection. Most significant for future generations of interpretation, perhaps, are the many historical sources published from the mid-1990s onwards. These include numerous local and regional studies, the more general and near definitive survey volumes mentioned above, and the (re)publication of many influential contemporary sources such as the eyewitness accounts of travellers Asenath Nicholson and Alexander Somerville, the memoir of Donegal teacher Hugh Dorian, and the powerful testimony of Quaker visitors and philanthropists, together with other detailed documentation, collected in *Transactions of the Central Relief Committee of the Society of Friends during the Famine in Ireland in 1846 and 1847* (1852, republished 1996).

history and representation

This wealth of publications makes available a rich, and at times overwhelming, array of historiographical material and it also necessitates a careful scrutiny of the nature of these sources, their influence and their limitations. The surviving eyewitness accounts, for example, are written almost always by privileged observers, such as philanthropists, relief officials or journalists, and thus may reveal, as historian David

Fitzpatrick argues, 'more about the assumptions of the observer than the experience of those observed'.[33] On the other hand, a sweeping dismissal fails to do justice to what is communicated and preserved through such personalised sources and by their depiction of individuals' fates. The representation of large-scale disaster is both a historical and imaginative act, whereby, in philosopher Paul Ricoeur's words, one 'counts the cadavers' and 'tells the story of the victims'.[34] Earlier famine historians, in particular the revisionist generation that began in the 1940s and continued into the 1980s, largely avoided eyewitness sources and testimonies, considering them to be unduly emotive. The best-selling *The Great Hunger* (1962) by Cecil Woodham-Smith was one of the first histories to make detailed use of these accounts, and to powerful effect. Her study in turn proved influential for other types of famine literature, including the famine poems of Seamus Heaney ('At a Potato Digging' and 'For the Commander of "the Eliza"') and Tom Murphy's play *Famine*.

Yet a gaping hole persists at the centre of famine source material, namely the testimony of its victims and their experience of what Philip Roth has called 'the relentless unforeseen'. The Irish-language songs and poems collected by Cormac Ó Gráda may come closest to communicating this, many of which are drawn from the archives of the Irish Folklore Commission.[35] One example is the poem, 'Na Fataí Bána' ('The White Potatoes') by Galway farmer Peatsaí Ó Callanáin (1791–1865), in which the narrator describes the packed poorhouse and hospital, with corpses laid out there 'deep in the clay', and the only meagre food fed to survivors being yellow meal two times a day.

> Tá teach an ospidéil is an poorhouse líonta,
> Agus coirp á síneadh ann go domhain i gcré,
> Is gann de sholamar de ló nó d'oíche,
> Ach praiseach bhuí acu dhá cheann an lae.[36]

In 'Amhrán na bPrátaí Dubha' (Song of the Black Potatoes), sung by Máire NÍ Dhroma from Ring, Co. Waterford, the notion of suffering being 'God-given' is sharply refuted and, as a result, the song was said to have generated the disapproval of local clergy:

> Ní hé Dia cheap riamh an obair seo,
> Daoine bochta a chur le fuacht is le fán,
> Iad a chur sa phoorhouse go dubhach is glas orthu,
> Lánúineacha pósta is iad scartha go bás.

(It wasn't God who devised that work, poor people to suffer cold and a life of vagrancy, to be put in the poorhouse in sorrow and under lock and key, married couples separated till death).[37]

The post-famine years saw a sharp decline in usage of the Irish language, with a disproportionately high number of Irish-language speakers among the famine dead and among emigrants. The extent of this cultural loss has been described by poet Nuala Ní Dhomhnaill as 'unconscionable':

> Unconscionable, because of what has been lost to consciousness, not just the tunes and the songs and the poetry, but because the memory that they were all in Irish – that they are part of a reality which was not English – has been erased so totally from our minds.[38]

Many historians and cultural commentators on the famine tend to pay lip service to the extent of linguistic change, without any in-depth investigation as to its significance or any acknowledgement of its consequences for their own historical practice.[39] On the other hand, recent studies of Irish-language material in the nineteenth century have highlighted the existence of a significant body of famine literature, written contemporaneously or soon after.[40] Together with aforementioned sources in the English language that have been restored to attention, these findings at the very least complicate the view of there being a 'silence' with regard to the Great Famine in Irish cultural history and make possible a much more detailed examination of recurring representational modes and motifs. One of the most enduring famine images depicts the difficulty experienced by those surviving as they attempt to bury their dead. This scene reappears in much of twentieth-century famine literature, including Liam O'Flaherty's best-selling novel *Famine*, where the old man's efforts to bury his wife are the closing image, and Seosamh Mac Grianna's powerful famine story, 'Ar an Trá Fholamh' (1929):

> Ba dhoiligh an úir a chur os cionn na haghaidhe sin, isteach i bpoll na sróine, tríd an fhéasóg. Bhí sé cosúil le marú duine. De réir a chéile chuaigh an cholainn as a amharc. Ar feadh tamaill fhada bhí an dá ghlúin, a bhí rud beag craptha, os cionn an ghainimh agus an fhéasóg ag gobabh aníos. Chuaigh sí i bhfolach, líonadh an uaigh go dtí go raibh sí ina mullóg cosúil leis na huaigheanna eile a bhí thart uirthi.
>
> 'Ar An Trá Fholamh'

It was hard to put the clay over that face, into the nostrils, through the beard. It was like killing someone. Slowly the trunk went out of sight. For a long time the knees, which were drawn up a little, were visible above the sand, and the beard kept sticking up. It disappeared. The grave was filled, until it was a little mound like the other graves around it.

'On the Empty Shore'[41]

famine 'trauma' and 'memory'

A notable feature of the treatment of famine in recent cultural studies is the deployment of concepts such as 'trauma' and of 'famine memory', with some controversial results. Historian Roy Foster is one of the sharpest critics of this practice and has criticised the commemorative period for what he sees as its perpetuation of a sense of victimisation both in Ireland and in Irish-America:

> But the effect of the commemoration year (or years) was to high-light the issues of guilt and pain, driven by the idea that some sort of empathy could be achieved, and a therapeutic catharsis brought about. The language of popular psychotherapy replaced that of his-torical analysis. This was popularised by a strange alliance of populist journalists, local political wheeler-dealers, erratic rock stars and those born-again newly Irish Eng. Lit. academics ... Meanwhile in the USA, a movement began among politicians in search of the ethnic vote; the Famine was defined as genocide in certain states and put on the curriculum of 'Holocaust Studies'.[42]

Foster's targets are not difficult to identify. Sinead O'Connor's rap song is one candidate, also cultural critic Terry Eagleton, author of the influ-ential work *Heathcliff and the Great Hunger*, would appear to be another. 'Populist' commentaries during 1995–7 certainly displayed a share of simplification and overstatement. One instance is the following comment by *Irish Times* journalist John Waters on the legacies of the Great Famine, 'its effects are also to be seen in the warped nature of our society, in the cravenness of our dependencies, in our fear of self-belief, in the culture of amnesia in which we live our lives, in our willingness to imitate anything rather than think for ourselves'.[43] And yet the practice of commemora-tion and its effects are far more complex than Foster allows. At its best, the commemorative period produced a substantial re-examining of views of the past, and their relationship to the present. The honouring of a major catastrophe, through commemorative ritual, memorial or other practice, does not inevitably mean the enshrining of victimisation or hatred, though this is a major danger, and in many of the specific activities sponsored by local communities in the mid-1990s, details conspicuously absent from Foster's account, this very challenge was negotiated in illuminating ways.[44] The work of historian Niall Ó Ciosáin is much more comprehensive in its analysis of what constitutes 'famine memory'. For example, Ó Ciosáin distinguishes between 'local memory', 'popular memory', and 'abstract or global memory' and traces the complex function of written accounts and of oral narratives in the construction and transmission of social memory.[45]

Irish historians have tended to save their sharpest critique for American commemorative practices, with generalised dismissals especially prevalent. As a result, the diversity of Irish-American engagement with Irish history, in memorial practices or in historiographical writing, remains undervalued. Efforts were made in 1995 to place the Great Famine on the curriculum of some American states and some of the resulting historiography did reproduce, unquestioningly, the Mitchelite argument. On the other hand, projects such as the New York Great Irish Famine Curriculum Project presented a scholarly and informed treatment of all aspects of the famine, including a detailed refutation of the genocide thesis, and drew significant links with contemporary hunger and famine.[46] The differences in significance accorded to the famine in Ireland and outside of Ireland represent an avenue of enquiry that is still largely unexplored. One visual illustration is the contrast between the famine memorial constructed in Boston in 1998 and the Irish National Famine Memorial in Murrisk, Co. Mayo. Both are images of emigration: in John Behan's Mayo 'famine ship', the rigging is made of life-size skeletons hanging from its masts. In the Boston memorial, two life-sized sculptural groups are presented, one a family leaving Ireland, dejected and impoverished; the second, a family arriving in Boston, purposeful and forward-looking. The disconcertingly substantial size of the second group has drawn considerable negative comment, both in Ireland and in the United States, but the memorial does capture the iconic significance of the famine for Irish-America, as charter-myth and foundational story.[47]

conclusions: why the past matters

The difficulty of positioning the past in relationship to the present continues to be a major challenge for commentators on the Irish famine. One discourse may tend to an excessive emphasis on victimisation, another extreme is the underscoring of 'survivor guilt' whereby the banality that we are all descendants of survivors attains the power to silence further comment. The question of the famine's relationship to modernity, which occupies economic and cultural theorists alike, also produces very different responses: should the famine be viewed as the first modern developmental crisis, as some economists argue, and if so to what effect? Is the famine instead the sign of the premodern, of Ireland's atavism, as was believed by many at the time, or of the 'non-modern', a term proffered by cultural critic David Lloyd to denote Ireland's anomalous condition? Lloyd has usefully drawn attention to another key discursive strand in the recent period of commemoration, whereby, underlying the language of official 'mourning', was, what he terms, 'a distinctly developmental narrative: if we could leave our dead and their suffering behind and overcome our melancholy, we could at last shake off the burden of the past and enter modernity as fully formed subjects'.[48] In other words, the past is to be commemorated so that it, and its potential to embarrass the present, can be fully left behind. In Lloyd's view, the commemoration of the famine thus 'becomes unhappily one with a set of current cultural and political tendencies in Ireland that are thrusting the country uncritically into European and transnational capitalist modernity'.[49] A spectacular illustration of his argument is provided by another famine memorial, the monument on Dublin's Custom House quay, situated to evoke the lives of thousands of emigrants who departed from the quays but also set against the towering backdrop of the International Financial Services Centre.[50]

Why famine continues to matter in studies of Ireland is a question that yields interesting insights into our current cultural condition. For some recent commentators, a comparative approach is preferable, either with historical famines or with the continuing incidence of world hunger, and much work remains to be done in this area. The Hunger Memorial in New York's Battery Park is named deliberately to forge such links and includes in its textual inscriptions lines by American traveller Asenath Nicholson, written in Dublin in 1847, 'never was a famine on earth, in any part, when there was not an abundance in some part to make up all the deficiency'.[51] Another response, evident in the educational programmes of Irish development agencies for example, is to explore the comparisons between Ireland's historical narrative of famine and emigration and the current experience of large-scale immigration. The debates regarding government responsibility and state intervention which have occupied such a large part of Irish famine historiography thus continue to have a relevance that extends not just to the economies of the developing world but to the geopolitical and economic system in which all of our political economies function.

notes

1. Philip Roth, *The Plot against America* (New York, Vintage, 2004), pp. 113–14.
2. Paul Ricoeur, 'Imagination, Testimony and Trust', in Richard Kearney and Mark Dooley (eds), *Questioning Ethics: Contemporary Debates in Philosophy* (London and New York, Routledge, 1989), p. 15.
3. Cormac Ó Gráda, *The Great Irish Famine*, Studies in Economic and Social History (London, Macmillan, 1989), pp. 48–9.
4. For a fuller account of famine demography, see Cormac Ó Gráda, *Black '47 and Beyond: The Great Irish Famine in History, Economy and Memory* (Princeton, Princeton University Press, 1999), chapter 3.
5. Peter Gray, *The Irish Famine*, New Horizons Series (London, Thames and Hudson, 1995), p. 94.
6. Ó Gráda, *The Great Irish Famine*, p. 19.
7. David Dickson, 'The Other Great Irish Famine', in Cathal Póirtéir (ed.), *The Great Irish Famine* (Cork and Dublin, Mercier Press and RTÉ, 1995), p. 55.
8. Ó Gráda, *The Great Irish Famine*, p. 20, p. 22.
9. Margaret Kelleher, *The Feminization of Famine: Expressions of the Inexpressible?* (Cork and Durham, Cork University Press and Duke University Press, 1997), p. 163.
10. Gray, *The Irish Famine*, pp. 38–42.
11. Reproduced in Ó Gráda, *Black '47 and Beyond*, pp. 38–9.
12. Letter from Captain Wynne to Lieutenant Colonel Jones, 24 December 1846, reproduced in Irish University Press Famine Series (Shannon, Irish Academic Press, 1970), VI, pp. 466–7.
13. See Gray, *The Irish Famine*, pp. 50–9.
14. Ó Gráda, *Black '47 and Beyond*, pp 44–5. See also James S. Donnelly, 'Mass Evictions and the Great Famine', in Póirtéir (ed.), *The Great Irish Famine*, pp. 155–73.
15. Gray, *The Irish Famine*, p.100.
16. Ó Gráda, *Black '47 and Beyond*, p. 105.
17. James S. Donnelly discusses the early politicisation of eviction memories among the Irish in America in *The Great Irish Potato Famine* (Gloucestershire, Shroud, 2002), pp. 209–45, especially p. 228.
18. Ó Gráda, *Black '47 and Beyond*, p. 107.
19. See Gray, *The Irish Famine*, p. 82; Ó Gráda, *Black '47 and Beyond*, p. 41.
20. Ó Gráda, *Black '47 and Beyond*, pp 43, 27; Cormac Ó Gráda, 'Famine, Trauma and Memory', *Béaloideas*, 69 (2001), pp. 121–43, p. 123.
21. Ó Gráda, *Black '47 and Beyond*, chapter 5.
22. Ó Gráda, *Great Irish Famine*, p. 50.
23. Ó Gráda, *Black '47 and Beyond*, p. 101; see also Mary E. Daly, *The Famine in Ireland* (Dundalk, Dundalgan Press and Dublin Historical Association, 1986), p. 100; and David Fitzpatrick, 'Women and the Great Famine', in Margaret Kelleher and James H. Murphy (eds), *Gender Perspectives in Nineteenth-Century Ireland: Public and Private Spheres* (Dublin, Irish Academic Press, 1997), pp. 50–69.
24. Ó Gráda, 'Famine, Trauma and Memory', pp. 124–6.
25. James S. Donnelly, 'Constructing the Memory of the Famine, 1850–1900', in *The Great Irish Potato Famine*, pp. 209–45.

26. The best discussion of this topic is by Peter Gray in his *Famine, Land and Politics* (Dublin, Irish Academic Press, 1999).
27. Donnelly, *Great Irish Famine*, pp. 214–5; Gray, *The Irish Famine*, p. 46.
28. William Carleton, *The Black Prophet* (1847, Shannon, Irish Academic Press, 1972), dedication.
29. Gray, *The Irish Famine*, p. 59, p. 95.
30. Ó Gráda, *Black '47 and Beyond*, p. 10, p. 6.
31. See Margaret Kelleher, 'Hunger and History: Monuments to the Great Irish Famine', *Textual Practice*, 16, 2 (2002), pp. 249–76. See also Peter Gray and Kendrick Oliver (eds), *The Memory of Catastrophe* (Manchester, Manchester UP, 2004).
32. Blair's statement included the following carefully chosen lines: 'Those who governed in London at the time failed their people through standing by while a crop failure turned into a massive human tragedy. We must not forget such a dreadful event.'
33. David Fitzpatrick, 'The Failure: Representations of the Irish Famine in Letters to Australia', in E. Margaret Crawford (ed.), *The Hungry Stream: Essays on Famine and Emigration* (Belfast, Institute of Irish Studies, 1997), p. 161.
34. Paul Ricoeur, *Time and Narrative* (1985, Chicago, University of Chicago Press, 1988), III, p. 188.
35. Cormac Ó Gráda, *An Drochshaol: Béaloideas agus Amhráin* (Dublin, Coiscéim, 1994). For a discussion of the famine in folklore, see Ó Gráda, *Black '47 and Beyond*, chapter 6.
36. Ó Gráda, *An Drochshaol*, p. 51; *Black '47 and Beyond*, p. 248.
37. Ó Gráda, *An Drochshaol*, p. 59.
38. Nuala Ní Dhomhnaill, 'A Ghostly Alhambra', in Tom Hayden (ed.), *Irish Hunger: Personal Reflections on the Legacy of the Famine* (Dublin, Wolfhound, 1997), p. 72.
39. A notable exception is the work of Niall Ó Ciosáin; see his article 'Gaelic Culture and Language Shift', in Laurence Geary and Margaret Kelleher (eds), *Nineteenth-Century Ireland: A Guide to Recent Research* (Dublin, UCD Press, 2005), pp. 136–52.
40. See Antain Mac Lochlainn, 'The Famine in Gaelic Tradition', *The Irish Review*, 17/18 (1995), pp. 90–108; also Neil Buttimer, '"A Stone on the Cairn": The Great Famine in Later Gaelic Manuscripts', in Christopher Morash and Richard Hayes (eds), *Fearful Realities: New Perspectives on the Famine* (Dublin, Irish Academic Press, 1996), pp. 93–109.
41. Seosamh Mac Grianna, 'Ar an Trá Fholamh', from *An Grá agus An Ghruaim;* (Baile Átha Cliath, Longman, Brún agus Ó Nualláin, 1929), pp. 73–9; transla-tion by Séamus Ó Néill, *Irish Writing*, 33 (1955), pp. 33–7.
42. Roy Foster, *The Irish Story: Telling Tales and Making it up in Ireland* (London, Allen Lane, the Penguin Press, 2001), p. 30.
43. John Waters, 'Confronting the Ghosts of our Past', in Tom Hayden (ed.), *Irish Hunger*, p. 29.
44. See Kelleher, 'Hunger and History', pp. 249–76 for a fuller discussion of this topic.
45. Niall Ó Ciosáin, 'Famine Memory and the Popular Representation of Scarcity', in Ian McBride (ed.), *History and Memory in Modern Ireland* (Cambridge, Cambridge University Press, 2001), pp. 95–117.

46. See Maureen Murphy and Alan Singer, 'New York State's "Great Irish Famine Curriculum"': A Report', *Éire-Ireland* XXXVII. 1 & 2 (Spring/Summer 2002), pp. 109–18.

47. See Kelleher, 'Hunger and History', pp. 265–7.

48. David Lloyd, 'Colonial Trauma/Postcolonial Recovery?', *Interventions*, 2.2 (2000), pp. 212–28, 221. See also Lloyd, 'The Political Economy of the Potato', *Nineteenth-Century Contexts*, 29.2 (2007), pp. 311–35 and his 'Mobile Figures', *Vectors: Journal of Culture and Technology in a Dynamic Vernacular* (2005), vol. 2, online resource.

49. Lloyd, 'Colonial Trauma', p. 222.

50. For a discussion of this monument and the ensuing controversy, see Kelleher, 'Hunger and History', pp. 261–3.

51. A. Nicholson, *Annals of the Famine in Ireland* (1851; republished Dublin, Lilliput Press, 1998) p. 48.

4

economic and labour history

niamh puirséil

introduction

Writing in 1997, Mary E. Daly observed that 'while the primary task facing Irish historians in the 1930s was the debunking of nationalist pieties, by now this process appears to have run its course and many of the earlier "revisionist" accounts are being subjected to critical scrutiny, though it is doubtful whether this process will result in the re-creation of a new "apostolic succession of national heroes"'.[1] In fact, Ireland's desire for national heroes seems undiminished; it is just that the heroes are rather different from the patriot idols of old. An indication of this trend came in 2002 when the organisers of the annual greatest Irish person award decided to go one better and create an award for the greatest living Irish person, an award bestowed to T. K. Whitaker, former secretary of the Department of Finance and later governor of the Central Bank. Public servants rarely enjoy such honours but as author of 'Economic Development' (1958), a policy document regarded as marking a turning point in Ireland's economic fortunes from the disastrous 1950s to the relatively prosperous 1960s, Whitaker, with the help of a generation of historians, developed a reputation as the man who saved Ireland (for a few years, anyway). The 'Whitaker revolution' did not last terribly long; by the 1970s and 1980s the optimism which had gone with it had evaporated entirely, but by the mid-1990s the economic boom of the 'Celtic Tiger' saw national despair give way to self-congratulation, leading the Whitaker revolution to be revisited. This focus on matters economic is not a product of the Celtic Tiger, however; the Irish middle class has long enjoyed the capacity to 'talk Christ and think money', as J. J. Lee has put it.[2] Perhaps this propensity to think about money but remain mute on the matter worked to hinder the development of

100

economic history in Ireland for so long. This chapter traces the development of Irish economic history and its sister discipline, labour history, to see how historians managed to think money and write history.

economic history

In recent years Ireland's economic profile has begun to eclipse the more traditional image of the country as contemporary Ireland established itself as a case study in rapid economic growth. Factors such as low corporate tax rates, reorientation to an information-based economy, membership of the European Union and the neo-corporatism of the social partnership wage agreements have helped turn the republic from the poor man of Europe to one of the continent's best performing economies in the space of perhaps 15 years. The Celtic Tiger boom marked a very belated economic advance for a country which identified itself as poor for so long that it almost became a self-fulfilling prophecy. Indeed, the subtitle of a recent best-selling book *Preventing the Future* reflects the new affluent Irish society; it is not a case of asking how policymakers and sectors of Irish society contributed to the new prosperity but of asking '*why was Ireland so poor for so long?'* For decades, indeed for centuries, the answer was simple. Since the eighteenth century, Irish patriots and nationalists attributed Ireland's economic underdevelopment, either real or perceived, to the malign British influence, believing that Ireland free would be Ireland prosperous. Conversely, unionists in the northeast of the country, held the link with Britain to be source of prosperity. Thus, as Mary E. Daly has put it, 'while Ireland's economic performance under the Union was not the sole factor fuelling the movement for independence, it is hardly a coincidence that Ulster, the most successful province of the Union, rejected independence'.[3] By the mid-twentieth century, blaming Britain for Ireland's economic ills was no longer a feasible response, but it took some time before Irish economic history attempted to tackle the question of Ireland's economic malaise, although the link between economics and politics in Irish history has always been strong, and as we shall see in the course of this chapter, it has often been the case that former has been overlooked by the latter.[4]

At the beginning of the twentieth century, history in Ireland was a very underdeveloped discipline. Little or no systematic primary research was undertaken and, predictably in the context of the political upheavals of the time, published histories were usually didactic treatise in which Ireland was subjected to every abuse imaginable by perfidious Albion. Lack of empirical research or analysis and dominance of a nationalist agenda meant there was a general acceptance that Ireland had always been poor, and that this was the malign effect of British policy in Ireland. Difficulties encountered by the Irish economy prior to the Act of Union in 1801 were put down to the British mercantilism, while the commercial arrangements contained in Article 6 of the Act of Union and later the British government's adherence to free trade were identified as being responsible for the deindustrialisation of Ireland after the union.[5] Disproportionate weight was placed on literary sources such as those of Jonathan Swift, Dean of St Patrick's Cathedral in Dublin during the early eighteenth century, who attacked English economic treatment of Ireland in satires such as his series of *Drapier's Letters* and who famously responded to the trade disadvantages imposed on Ireland by its neighbour with the instruction that Irish people should 'burn every English except their coal'.

The problem was that these texts tended to be reproduced without any critical examination of, for instance, levels of regional or national income or assessing the impacts of factors beyond Britain.[6] The first significant works of Irish economic history, George O'Brien's *Economic History of Ireland in the Eighteenth Century* (1919) and his *Economic History of Ireland from Union to Famine* (1921) were prime examples of this type of study. Published at the height of the Irish revolution, when economic self-reliance was being espoused by Sinn Féin (literally 'ourselves alone') as a vital part of Ireland's independence project, O'Brien's work simply rehashed received nationalist opinion without any rigorous analysis of independent factors. Agit-prop rather than history, even O'Brien's contemporary, the zealous Irish-Irelander D. P. Moran, lamented the nonsense of whining about 'how England stole our woollen industries some hundreds of years ago'.[7] The lack of readily available statistical data made rigour difficult, not to mention the fact that O'Brien, with no formal training in economics or its methodologies, might have been characterised as an amateur economist had he not been in receipt of a lecturer's salary in the subject,[8] but the fact remains that the study of the Irish economy at this time was characterised by a combination of bad history and bad economics.[9] It would be churlish at this distance to criticise Professor O'Brien for his lack of detachment, but what was disappointing is that it would take almost 50 years before there was any attempt to publish economic history surveys which attempted to supersede his work.

A revolution in Irish history began with the establishment of the journal *Irish Historical Studies* in 1939 by two young academics: T. W. Moody and R. Dudley Edwards. The central tenet behind the journal was to promote a more scientific approach in the writing of Irish history and thus discard the morality tales which had dominated Irish historiography until then. From the late 1930s, a new generation of historians set about tackling many of the old orthodoxies of historical thought, re-evaluating primary sources to draw more nuanced portraits of the country's past. Welcome as this project of 'revisionism' was, its focus was very narrowly political, and while its practitioners set about questioning and dismantling the myths of the nation builders, other areas remained unexplored. Economic history was making considerable progress in Europe and particularly in Britain throughout the 1930s and 1940s, but the subject failed to capture Irish imaginations. It was not that Irish historians were ignorant of international trends in historiography. Moody and Edwards, like most of their contemporaries, were recently returned from graduate studies in England and kept close links with colleagues from outside Ireland. They remained focused on their politically revisionist project with Ireland's relationship with Britain remaining the cynosure of the Irish historical establishment. The single notable exception to this avoidance of economic history was a significant collection of pieces on the famine which gestated during the 1940s and 1950s and which appeared eventually in early 1957 as *The Great Famine: Studies in Irish history 1845–52*. Edited by R. Dudley Edwards and T Desmond Williams, the book, which was supposed to have come out to mark the famine's centenary but was long delayed through the dilatory approach of historians involved, represented a welcome, but unusual, deviation into social and economic history. Significantly, the impetus for this study came not from historians themselves but from the Taoiseach, Eamon de Valera, who had proposed a book on the subject in early 1944.[10]

By the early 1950s a cultural shift had occurred in the republic which saw the political establishment give up green flag-waving in favour of campaigning on economic questions. As historian and contemporary commentator T. Desmond Williams observed in 1953, 'one of the most striking features of Irish politics in recent years has been the frequency with which politicians employ economic phraseology,' a trend which, he noted, had become a universal phenomenon.[11] This shift began to filter into Irish academe, including history. Queens University Belfast made the first significant advance when it appointed Ken Connell as a senior lecturer in economic and social history in 1952. Connell was a graduate of the London School of Economics, one of the centres of research and teaching in economic history in Britain, and was the author of the groundbreaking *Population of Ireland, 1750–1845* (1950), the first major study of its kind on Irish demography.[12] Significantly, while Connell's book was cited consistently whenever the subject of population growth was discussed outside Ireland, it was not until the 1960s that his work received critical appraisal at home.[13] He remained the only dedicated economic historian in Irish academia for nearly ten years, joined in 1963 by the young Joe Lee, whose doctoral research was on nineteenth-century railways in Ireland, and who was recruited by University College Dublin to lecture on economic history. Nevertheless, while economic historians may have been lacking in faculty, the role played by academic economists at this time should not be overlooked. In University College Dublin, for instance, economists like James Meenan, Patrick Lynch and Alexis Fitzgerald 'brought a highly developed historical sense to their teaching'.[14] Lynch, whose sojourn as a gifted economic adviser within the civil service has placed him in the history books as well as writing them, made a significant early contribution to the corpus of economic history with his study *Guinness's Brewery in the Irish economy, 1759–1876* (1960), co-written with John Vaizy, while Meenan's *Irish economy since 1922* (1970) was the first study of its kind on the period after independence. Meanwhile, by 1965, L. M. Cullen had joined the teaching staff of Trinity College Dublin where he lectured in economic history, publishing two key studies, *Anglo-Irish Trade 1660–1800* and *Life in Ireland* in 1968. Obviously the presence of specialist economic historians on the faculties of the larger universities in the country represented a significant foothold for the subject, but it was a while before this was reflected in a significant advance in the writing on the subject, and many of those trying to teach in third level found the lack of accessible texts a difficulty. As J. J. Lee put it,

> The inadequacy of the standard work on the 1600–1845 period, coupled with the absence of even inadequate general works on earlier and later periods, proved a serious obstacle to systematic advance. There was simply no coherent framework into which researchers could integrate their findings with the result that Irish economic history, despite the occasional impressive monograph, remained very much a patch-work quilt throughout the 1950s and 1960s.[15]

After a very slow start, economic history finally came into its own in the 1970s. Publishers noticed the increased demand for economic history material and responded initially with reprints of primary material such as Arthur Young's *A Tour in Ireland, 1776–1779* and a compendium of documents, some of which relating to trade, published as *Aspects of Irish Social History, 1750–1800*. 1971 saw the publication of F. S. L. Lyon's groundbreaking survey *Ireland since the famine*, in which a strong economic emphasis complemented the political history, while economic issues featured strongly in Gearoid Ó Tuathaigh's *Ireland before the Famine, 1798–1848*, published the following year, and its companion volume *The Modernization of Irish Society, 1848–1914* (1973) by J. J. Lee. 1972 also saw the publication of L. M Cullen's *An Economic History of Ireland since 1660* which added a few extra squares to the quilt and provided teachers and students with the first comprehensive text on the subject since George O'Brien's series 50 years earlier. Cullen's work represented an about-turn in writing on Irish economic history, arguing that the Irish economy functioned quite well and where it did not it was less as a result of pernicious legislation from London than other factors of production or terms of trade. Cullen also played an important role in the subject's development when he and Ken Connell provided the driving force behind the founding of the Irish Economic and Social History Society which held its first meeting in Belfast in 1968, a mere 40 odd years after its sister organisation the Economic History Society had been founded in London. It was, according to one historian, the most important new departure in Irish historiography since the setting up of *Irish Historical Studies*.[16] Its journal *Irish Economic and Social History* (of which David Dickson and Peter Roebuck were founding editors) published annually since 1974 has provided a home for the growing number of articles in the area, although the number of pieces on social history usually outnumbered those on economics.[17] Studies for the most part focused on various aspects of the microeconomy in the early modern and modern periods and tended to look at key industries such as linen and wool, land, diet and population while local studies were extremely popular, with researchers helped immeasurably by the fact that estate records had recently become widely accessible.[18] The numbers of graduate students engaged in research in economic history also mushroomed as an examination of research on Irish history in Irish universities at this time attests.[19] A great number of these students were based in the department of economic and social history in Queens which was a decade old by 1972. Ken Connell and Miriam Daly supervised numerous dissertations there, although by this stage every university in the country had at least one postgraduate engaged in research on economic history.[20]

This new research began to be assimilated into mainstream history within general texts. The 1971 edition of *Ireland since the Famine* had seen Lyons opine that so many gaps remained in the knowledge of

economic history that 'the general historian [had] either to admit ignorance and pass by on the other side, or else do some of the spade work
himself'; by the second edition two years later he was able to point
to the 'extraordinarily large volume of specialised work' which had
appeared in the meantime.[21] Now the greatest problem facing the general historian was how to keep up with the literature, rather than there
being insufficient research, with one survey finding over one thousand
items published on economic history since 1968.[22] During the 1960s
the Irish Historical Society began to organise the *New History of Ireland*,
a series of collected essays which would cover Ireland's history from pre-
historic times to 1945. Those guiding the project wanted economic and
social history to 'have its place in the primary narrative' while treating
of it in specialist chapters also.[23] Ken Connell, one of the New History's
editorial committee, tried in vain to have a dedicated economic history
included in the New History project (the notion of such a specialised
text was deemed contrary to the spirit of the scheme) and began to
put together an economic history of Ireland since 1760. Unfortunately
Connell's volume never came to fruition but the New History of Ireland
(whose first volume appeared in 1972) has been reasonably successful
in its remit of including economic and social history in its books, if not
always within the narratives.

By the 1970s it was a commonly held view that economic history had
become the most fertile area of new research; indeed by the mid-1980s
Ronan Fanning, himself a political historian, complained that a 'growing vogue for social and economic history' was deflecting the energy of
historians from working on political history.[24] Fanning attributed this
shift to two factors, firstly to belated notice being taken to international
trends, and secondly to the 'reaction against the political in favour of the
socio-economic' which had followed the premiership of Seán Lemass
in the late 1950s and 1960s.[25] Lemass was a nationalist for whom economic success was an intrinsic part of the nations development. He had
played a key role in implementing Sinn Féin economics of protectionism and building up native industry while Minister for Industry and
Commerce in the 1930s but after a decade of mass unemployment and
emigration in the 1950s, decided that free trade with Britain and within
the European Economic Community and foreign direct investment
would be the key to Ireland's prosperity. It was only natural that the
focus on economic development by the political elite and the media would
be reflected in the academia, and in history in particular. Fanning also
suggested that the subject was consolidating its position as, with most
able and energetic historians attached to history departments in Irish

universities specialising in socio-economic history and so, inevitably, would their best graduate students,[26] but this hypothesis was not borne out by events. If the 'best graduate students' followed their professors into research in economic history, few of them got jobs. Queens University Belfast remained home to the only economic history department on the island of Ireland until 2002 when it was closed down. Even at the time when it had reached its zenith of popularity, L. A Clarkson suggested that if those lecturing in economic history in universities north and south were gathered together, one would be 'hard pressed to raise a rugby team.'[27] The numbers teaching economic history remained static after the 1970s, but the output of publications remained high with those researching the topic numbering some of the most prolific of Irish historians.

Research on the nineteenth-century economy continued to develop during the 1980s, in particular the study of the country's economic position before the famine, with the American-based economic historian Joel Mokyr's *Why Ireland Starved* (1983) and the work of Cormac Ó Gráda going some way to revise the revisionists.[28] Ó Gráda, based in the School of Economics in University College Dublin is one of Ireland's leading economic historians, whose more recent texts have included *Ireland: A New Economic History 1780–1939* (1994) and *A Rocky Road: The Irish Economy since the 1920s* (1997).[29] On the nineteenth- and twentieth-century rural economy, Carla King and Liam Kennedy have examined the development of co-operative societies which played such an important role in the modernisation of the Irish countryside.[30] Another very strong trend during the 1980s was a synthesis between economic and political history, focusing on the twentieth century which, with a couple of notable exceptions, had been overlooked previously. The neglect of contemporary history is largely explained by two factors: resistance from the historical establishment (for instance it was not until 1978 *Irish Historical Studies* began to publish work dealing with events after 1925)[31] but more importantly the lack of readily accessible government records, as it was not until the implementation of the National Archives Act, 1986 that there was any systematic release of state papers. Before then twentieth-century economic history had either been the work of economists and based on published reports or statistics, most notably James Meenan's 1970 text and Kennedy and Dowling's *Economic Growth in Ireland. The Experience since 1947* (1975), or official histories. 1975 saw the publication of *Currency and Central Banking in Ireland 1922–60* by Maurice Moynihan, a former senior civil servant and Governor of the Central Bank (1961–9), followed three years later by Ronan Fanning's *Irish Department of Finance 1922–1958*, for which the author was granted unprecedented access to the Department's files. The study emphasised the continued dependence of the Irish economy on that of Great Britain and the limits this played on issues such as fiscal policy after independence as well as elucidating the many disagreements between different governments and the conservative secretariat ensconced in the Department of Finance throughout the period in question. Another study which placed the development of the southern states macroeconomic policy to the fore was the 1982 book *Seán Lemass and the Making of Modern Ireland 1945–66* by two northern-based Marxist political scientists, Paul Bew and Henry Patterson. At the centre of this book was the authors' desire to explain the basis of Fianna Fáil hegemony since 1932, and the role played by Seán Lemass in consolidating working class support for the party over the years, particularly with reference to his links with the Irish trade union movement. Bew and Patterson's Marxist perspective was the exception to the rule in Irish economic history which avoided not only Marxism but the taint of models generally.[32] Arguably, these were not economic histories in the pure sense, but political histories which devoted a great deal of attention to economic issues, but they illustrate nevertheless how economic history had become part of the mainstream by this stage.

1987 saw the publication of Joe Lee's magisterial *Ireland 1912–1985. Politics and Society*. Here was an economic historian writing a political history in which Ireland's economic performance took centre stage throughout. Lee's main thesis was that since independence the economy of the southern Irish state had failed, and he sought to explain this, not merely in terms of the impact of government policy but also in terms of the national culture, pointing to a lack of entrepreneurialism and a tendency towards begrudgery within Irish society. A number of Lee's themes have been expanded further in a recent study by the political scientist Tom Garvin, *Preventing the Future: Why was Ireland so Poor for so Long?* (2004), which most notably blames the failure to provide adequate levels of education for the majority of the population for arresting Ireland's development for so long.[33] One important aspect to Lee's study was its comparative emphasis that had often been lacking.[34] International comparisons of economic performance are invaluable, but it is worth remembering that for much of the twentieth century, independent Ireland, though obviously affected by international markets was a closed economy with little in the way of exports outside of agricultural produce which were destined, almost without exception, for Britain. This market was cut off for most of the 1930s when a trade war known as the Economic War, in Ireland, broke out between the two countries over the Fianna Fáil government's non-payment of land annuities.[35] Independent Ireland's efforts to find its feet economically after 1922 is traced by Brian Girvin in *Between Two Worlds: Politics and Economy in Independent Ireland* (1989) and by Mary E. Daly in her study of *Industrial Development and Irish National Identity 1922–1939* (1992). It was not until after the Second World War that Ireland's economy began halting steps towards opening itself up to international trade. Ireland's (lesser) inclusion in the European Recovery Plan is dealt with in Bernadette Whelan's forensic *Ireland and the Marshall Plan 1947–1957* (2000) and a recent collection of essays,[36] while the political struggles to reorient the Irish economy towards a free market which took place during the late 1950s are dealt with in Fanning's *The Irish Department of Finance, 1922–1958* (1978). One of the most important factors in Ireland's economic development has been its decision to engage with Europe which saw it join the European Economic Community in 1973 after a couple of false starts in the 1960s, this issue has been dealt with comprehensively in Gary Murphy's *Economic Realignment and the Politics of EEC Entry, Ireland, 1948–1973* (2003), in which the role played by sectional economic interests such as the trade union movement and farmers' representatives in influencing government economic policy is clear throughout. On the subject of sectional interests, it is worth noting the relative neglect in economic history of the agricultural sector. Important works have been published, most notably Raymond Crotty's *Irish Agricultural Production* (1966) and Mary E. Daly's recent *History of the Department of Agriculture* (2002), while J. J. Lee's *Ireland 1912–1985* (1989) is excellent on the subject, but when one considers the centrality of agriculture within the Irish economy it would be hard to disagree that it has not been overlooked.[37] This is all the more surprising when issues relating to the land have preoccupied economic historians who have examined other periods, especially in relation to the mid-nineteenth century and the famine.

Economic history is a discipline in decline in Ireland as it is elsewhere. Since 2002 there has been no specialised department on the island of Ireland and there are very few courses currently available to undergraduates while 2005 marked the last time that economic history was examined on the Leaving Certificate. Of the 116,000 students sitting Leaving Certificate history that year, only 352 students sat the economic history paper. Although the Economic and Social History Society of Ireland and its journal are still going strong, the emphasis of its members seems to be more and more on the social than the economic. There seems to be almost a sense that economic history has been done, important original research has been completed and the results filtered into the mainstream and that now its time to move on to different things. As Louis Cullen, the great pioneer of new economic history in Ireland, remarked of his own decision to shift towards cultural and political history: 'In my formative years in the 1950s I shared the view that economic history was central and that it could answer almost every question. The optimism was misplaced.'[38] There is also the extent to which economic history has become more specialised; the development of more econometric models can sometimes diminish its appeal to those without advanced training in the area, so that ironically, the better the economic history, the more difficult it is to find an audience for it. The problems of specialism notwithstanding, there remain lively and accessible areas of scholarship, particularly in the area of local histories.[39] Another way in which economic history is likely to develop is as an adjunct of other disciplines such as urban geography, local studies and women's studies. In the latter case the economic position of women within and without the workforce is a subject which has been gaining increased attention over recent years, and is an excellent example of how less conventional economic history is in fact making progress in spite of the topic's fall from fashion.

labour history

Ireland has long been of interest to those of a left-wing persuasion. In the mid-nineteenth century, Fredrich Engles and Karl Marx wrote reams on Ireland to and how it was as, as Anthony Coughlan put it, 'English intervention in Ireland rather than internal Irish conditions which had historically been the prime political cause of the country's problems'.[40] However, Marx and Engles were always more interested in Ireland than Ireland was in them. Generally speaking, the Irish have proved remarkably resistant to left-wing politics, radical or otherwise. The dominance of nationalism, the inherent conservatism of the small landholder and the impact of the Catholic Church's hostility towards socialism or anything that smacked of it, this troika of 'priest, peasant and patriot'[41] did much to hinder the development of a left-wing or class-based political movement, and the relative dearth of manufacturing industry beyond the northeast meant that the traditional working class was comparatively small. Notwithstanding the absence of a strong political presence, however, labour has nevertheless played an important role in Irish political and economic life. Levels of trade union membership were traditionally high, and the co-operation between sections of the trade union movement and the government, at an unofficial or official level, has at times been very close.

The importance of workers as a section of Irish society or of the labour movement as an interest group has not been reflected in the history books. As with so many history genres in Ireland, labour history remained undeveloped and at the margins of general history until the 1970s as the fashion for pure political history waned, and in this case, as interest in things left-wing flourished on top of the radicalism and the new left that grew out of the 1960s. However, unlike economic history (for instance) it never enjoyed institutional support within universities, a factor which has limited its progress from the outset and contributed to its failure to enter mainstream historical discourse. Labour is present in the iconography of Irish history and society to the point of cliché (the photograph, subsequently the basis of a statue erected in the middle of O'Connell Street in 1979, of the trade union leader Jim Larkin, arms aloft, preaching revolt to a Dublin crowd during the 1920s is one of the most recognisable images of the twentieth century) while the worker and his or her organisations remain missing from the narrative. *Seven Ages*, a landmark series charting the history of independent Ireland shown by the Irish national broadcaster Radio Telefís Éireann (RTÉ) in 2000 managed to chart 70 years of Irish life without any mention of labour history. This is but one example of many. Significantly, it is not the case that labour history is being written out of Ireland's history; rather that labour historians, for the most part, have failed to have it written in to Irish history in the first place.

Traditionally, one of the strongest factors which hindered labour history's development and advance was the pre-eminence of the national question. History was a story of good guys and villains in which labour did not always fit comfortably. As nationalists tried to forge a sense of identity around the movement for independence and later, as the new state endeavoured to establish itself, efforts to cast light on exploitative native capitalists was regarded as divisive and unpatriotic. Contrast, for instance, the treatment of the land wars of the nineteenth century and that of the 1913 Lockout and the squalid living conditions of so many workers in Dublin, a city which held some of the worst slum housing in Europe. The former had significant propaganda value as the Britain and the Anglo-Irish landlords could be cast as the miscreants, but the lockout by Catholic–Irish employers and the slum tenements of the capital, many owned by Catholic–Irish landlords, was best forgotten. Without an anti-British angle to it, working class movements would have to be without regard.

Few tried to tackle this nationalist orthodoxy but the first example remains perhaps the best known. Labour history first emerged in Ireland at the beginning of the twentieth century far from the confines of ivory towers, written not by professional practitioners but by activists for whom its purpose was propagandist. It was part of the 'new unionism' then establishing itself in Ireland, which saw the creation of militant labour organisations geared towards looking after the unskilled general workers who suffered from the greatest insecurity and worst conditions of all workers, and who had, until then, been ignored by the traditional trade union movement which looked after the interests of artisans and the 'labour aristocracy'. At the forefront of this movement was James Larkin, usually known as Big Jim, who came to Belfast, then Cork, as an organiser of the National Union of Dockers before moving to Dublin and founding the Irish Transport and General Workers Union (ITGWU) in 1909. Part of the work done by Larkin and his comrades was to inculcate a labour and trade union consciousness among the general workers, but while Larkin was a consummate rabble-rouser, skilled in the art of inspiring dissent, his talents to not extend to more sober analyses of Irish working class history.[42] It was his colleague James Connolly, described as the lighthouse to Larkin's tornado, who provided the historical background to the contemporary struggle, using history to impress on workers the necessity of a labour point of view, first in the pages of the labour newspapers he edited,[43] and subsequently in his Marxist history of Ireland, *Labour in Irish History*, published in 1910.[44] Connolly was open about the didactic nature of his work, to detail 'the position of the Irish workers in the past, and the lessons to be derived from a study of that position in guiding the movement of the working class today', and he was also clear that it was not his intention of writing a history of labour in Ireland, but rather to examine Irish history from a labour viewpoint.[45] It was a landmark historical work, particularly significant for placing previously ignored working class or socialist endeavours, such as that of the short-lived Ralahine commune in 1830s' Cork, into the narrative of Irish history and also in the way that it cast Connolly as one of the first historical revisionists, as he tackled the historical orthodoxies of his nationalist contemporaries. He was scathing in his treatment of Daniel O'Connell, a man more commonly known to Irishmen as 'the Liberator' but who was dubbed by Connolly as 'the most bitter and unscrupulous enemy of trade unionism that Ireland has yet produced'.[46]

Notwithstanding the attacks on nationalist untouchables such as O'Connell, Connolly's socialist analysis was far from popular with the

Catholic Church proving particularly hostile. Connolly had argued that it was possible to be a good Catholic and a good socialist (an argument rejected in the 1891 papal encyclical *Rerum Novarum*), and in *The Reconquest of Ireland*, published in 1915, he portrayed socialism as a native philosophy by painting a picture of Gaelic civilisation before the Norman conquest as an early communist society which was ultimately corrupted by notions of private ownership imposed by the invaders. By this point Connolly was devoting most of his time to planning an armed rebellion against the British presence in Ireland. In Easter 1916 he led a small band of men and women from the Irish Citizen Army alongside the larger Irish Volunteers to fight in the unsuccessful rebellion. Connolly was captured and executed for his role in planning the rising, costing the Irish labour movement its greatest thinker, and Irish labour history its only proponent. As J. J Lee put it, 'for sheer originality, his writings, despite many flaws, [are] worth those of all his professional contemporaries combined'.[47]

In *Labour in Irish history* Connolly had cast himself as a sort of labour history John the Baptist, claiming he was merely laying the ground work for 'more abler pens' to continue the project,[48] but immediately after his death those willing to pick up where he had left off proved few and far between. 1919 saw the publication of *The Irish Labour Movement from the Twenties to Our Own Day* by W. P. Ryan, a left-wing journalist from England, on commission from a Dublin publishing company.[49] It was a history of the evolution of organised labour in Ireland, beginning with the early artisan combinations in the first half of the nineteenth century before charting more contemporary developments in the labour movement, looking at how the trade union movement had transformed from a conservative representative body for skilled labourers to a militant faction fighting for the unskilled, and until recently unorganised, workers in Ireland, influenced in part by the teaching of Connolly but more often than not by the oratory of Larkin and the organising abilities of others. This shift from the craft-based 'old unionism' to the militant new unionism (often referred to in the Irish context as Larkinism) was the subject of *Labour and Nationalism in Ireland*, the first academic study of the Irish labour movement, published in 1925. As was so often the way in Irish academia, the pioneer came from abroad, in this case an American professor, J. D. Clarkson, and the book, published in New York was not available in Ireland and made little impact on publication as a result.

The trade union movement had enjoyed a period of growth in numbers and militancy during the second decade of the twentieth century, which culminated in the outbreak of syndicalist activity and in the early 1920s but its fortunes were on a downward trajectory soon after. It was a difficult time for workers at an individual level and for organised labour as a whole. The economic situation in the south after five years of conflict from the war of independence to civil war was dire, and with an economically conservative government ensconced in the new Dublin parliament with a secure majority, labour was effectively marginalised in Irish politics. Matters were not helped by the schism within the country's largest union, the ITGWU, prompted by the return to Ireland of its general secretary James Larkin in 1923, after ten years in the United States. Larkin's efforts to resume his duties on return were resisted by the officers who had held the fort in his absence and the row which ensued between the two factions saw a breakaway Workers Union of Ireland formed by Larkinites who then engaged in a campaign of vilification against the Labour Party, which Larkin himself had helped found in 1912. During this time there was little written in labour history, or nothing if we discount the self-serving accounts of the recent past which were put out by the opposing sides in an attempt to put down their opponents.[50] If history is only written by the victors, it explains why for so long there was no labour history; the diversion into infighting made losers out of all sides within the labour movement.

So it was that throughout the 1920s and 1930s studies of labour history, be they academic or pamphleteering, were conspicuous by their absence.[51] It was only in the 1940s that the Dublin-based English journalist R. M. Fox, himself a socialist, began to write a series of very popular books of labour interest, including *A History of the Irish Citizen Army* (1943), *James Connolly. The Forerunner* (1946) and *James Larkin. Irish Labour Leader* (1957). Fox was also the author of 'Labour and the national struggle', a propagandist pamphlet published by the Irish Labour Party in 1945 after a young West Cork worker had complained to the party that public ignorance of its principles was partly due to the 'teaching of history in the primary schools, where proper credit is not given to the work of James Connolly and other Labour thinkers and leaders in our national life'.[52] But Fox's journalistic work represented almost the sum total of writing on Irish labour history at this time. While the end of the Second World War saw the discipline flourish in other countries, in Ireland it remained dead in the water. As was noted in the case of economic history, the attention of academic historians was focused entirely on questions of nationalist history while other aspects of Irish life were ignored, but there was more to it than this. In Britain, in particular, its study was being driven by committed Marxist academics, particularly members of the Communist Party Historians Group, such as Eric Hobsbawn who wrote highly readable histories of the working class. Ireland had no professed Marxist historians. Indeed, historians aside, the number of self-professed Marxists in Ireland could probably have been counted on the fingers of one hand, as the general antipathy towards communism, and an often deliberate blurring of the boundaries between communism and socialism, became all the more virulent with the onset of the Cold war. Trinity College Dublin, as a protestant university had a reputation for being home to somewhat unorthodox characters a number of whom were thought to have social-istic tendencies, but University College Dublin was closely monitored by the Catholic clergy for suspect teaching so that it might remain a suitable haven for impressionable young Irish minds. Efforts outside the universities to educate workers on labour history, or indeed, other mat-ters were also frustrated by the political climate. The Peoples' College, through which the Irish Trade Union Congress ran adult education courses, was opposed by the Catholic Church as 'a tentacle of commu-nism' because the Church had no input in its curricula, while a library established in the premises of the Bakers Union by John Swift, a trade union activist, was sold off amid accusations that it held communist tracts unfit for the eyes of Catholic workers.[53] Swift had a deeply held belief in need to write and preserve the history of labour; his *History of the Bakers' Union and Others* (1948) was one of the earliest histories of its kind but of greater impact in the long term was his role as a founder member of the Irish Labour History Society in 1973.

By the late 1950s there was a slow awakening of interest in labour his-tory. A handful of doctoral dissertations were completed (including one by John W. Boyle who began to lecture in the Department of Economic and Social History in Queens n 1965),[54] while the early 1960s saw the publication of two significant studies of labour personalities, C. Desmond Greaves' *The Life and Times of James Connolly* (1961) and Emmet Larkin's biography *James Larkin* (1965). Greaves, whose study in many ways remains a classic account of Connolly's life, was a London-based communist with strong republican sympathies[55] while Emmet Larkin was an American historian who had written his doctoral disserta-tion for Columbia University on his labour namesake. These were joined by a number of home-grown shorter studies, including *the Fiery Cross*, a short propagandist study of Jim Larkin published by the communist Irish Workers' League in 1963 (printed in England because no Irish printer at this time was prepared to touch communist literature)[56] and *Leaders and Workers* in 1966, a collection of brief biographical studies of significant labour activists edited by John W. Boyle.[57] Although a welcome addition to a still neglected area, *Leaders* of *Workers* might have been a more appropriate title, for as with the majority of its predecessors, the role of the ordinary workers within the labour movement was overlooked in favour of the big personalities. This rather slim volume remained the key text on the Irish labour movement for many years as there remained little dedicated study in the area. The young American scholar Arthur Mitchell managed to spend four years of doctoral research on the Irish labour movement in Trinity College Dublin (beginning in 1963) without meeting anyone working on the same area.[58] By the end of the sixties however, change was afoot. The often-hysterical anti-communism of previous decades had begun to dissipate by around 1963 and by the time of the 1916 Easter Rising Jubilee celebrations there was increasing interest around the figure of James Connolly, who had long been over-shadowed by more politically orthodox figures such as Patrick Pearse. Reprinted editions of Connolly's works began to reach a new audience as the younger generation, influenced by student radicalism abroad, began to embrace the politics of the left. This wave of left-wing activism engendered a new interest in the area of labour history. As with economic history, labour history developed remarkably rapidly during the 1970s. Among the first publications to emerge from this generation of 1960s left-wing activists were two efforts to update the work of Connolly half a century earlier: D. R. O'Connor Lysaght's *The republic of Ireland* (1970), a very readable Marxist exposition of Irish history from 400AD to 1969 and Peter Beresford Ellis's *A History of the Irish Working Class*, first published in 1972 and was last reprinted in 1996. The leftist leanings of many of those involved in the Civil Rights Movement in Northern Ireland (the student group Peoples Democracy in particular) and the outbreak of the troubles in the late 1960s reinforced this trend towards a more leftist view of the history of the island of Ireland.

In 1973, a number of young University College Dublin academics, including Fergus D'Arcy and Ken Hannigan, secured the support of veteran trade unionist John Swift among others to establish the Irish Labour History Society (ILHS) for the purpose of encouraging the study of labour history and preserving the records of the trade union movement.[59] The activities of the society itself, and particularly the publication of its journal *Saothar* (the Irish for work or labour), which appeared annually from May Day 1975 were of vital importance to the subject's development. *Saothar* provided a forum for the increasing number of works on labour history and contained contributions from academics and worker historians alike. The focus of many of the early articles was on labour organisations, often during the nineteenth century, but even if labour history remained 'overwhelmingly institutional'[60] by the end of the 1970s, this represented a significant advance on previous personality-based histories. Among the institutional histories published during the 1970s were Arthur Mitchell's *Labour in Irish Politics 1890–1930* (1974), Charles McCarthy's *Decade of Upheaval: Irish trade unions in the* 1960s (1973) and *Trade Unions in Ireland 1894–1960* (1977), C. Desmond Greaves' *The Irish Transport and General Workers' Union: The formative years 1909–1923* (1982) and Dermot Keogh's *The Rise of the Working Class: The Dublin Trade Union Movement and Labour Leadership 1890–1914*, (1982). These works benefited immeasurably from newly available sources, in particular the papers of William O'Brien, which had been deposited in the National Library of Ireland in the late 1960s. A union leader during the revolutionary period and far beyond, infamous in labour history for his long running enmity with Jim Larkin, O'Brien was vilified as a paper pusher by his enemies within the movement; he was described by Seán O'Casey as a man 'who had time to index everything'.[61] But if this was bad for his members it was a godsend to historians who now had access to printed papers and private documents for the whole of O'Brien's public life. Also to be found in the National Library were the papers of Thomas Johnson, leader of the Labour Party until 1927 and active in politics for many years after, which formed the basis of J. Anthony Gaughan's exhaustive biography *Thomas Johnson, 1872–1963*, published in 1980.

The availability of high-quality sources and the general historical trend towards more contemporary topics saw studies of twentieth-century labour come to the fore. As was the case with economic history, labour history began to look increasingly at the political. Whereas historians usually seek the answers to five questions, namely, when, where, why, what and how, in Ireland, where political historians are faced with a catalogue of failed revolutions, the last question is changed to 'why did it go wrong?'. This is particularly so for those studying the Irish Left whose marginal status in Ireland after the revolutionary period became one of the key questions in labour history as historians examined why labour or the Left had always remained on the fringes.[62] Among the major studies in this vein were E. Rumpf and A. C. Hepburn's *Nationalism and Socialism in Twentieth-Century Ireland* (1977), Mike Milotte's *Communism in modern Ireland. The pursuit of the Workers' Republic since 1916* (1984) and Richard English's *Radicals and the republic. Socialist Republicanism in the Irish Free State, 1925–1937* (1994). We could also include Emmet O'Connor's *Syndicalism in Modern Ireland, 1917–23*

(1988) and *A Labour History of Ireland 1824–1960* (1992) – the latter the first and only survey of its kind on Irish labour history. One reason for the political left's failure has been its schismatic tendency (it is said that when an Irish left-wing or republican group has its inaugural meeting the first item on the agenda is when the split will take place) but there is truth in the argument that an inordinate amount of time has been devoted to looking at marginal leftist groups or splinter factions rather than the more mainstream, if perhaps less glamorous, labour tendency in Ireland. For instance, one commentator criticised the attempts to give the short-lived 1930s socialist Republican Congress 'a posthumous standing not enjoyed by it in its life time' as 'yet another example of the extraordinary capacity of the blindly committed to turn the foot-notes of history into pages of text. It may be good show-business, but it is scarcely good history'.[63] A harsh observation perhaps, but contrast the number of biographies of the Republican Congress leader Peadar O'Donnell, a conspirator with few tangible achievements in political or trade union life with the lack of even a single article on the Labour Party leader William Norton, a man who put Fianna Fáil in government in 1932 and who served as Tánaiste (deputy prime minister) on two occasions in the 1940s and 1950s.

That is not to say that the Irish Labour Party has been ignored, it is the subject of three books, Arthur Mitchell's *Labour in Irish Politics,* (1974) Michael Gallagher's *Irish Labour Party in transition 1957–82* (1982) and the *History of the Irish Labour Party 1922–73* (2007) by the present author as well as a sizeable number of articles and theses. In the context of the lack of academic studies of Irish political parties it has not done too badly, but past studies have focused on periods for which records were easily available and the party's history has been somewhat skewed as a result.[64] Another factor in the Left's or Labour's comparatively low level of support has been Fianna Fáil's success in establishing itself as a catch-all party, winning the vast majority of working class support and thus exerting a remarkably tenacious grip on office. The sometimes fraught but often close relationship between Fianna Fáil, and particularly Seán Lemass, and the trade union movement, has been central to studies such as Richard Dunphy's *The Making of Fianna Fáil Power in Ireland 1923–1948* (1995), Kieran Allen's *Fianna Fáil and Irish labour* (1997), Paul Bew, Ellen Hazelkorn and Henry Patterson's *The Dynamics of Irish Politics* (1989) as well as Bew and Patterson's *Seán Lemass and the Making of Modern Ireland, 1945–66* (1982) and Brian Girvin's *Between Two Worlds,* (1989) both mentioned above. Most of these are written from a Marxist perspective and significantly none of the authors are based in history departments, with all bar one (Kieran Allen, a sociologist) working as political scientists. Irish history continues to operate without utilising any expressed ideological models, and Marxist readings of Irish history remain firmly on the margins. Indeed, it could be said that a perception that much of the work on labour history generally has a 'strong ideological flavour'[65] has hampered its development as a distinct subject. It might be going too far to suggest an institutional bias against labour history but the case that 'the history of the working class probably lags partly because of the social composition of academia' is not one which cannot be discounted out of hand.[66] It continues to be the case that much of the impetus for research and publication on trade unions has come from the trade unions themselves (this is very similar to the current status of agricultural history noted above).[67] However, this tendency towards labour history by the unions, essentially *for* the unions, has helped consolidate its ghetto status, expending most of its energy preaching to the converted rather than expanding its audience.

If, as Clarkson suggested, it was difficult to find sufficient economic historians to put together a rugby team, a labour historian might be hard pressed to find a partner for a game of tennis, and a game of doubles would be almost out of the question. Without wanting to exaggerate the situation, it is nevertheless the case that labour history remains largely absent from university curricula. There are only a handful of dedicated courses in labour history at third level and many of those who emerged in the first wave of labour historians have diversified into political or social history. This is in line with the international trend in the discipline which has been taking a broader view of what constitutes labour history since the fall of the Berlin wall.[68] The degree to which labour history has filtered into the historical mainstream has been poor.[69] The outstanding area of development in this regard has been the growth of studies on women and work. The pioneering work of Mary E. Daly on this subject,[70] has been followed by a significant number of studies ranging from institutional histories and biographical works on women trade union leaders[71] to studies of status and working conditions within and without the paid workforce.[72] It is worth noting that the use of oral history by historians of women in work has meant that this area has developed a distinctly grassroots approach that has been absent from institutional labour histories.[73] It is likely that many of the gaps in labour history such as the history of the rural labourer[74] will be filled as a result of oral history projects. In this sense labour history can only hope to gain from the blurring of boundaries between subdisciplines of history. In many ways labour history has a lot to gain from the post-revisionist school of history which has been growing in strength in Ireland since the mid-1990s. Its focus on the social, cultural and political attitudes and activities of ordinary Irish people means that working class history, that is, the lives of workers, their sporting and leisure activities, their religious and political beliefs, what they enjoyed reading and so on – will enrich the more narrowly based labour history which has tended to focus on workers in a political-economic context. In labour history, as in economic history, interest in local studies continues to sustain and nourish the discipline.[75]

Ultimately Irish labour history has shown itself to be remarkably hardy. Despite the profound indifference of the academic establishment it continues to attract the interest of research students and interested laymen and women. As researchers continue to unearth previously unused sources, both at home and abroad, for instance, the opening up of the former Soviet archives in Russia has provided material for Emmet O'Connor's controversial biography of James Larkin and his study of the relationships between Irish communists and the Comintern;[76] a more nuanced view of labour history, politically and culturally, will emerge and it is likely that the new emphasis in grassroots history will see the emergence of a more class-based view of Irish history generally.[77] If it fosters these kinds of studies alongside its more traditional organisational focus, it is quite possible that labour history is about to enter its most vital phase yet.

notes

1. Mary E. Daly, 'Recent Writings on Irish History. The Interaction between Past and Present', *The Journal of Modern History*, vol. 69, no. 3 (September, 1997).
2. J. J. Lee, *Ireland 1912–1985* (Cambridge, Cambridge University Press, 1989), p. 542.
3. Mary E. Daly, *Industrial Development and Irish National Identity 1922–1939* (Dublin, Gill and Macmillan, 1992), p. 3.
4. One area that looms large over economic history is that of the Great Famine of 1845–51. As this is the subject of another chapter, work on the famine has been largely avoided in this essay.
5. See Cormac Ó Gráda, *Ireland. A New Economic History 1780–1939* (Oxford, Oxford University Press 1994), p. 314.
6. Louis M. Cullen, *An Economic History of Ireland since 1660*. (London, Batsford, 1972), p. iv.
7. Quoted in R. F. Foster, 'We are All Revisionists Now', *Irish Review*, 1986, p. 2.
8. To be fair, O'Brien was one of many dilettante economists around at this time (although he was probably the only one to hold a senior teaching post in the discipline). Cranky economics was a favoured intellectual pursuit of many Irish polymaths of the time, with academics such as Professor Alfred O'Rahilly of UCC, for instance, writing more on economics than his own field of mathematical physics.

9. George O'Brien's antipathy towards statistics remained undiminished over time, as can be seen in his arguments with his contemporary, Roy Geary, Ireland's leading statistician and later director of the Central Statistics Office and the Economic Research Institute. See Mary E. Daly, 'The Society and its contribution to Ireland: past present and future', *Journal of the Statistical and Social Inquiry Society of Ireland*, vol. XXVII, Part V, 1998.

10. See Cormac Ó Gráda, 'Introduction to the New Edition', R. Dudley Edwards and T. Desmond Williams *The Great Famine. Studies in Irish History 1845–52*, 2nd Edition (Dublin, Lilliput Press, 1994).

11. Quoted in Tom Garvin, *Preventing the Future. Why was Ireland so Poor for so Long?* (Dublin, Gill and Macmillan, 2004), p. 100.

12. For an account of Kenneth H. Connell's academic career see R. M. Hartwell, 'Kenneth H. Connell: An apreciation', in *Irish Economic and Social History Volume 1* (1974); M. Drake, 'Professor K. H. Connell', in *Irish Historical Studies, XIX*: 73 (March 1974).

13. M. Drake, 'Professor K. H. Connell', in *Irish Historical Studies XIX*: 73 (March 1974), p. 83.

14. G. Henry, 'Peripatetic Professor', in *History Ireland*, Summer 1995.

15. J. J. Lee, 'Irish Economic History since 1500', in J. J. Lee (ed.) *Irish Historiography 1970–79* (Cork, Cork University Press, 1981), p. 173.

16. Ronan Fanning, '"The great enchantment": Uses and Abuses of Modern Irish History', in Ciaran Brady (ed.) *Interpreting Irish History. The Debate on Historical Revisionism* (Dublin, Irish Academic Press, 1994), p. 153.

17. *Irish Economic and Social History*, volume 1, 1974.

18. See V. Pollock, *Irish Economic and Social History*. Index to volumes I–XV (1974–88).

19. T. W. Moody, 'Research on Irish History in Irish Universities, 1971–2', in *Irish Historical Studies XVIII*, 69, March 1972.

20. The English historian L. A. Clarkson had been teaching in the department in Queens since the mid-1960s, but he did not turn his attention to Irish economic history until the mid-1970s. See Clarkson, 'From England to Australia to Ireland: A Cultural Odyssey', in P. Hudson and R. Bowen (eds), *Living Economic and Social History* (Glasgow, Economic History Society, 2001), p. 13.

21. F. S. L. Lyons, *Ireland since the Famine* (2nd Edition London, Fontana, 1973), p. 7.

22. L. A. Clarkson, 'The Writing of Irish Economic and Social History since 1968', in *Economic History Review*, cited in Lee, 'Irish Economic History since 1500'.

23. T. W. Moody, 'A New History of Ireland', in Brady (ed.) *Interpreting Irish History: The Debate on Historical Revisionism*, p. 45.

24. Fanning, 'The Great Enchantment', p. 152.

25. Fanning, 'The Great Enchantment', p. 153.

26. Fanning, 'The Great Enchantment', p. 153.

27. Quoted in Lee, 'Irish Economic History since 1500', p. 194.

28. C. Ó Gráda, *Ireland before and after the Famine: Explorations in Economic History, 1800–1925* (Manchester, Manchester University Press, 1988).

29. For an examination of the development of econometrics in Ireland see Liam Kennedy, 'Studies in Irish Econometric History', *Irish Historical Studies XXIII*, 91 (May 1993).

30. See Liam Kennedy, *Colonialism, Religion & Nationalism in Ireland* (Institute of Irish Studies, Belfast) 1996 and *The Modern Industrialisation of Ireland, 1940–1988* (Studies in Irish Economic & Social History, Dublin) 1989; Carla King, 'Co-operation and Rural Development: Plunkett's Approach', in John Davis, (ed.) *Rural Change in Ireland* (Belfast, Institute of Irish Studies, 1999); 'The Early Development of Agricultural Co-operation: Some French and Irish Comparisons', in *Proceedings of the Royal Irish Academy*, 96 C, no. 3 (1996).

31. Fanning, 'The Great Enchantment', p. 151.

32. See L. A. Clarkson, 'Irish Social and Economic History 1974–2000 and Beyond', *Irish Economic and Social History XXVIII* (2001), p. 2.

33. Free secondary education was not introduced in Ireland until 1967 and, with the exception of a small number of scholarship students, higher education was the preserve of the wealthy. It was not until the 1970s, with the establishment of Regional Technical Colleges in the 1970s, that the expansion in university education and the growth in numbers educated up to Leaving Certificate level that Ireland's workforce could hope to compete in an international context.

34. See David Fitzpatrick, 'Was Ireland Special? Recent Writing on the Subject of the Irish Economy and Society in the Eighteenth Century', *Historical Journal*, 33: 1 (1990) with regard to economics and society in Scotland and Ireland. Among the comparative studies of Scotland and Ireland are: L. M. Cullen and T. C. Smout (eds), *Comparative Aspects of Scottish and Irish Economic and Social History, 1600–1900* (Edinburgh, John Donald, 1977); T. M. Devine and D. Dickson, *Ireland and Scotland, 1600–1850: Parallels and Contrasts in Economic and Social Development* (Edinburgh, John Donald, 1983); R. M. Mitchison and P. Roebuck (eds) *Economy and Society in Scotland and Ireland 1500–1939* (Edinburgh, John Donald, 1988); S. J. Connolly, R. A. Houston and R. J. Morris (eds) *Conflict, Identity and Economic Development: Scotland and Ireland, 1600–1939* (Preston, Carnegie, 1995). On Ireland and the wider world see Kevin H. O'Rourke, 'Ireland and the bigger picture', in David Dickson and Cormac Ó Gráda (eds) *Refiguring Ireland. Essays in Honour of L. M. Cullen* (Dublin, Lilliput Press, 2003).

35. Under the land acts of the late nineteenth century and early twentieth century loans were made available for tenant farmers to purchase their land holdings. Under the terms of the 1922 Anglo Irish treaty it was agreed that the Irish government would continue to collect the annuities and forward the money to the British exchequer. When Fianna Fáil came into government in 1932 they continued to collect the annuities but refused to hand the moneys over to the British government which responded by placing heavy tariffs on Irish cattle imports. Normal trading between the two states did not resume until Britain backed down in the context of war looming in Europe. For economic aspects of the war see in particular David Johnson, *The interwar economy in Ireland* (Studies in Irish Economic and Social History); Mary Daly, *Industrial Development and Irish National Identity, 1922–39*; (Dublin, Gill and Macmillan, 1992); J. Peter Neary and Cormac Ó Gráda, 'Protection, Economic War and Structural Change: The 1930s in Ireland', in *Irish Historical Studies*, vol. 27, no. 107, May 1991, pp. 250–66.

36. Till Geiger and Michael Kennedy, *Ireland, Europe and the Marshall Plan* (Dublin, Four Courts Press, 2004). There are a number of economic histories in the book, although it deals for the most part on politics and international relations.

37. D. Hoctor, *The Department's Story: A History of the Department of Agriculture* (Dublin, Institute of Public Administration, 1971); John Neill-Watson, *A History of Farm Mechanisation: Ireland 1890–1990* (Dublin, Farm Tractors and Machinery Trade Association, 1993); Louis P. F. Smith and Sean Healy, *Farm Organisations in Ireland: A Century of Economics and Politics* (Dublin, Four Courts Press, 1996); Paul O'Grady (ed.), *Leaders of Courage: The Story of the ICMSA* (Limerick, Irish Creamery Milk Suppliers Association, 2000); Paul Rouse, *Ireland's Own Soil: Government and Agriculture in Ireland, 1945–1965* (Dublin, Irish Farmers' Journal, 2000); Mary E. Daly, *The First Department: A History of the Department of Agriculture* (Dublin, Institute of Public Administration, 2002); Cormac Ó Gráda, 'Irish Agriculture North and South since 1900', in Bruce Campbell and Mark Overton (eds) *Land, Labour and Livestock: Historical Studies in European Agricultural Productivity* (Manchester, Manchester University Press, 1991) and Cormac Ó Gráda, 'Irish Agricultural History: Recent Research', in *Agricultural History Review*, vol. 38, no. 2, 1990, pp. 165–73.
38. Kevin Whelan, 'Watching the Detective', in *History Ireland*, summer 1994, pp. 10–12.
39. See for example, David Dickson, *Old World Colony: Cork and South Munster 1630–1830*, (Cork, Cork University Press and University of Wisconsin Press, 2005); Andy Bielenberg, *Cork's Industrial Revolution, 1780–1880* (Cork, Cork University Press, 1991).
40. Anthony Coughlan, 'Ireland's Marxist Historians', in Brady (ed.) *Interpreting Irish History. The Debate on Historical Revisionism*, p 288. The pair's writings on the subject have been collected and published by a Moscow publisher as *Ireland and the Irish Question* (1978).
41. J. J. Lee, *The Modernisation of Irish Society 1848–1918* (Dublin, Gill and Macmillan, 1973), p. 151.
42. This is not to suggest that Larkin was under the influence of anything stronger than tea. He was a convinced abstainer from alcohol which he regarded as a blight on the lives of the working class. One of his best remembered successes as a trade union organiser was the ending of the payment of dockers in public houses.
43. J. D. Clarkson, *Labour and Nationalism in Ireland* (New York, Columbia University, 1925), p. 211.
44. Connolly had been a trade union official and founder of the Irish Socialist Republican Party in Dublin before his emigration to the United States in 1903 where he became an organiser with Daniel De Leon's Socialist Labour Party, subsequently becoming one of the founders of the Industrial Worker of the World, or 'Wobblies'.
45. James Connolly, *Collected Works*, Volume One (Dublin, New Books, 1987), p. 26.
46. Connolly, *Collected Works*, p. 137.
47. See Lee, *Modernisation*, p. 151; Patrick Lynch, 'William Thompson and the Socialist Tradition', in J. W. Boyle (ed.) *Leaders and Workers* (Cork, Mercier, 1966), p. 9.
48. Connolly, *Collected Works*, p. 27.
49. See William O'Brien and Edward MacLysaght, *Forth the Banners Go* (Dublin, Irish Transport and General Workers Union, 1969), p. 23.

50. For instance, William O'Brien contested Jim Larkin's account of why he went to the United States in 1913, and his efforts to discount Larkin's version appeared weekly in the pages of the ITGWU's newspaper the *Voice of Labour* in 1923.

51. The only exception to this was a small number of biographies and autobiographies written by activists, for instance P. Ó Cathasaigh [Seán O'Casey], *The Story of the Irish Citizen Army* (Dublin and London, Maunsel, 1919); Nora Connolly O'Brien, *Portrait of a Rebel father* (London, Rich and Cowan, 1935) and; J. R. White, *Misfit* (1930), but these represented highly subjective accounts of the period. O'Casey's in particular was an exercise in point scoring after the fact, a style he continued in his later forays into autobiography.

52. R. J. C. Connolly, 'Introduction', in R. M. Fox, 'Labour in the National Struggle' (Dublin, Labour Party Propaganda department, n. d. [1945]), p. 2.

53. See Ruaidhrí Roberts, *The Story of the People's College* (Dublin, 1986); John P. Swift, *John Swift: An Irish Dissident* (Dublin, Gill & Macmillan, 1991), pp.143–9.

54. J. J. Judge, 'The Labour Movement in the Republic of Ireland' (UCD, 1955); Emmet Larkin, *James Larkin and the Irish Labour Movement* (Columbia University, 1957); and John W. Boyle, *The Rise of the Irish Labour Movement, 1888–1907* (University of Dublin, Trinity College, 1961).

55. See Anthony Coughlan, '*C. Desmond Greaves: An Obituary Essay*' (Dublin, Studies in Irish Labour History, 1990).

56. See Francis Devine and Niamh Puirséil, 'Joseph Deasy and the Fiery Cross', in J. Deasy, *Fiery Cross. The Story of Jim Larkin* (Dublin, Studies in Irish Labour History, 2004).

57. J. W. Boyle, (ed.) *Leaders and Workers* (Cork, Mercier Press, 1966)

58. A. Mitchell, 'The Course of Irish History', *Saothar*, 22 (1997).

59. See Swift, *Swift. An Irish dissident* pp. 195–7; Francis Devine 'Saothar, the Irish Labour History Society and Labour History, 1973–2000', in Francis Devine (ed.) *Saothar Index* (Dublin, Irish Labour History Society, 2000), p. 12.

60. J. J. Lee, *Irish Economic History*, p. 188.

61. Seán O'Casey to Jack Carney, 2 August 1948 in David Krause (ed.) *The Letters of Seán O'Casey1942–54*, Volume 2 (New York, Macmillan, 1980), p. 546.

62. See Francis Devine and E. O'Connor, 'The Course of Labour History', *Saothar*, 12 (1987).

63. Brendan Ó hÉither, *The Begrudger's Guide to Irish Politics* (Dublin, Poolbeg Press, 1986), pp. 58–9. The focus on the Republican Congress had a lot to do with contemporary events and the efforts by left-wing republicans to establish legitimacy for their project in the 1970s and 1980s after their split with more orthodox physical force republicans in the Provisional IRA. On Republican Congress and O'Donnell see Henry Patterson, *The Politics of Illusion: A Political History of the IRA* (London: Serif, 1997) and Richard English *Radicals and the Republic. Socialist Republicanism in the Irish Free State, 1925–1937* (Oxford, Clarendon Press, 1994); notwithstanding my complaints about the surfeit of work on O'Donnell, Donal Ó Drisceoil's *Peadar O'Donnell* (Cork, Cork University Press, 2001) is a brilliant and valuable study.

64. The central records of the Irish Labour Party were destroyed in the late 1960s. While the papers of individual Labour members (such as those of William O'Brien and Thomas Johnson mentioned above) are a valuable source, they are far from a complete record of the party and are, naturally, only useful for the periods when these individuals were active. However, the

annual reports of the party (the only Irish party which did so) which, until
the early 1940s contained a verbatim report of the party's annual conference
have proved useful to historians, even if there has been a tendency to use
them somewhat uncritically. The party's sometime publication of weekly
newspapers has also provided a useful, if often underused, source. See Niamh
Puirséil, 'Reading between the Lines. The Labour Party Press until 1949', in
Irish Archives (Winter 2003).

65. L. A. Clarkson quoted in Francis Devine and John Horne, 'Editorial', *Saothar*,
6 (1980), p. 3.
66. F. Lane, 'Review of Francis Devine (ed.) An Index to Saothar', in *Saothar*, 26
(2001), p. 88.
67. For example John Swift, *History of the Dublin Bakers and Others* (Dublin, Irish
Bakers' Confectioners' and Allied Workers Union, 1948); T. J. O'Connell, *The
100 Years of Progress. The Story of the Irish National Teachers' Organisation 1868–
1968.* (Dublin, Irish National Teachers' Organisation, 1968); Desmond Greaves,
The Irish Transport and General Workers Union: The Formative Years (Dublin, Gill
and Macmillan, 1982); Paul Doyle and John O'Dowd, *The Parliament of Labour.
100 Years of the Dublin Council of Trade Unions.* (Dublin, Dublin Council of Trade
Unions, 1986); David Nevin, *Trade Union Century* (Dublin, Mercier Press, 1994);
Martin Maguire, *Servants to the Public: A History of the Local Government and
Public Services Union, 1901–1990* (Dublin, Institute of Public Administration,
1998); Marie Coleman, *IFUT A History. The Irish Federation of University Teachers
1963–99* (Dublin, IFUT, 2000). See also the Studies in Irish Labour History series
published by the Irish Labour History Society.
68. See for example F. Lane and E. O'Connor, 'Ebb Tide or Fifth Wave', in
Saothar, 27 (2002) and 'Labour History: Broadening the Field?', in *Labour
History Review*, 68: 3 (December 2003).
69. See M. McGinley, 'Labour pro bono publico?', *Saothar*, 23 (1998), p. 73.
70. Mary E. Daly, 'Women, Work and Trade Unionism', in Margaret MacCurtain
and Donncha Ó Corráin (eds) *Women in Irish Society: The Historical Dimension*
(Dublin, Women's Press, 1978).
71. Mary Jones, *These Obstreperous Lassies: A History of the Irish Women's Workers
Union* (Dublin, Gill and Macmillan, 1988); Rosemary Cullen Owens,
Louie Bennett (Cork, Cork University Press, 2002); Mary Cullen and Maria
Luddy (eds) *Female Activists: Irish Women and Change, 1900–1960* (Dublin,
Woodfield Press, 2001); Marianne Heron and Sheila Conroy. *Fighting Spirit*
(Dublin, Attic Press, 1993).
72. See Maria Luddy, 'An Agenda for Women's History in Ireland, Part II:
1800–1900', in *Irish Historical Studies XXVIII*: 109 (May 1992), for a lengthy
examination of work in this area p. 29–31; idem, 'Working Women, Trade
Unionism and Politics in Ireland, 1830–1945', in Fintan Lane and Donal Ó
Drisceoil (eds), *Politics and the Irish Working Class, 1830–1945* (Basingstoke,
Palgrave Macmillan, 2005); Joanna Bourke, *Husbandry to Housewifery: Women,
Economic Change, and Housework in Ireland, 1890–1914* (Oxford, Clarandon,
1993); Mary E. Daly, *Women and Work in Ireland* (Dundalk, Economic and
social history society of Ireland, 1997); Catriona Clear, *Women of the House:
Women's Household Work in Ireland, 1926–61: Discourses, Experiences, Memories*
(Dublin, Irish Academic Press, 2000); Bernadette Whelan (ed.) *Women and
Paid work in Ireland 1500–1930* (Dublin, Four Courts Press, 2000).

73. See for example Clear, *Women of the House*; Mary Muldowney, *The Second World War and Irish Women: An Oral History* (Dublin, Irish Academic Press, 2007); Elizabeth Kiely and Máire Leane, 'Money Matters in the Lives of Working Women in Ireland in the 1940s and the 1950s', in Fintan Lane, Francis Devine and Niamh Puirséil (eds), *Essays in Irish Labour History: A Festschrift for John W. and Elizabeth Boyle*. (Dublin, Irish Academic Press, 2008); idem, 'Female Domestic and Farm Workers in Munster, 1936–60: Some Insights from Oral History', *Saothar*, 29 (2004); M. Elders, E. Kiely, M. Leane and C. O'Driscoll, 'A Union in those Days was Husband and Wife: Women's Narratives on Trade Unions in Munster, 1939–60', *Saothar*, 27 (2002); *Saothar* has also published a number of oral histories of individual labour activists which provide a valuable resource for historians. See Francis Devine, *Index to Saothar*, p. 82.

74. Fintan Lane and Emmett O'Connor, 'Speed the Plough', in *Saothar*, 26 (2001), p. 3; on rural labourers see F. Lane, 'Rural Labourers, Social Change and Politics', in Lane and Ó Drisceoil, *Politics and the Irish Working Class*.

75. Notable local studies include Maura Cronin, *Country, Class or Craft? The Politicisation of the Skilled Artisan in Nineteenth-Century Cork* (Cork University Press, 1994); John Cunningham, *Labour in the West of Ireland* (1995).

76. Emmet O'Connor, *James Larkin* (Cork, Cork University Press, 2002); *Reds and the Green: Ireland, Russia and the Communist Internationals, 1919–1943* (Dublin, UCD Press, 2005).

77. For class and politics see Lane and Ó Drisceoil (eds) *Politics and the Irish Working Class*.

5

conceiving irish diasporas: irish migration and migrant communities in the modern period

william murphy

introduction

The notion that the sum of Irishness is not confined to a small island off the west coast of Europe is not new. This could hardly be otherwise; the Irish have long been represented as having a particular propensity towards migration. Enda Delaney opened his first full-length study of Irish migration to Britain by recalling the words of an eighth-century abbot who remarked upon 'the Irish habit of going away';[1] while debating the Republic of Ireland Bill (1948) John A. Costello stated that the 'Irish at home are only one section of a great race which has spread itself throughout the world'.[2] In the modern period Irish people have trickled, rushed, flowed and been flushed out of their homeland to various destinations at various times. Some travelled in sorrow and others with enthusiasm, participating in a 'complex phenomenon' prompted by a 'mix of elements of dynamism, persecution, and poverty'.[3] Every conceivable category of native Irish person has been represented in this enormous movement and in moving the migrants, and their descendants, have created a multiplicity of new categories of Irishness. Increasingly, Irish emigrants and their multigenerational progeny are encompassed within a single entity or analytical framework: the Irish diaspora.

The size of the Irish diaspora, if we accept that it exists, has continually fluctuated over time, depending on such factors as the rate of migration from Ireland, the rate at which the Irish abroad are fruitful and multiply, and the extent to which they pass their Irish identity on through the generations. In truth, all these variables, particularly the last, make it difficult to accurately quantify the Irish diaspora. The figure most often reached is that given by Mary Robinson in 1990.[4] She stated that there were then over 70 million people around the world, claiming Irish descent; the figure was speculative and has since been characterised alternatively as 'fabled'[5] and 'plausible'.[6] Writing on the Irish diaspora is a phase in a long and mixed tradition of writing, both academic and popular, on Irish migration and the Irish abroad.[7] In recent years, however, there has been an extraordinary expansion in the literature on the Irish abroad, linked very often to a growing interest in the notion of an Irish diaspora.[8] As a result it is necessary to make the observation, which is also a caveat, that the literature exploring Irish emigration and the multi-generational consequences has become almost as vast as the phenomenon described.[9] Consequently, this chapter must of necessity ignore much that is fascinating in the field. It will, however, attempt to explore the process through which the Irish acquired a diaspora. It will also consider the current influence of the concept, and touch on some of the questions of definition and contentious debates within the field.

emigration from ireland

Before the diaspora there was emigration. It has been described, accurately, as 'one of the great formative factors in modern Irish history'. Anyone familiar with Irish history is aware of the mass exodus from Ireland during the nineteenth century which reached its peak during the decade of the Great Famine. In ten years between 1846 and 1855 as many as 2.5 million people – from a population of just over 8 million – left the island.[10] The Irish have, however, emigrated throughout the modern period. Irish migration in the seventeenth and eighteenth centuries has not impinged on the popular imagination to the same extent and was in real numbers much smaller than later movements, although, as Louis Cullen has noted, it 'represented a higher proportion of the total movement of people who crossed national boundaries within and out of Europe than did the nineteenth century outflow'.[11] No area of Irish migration studies is completely free from problems of quantification, but this is a period for which reliable census material is not available and the sheer divergence in figures is enough to induce despair. In 1985 Kerby A. Miller argued that between 300,000 and 500,000 people migrated from Ireland to the American colonies in the years 1600–1776,[12] whereas Cullen estimated in 1994 that the total may be a fraction of this.[13] In a recent essay with Liam Kennedy, Miller has responded and still stands adjacent to his original figures and very far from Cullen's,[14] others occupy ground in between.[15] Figures for the substantial Irish migrations to Europe and Britain during this period are hard to come by, although, again, Cullen has offered conservative estimates.[16]

During the Napoleonic wars there was a lull in Irish migration, but between 1815 and the Great Famine emigration from Ireland is estimated at 'well over a million'.[17] Kerby Miller, whose estimates tend towards the upper end in most debates around the quantification of Irish migration, has consistently suggested that during this period 800,000 to a million went to North America alone,[18] while 'perhaps' another half a million migrated to Britain, 35,000 to Australia and smaller numbers to other exotic areas of the British Empire and beyond.[19] In the decades after the Great Famine Irish emigration remained high. Approximately a further four million people left Ireland between 1855 and the outbreak of World War I in 1914,[20] ensuring that in 1891 at least 38.3 per cent of Irish born people lived outside of Ireland.[21] Between 1921 and the end of the twentieth-century emigration continued to affect most Irish families, but was significantly lower than the nineteenth-century out-flow and the proportion of Irish born persons living outside of Ireland dropped.[22] It is estimated that during this period a half million left the northern (six-county) state while 1.5 million people left the southern (26-county) state.[23] These figures hide the fluctuations within the period; emigration from the southern state spiked between 1945 and 1960 when over half a million left,[24] and in the 1980s when there was net outward migration of over 200,000.[25]

discovering the irish diaspora

The word diaspora is Greek in origin, meaning scattering. The conventional usage of the word, to describe the Jewish people in exile, ensured that quite specific characteristics became associated with it. A diasporic group had been driven from their homeland by catastrophe and scattered across many territories. They maintained a strong sense of their own cultural identity, passing this down through the generations, while a crucial aspect of this identity became a consistent desire to return to the home country.[26] In applying the term to other ethnic groups all or most of these characteristics were at first adhered to, however, incrementally academics have come to use the word diaspora and related terms much more loosely as

> metaphoric designations for several categories of people – expatriates, expellees, political refugees, alien residents, immigrants, and ethnic and racial minorities *tout court* – in much the same way that 'ghetto'

has to come to designate all kinds of crowded, constricted, and disprivileged urban environments, and 'holocaust' has come to be applied to all kinds of mass murder.[27]

It is not clear at what point this process ceases to add layers of meaning to the word and begins to leach it of any defining characteristics, but Kachig Tölölyan was certainly correct when he coined the aphorism 'Where once were dispersions, there now is diaspora.'[28] Robin Cohen and Gabriel Sheffer have both suggested that increased globalisation contributed significantly to this burgeoning enthusiasm for diaspora,[29] while Rogers Brubaker has amusingly described the result as a '"diaspora" diaspora' or 'a dispersion of the meanings of the term in semantic, conceptual and disciplinary space'.[30]

It was only a matter of time before academics of Irish migration and settlement abroad picked up on developments in the international literature of migrant communities[31] and the Irish too acquired a diaspora. Sporadically the unfamiliar word 'diaspora' began to appear in scholarly work on the Irish emigrant experience. During the 1970s and 1980s it graced a handful of titles.[32] In 1990s, however, 'the Irish diaspora' seemed to become the expression of choice among academics when describing emigrants from Ireland and their descendants. The term is now commonly used in the titles of general studies,[33] collections,[34] and articles.[35] In the Republic of Ireland the recently revised history curriculum at Leaving Certificate level has a section devoted to 'The Irish diaspora, 1840–1966',[36] ensuring that more and more Irish people are familiar with a term which was alien to the Irish public less than 20 years ago.

The pattern discernible in academic discourse has been matched in the language of public life in Ireland. 'Diaspora' was first used in Dáil Éireann in November 1963 by James Dillon (a man who liked to display his erudition) when he described John F. Kennedy as 'this fine flowering of our people's worldwide diaspora'.[37] In succeeding decades the term continued to appear, although rarely at first, on the Dáil record. There was, nevertheless, an almost imperceptible trend towards its adoption.[38] As President of Ireland, Mary Robinson did much to popularise the idea. On 2 February 1995 she addressed a joint session of the Dáil and Seanad on the topic of 'Cherishing the Irish Diaspora'.[39] Suddenly the phrase 'the Irish diaspora' verged on commonplace.[40] Donald Harman Akenson,[41] perhaps the leading advocate of the idea in an Irish context, has admitted that diaspora was threatening 'to become a massive linguistic weed'.[42] Typical of this was the headline over a newspaper article published in 2005 on three Irish professional rugby players who were plying their trade in England and France; 'Rugby's new diaspora'.[43]

In 2000 Enda Delaney noted that the 'historical study of migration from Ireland is striking in that little or no heed is paid to the vast and burgeoning literature on possible theoretical frameworks which attempt to explain and understand' migration as a phenomenon.[44] This has been true not only of studies of the process of migration, but of studies which have sought to examine the experiences of the consequent Irish migrant communities. In adding an Irish variety to the world's growing list of diasporas, have academics and politicians simply adopted a more pretentious and modish way of saying the Irish abroad or have they embarked upon a serious engagement with a theoretical framework? Are they mere followers of intellectual fashion or have they reached for the concept with a purpose or purposes? In recent years, as the label the 'Irish diaspora' attained a dominance approaching ubiquity, some scholars have displayed negligible engagement with the ideas implied by the label never mind any acknowledgement that these ideas are contested and complicated. Perhaps the most egregious instance of such woolly thinking – and unfortunately the most popular book on the Irish diaspora – is Tim Pat Coogan's *Wherever Green is Worn: The Story of the Irish Diaspora*. Infected by Celtic Tiger and peace process triumphalism it is a concoction of hokum of the 'aren't we a great little nation, you can kick us but you can't keep us down' variety and embassy drinks reception anecdote as history.[45]

The sense that some scholars of Irish emigration had adopted the term diaspora with rather more haste than thought has been arrested somewhat in recent years with the appearance of a number of articles which have begun to question the implications of terms such as the 'Irish diaspora', while speculating on the future of the emergent discipline 'Irish diaspora studies'. In a 1995 article Akenson interrogated the promiscuous use of 'diaspora' and warned that the concept 'should be approached with a fair degree of scepticism'. He acknowledged that the 'genie is out of the bottle', but insisted that the term must retain meaning even if this meaning was inevitably less restricted and not so easily defined as in the past.[46] Enda Delaney has cautioned against seeking to present various phases of Irish migration as having a coherence when 'what occurred was a series of diverse migrations, unconnected in may respects, apart from the fact that people left the same island'.[47] Kevin Kenny has warned that a diasporic approach 'can underestimate the enduring power of nation states and the emergence within them of nationally specific enthnicities that sharply differentiate an ostensibly unitary "people"'.[48] Also Joe Lee has posed many pertinent questions, flagging some of the theoretical and practical problems in the use of the concept. Perhaps most fundamentally, he suggested that if issues of definition were not attended to there was a danger that 'scholars, to say nothing of non-scholars, will find the diaspora they want.'[49] So how have scholars defined the Irish diaspora: which diasporas have they sought?

defining the irish diaspora: a persecuted people

Those scholars who are experts in theories of diaspora, but not Irish migration history have tended to acknowledge the existence of an Irish diaspora, while stressing a narrative of oppression, victimhood and exile. The 'exodus' during the Great Famine and in its immediate aftermath has loomed largest in the minds of these writers. This is undoubtedly because famine migration is the period of Irish migration which can most easily be described in terms which conform to traditional models of diaspora. Cohen, referring to the work of Christine Kinealy on the Great Famine, placed the Irish diaspora in a category described as 'victim/refugee' along with the Jewish, Armenian, African and Palestinian diasporas. The practices he associated with these diasporas are 'expulsion, deportation, genocide and "ethnic cleansing"'.[50] Gérard Chaliand and Jean-Pierre Rageau included the Irish diaspora in *The Penguin Atlas of Diasporas* which was originally published in French in 1991. Their primary definition of diaspora was '*the collective forced dispersion of a religious and/or ethnic group,* precipitated by a disaster, often of a political nature.' They seemed satisfied that the Irish met this definition, although they questioned whether the Irish movement constituted a mere migration because 'the overwhelming majority of migrants have gone to a single country, or indeed two or three countries, often linguistically similar to their home country?'[51] Their brief chapter on the Irish diaspora had the Great Famine and Irish-America as its focus. They stressed that Ireland was 'under the thumb of England' and emphasised the attachment of the Irish diaspora to Catholicism and nationalist politics.[52]

This picture is no doubt representative of the image some in the Irish diaspora have of themselves. Kerby Miller has argued in his brilliant study *Emigrants and Exiles* that the dominant tendency among Irish migrants to North America was to view themselves as 'involuntary, nonresponsible "exiles", compelled to leave home by forces beyond individual control, particularly by British and landlord oppression'.[53]

Alan O'Day has observed, however, that recent work has complicated this image and emphasised

> the importance of 'pull' factors in the decision to emigrate and choice of location. Furthermore, the myth that the Irish either left Ireland in large numbers because of political considerations or selected their destinations for these reasons is dispelled. Additionally, the emigration pattern is now seen as a Protestant as well as Catholic phenomenon.[54]

The Irish diaspora as characterised by general theorists of diaspora such as Cohen reflects neither these developments nor the tendency to acknowledge the importance of generations of migrants either side of the Great Famine. Similarly this construction of the Irish diaspora ignores decades of revisionist historiography which has attempted to complicate the British/oppressor versus Irish/victim dichotomy. It is surely with this in mind that Houston and Smyth have suggested that the 'concept of diaspora, with its emphasis upon the displacement of people from their homeland and its connotations of exile, is a compelling but limited description of the Irish experience.'[55]

defining the irish diaspora: we may be sectarian but we are all irish

Among the most vociferous promoters of the idea of the Irish diaspora there has been an openly (even combatively) expressed desire that the concept should facilitate a redefining of Irishness in as liberal and inclusive a manner as possible. This was in part a reaction to the historic tendency among many Irish nationalists, particularly those influenced by the Irish-Ireland movement, to define those from a Gaelic and Catholic tradition as 'fíor-ghael' (true-Irish) whereas those from an Anglo-Irish and Protestant tradition were represented as less Irish or not Irish at all. This position was inconsistently opposed by non-sectarian nationalists and a large part of the revisionist project in Irish history has been a refutation of these assumptions and the presentation of a more complicated picture. The aspiration to reject narrow characterisations of, or hierarchies within, Irishness has been an important touchstone for Akenson in his advocacy of diaspora. He defined an Irish person as 'anyone who lived permanently within the social system that was the island of Ireland' and an Irish migrant as 'a woman or man, girl or boy, who either was born in Ireland or was a permanent resident of Ireland before embarking for some new world'.[56] He rejected any other conception of Irishness because it would open the door to 'exclusivist mentality lunacy'; in other words the association of Irishness with a particular creed or lineage. He also forwarded a methodological reason for the dangers of any other approach; 'if one is absolutely committed to the particularistic and exclusive view that not all the Irish emigrants in the tallies were "truly" Irish, then one can follow only one course: burn all the data on Irish emigration as useless and thereafter wander into the historical darkness.'[57]

This motivation is again apparent when one examines the introduction of the notion of the Irish diaspora into political and popular discourse. As Piaras Mac Éinrí has argued, the entry of diaspora into the 'public discourse' signified 'a new willingness to embrace a more inclusive and less territorially bounded notion of Irishness'.[58] Robinson gave expression to this liberal approach in her 'Cherishing the Irish Diaspora' speech when she stated:

> If we expect that the mirror held up to us by Irish communities abroad will show us a single familiar identity, or a pure strain of Irishness, we will be disappointed. We will overlook the fascinating diversity of culture and choice which looks back at us. Above all we will miss the chance to have that dialogue with our own diversity which this reflection offers us.[59]

She insisted that the term 'the people of Ireland' resists 'any fixed or narrow definition' and argued that 'far from seeking to categorise or define it, we widen it still further to make it as broad and inclusive as possible'.[60] Breda Gray has characterised this as an attempt to 'give legitimacy to the many spaces of Irishness and the "multiculturalism" that marks them all, whether "at home" or abroad'.[61] This call for change presumes an underexplored aspect of the Irish diasporic experience, the ways in which the culture of the homeland excludes or negatively represents migrants and their descendants. Such negativity ranges from the extreme, where in the past some voices within the Irish-Ireland movement represented emigrants as traitors who were intent on committing race suicide,[62] to the more mundane, if fundamental, disbelief among the Irish-born when the diasporan of the second or third generation describes himself or herself as 'Irish'.[63] The concept of the Irish diaspora is then to some extent a vehicle for disseminating positive images of the migrant.

The Irish state has come to reflect, although not fully embrace, these diasporic tendencies. In March 1996 the Minister for the Environment, Brendan Howlin, announced that one of his legislative priorities for the year was the introduction of a constitutional amendment bill, allowing for the election of three members of the Irish Senate by emigrants.[64] By November 1996, however, the proposal had been abandoned.[65] In the context of the Good Friday agreement of 1998, Article Two of the Irish constitution was amended to include a rather wishy-washy intimation of ethnic fellow-feeling which, nonetheless, marks a significant symbolic acknowledgement of a transnational Irish identity. The new wording states that 'The Irish nation cherishes its special affinity with people of Irish ancestry living abroad who share its cultural identity and heritage.'[66] This was not entirely new; between 1936 and 1986 around 16,500 diasporans applied for, and were granted, Irish citizenship under provisions in the Irish Nationality and Citizenship Acts of 1935 and 1956.[67] Irish law continues to afford citizenship rights to the children and grandchildren of those born in Ireland, but living abroad. It is not yet clear how the recent trend towards significant inward migration will impact on debates surrounding Irishness and as a consequence debates about diaspora. It is likely that Irishness will become an even more capacious category, although the phenomenon has also been accompanied by the 27th amendment to the Irish constitution passed in 2004 which restricted rights to Irish citizenship in the face of alleged exploitation by immigrants.

defining the irish diaspora: pushmi-pullyu

In the past Irish migrants were almost universally represented as suffering at the hands of the British imperial masters whereas recently historians have begun to assert the significance of the Irish as colonisers.[68] This not only brings into focus the Irish in India or South Africa,[69] but acknowledges that one of the consequences of Irish migration to Europe in the seventeenth and eighteenth centuries was Irish participation in Spanish imperialist campaigns in various South American locations at this time.[70] Many of the early Irish inhabitants of the Americas were rebels and vagrants who were transported there – Akenson estimates that 10,000 Irish were transported to the West Indies in the Cromwellian era[71] – but others were eager participants in colonial projects. Irish people willingly contributed to British imperial experiments not only in the colonies which were to become the bedrock of the United States, but in the West Indies.[72] Several Irish families were among the most significant slave-owning families in the Caribbean in the eighteenth century and early nineteenth century. James Blair Jnr, the son of a Newry family that had settled in Saint Eustatia, received the enormous sum of £83,530 in compensation when his 1,538 slaves were emancipated.[73] Consequently, Akenson has insisted that

> the Irish polity, through the historians who are the keepers of its collective memory, must cease to view the emigrants from Ireland as forever-passive victims, and therefore as persons who were incapable of hard dealing. One of the fundamental stories of the Irish diaspora is of Irish emigrants choosing to do unto others what had already been done unto them. In neither case was that a matter of kid and tender mercies.[74]

This has become a key emphasis in Irish diaspora studies, albeit often expressed with less rhetorical colour. Andy Bielenberg devoted considerable space in his edited volume to the imperial diaspora,[75] while Fintan O'Toole's recent biography of William Johnson is a portrait of a man who is in many ways a personification of the Janus-faced colonised/coloniser. From a dispossessed Irish family, Johnson migrated to the American colonies where he integrated with the Iroquoi, furthering the British colonising mission in the process.[76] A lesser-known Irishman was not nearly so enthusiastic about friendly relations with Native Americans. Francis Campble, an Irish Presbyterian living in Shippenburg in the Cumberland Valley in Pennsylvania, recorded in his diary in 1740 that he had 'no confidence in the friendship with these savages, and have always felt that we have been warming a viper which will some day show us its fangs'.[77]

A member of the Irish diaspora does not have to be portrayed as either a victim or an imperialist. There were middling stations in life. Most migrants left Ireland due to a combination of push- and pull-factors. During the 1850s Irish migration to Australia peaked in large part as a consequence of the discovery of gold.[78] In 1853 the McCance family travelled from County Down to Victoria as assisted immigrants. Financial support to the migrant (on occasion from Irish landlords, but more frequently from government) was a significant factor in nineteenth-century Irish migration to Australia. John McCance took his family to the Forest Creek goldfield where he observed the township of Chewton 'growing as if it were by m[a]gic' due to the lure of gold.[79] Military historians have showered attention upon the military exiles who left Ireland to fight in the armies of various European powers.[80] In the past this has been shot through with a romantic attitude toward the 'celebrated and lamented Wild Geese' or has taken the form of vast biographical and brigade histories which concentrated on the officer class.[81]

There has, however, been a change in emphasis. A narrative of four large and distinct outflows in the 1580s, 1603, 1652 and 1691, following defeats for the Catholic cause in Ireland, has been qualified. Greater weight is attached to enduring poverty in Ireland which when combined with consistent opportunities for employment in the expanding armies of Europe generated 'a smaller but regular outflow' at least until the 1730s.[82] Most importantly, the military community which surrounded the soldier migrants has come to achieve greater prominence. Gráinne Henry's work on the Irish in Spanish Flanders is the outstanding example of this approach. The wives, parents and children of the soldiers come into view as do various camp followers such as prostitutes. The vital relationships between the Irish military units and Irish siblings and cousins in the Irish colleges (who often ministered to the soldiers) and in the merchant classes (who sometimes supplied the army) are exposed. Their continuing links with, and aspirations to return to Ireland, surface. In short, the full diasporic dimensions of these individuals' experiences emerge.[83] Excavating the experiences of women and the poor is central to this less restricted approach.[84] Research on the Ireland's European diaspora received a considerable boost in 1997 with the establishment of the 'Irish in Europe' project. Based at NUI, Maynooth, this initiative has provided a focus for Irish and European scholars. Through an excellent website,[85] conferences and the publication of three volumes of articles[86] the 'Irish in Europe' project has brought a new vigour to this field. Simultaneously, Thomas O'Connor has utilised his position as editor of *Archivium Hibernicum* to revive that journal's tradition of providing an outlet for those writing on the Irish in Europe.

defining the irish diaspora: local, comparative, transnational

Discreet studies of the Irish in particular countries such as the United States and Britain, or in particular regions or cities such as Galicia, Cornwall, New York and Durham[87] remain the primary building blocks of research into Irish migration and its effects. More and more, however, these groups are examined in the context of an enormous worldwide phenomenon: the Irish diaspora. To conduct a local, regional or national study of an Irish migrant community and not to acknowledge the connections and comparisons with multiple other Irish migrant experiences is increasingly perceived as a wilful ignoring of complexity and wonder. Donald MacRaild has insisted that 'the core meaning of diaspora comprises a triangular dialogue between the homeland and multiple new communities, as well as a consciousness of being part of an international community',[88] while Akenson has compared the Irish diaspora to a Fabergé egg and insisted that 'the story of the Irish in America makes sense only within the context of a world-circling history'.[89] As an absolute basic requirement he demanded that

> diaspora histories, if they are not merely to use the word 'diaspora' as a flag of convenience, must be *multipolar*. They must deal with the homeland and with two or more countries of reception. Otherwise, one is not studying diaspora, but simple migration from one point to another.[90]

Akenson associates the tendency to use the word diaspora in unipolar studies with what he has described as the 'baneful hegemony of U.S. work on the history of the Irish diaspora'.[91]

In 2000 Lawrence J. McCaffrey was provoked to a defence against the allegation that he and other American scholars were guilty of perpetuating 'the nocent obsession with national focus and analysis which dominates so much of the American literature'.[92] McCaffrey feared, perhaps correctly, that under Akenson's influence a hierarchy was being created within the study of the Irish abroad which awarded primacy to a transnational approach. McCaffrey had been among the first to employ the term 'Irish diaspora' in his study of the Irish in America,[93] but his work was not 'multi-polar' and therefore he stood accused of adopting a 'flag of convenience'. He counterattacked on a series of fronts, but primarily by labelling Akenson's approach as 'comparative diaspora studies' thereby implying that 'diaspora studies' is not of its nature comparative and in this way attempting to create a legitimate space for national or local studies within the diasporic tent. Further, he warned that comparison with Canada, Australia or New Zealand was unlikely to reveal much about the Irish in the United States and that instead complexity should be sought through in-depth regional studies. He insisted that, 'Before embarking on comparative Irish diaspora explorations, scholars of Irish America should realize that their first priority should be sorting out the complexity of their own area of study' and concluded in an even more dogmatic fashion.

> While comparative diaspora studies offer tempting possibilities, they do not exceed the challenge of uncovering the many hidden facets of Irish America. At present, many young scholars spend their research time in Dublin's National Library of Ireland or Belfast's Public Records Office, working on topics relating to Ireland. They might find it more

creative, interesting, and professionally profitable to search for Irish-American material in American city and state historical society librar-ies and in the columns of old American newspapers. In fact, the best future in Irish studies for Americans is right here at home.[94]

Akenson would no doubt regard McCaffrey's career advice as apposite, but insist that it amounted to the abandonment of a genuinely diasporic approach. He himself warned 'any young Canadian historian of English-speaking Canada who prudently considers his or her future would do well to avoid diaspora history.... The safe route is to be a local hero'.[95]

Joe Lee examined, with not a little sarcasm, the vituperation and hyper-bole engaged in by both sides of this argument, noting that both the local and the diasporic approaches have merit, before concluding, 'who says diaspora says comparison'.[96] Kevin Kenny, however, is concerned that much diasporic history may not be in the true sense comparative. He has sought to draw a distinction between diasporic or 'transnational' and comparative or 'cross-national' approaches. For Kenny, diasporic analyses seek 'to transcend the nation-state as the primary unit of his-torical analysis, searching for reciprocal interactions and the sensibilities they nurture among globally scattered communities', while comparative analyses 'examine specific similarities and differences in the experiences of similar migrants who have settled in different nations or national regions'.[97] If diaspora tends to emphasise what is shared by a group by virtue of their ethnicity, while comparison tends to emphasise the ways in which different environments leave distinctive marks upon the group, then Kenny is surely right that what 'is needed is a migration history that combines' these schools. Any sensible historian of the Irish diaspora, however, must not only engage with difference across the phe-nomenon, but constantly ask the question, are the differences in reality so great that the model has ceased to have any practical value? Donna R. Gabaccia has written of *Italy's Many Diasporas*:[98] Are there Irish diasporas rather than an Irish diaspora? If so what do we gain by the use of the term? Why not revert to Irish-Americans and London-Irish or begin to talk about the Leinster-Canadians and Clare-Australians?

defining the irish diaspora: does the diaspora fade away?

Perhaps the most important aspect of diaspora studies is that it emphasises not solely the migrant generation (who are the primary focus of migra-tion studies) but their children, their children's children and beyond. This is also one of the most problematic aspects of the framework. Akenson conceded that defining an 'ethnic group' or 'what constitutes a sense of ethnicity' is a contentious area, but insisted that 'the Irish ethnic group is a multigenerational phenomenon. In historical discussion it includes not only the migrant generation but their direct offspring, and, often, subsequent generations of descendants.'[99] The difficulties quickly become apparent. Kevin Howard has pointed out that a mere 691,412 people identified themselves as ethnically Irish in the 2001 census in Great Britain. This is fewer than the number of people who ticked the born-in-Ireland box and far fewer than the number that the Irish lobby expected to declare an Irish ethnicity. This raises all sorts of interesting questions about the concept of an Irish diaspora in the contemporary British context.[100]

The Irish in Europe were rarely replenished by new migrants between the middle of the eighteenth century and the late twentieth century and, due to the process of 'ethnic fade', there can be very few progeny of the early modern Irish migration to Europe who maintain an attachment to the homeland and its culture. If the early modern Irish diaspora in Europe ceased to exist, when did this happen? What are the criteria we use to judge this? How important a role should Irish heritage occupy in a person's identity if they are to be labelled an Irish diasporan? Might some descendants of these migrants awaken to the idea, like the American activist Tom Hayden, that they are *Irish on the Inside*[101] and become diasporans reborn? Such ambiguities have prompted Lee to argue that the 'whole concept of the "multi-generational ethnic group" requires clarification for every diaspora in every destination'.[102]

conclusion

As a relatively new and enormous category, it is not yet clear to what extent the Irish diaspora elides or illuminates the stories of millions of individuals who 'occupy no singular cultural space but are enmeshed in circuits of social, economic, and cultural ties encompassing both the mother country and the country of settlement'.[103] The longevity of the Irish diaspora as a historiographical phenomenon is even more speculative than its longevity as a historical phenomenon. Aihwa Ong has argued that the current intellectual

> Interest in diasporas and cosmopolitanism registers a special moment in interdisciplinary studies that seeks to invoke political significance in cultural phenomena that can be theorised as resisting the pillaging of global capitalism, as well as the provincialism of metropolitan centres.[104]

Among scholars (diasporans and natives) of the Irish, the new interest in diaspora coincided with a moment when the urge to create a more plural definition of Irishness dominated. The diaspora's moment will no doubt pass, but it seems certain to remain a productive model for some time to come. For the sceptics it will continue to be a nebulous concept which raises too many unanswerable questions, but for enthusiasts it will remain a 'challenging' and 'rich' concept.

notes

1. Enda Delaney, *Demography, State and Society: Irish Migration to Britain, 1921–1971* (Liverpool, Liverpool University Press, 2000), p. 1.
2. *Parliamentary Debates Dáil Éireann*, cxiii, 393, 24 November 1948. See Mary E. Daly, 'Irish Nationality and Citizenship since 1922', in *Irish Historical Studies*, xxxii (2001), p. 377
3. L. M. Cullen, 'The Irish Diaspora of the Seventeenth and Eighteenth Centuries', in Nicholas Canny (ed.), *Europeans on the Move: Studies on European Migration* (Oxford, Oxford University Press, 1994), p. 114.
4. It is likely that Robinson's source for this figure was Richard Kearney, *Across the Frontiers: Ireland in the 1990s* (Dublin, Wolfhound Press, 1988), p. 1.
5. J. J. Lee, 'The Irish Diaspora in the Nineteenth Century', in Laurence Geary and Margaret Kelleher (eds), *Nineteenth-Century Ireland: A Guide to Recent Research* (Dublin, University College Dublin Press, 2005), p. 185.
6. Donald Harman Akenson, *The Irish Diaspora: A Primer* (Belfast, Institute of Irish Studies, 1993), p. 15.
7. One of the best overviews of trends in writing about the Irish diaspora since the mid-nineteenth century is Alan O'Day, 'Revising the Diaspora', in D. George Boyce and Alan O'Day (eds), *The Making of Modern Irish History* (London, Routledge, 1996), pp. 188–215.
8. David Noel Doyle, 'Cohesion and Diversity in the Irish Diaspora', in *Irish Historical Studies*, xxi (1999), pp. 411–34, is a stimulating examination of some recent work, including Patrick O'Sullivan's six volume collection on the Irish World Wide (1992–7).
9. Lee for example begins by acknowledging 'The challenge of addressing even a few of the issues that arise from the voluminous literature of the last decade on the Irish Diaspora'. See Lee, 'The Irish Diaspora in the Nineteenth Century', p. 182.
10. David Fitzpatrick, *Irish Emigration 1801–1921* (Dundalk, Economic and Social History Society of Ireland, 1984), pp. 1–3.
11. Cullen, 'The Irish Diaspora of the Seventeenth and Eighteenth Centuries', p. 113.
12. Kerby Miller, *Emigrants and Exiles: Ireland and the Irish Exodus to North America* (New York, Oxford University Press, 1985), p. 137.
13. Cullen, 'The Irish Diaspora of the Seventeenth and Eighteenth Centuries', p. 140.
14. Kerby Miller and Liam Kennedy, 'Apendix 2: Irish Migration and Demography, 1659–1831', in Kerby A. Miller, Arnold Schrier, Bruce D. Boling

David N. Doyle (eds), *Irish Immigrants in the Land of Canaan: Letters and Memoirs from Colonial and Revolutionary America, 1675–1815* (Oxford, Oxford University Press, 2003), pp. 656–78.

15. R. J. Dickson, *Ulster Emigration to Colonial America, 1718–1775* (New York, Humanities Press, 1966); Marianne Wokeck, *Trade in Strangers: the Beginnings of Mass Migration to North America* (Pennsylvania, Pennsylvania State University Press, 1999). Trevor Parkhill discussed these debates in a fine paper, 'Emigration Studies, 1973–2003: How Far Have We Travelled?', at the annual conference of Economic and Social History Society of Ireland at Coleraine in 2003. Thanks to Trevor for allowing me to read this paper.

16. Cullen, 'The Irish Diaspora of the Seventeenth and Eighteenth Centuries', pp. 113–49.

17. Fitzpatrick, *Irish Emigration 1801–1921*, p. 3.

18. Kerby A. Miller, *Emigrants and Exiles*, p. 193.

19. Kerby A. Miller, 'Emigration from the Seventeenth Century to 1845', in James S. Donnelly Jnr (ed.), *Encyclopedia of Irish History and Culture, I* (Detroit, Thompson Gale, 2004), pp. 431–5.

20. Fitzpatrick, *Irish Emigration 1801–1921*, p. 3.

21. Donald Harman Akenson, *The Irish Diaspora*, p. 54.

22. Damien Courtney, 'A Quantification of Irish migration with Particular Emphasis on the 1980s and 1990s', in Andy Bielenberg (ed.), *The Irish Diaspora* (Essex, Pearson Education, 2000), pp. 287–8.

23. Enda Delaney, *Irish Emigration Since 1921* (Dundalk, Economic and Social History Society of Ireland, 2002), p. 1.

24. Enda Delaney, 'Emigration and Immigration since 1950', in Donnelly, *Encyclopedia of Irish History and Culture I*, pp. 439–42.

25. Breda Gray, 'From "Ethnicity" to "Diaspora": 1980s Emigration and "Multicultural" London', in Bielenberg, *The Irish Diaspora*, p. 66.

26. Robin Cohen, *Global Diasporas: An Introduction* (London, UCL Press, 1997), pp. 1–26; Gérard Chaliand and Jean-Pierre Rageau, *The Penguin Atlas of Diasporas* (London, Penguin Press, 1995), pp. i–xx; Kachig Tölölyan, 'Rethinking Diaspora(s): Stateless Power in the Transnational Movement', in *Diaspora*, 5 (1996), pp. 9–15; William Saffran, 'Diasporas in Modern Societies: Myths of Homeland and Return', in *Diaspora*, 1 (1991), pp. 83–97. All of these offer etymological explanations in more or less the same terms as this.

27. Saffran, *'Diasporas in Modern Societies'*, p. 83.

28. Tölölyan, 'Rethinking Diaspora(s)', p. 3.

29. Robin Cohen, 'Diasporas, the Nation State and Globalisation', in Wang Gungwu (ed.), *Global History and Migrations* (Boulder, Westview Press, 1997), p. 137; Gabriel Sheffer, *Diaspora Politics: At Home Abroad* (Cambridge, Cambridge University Press, 2002), pp. 240–1. This is the second edition of Sheffer's book. When originally published in 1986, *Diaspora Politics* was an important contribution to the phenomenon Sheffer describes in the second edition.

30. Rogers Brubaker, 'The "diaspora" diaspora', in *Ethnic and Racial Studies, 28* (2005), p. 1.

31. For useful introductions to the general reading on diaspora see Cohen, *Global Diasporas*; Chaliand and Rageau, *The Penguin Atlas of Diasporas*; William Saffran, *'Diasporas in Modern Societies'*, pp. 83–97.

32. Lawrence J. McCaffrey, *The Irish Diaspora in America* (Bloomington, Indiana University Press, 1976); T. Morrissey, 'The Irish Student Diaspora in the Sixteenth Century and the Early Years of the Irish College at Salamanca', in *Recusant History*, xiv (1978), pp. 242–60. Sheridan Gilley, 'The Roman Catholic Church and the Nineteenth-century Irish Diaspora', in *The Journal of Ecclesiastical History*, xxxv (1984), pp. 188–207; E. J. Gallagher, 'Some Spiritual Empire: The Irish Nationality and Community Act of 1956 and the Irish Diaspora', in *Etudes Irlandaises*, xiii (1988), pp. 131–9.

33. Akenson, *The Irish Diaspora*; Mathew Fry Jacobson, *Special Sorrows: The Diasporic Imagination of Irish, Polish and Jewish immigrants in the United States* (Harvard, Havard University Press, 1995).

34. Arthur Gribben (ed.), *The Great Famine and the Irish Diaspora in America* (Amherst, University of Massachusetts Press, 1999); Bielenberg (ed.), *The Irish Diaspora*; Charles Fanning (ed.), *New Perspectives on the Irish Diaspora* (Carbondale, Southern Illinois University Press, 2000).

35. A few further examples of the at least 50 articles which have appeared since 1990 are J. Bowyer Bell, 'The transcendental Irish republic, the dream of diaspora', in *Journal of Political Science*, xviii (1990), pp. 148–68; Paul Arthur, 'Diasporan Intervention in International Affairs: Irish America as a Case Study', in *Diaspora*, i (1991), pp. 143–59; Joe Bradley, 'Facets of the Irish Diaspora: "Irishness" in 20th Century Scotland', in *Irish Journal of Sociology*, vi (1996), pp. 79–100; James S. Donnelly Jnr, 'The Construction of the Memory of the Famine in Ireland and the Irish diaspora, 1850–1900', in *Éire-Ireland*, xxxi (1996), pp. 26–61; Allen Feldman, '"Gaelic Gotham": Decontextualising the Diaspora', in *Éire-Ireland*, xxxi (1996), pp. 189–201; Mary Hickman, '"Locating" the Irish Diaspora', in *Irish Journal of Sociology*, 11, (2002), pp. 8–26; Kevin Kenny, 'Diaspora and Comparisons: The Global Irish as a Case Study', in *Journal of American History*, 90, (2003), pp. 135–62; Patrick O'Sullivan, 'Developing Irish Diaspora Studies: A Personal View', in *New Hibernia Review*, 7 (2003), pp. 130–48.

36. This is Topic 4 in the 'Later Modern Ireland' module of the Leaving Certificate History Syllabus. Details can be found on the website of the Irish Department of Education and Science at www.education.ie.

37. *Parliamentary Debates Dáil Éireann*, ccvi, 4, 26 November 1963.

38. The term appears on the Dáil record – 'in speeches or in questions' – on two further occasions in the 60s, then twice in the 70s, and on a grand total of seven occasions in the 80s. Such a survey would have been difficult ten years ago, but is now relatively easy using www.oireachtas-debates.gov.ie.

39. *Parliamentary Debates Dáil Éireann*, cdxlviii, 1146–55, 2 February 1995.

40. There is a watershed in the use of the term and it occurs in the mid-1990s. 'Diaspora' apeared on the Dáil record eight times from 1990 until Robinson's speech. During the remainder of the decade it appeared 35 times. Some might argue that it is still surprisingly rare but the spike is obvious.

41. Akenson has laid out his arguments at greatest length in *The Irish Diaspora*. He has, however, numerous other publications on the subject, some of which are referenced below.

42. Donald Harmon Akenson, 'The Historiography of English-speaking Canada and the Concept of Diaspora: A Sceptical Apreciation', in *The Canadian Historical Review*, lxxvi (1995), p. 382.

43. *Sunday Tribune*, 11 September 2005.
44. Delaney, *Demography, State and Society*, p. 7.
45. Tim Pat Coogan, *Wherever Green is Worn: The Story of the Irish Diaspora* (Basingstoke, Palgrave Macmillan, 2000).
46. Akenson, 'The Historiography of English-speaking Canada and the Concept of Diaspora: A Sceptical Appreciation', pp. 377–409.
47. Enda Delaney, 'The Irish Diaspora', in *Irish Economic and Social History*, xxxiii (2006), pp. 35–45.
48. Kenny, 'Diaspora and Comparisons: The Global Irish as a Case Study', p. 135.
49. J. J. Lee, 'The Irish Diaspora in the Nineteenth Century', pp. 182–222.
50. Cohen, *Global Diasporas*, p. 178.
51. Chaliand and Rageau, *The Penguin Atlas of Diasporas*, pp. xiv–xv.
52. Chaliand and Rageau, *The Penguin Atlas of Diasporas*, pp. 157–62.
53. Kerby Miller, *Emigrants and Exiles*, p. 556.
54. Alan O'Day, '*Revising the Diaspora*', p. 196.
55. C. J. Houston and W. J. Smyth, 'The Irish Diaspora: Emigration to the New World, 1720–1920', in Brian J. Graham and Lindsey J. Proudfoot (eds), *An Historical Geography of Ireland* (London, Academic Press, 1993), p. 338.
56. Akenson, *The Irish Diaspora*, pp. 6–9.
57. Akenson, *The Irish Diaspora*, pp. 6–9.
58. Piaras Mac Éinrí, 'Introduction', in Bielenberg, *The Irish Diaspora*, p. 4.
59. *Parliamentary Debates Dáil Éireann*, cdxlviii, 1146–55, 2 February 1995.
60. *Parliamentary Debates Dáil Éireann*, cdxlviii, 1146, 2 February 1995.
61. Breda Gray, 'From "Ethnicity" to "Diaspora": 1980s Emigration and "Multicultural" London', in Bielenberg, *The Irish Diaspora*, pp. 80–1.
62. D. P. Moran, *The Philosophy of Irish Ireland* (Dublin, James Duffy, 1905), pp. 16–7.
63. I have regularly encouraged Irish-American students studying the Irish diaspora while in Dublin (a strange place to study the diaspora you might say) to describe themselves as Irish when speaking to Dubliners during their everyday socialising and sample the reactions. It is a consistently interesting experiment.
64. *Parliamentary Debates Dáil Éireann*, cdlxii, 1943–4, 7 March 1996.
65. *Parliamentary Debates Dáil Éireann*, cdlxxi, 1022, 13 November 1996.
66. Bunreacht na hÉireann at www.taoiseach.gov.ie/upload/static/256.pdf (accessed on 28 September 2005).
67. Daly, 'Irish nationality and citizenship since 1922', pp. 377–407.
68. Houston and Smyth, 'The Irish Diaspora: Emigration to the New World, 1720–1920', p. 338.
69. Michael Holmes, 'The Irish and India: Imperialism, Nationalism and Internationalism', in Bielenberg, *The Irish Diaspora*, pp. 235–50; Donal P. McCracken, 'Odd Man Out: The South African Experience', in Bielenberg, *The Irish Diaspora*, pp. 251–71.
70. Patrick McKenna, 'Irish emigration to Argentina: A Different Model', in Bielenberg, *The Irish Diaspora*, pp. 194–212.
71. Donald Harman Akenson, *If the Irish Ran the World: Montserrat 1630–1730* (Liverpool, Liverpool University Press, 1997), p. 63.

72. Joyce Lorimer (ed.), *English and Irish Settlements on the River Amazon, 1550–1646* (London, Hakluyt Society, 1989); Donald Harman Akenson, *If the Irish Ran the World*.

73. Nini Rodgers, 'The Irish in the Caribbean 1641–1837: An overview', in *Irish Migration Studies in Latin America*, 5: 3 (November 2007), pp. 145–56.

74. Akenson, *If the Irish Ran the World*, p. 175.

75. Andy Bielenberg, 'Irish Emigration to the British Empire, 1700–1914', in Bielenberg, *The Irish Diaspora*, pp. 215–34. This is one of four chapters in the volume devoted to 'The Empire'.

76. Fintan O'Toole, *White Savage: William Johnson and the invention of America* (London, Farrar, Straus and Giroux, 2005).

77. Miller, Schrier, Boling, Doyle (eds), *Irish Immigrants in the Land of Canaan*, p. 320.

78. Akenson, *The Irish Diaspora*, p. 96 and p. 101.

79. David Fitzpatrick, *Oceans of Consolation: Personal Accounts of Irish Migration to Australia* (Cork, Cork University Press, 1994), p. 213.

80. The military history journal, the *Irish Sword*, must be the first port of call for anyone interested in this subject, while interesting recent general introductions include Harman Murtagh, 'Irish Soldiers Abroad, 1600–1800', in Thomas Bartlett and Keith Jeffrey (eds), *A Military History of Ireland* (Cambridge, Cambridge University Press, 1995), pp. 294–314 and John McGurk, 'Wild Geese: The Irish in European armies (sixteenth to seventeenth centuries)' in Patrick O'Sullivan (ed.), *Patterns of Migration* (London, Leicester University Press, 1992), pp. 36–62.

81. J. C. O'Callaghan, *History of the Irish Brigades in the Service of France* (Glasgow, Cameron and Ferguson, 1870); Richard F. Hayes, *Irish swordsmen of France* (Dublin, M. H. Gill and Son Ltd, 1934).

82. Cullen, The Irish Diaspora of the Seventeenth and Eighteenth Centuries', pp. 121–5.

83. Grainne Henry, *The Irish Military Community in Spanish Flanders, 1586–1621* (Dublin, Irish Academic Press, 1992).

84. Mary Ann Lyons, '"Vagabonds", "Mendiants", "Geux": French Reaction to Irish Immigration in the Early Seventeenth Century', in *French History*, xiv (2000), pp. 363–82; David Bracken, 'Piracy and Poverty: Aspects of the Irish Jacobite Experience in France, 1691–1720', in Thomas O'Connor (ed.), *The Irish in Europe, 1580–1815* (Dublin, Four Courts Press, 2001), pp. 127–42; Grainne Henry, 'Women "Wild Geese", 1585–1625: Irish Women and Migration to European Armies in the Late Sixteenth and Early Seventeenth Centuries', in Patrick O'Sullivan, *Irish Women and Irish Migration* (London, Leicester University Press, 1995), pp. 23–40. It should be noted that a beginning was made in this area by Micheline Walsh, 'Some Notes Towards a History of the Womenfolk of the Wild Geese', in *Irish Sword*, v (1961–2), pp. 98–106 and Micheline Walsh, 'Further Notes Towards a History of the Womenfolk of the Wild Geese', in *Irish Sword*, v (1961–2), pp. 133–45.

85. www.irishineurope.com (accessed 20 April 2007).

86. Thomas O'Connor (ed.), *The Irish in Europe, 1580–1815* (Dublin, Four Courts Press, 2001); Thomas O'Connor and Mary Ann Lyons (eds), *Irish Migrants in Europe After Kinsale, 1602–1820* (Dublin, Four Courts

Press, 2003); Thomas O'Connor and Mary Ann Lyons (eds), *Irish Communities in Early Modern Europe* (Dublin, Four Courts Press, 2006).

87. Among the most recent examples are Kevin Kenny, *The American Irish: A History* (Harlow, Pearson Education Ltd, 2000); Donald M. MacRaild, *Irish Migrants in Modern Britain, 1750–1922* (New York, St Martin's Press, 1999); Ciaran O'Scea, 'The devotional World of the Irish Catholic Exile in Early-modern Galicia, 1598–1666', in O'Connor, *The Irish in Europe*, pp. 27–48; Louise Miskell, 'Irish Immigrants in Cornwall: The Camborne Experience, 1861–82', in Roger Swift and Sheridan Gilley (eds.), *The Irish in Victorian Britain: The Local Dimension* (Dublin, Four Courts Press, 1999), pp. 31–51; Ronald H. Bayor and Timothy J. Meagher (eds), *The New York Irish* (Baltimore, The Johns Hopkins University Press, 1996); Roger Cooter, *When Paddy met Geordie* (Sunderland, University of Sunderland, 2005).

88. Donald M. MacRaild, '"Diaspora" and "Transnationalism": Theory and Evidence of the Irish World-wide', in *Irish Economic and Social History, xxxiii* (2006), pp. 51–8.

89. Akenson, *The Irish Diaspora*, pp. 3–5.

90. Akenson, 'The Historiography of English-speaking Canada and the Concept of Diaspora: A Sceptical Apreciation', pp. 377–409.

91. Donald Harman Akenson, 'Irish Lives: Confession of a Biographical Recidivist', in Rebecca Pelan (ed.), *Irish-Australian Studies: Papers Delivered at the Seventh Irish-Australian Conference July 1993* (Sydney, Crossing Press, 1994), p. 139.

92. Donald Campbell, 'Exploring Comparative History: The Irish in Australia & the United States', in Pelan, *Irish–Australian Studies*, p. 343.

93. McCaffrey, *The Irish Diaspora in America*.

94. Lawrence J. McCaffrey, 'Diaspora Comparisons and Irish-American Uniqueness', in Fanning (ed.), *New Perspectives on the Irish Diaspora*, pp. 15–27.

95. Akenson, 'The Historiography of English-speaking Canada and the Concept of Diaspora: A Sceptical Apreciation', p. 389.

96. Lee, 'The Irish Diaspora in the Nineteenth Century', p. 211.

97. Kenny, 'Diaspora and Comparisons: The Global Irish as a Case Study', p. 135.

98. Donna R. Gabaccia, *Italy's Many Diasporas* (Seattle, University of Washington Press, 2000).

99. Akenson, *The Irish Diaspora*, p. 9.

100. Kevin Howard, 'Constructing the Irish of Britain: Ethnic recognition and the 2001 UK Censuses', in *Ethnic and Racial Studies*, 29 (2006), pp. 104–23.

101. Tom Hayden, *Irish on the Inside* (New York, Verso, 2001).

102. J. J. Lee, 'The Irish Diaspora in the Nineteenth Century', pp. 183–5.

103. Smadar Lavie and Ted Swedenbury, 'Introduction', in Lavie and Swedenbury (eds), *Displacement, Diaspora and Geographies of Identity* (Durham, Duke University Press, 1996), p. 14.

104. Aihwa Ong, *Flexible Citizenship: The Cultural Logics of Transnationality* (Durham, Duke University Press, 1999), p. 14.

6
local history

maura cronin

introduction

Local history is the history of place, but, though place is central to its meaning, it is much more than this. Local historical research, in the first place, teases out the interplay of landscape, economy, culture and population to explain the shaping of the local community over time. Secondly, by asking 'big questions about small places', it prompts the reassessment of assumptions about developments over a wider spatial canvas.[1] Thus, local history is about both people and place, and it provides a lens through which one can view the evolution of both the micro world of the locality and the wider world composed of many such localities. Modern Irish local history has been in the making since the mid-eighteenth century, the first significant landmark in its development being the work of the Physico-Historical Society. Established to investigate the roots of contemporary economic development and to combat Ireland's image as a barbaric country, this society initiated a series of county studies, only four of which were published.[2] Though primarily economic in focus, these surveys into 'the ancient and present state' of the counties in question effectively linked past with present, and prefigured the interdisciplinary approach of two centuries later by combining elements of geographical, economic, historical and political enquiry.[3] Similar studies were continued by the nineteenth century's dedicated amateur historian-antiquarians, and from the 1850s onwards Kilkenny, Wexford and Limerick saw the publication of local studies, all primarily genealogical, historical, scenic and antiquarian in focus.[4] It was during this period, too, that there came into existence a number of long-lived periodical publications: the *Ulster Journal of Archaeology*, established in 1853, was one of the first, with the *Ossory Archaeological*

Journal following in the mid-1870s, and the *Kildare Archaeological Journal*, the *Journal of the Waterford and South East of Ireland Archaeological Society* and the *Journal of the Cork Historical and Archaeological Society* in the1890s.[5] While most of these works focussed on the county or a wider region, other contemporary studies like Lenihan's *Limerick: its history and antiquities* or Gibson's *History of the County and City of Cork* (1866) celebrated the history of a particular urban centre in its broader regional setting.[6]

For Lenihan, Gibson and the other dedicated men of letters in the eighteenth and nineteenth centuries, there was little difficulty in defining 'local' and in deciding the spatial unit on which to base their studies. Their primary unit of investigation and celebration was the county, diocese and/or city, the focus of attention was on 'great men' and 'great events', and the stress was on gathering and listing information rather than on posing and answering questions regarding the nature and dynamics of local communities. Gibson's work was dedicated to Lord Fermoy, and Lenihan's to the Earl of Dunraven, while their chapters concentrated on leading figures of the past like the Earl of Desmond, Florence McCarthy and Daniel O'Connell, and on chronological 'landmarks' like the Battle of Kinsale, the 1798 rebellion and Catholic Emancipation.[7] This pattern continued into the twentieth century, virtually untouched by the *Annales* School of the 1920s, which emphasised the need to explore historical themes through the multiple lens of a wide range of disciplines. Rev. John Begley's monumental *Diocese of Limerick* is characteristic of the 'old style'. This work was complied over a 30-year period but the approach remained essentially antiquarian, the third volume (published in 1938), just like the first, being divided into chapters determined by century, and dedicated to the bishop and the diocese.[8]

The real turning point in the approach to Irish local history can be dated to the 1970s, and it was influenced by three parallel developments. The first such development was the increasing popular interest in local history, culminating in the founding in 1981 of the Federation of Local History Societies whose purpose was to encourage research in history, archaeology and folklore and to provide a forum for those so involved.[9] During this period, too, there was an awakening consciousness of the potential of local history to act as an influence of reconciliation in divided communities. The Ulster Scots Historical Foundation, originally set up in 1956, changed its title in 1975 to the Ulster Historical Foundation, still stressing its unique regional identity but in a less exclusive manner than heretofore. Two decades later, parallel to attempted solutions to Northern Ireland's complex political situation, the Border Counties Historical Collective was set up to 'reconcile identities, create relationship and celebrate unique ways of life and cultural tradition'.[10] The second formative influence on the development of local history in late twentieth-century Ireland was that of the University of Leicester's Local History Department, founded in 1948 and, by the 1970s making its mark on the work of Irish local historians. The Leicester school stressed an analytical and quantitative approach, emphasising the broader contextualisation of regional experience, and shifting the focus from elites to the broader local community. The third influence was the emerging revisionist trend within both geographical and historical scholarship, and the parallel increase in emphasis on Irish social, economic and labour history.[11] Though the main emphasis remained more on re-examining the grand narrative through concentration on local variations and aberrations than on analysing the local community *per se*, these three influences accelerated the growth-rate of locally based studies on issues including urban growth, popular politicisation and regional agrarian change, using the regional experience to cast new light on broader historical developments in the island as a whole.[12]

In the 1980s the approach to local historical research was further sharpened and refined by the contribution of historical geographers, a development prompting among historians a more open attitude to the interdisciplinary nature of local history and a greater awareness of the importance of examining the *locale* in its own right. This was reflected in Geography Publications' launching of the groundbreaking *History and Society* series, interdisciplinary studies which sought to 'explore at county level the dynamics of economic, cultural and social change'.[13] The emerging pre-eminence of the 'new' local history was also made manifest in the establishment in the 1990s of local history degree and certificate courses at the National University of Ireland Maynooth, the University of Limerick and University College Cork.[14] Stressing the interdisciplinary nature of local history, and influenced especially by the Leicester school, these courses fostered co-operation between university-based and 'amateur' local historians, posed questions regarding the interpretation of terms like 'local' and 'community' and promoted research at micro-level, concentrating on smaller communities and territorial divisions than those of county, diocese or city.

From the 1970s onwards, therefore, Irish local history has been opened up to explore a broad range of issues which both elucidate the local and regional experience, and prompt reassessment of island-wide developments: the evolution of the local landscape; the process of landscape change and shifting boundaries; the contact between the local and the wider world; and the dynamics of intergenerational conflict, all traceable through topography, the evolution of settlement patterns and the development of the local cultivated and built environment. The study of this 'living landscape', shaped by the confluence of environmental conditions and economic processes, has been possible only through the interdisciplinary approach, the contribution of geographers, anthropologists, sociologists and archaeologists being equal in importance to that of economic and social historians.[15] Archaeological research, in particular, has greatly advanced the understanding of early Irish urban settlement in its regional and wider setting. New questions have been posed regarding pre-Viking agricultural and exchange systems by excavations on Ulster ring-forts by McCormick, while work by Bradley, Hurley and others, has been used in conjunction with documentary sources ranging from Giraldus Cambrensis' *Expugnatio Hibernica* to *The Song of Dermot and the Earl* to reconsider the pre-Viking, Viking and Norman genesis of centres like Waterford, Cork, and Dublin.[16] Archaeological research, especially that by Orser in the context of Co. Roscommon, has also begun to contribute to our understanding of the material culture of pre-famine clachan settlements, while industrial archaeology has added immeasurably to our understanding of the development of the eighteenth- and nineteenth-century city.[17]

A similar interdisciplinarity, this time between history and geography, is evident in recent research into settlement patterns over time. Geographers' and historians' exploration of the history of the names of fields, townlands and streets has facilitated the tandem tracing of socio-economic and landscape/streetscape change from the seventeenth to the nineteenth century.[18] History and geography have also combined to trace the ebb and flow of settlement from the seventeenth century onwards, not only in the more intensively planted Ulster region, but through the island generally.[19] Smyth's examination of 'property, patronage and population' in mid-seventeenth century Tipperary traces the long-term effects of the Cromwellian conquest and the growth of a new landowning elite, while O'Dowd's study of Sligo in the same period reveals the complexities of Gaelic society, the progress of settlement in an area outside the main locus of government-sponsored plantation, and the effects of such plantation on the subsequent character of the county.[20] The nature of plantation and its effects are analysed in David Dickson's monumental work on Cork as 'Old World Colony' which, like Jacqueline Hill's study of Dublin Protestantism,

reaches forward into the early nineteenth century to trace the undermining of 'ascendancy' and the parallel acceleration of social and
demographic research which would have been impossible without the
local and regional focus, and it again owes much to the geographers
who by mapping population clusters and surname distribution, tracing
the rise and decline of high- and medium-status families, and examining the distribution and shape of villages and the nature of parochial
structures, have traced patterns of population expansion and contrac-
tion, land reclamation and abandonment over a span of some four
centuries.[21] Parallel to this, historical and anthropological researches
into the means of production, such as Bell's study of farming methods
in nineteenth-century County Derry and Cohen's examination of linen
production in Down, allow the examination of contemporary social
gradations and entrepreneurial attitudes through the lens of 'improved'
and 'traditional' farming.[22]

Fundamental to place-centred research is an ever-growing awareness
of the centrality of mapping; though no surprise to geographers,
admittedly, it was underplayed by most Irish historians before the
1980s. This stress on the spatial aspect of local history, epitomised in the
ongoing *Irish Historic Towns Atlas* project,[23] has resulted in the emergence of two types of map-related research over the past two decades:
(1) studies identifying and discussing contemporary motives for surveying and mapping and (2) those using maps as the primary lens through
which to examine local and regional developments. J. H. Andrew's
study of map-making in Wexford, for instance, highlights the role of
the 1798 rebellion as a major incentive to mapping, while Patrick
Power's examination of Wicklow maps in the early modern period
throws light not only on the development of surveying, but also on
parallel changes in both the landscape and in the complex political
structures of the time.[24] Two invaluable map-centred works examining
both rural and urban evolution over time have been published in the
recent past. The *Atlas of the Irish Rural Landscape*, (1997) though not a
local study, uses local and regional case studies to explore issues of
settlement, production and communication, while the *Atlas of Cork City*
(2006) takes a more deliberately local vantage point.[25] Perhaps the most
assiduous recent use (and deconstruction) of maps in researching local
socio-economic change is by Jacinta Prunty, whose *Dublin Slums 1800–
1925* (1998) discusses and maps living conditions, industrial location
and the relationship between property valuation and social position.[26]
Other studies fit, like Prunty's, into the rapidly developing area of
Irish urban history. Particularly revealing are Clarkson's examination

of late eighteenth-century Armagh and King's study of Carlow in its transition from manor to town over the course of the late seventeenth and early eighteenth centuries.[27] Anngret Simms' *Irish Country Towns* and *More Irish Country Towns* (1995) and Howard Hughes' *Irish Cities* (1995), by bringing together studies on 37 individual urban centres ranging in size from Downpatrick to Dublin, and from Carrickmacross to Cork, have provided an overview of, and an agenda for, Irish urban history.[28] Originally broadcast in the Thomas Davis Lectures on Radio Teilifís Eireann (RTE) between 1991 and 1995, these particularly accessible urban studies explore not only the spatial and socio-economic development of the centres in question, but also the more elusive matter of the local character and sense of place.

a sense of place

The precise delineation of 'place' remains the primary question facing every potential researcher in the field of local history. The administrative unit of the county, so beloved of the earlier antiquarians, still continues to provide a vital focus for local studies. Now, however, its study moves far beyond the recording-listing function to that of reassessing the grand narrative. Dickson's work on Cork and O'Dowd's on Sligo, for instance, explore not only the forces defining 'region', but also the nature and impact of colonisation and settlement over a broader geographical canvas, while Jordan's *Land and Popular Politics in Ireland* (1994) traces the economic transition from subsistence to agrarian capitalism from the vantage point of County Mayo, discussing the varieties of economic region and experience initially masked by arbitrary county divisions – a theme also captured in the aptly named *Various Country: Essays in Mayo History* (1987) edited by Gillespie and Moran.[29] The county-centred study has also contributed hugely to our understanding of the background to, and dynamics of, nationalist politics and militancy in the period 1910–23, beginning with David Fitzpatrick's groundbreaking study of Clare, and now extending to the various, yet linked, experiences of the War of Independence in several parts of the island, especially Tipperary, Cork, Derry and Longford.[30] While taking the county as their primary focus, these works continue, like those centred on earlier land-related themes, to highlight the varieties of experience within each county, Derry's nationalism, for instance, being more radical in the city and the eastern portion of the county than in the more westerly areas.[31] The *History and Society* series, too, stresses the parallel cohesion and diversity within counties by combining the county focus with that on smaller spatial units, each of the 16 county volumes so far published comprising a number of thematic chapters which together build up not only a profile of the dynamics of long-term economic, cultural and social change but also stress the combined cohesion and diversity of county experience.

The smaller spatial units upon which the more recent studies are focussed range downwards in size from the Poor Law Union to the townland. The Poor Law Union, in existence since the late 1830s and early 1840s, was an important public administrative unit over a span of more than 80 years, and the survival of impressive (if incomplete) runs of minute books and registers ensures that the unions provide a useful lens through which to study the regional experience.[32] Landed estates, too, for which a variety of records survive in both private hands and in public repositories, have provided a focus for the historian of local social and community networks. Donnelly's seminal study of Cork landed estates has been followed by another by him on the Kerry Kenmare estates, by Lyne's examination of the Lansdowne Estate in the same county and by Connell's examination of agrarian changes in Meath in the century preceding the famine.[33] Similarly, the diocese and parish, widely used as the unit of investigation by clerical local historians in the nineteenth century, still provide a useful focus, while at a micro-level, village and townland open windows into the locale.[34] Though the townland (the smallest territorial division in the Irish context) can prove difficult to research, lying as it does beyond the reach of many sources, it has been successfully unearthed by the interdisciplinary approach, with the emphasis not only on topography and archaeology, but also, like Scally's work on the county Roscommon townland of Ballykilcline and Carr's study of Portavo in county Down, on tracing the inward and outward movement of influences and families over time.[35] Villages too, have proved a useful keyhole into the broader society; the last ten years have seen published O'Flanagan's work on Co. Cork villages, those by Lawlor on Dunlavin and Hunt on the Co. Waterford industrial village of Portlaw and two collections of seminal essays exploring individual villages shaped by forces ranging from topography and monastic and manorial settlement, to the economics of fairs, markets and fishing.[36] The parish, too, as 'a place of neighbours, kin, marriage alliances and community solidarity', has provided a useful lens through which to view the dynamics of local communities.[37] Work on Catholic parishes in Counties Dublin, Longford and Leitrim considers the interlinked issues of religious observance, parish loyalty and attitudes to economic change, while Devereux's piece on 'negotiating community' in the Limerick urban parish of St. Mary's explores the role of local development groups and parish-based activists in the later twentieth century.[38] Moffit's and Crawford's studies of Church of Ireland Parishes in Connaught and Dublin respectively explore the experience of communities within broader communities, a theme also explored at city and county level by D'Alton in relation to Cork and Tunney in reference to Donegal.[39]

This focus on the local experience has also enabled a deeper exploration of the issue of place beyond place – i.e. the complex interdependence between family and locality on the one hand, and Ireland abroad on the other. Studies by McCarron and Mannion on prosperous Offaly and the moving of Wexford farming and milling families to New England and Newfoundland in the eighteenth century explore their relations with their peers at home, their marriage-cemented status and their upward thrust in economically liberating but politically constrained colonial societies.[40] Further down the social scale, and echoing Fitzpatrick's *Oceans of Consolation* (1994) in a more local context, O'Mahony and Thompson's appropriately named *Poverty to Promise* (1994) documents the experiences and emotions of the assisted emigrants from the county Limerick Monteagle estate in the immediate pre- and post-famine years.[41]

It is at a micro-level that the examination of the mechanisms of social and economic control can best be carried out, and the internal competition for power within local communities informs several recent studies, challenging any simplistic view of individual or group power as entirely dependent on, or proportionate to, social status. As indicated by several such studies from as far apart as Waterford and Monaghan, landlords were not always in control, nor were tenants without power. While improving landlords had a major role in shaping the local landscape and economy through house-building, hedge planting and clearing stones from fields, absentee landlords lost out on the chance to improve and modernise their estates. In the proprietor's absence, consolidation and the elimination of the prevailing clachan and rundale system were prevented, or at least inordinately delayed, as tenants seized 'control of the landscape'.[42] Local studies also enable the tracing of a social hierarchy stretching from the strong farmer down to the labourer, Burtchael and Stout making particularly astute use of Griffith's Valuation to confirm the occupancy of prime land and sites by the strongest farmers, with smaller holders and cottiers relegated to the margins.[43] Status exploration at local level has also been painstakingly and convincingly analysed over the past two decades.

Terence Dooley's micro-study of the agrarian murders at Wildgoose Lodge on the Louth-Monaghan border presents a snapshot of local community tensions as well as the complex relationships between state and community in early nineteenth-century Ireland.[44] Over a broader time-span, the work of anthropologists Gulliver and Silverman on the Thomastown neighbourhood of Co. Kilkenny, spanning a century and a half, explores the complex issues of respectability and status through the lens of the local labouring and shopkeeping classes, while Cohen's work on the linen-producing County Down parish of Tullylish casts much light on the varieties of class formation, paternalism, neighbourliness, interdependence and gender over two centuries.[45]

The study of powerful families and prominent individuals, part of local history since the eighteenth century, maintains its attraction into the twenty-first century. However, while the celebratory and adulatory emphasis continues to dominate popular history, more serious studies effectively use the family or individual focus to open a window on the local and wider society.[46] Land ownership and lordship changes – some sweeping, some faltering – continue to be examined most effectively through the varied experiences of powerful regional septs and families in Gaelic and Norman Ireland, as locally based power was challenged first by ambitious families who set their sights on a more centralised power, and later by the evolving administrative apparatus accompanying Plantagenet and Tudor state building.[47]

Centenaries and anniversaries have contributed their fair share of local studies, the best of which have prompted a re-examination of wider issues. The 1798 rebellion, itself generated by an uneasy mixture of national and international forces confused by local rivalries, prompted in its bicentenary year a multiplicity of regional studies re-examining intergenerational political transmission and the complexity of regional economic networks. A number of these works concentrated on families or individuals involved in the disturbed events of the 1790s, exploring the complexities of personal, family and regional loyalties, particularly in Wexford and Wicklow.[48] The 150th anniversary of the famine, too, produced its own crop of local studies revisiting the nature of poverty and the difficulties experienced by both state and local elite in dealing with the crisis, while the centenary of a very different event – the 1899 reform of Irish local government – gave rise to a number of local studies prompting a re-assessment of both political developments on the threshold of the twentieth century and the evolution of Irish democracy.[49]

Some of the most useful individual local histories of the past two decades have centred on landlords in the context of their estates

and wider society. Robert French of Monivea, Ulick John de Burgh
of Portumna and John Hamilton of Donegal are among those whose
careers highlight the dilemmas facing Irish landed proprietors in their
role as brokers between locality and metropolis, caught between the
conflicting motives of humanitarianism and economic survival in
the eighteenth and nineteenth centuries.[50] The complex relationships
between landlord family, servants, tenantry and community in a later
period are confronted in Terence Dooley's study of the 'big house'
(concentrating largely on the Leslie estate in Co. Monaghan) and that
by Purdue on the MacGeough Bonds of Co. Armagh, both teasing out
the interwoven strands of deference, affection, paternalism and resentment and the passing in the early twentieth century of a whole world
which had once seemed immutable.[51] This world of the estate, its *locale*,
social function and economic importance, is further facilitated since
2004 by the work of the Centre for the Study of Historic Houses and
Estates at NUI Maynooth, with its evolving research database and its
annual conferences.

The urban social and political milieu has been further opened up to
scrutiny through a number of place-centred studies concentrating on
individual businessmen and public. An analysis of the career of Thomas
Synnott, a forgotten but significant representative of Dublin's emerging shopocracy in the 1840s, throws considerable light on the civic,
philanthropic and professional role of the upwardly mobile Catholic
middle class in an age of ferment, while further down the social scale,
the world of Cork city radicalism, in a slightly earlier period, has been
explored through the public life of Thomas Sheehan, newspaper editor
and political activist.[52] From a somewhat different but no less revealing
vantage point, Irish middle class social and intellectual life has been
unveiled in Nuala McAllister's examination of music in nineteenth-
century Londonderry, raising questions for further studies on leisure,
status and the overlapping of the public and private spheres.[53] Studies
on individual singers and regional musical styles outside the urban setting have also raised questions of local cultural identity, Ó Cróinín's
study of Elizabeth Cronin and her songs throws light not only on
musical issues, but also on local norms of humour, status and hospitality.[54] On the politico-religious front, studies of individual church-
men in their local-cum-national context have opened up the area of
ecclesiastical politics, McGrath's work on James Doyle (the redoubtable
J. K. L.), Bolster's examination of William Delany of Cork and Bane's
work on John McEvilly of Galway all explore the higher ranks of the
Irish Catholic Church at diocesan and national levels, while the more

populist aspects of religion are discussed in regionally based studies on Catholic pilgrimage and Presbyterian revivalism.[55]

The evolving ascendancy of the strong farmer in late nineteenth-century Ireland has attracted growing attention among researchers, and a number of recent family-centred local studies focussing on the farming class have contributed to our understanding not only of particular regions, but of broader developments over time. Urwin's research into the O'Hanlon-Walshes discusses not only one Wexford family's leading role in late nineteenth-century land agitation, but also touches on the issue of women as agitators and the combined role of the priest as popular leader and as representative of strong farming society. The private face of status building in a similar farming milieu is explored in Fallon's *County Roscommon Wedding 1892* (2004), which gives rare insights into a family's marriage-cemented attempts to ensure consolidation, prosperity and status for the next generation.[56] Further down the social scale O'Neill's invaluable Killeshandra study reconstructs family and household structures in South Cavan, raising questions regarding status, dependence and patronage. Based on an in-depth analysis of the family census forms of 1841, the only such set to have survived intact in the Four Courts fire of 1922, this study focusses on population (both in its size and its socio-economic profile) as product and shaper of place. The relevance of the study extends far beyond Killeshandra, raising questions regarding pre-famine society by challenging the picture of an uncontrolled demographic explosion among the labouring classes, and supporting the view of the precedence of market over consumption-driven forces in the pre-1840s' economy.[57]

Identification and analysis of power networks is one of the primary quests of local history, particularly feasible in the area of public administration at local level. The complexity of such networks is amply illustrated in Windrum's analysis of prison reform in County Down from the late eighteenth to the early twentieth century.[58] Similarly, exploration of the experiences of different Poor Law Unions has facilitated a reassessment of not only local living conditions and the administration of poor relief, particularly in times of crisis, but also the interweaving of politico-denominational with welfare issues, as well as the complex relationships between relief recipients, local elite and central authorities.[59] Such contact and conflict between the regional and the central have also been successfully explored in several studies of events that, at first sight, appeared purely local in their impact. Tensions between community values and beliefs on the one hand and the apparatus of the modern state on the other underlie Bourke's study of the burning of Bridget Cleary in South Tipperary in 1895, an incident sparked off by a combination of interpersonal tensions and a common, if imprecise, belief in fairies. Similarly, the murder of Connor Boyle in northwest Donegal in 1898 explores the intrusion of the state apparatus into a small remote community whose Gaelic culture was in retreat.[60] Nor are such studies of central-peripheral conflict confined to the nineteenth century: more recent conflicts such as those concerning the status of Magee College in Derry have opened the way for further exploration of how faulty communication between central powers, civil service and locality can complicate already smouldering political and sectional rivalries in a divided society.[61]

conclusion

Irish local historical research has changed considerably since the Physio-Historical society set about investigating the past-shaped situation of Irish counties in the late eighteenth century and since the committed antiquarians of the nineteenth century framed their county studies to fit the grand narrative of history. The break with these founding fathers is not, of course, total. The county still remains a primary focus for local historians in the early twenty-first century, but the focus stresses 'micro' rather than 'macro', and the concentration is less on prominent individuals and families than on those (of both high and low status) who provide a historical lens through which the community's past can be examined. The contribution of Irish universities, publishers and local historical societies to this maturing of Irish local historical study is considerable, and pride of place must surely go to NUI Maynooth, the Institute of Irish Studies, Four Courts Press and Geography Publications, not only in terms of published research, but in relation to the initiative shown in producing research guides compiled by experts in the field, which point the way forward for both seasoned and apprentice researchers.[62]

One suggested way forward, building on all that has been researched and written since the 1970s, involves a more in-depth exploration of the elusive nature of local identity which, despite its tangibility, has been given only cursory attention up to now. There can be no doubting the role of the county as a prime shaper of regional identity, as borne out by the avowed objectives of historical societies, the names of local heritage groups and the incidental comments of academic historians.[63] While the county's vital role as identity shaper is generally attributed to the influence of the Gaelic Athletic Association from the 1880s onwards, there is some evidence, well worth further investigation, that county-centred loyalties stretch back at least as far as the 1830s when O'Connell's public speeches took care to play on the perceived superiority of his audience's native county.[64] And what of that parish and locality identity which has generated shelves full of popular histories of sporting clubs, musical bands and – in one region, at least – Orange lodges?[65]

Local identity within the urban setting has been subjected to more analysis, and identifying labels (partly stereotypical, partly well-grounded) have changed very little over time. A pre-famine visitor described Cork character as 'rather sharp. They like to make themselves merry at other people's expense ... and are merciless in the use of their keen but cutting sarcasms.'[66] A century and a half later, John A. Murphy noted much the same qualities in Corkonians: 'cute (in the Irish rather than the American usage) if not wily and cunning, opinionated, self-satisfied and self-confident, sometimes to the point of *hubris*', even their county brothers being excluded from 'the plenitude of Corkiness, so to speak, being merely "Kerrymen with shoes", to quote a contemporary Cork comedian'.[67]

Researchers and writers outside the ranks of the historians have also contributed to the discussion on identity. A number of largely literary anthologies representing the principal urban centres have appeared since the early 1990s, all evoking landmarks, events, characters and attitudes capturing the essential 'character' of place.[68] The celebration of local identity has also taken the form of a multiplicity of personal memoirs, some literary, some popular, on life in Dublin, Cork and Limerick. The most well-known, the controversial *Angela's Ashes*, centred on Limerick City in the 1930s, provoked reactions underlining just how alive passions are, even in the early twenty-first century, regarding the portrayal and reputation of localities.[69] Oral testimony, too, now used increasingly in local studies, deserves more considered analysis. Flynn's groundbreaking study on Dundalk, combining oral and documentary evidence, has paved the way for similar work, including McGrath's study of social life and identity in the Limerick City parish of St. Mary's in the early twentieth century, while Grace's work on a Tipperary parish is an exemplar of accessible historical scholarship, combining exhaustive documentary evidence with local knowledge and personal memory.[70]

Similar attention might be given to the local sense of community generated on those landed estates whose world ended sometime between the two world wars, and the combined fragility and solidity of whose identity is expressed in two separate but related anecdotes. The first, noted by Dooley in his *Decline of the Big House*, (2001) sums up the bewilderment of the 'big house' occupants who, following the burning of the house, found all the doors in the village closed to them: 'No one would take us in. I knew every one of them, their fathers and mothers, their grandparents, all their children, and I thought they were my friends'.[71] The second anecdote centres on the recent experience of an undergraduate student who wished to interview an elderly friend who had worked as head stable hand in a South Leinster 'big house'. The friend was very willing to be interviewed on his memories of working on the estate, but as the interviewer got his recorder ready, his potential interviewee faltered, then baulked. 'I can't bring myself to do it', he said, 'I can't let them down. It wouldn't be right'. His personal loyalties to his former employer and the world he represented were too strong to discuss with an outsider – a tenacious, yet seldom recognised, sense of local identity which has transcended the changes wrought by time.[72]

notes

1. Lawrence J. Taylor, Easton, Pennsylvania, in lecture at University College, Cork, 3 July 1992; Raymond Gillespie and Myrtle Hill (eds), *Doing Local History, Pursuit and Practice* (Belfast, Institute of Irish Studies, Queen's University, 1998), p. 16.
2. Eoin Magennis, '"A land of milk and honey", the Physico-Historical Society, Improvement and the Surveys of Mid-eighteenth-century Ireland', *Proceedings of the Royal Irish Academy* 102C (6) 2002, pp. 199–217.
3. Walter Harris, *The Ancient and Present State of the County of Down* (Dublin, 1744); Charles Smith, *The Ancient and Present State of the County of Cork* (Dublin, 1750), *The Ancient and Present State of the County and City of Waterford* (Dublin, 1746), *The Ancient and Present State of the County of Kerry* (Dublin, 1756).
4. 'Printing at Trim', *Irish Book Lover* 1, 77; vi, p. 103; Thomas Shannon, *Antiquities and Scenery of the County Kilkenny* (Kilkenny, Robertson, 1851); Revd William Healy, *History and Antiquities of Kilkenny* (Kilkenny, Egan, 1893); George Griffiths, *Chronicles of the County Wexford, Being a Record of Memorable Incidents, Disasters, Social Occurrences and Crimes, also Biographies of Eminent Persons, Brought down to the Year 1877* (Enniscorthy, Watchman Office, 1878); Revd James O'Dowd, *Round about the County of Limerick* (Limerick, McKern, 1896), *Irish Book Lover*, pp. vi, 194–5; pp. xxi, 31.
5. Linenhall Library Belfast, online catalogue, March 2004, 313124; *Irish Book Lover* xviii, p. 25; *Transactions of the Ossory Archaeological Society* (Kilkenny, Journal Office, 1879); *Journal of the Waterford and South East of Ireland Archaeological Society* (Waterford, Harvey, 1894), *Journal of the Cork Historical and Archaeological Society* (Cork, Guy, 1895). The Cork publication first

appeared in 1892, but was discontinued briefly and resumed publication in 1895.

6. Maurice Lenihan, *Limerick, its History and Antiquities, Ecclesiastical, Civil and Military* (Dublin, Hodges and Smith, 1866); Rev. C. B. Gibson, *The History of the County and City of Cork*, 2 Vols. (London, Thomas Newby, 1861); Michael Comerford, *Collection relating to the diocese of Kildare and Leighlin* (Dublin, J. Duffy, 1886); *John* Davis Whyte, *History of the Family of White* (Cashel, Whyte, 1887); *Cashel of the Kings* (Clonmel, *Chronicle Office*, 1863; Cashel, Whyte, 1866); *Guide to the Rock of Cashel* (Cashel, Whyte, 1877, 1888); Revd James O'Dowd, *Limerick and its Sieges* (Limerick, McKern, 1890).

7. Gibson, *History of Cork*, vol. 1, pp. v, vii–viii; Lenihan, *Limerick*, pp. 396–7, pp. 481–2.

8. Rev. John Begley, *The Diocese of Limerick* (3 vols.) (Dublin, Browne and Nolan, 1906, 1927, 1938).

9. Federation of Local History Societies, http://homepage.eircom.net/~localhist 17 October 2005. Other historical societies founded in this period were the Ormond Historical Society (1977).

10. http://homepage.eircom.net/~historycollective/projectoffice.html,   17 October 2005.

11. The pioneering work of John Andrews in archival map research was particularly influential. See Kevin Whelan, 'Beyond a Paper Landscape, John Andrews and Irish Historical geography', in F. A. A. Aalen and Kevin Whelan (eds), *Dublin City and County, from Prehistory to Present* (Dublin, Geography Publications, 1992), pp. 181–228.

12. Mary Daly, *Dublin, the Deposed Capital* (Cork, Cork University Press, 1984); Maura Murphy, Repeal and Young Ireland in Cork City and County (unpublished M.A. thesis, University College Cork, 1975); James S. Donnelly Jr, *The Land and People of Nineteenth-Century Cork* (London, Routledge and Kegan Paul, 1975).

13. Kevin Whelan, *Wexford, History and Society* (Dublin, Geography Publications, 1992), p. v.

14. The History Department and the Department of Adult and Continuing Education, University College Cork, and the Department of Modern History, National University of Ireland Maynooth, offer certificate and primary degree courses as well as taught and research higher degrees in local history and regional studies. The University of Limerick and Mary Immaculate College, Limerick run a joint taught MA course and supervise research towards higher degrees in local history.

15. Frank Mitchell and Michael Ryan, *Reading the Irish Landscape* (Dublin, Townhouse, 2001, first published 1986).

16. Finbar McCormick, 'Early secular settlement in County Fermanagh', in E. E. Murphy and W. J. Roulston, *Fermanagh, History and Society* (Dublin, Geography Publications), pp. 57–75; 'Economic and Agricultural Change in Early Medieval Ireland', paper delivered at the Economic and Social History Society of Ireland Annual Conference, 11 November 2005; Michael Moore and Peter Woodman, 'The Prehistory of County Waterford'; Maurice Hurley, 'Late Viking Age Settlement in Waterford City'; John Bradley and Andrew Halpin, 'The Topographical Development of Scandinavian and Anglo-Norman Waterford City', all in William Nolan and Thomas P. Power, *Waterford,*

History and Society (Dublin, Geography Publications, 19920, pp. 1–26, 49–72, pp. 105–30; John Bradley and Andrew Halpin, 'The Topographical Development of Scandinavian and Anglo-Norman Cork', in Patrick O'Flanagan and Cornelius Buttimer, *Cork, History and Society* (Dublin, Geography Publications, 1994), pp. 15–44; John Bradley, 'The Topographical Development of Scandinavian Dublin', in Aalen and Whelan, *Dublin City and County*, pp. 43–56.

17. Colin Rynne, *The Archaeology of Cork City from the Earliest Times to Industrialisation* (Cork, Collins Press, 1993); John Crowley, Robert Devoy, Denis Linehan, Patrick O'Flanagan and Michael Murphy, *Atlas of Cork City* (Cork, Cork University Press, 2005).

18. Patrick O'Flanagan and S. Ó Catháin, *The Living Landscape, Kilgalligan, Co. Mayo* (Dublin, Comhairle Béaloideas Éireann, 1975); T. Jones Hugues, 'Town and Baile in Irish placenames', in Nicholas Stephens and Robert Glascock (eds) *Irish Geographical Studies* (Belfast, Queen's University, 1970), pp. 244–58; F. H. A. Aalen, Kevin Whelan and Matthew Stout (eds), *Atlas of the Irish Rural Landscape* (Cork, Cork University Press, 1997). Maura Cronin, 'From the "flat o' the city" to the top of the hill, Cork since 1700', in Howard Clarke (ed.), *Irish Cities* (Cork, Mercier, 1995), pp. 55–68.

19. Robert J. Hunter, 'The Plantation in Donegal', in William Nolan, Liam Ronayne, Mairéad Dunleavy (eds), *Donegal, History and Society* (Dublin, Geography Publications, 1995), pp. 283–324; Monica Brennan, 'The Changing Composition of Kilkenny's Landowners', in William Nolan and Kevin Whelan (eds) *Kilkenny, History and Society* (Dublin, Geography Publications, 1990), pp. 161–97.

20. Mary O'Dowd, *Power, Politics and Land, Early Modern Sligo 1568–1688* (Belfast, Institute of Irish Studies Queen's University, 1991).

21. Jack Burtchaell, 'A Typology of Settlement and Society in County Waterford c. 1850', in Nolan and Power, *Waterford, History and Society*, pp. 541–78; William Nolan, 'Patterns of Living in Tipperary 1750–1850'; T. Hughes Jones, 'Landholding and Settlement in County Tipperary in the Nineteenth Century', in William Nolan and Thomas G. McGrath, *Tipperary, History and Society* (Dublin, Geography Publications, 1985), pp. 288–325, pp. 339–67; O'Flanagan, Patrick, 'Three Hundred Years of Urban Life, Villages and Towns in County Cork. c. 1600–1901', in O'Flanagan and Buttimer, *Cork, History and Society*, pp. 391–468; William Nolan, 'Society and Settlement in the Valley of Glenasmole c. 1750–1950', in Allen and Whelan (eds), *Dublin City and County*, pp. 181–228.

22. Jonathon Bell, 'Changing Farming Methods in County Derry', in Gerard O'Brien (ed), *Derry and Londonderry, History and Society* (Dublin, Geography Publications, 1999), pp. 405–14; Marilyn Cohen, *Linen, Family and Community in Tullylish, Co. Down 1690–1941* (Dublin, Four Courts, 1997).

23. Anngret Simms, H. B. Clarke, Raymond Gillespie, J. H. Andrews and Sarah Grearty (eds) *Irish Historic Towns Atlas* (Dublin, Royal Irish Academy, 1981–) This project, part of the wider European scheme of the European Atlases of Historic Towns, was established in 1981, with the aim of recording the topographical development of a selection of Irish towns. Fourteen atlases have been published up to 2005, and a number of others are under consideration.

24. John Andrews, 'Landmarks in early Wexford cartography', in Whelan, *Wexford, History and Society* (Dublin, Geography Publications, 1992), pp. 447–66; Patrick Power, 'A Survey, some Wicklow Maps 1500–1800', in Ken Hannigan and William Nolan (eds.) *Wicklow, History and Society* (Dublin, Geography Publications, 1994), pp. 723–60.

25. Aalen, Whelan and Stout, *Atlas of the Irish Rural Landscape*; Crowley, Devoy et al., *Atlas of Cork City*.

26. Jacinta Prunty, *Dublin Slums 1800–1925, A Study in Urban Geography* (Dublin, Four Courts Press, 1997).

27. Leslie Clarkson, 'Portrait of an Urban Community, Armagh 1770', in David Harkness and mary O'Dowd (eds.) *The Town in Ireland, Historical Studies*, xiii (Belfast, Appletree Press, 1981), pp. 81–102; Leslie Clarkson, 'Doing Local History, Armagh in the Late Eighteenth Century', in Gillespie and Hill, *Doing Irish Local History*, pp. 81–96; Bob King, *Carlow, the Manor and Town*, Maynooth Studies in Local History (Dublin, Irish Academic Press, 1997).

28. Anngret Simms, *Irish Country Towns* (Cork, Mercier, 1994); *More Irish Country Towns* (Cork, Mercier, 1995); Howard Hughes, *Irish Cities* (Cork, Mercier, 1995).

29. David Dickson, *Old World Colony* (Cork, Cork University Press, 2005); Mary O'Dowd, *Power, Politics and Land*; Donald Jordan, Jr, *Land and Popular Politics in Ireland, County Mayo from the Plantation to the Land War* (Cambridge, Cambridge University Press, 1994); Raymond Gillespie and Gerard Moran (eds.) *A Various County, Essays in Mayo History1500–1900* (Westport, Foilseacháin Nisiunta Teo Mayo, 1987).

30. David Fitzpatrick, *Politics and Irish life, 1913–1921, Provincial Experience of War and Revolution* (Dublin, Irish Academic Press, 1996); Joost Augusteijn, *From Public Defiance to Guerrilla Warfare: the Experience of Ordinary Volunteers* (Dublin, Irish Academic Press, 1996); Peter Hart, *The IRA and its Enemies: Violence and Community in Cork 1916–1923* (Oxford, Clarendon, 1998); Maria Coleman, *County Longford and the Irish revolution, 1910–1923* (Dublin, Irish Academic Press, 2003).

31. Ronan Gallagher, *Violence and Nationalist Politics in Derry City, 1920–1923*, Maynooth Studies in Local History (Dublin, Four Courts Press, 2003); Joost Auguusteijn, 'Radical and Nationalist Activities in County Derry 1900–1921', in O'Brien (ed.) *Derry and Londonderry, History and Society*, pp. 573–600.

32. James Grant, 'The Great Famine in County Down', in Leslie Proudfoot (ed.) *Down, History and Society* (Dublin, Geography Publications, 1997), pp. 353–82; Eva O Catháin, 'The Poor Law in County Wicklow', in Hannigan and Whelan (eds), *Wicklow, History and Society*, pp. 503–80.

33. Donnelly, *Land and People of Nineteenth Century Cork*; 'The Kenmare Estates During the Nineteenth Century', in *Kerry Historical and Archaeological Journal* no. 21, 1988, pp. 1–41, 22; 1989, pp. 96–7, 23; 1990, pp. 5–43; Gerard J. Lyne, *The Lansdowne Estate in Kerry under the Agency of William Steuart Trench 1849–72* (Dublin, Geography Publications, 2001); Peter Connell, *The Land and People of County Meath, 1750–1850* (Dublin, Four Courts Press, 2004).

34. Donal McCartney, 'Canon O'Hanlon, Historian of the Queen's County', in Timothy P. O'Neill and William Nolan (eds), *Offaly, History and Society* (Dublin, Geography Publications, 1998), pp. 585–600; Henry A. Jeffrries and Ciarán Devlin (eds) *History of the Diocese of Derry from earliest times*

(Dublin, Four Courts Press, 2000); James Kelly and Dáire Keogh, *History of the Catholic Diocese of Dublin* (Dublin, Four Courts Press, 2000).

35. Gabriel O'Connor, 'Clonfush, County Galway, a Self-contained Townland Adjacent to the Town of Tuam', in Brian Ó Dálaigh, D. A. Cronin and P. Connell (eds), *Irish Townlands* (Dublin, Four Courts Press, 1998), Peter Carr, *Portavo, An Irish Townland and its Peoples, Earliest Times to 1844* (Belfast, White Row Press, 2003).

36. Patrick O'Flanagan, 'Three Hundred Years of Urban Life, Villages and Towns in County Cork, c. 1600–1901', in Flanagan and Buttimer, *Cork, History and Society*, pp. 391–469; Karina Holton, Liam Clare and Brian Ó Dálaigh (eds), *Irish Villages, Studies in Local History* (Dublin, Four Courts Press, 2004); D. A. Cronin, J. Gilligan and K. Holton, *Irish Fairs and Markets* (Dublin, Four Courts Press, 2001); Tom Hunt, *Portlaw, County Waterford 1825–76, Portrait of an Industrial Village*, Maynooth Studies in Local History (Dublin, Irish Academic Press, 2000); Chris Lawlor, *Canon Frederick Donovan's Dunlavin 1884–1896*, Maynooth Studies in Local History (Dublin, Irish Academic Press, 2000).

37. P. J. Duffy, 'Locality and Changing Landscape, Geography and Local History', in Gillespie and Hill, *Doing Irish Local History*, p. 34.

38. Elizabeth Cronin, *Fr Michael Dungan's Blanchardstown 1836–1868*, Maynooth Studies in Local History (Dublin, Four Courts, 2002); Francis Kelly, *St. Mary's Parish, Granard, Co. Longford 1933–68*, Maynooth Studies in Local History (Dublin, Irish Academic Press, 1996); Liam Kelly, *Kiltubrid. County Leitrim, Snapshots of a parish in the 1890s*, Maynooth Studies in Local History (Dublin, Four Courts, 2005); Eoin Devereux, 'Negotiating Community, the Case of a Limerick Community Development Group', in Chris Curtin (ed.), *Irish Urban Cultures* (Belfast, Institute of Irish Studies, Queen's University, 1993).

39. John Crawford, *St Catherine's Parish, Dublin, Portrait of a Church of Ireland Community*, Maynooth Studies in Local History (Dublin, Irish Academic Press, 1996); Miriam Moffit, *The Church of Ireland community of Killala and Achonry 1870–1940*, Maynooth Studies in Local History (Dublin, Irish Academic Press, 1999); Ian D'Alton, 'Keeping Faith, an Evocation of the Cork Protestant Character, 1820–1920', in O'Flanagan and Buttimer, *Cork, History and Society*, pp. 755–93; John Tunney, 'The Marquis, the Reverend, The Grand Master and the Major, Protestant Politics in Donegal 1868–1933', in Nolan, Ronayne and Dunleavy, *Donegal, History and Society*, pp. 675–96.

40. Edward T. McCarron, 'In Pursuit of the "Maine" Chance, the North Family of Offaly and New England 1700–76', in O'Neill and Nolan (eds), *Offaly, History and Society*, pp. 332–70; John Mannion, 'A Transatlantic Merchant Fishery, Richard Welsh of New Ross and the Sweetmans of Newbawn in Newfoundland 1734–1862', in Whelan, *Wexford, History and Society*, pp. 373–421. See also Cyril Byrne, 'The Waterford Colony in Newfoundland', in Nolan and Power, *Waterford, History and Society*, pp. 351–72.

41. Christopher O'Mahony and Valerie Thompson, *Poverty to Promise, the Monteagle Emigrants 1838–58* (Darlinghurst, New South Wales, Crossing Press, 1994); David Fitzpatrick, *Oceans of Consolation* (Cork, Cork University Press, 1994).

42. Matthew Stout, 'Historical Geography', in Geary and Kelleher, *Nineteenth Century Ireland, A Guide to Recent Research* (Dublin, UCD Press, 2005), p. 91; Lindsay Proudfoot, 'Landownership and Improvement c. 1700 to 1845', in Proudfoot, *Down, History and Society*, pp. 203–38.

43. Jack Burtchael, 'A Typology of Settlement in County Waterford', in Nolan and Power, *Waterford, History and Society*, pp. 541–578; Geraldine Stout, *Newgrange and the Bend of the Boyne* (Cork, Cork University Press, 2002); P. J. Duffy, *Landscapes of South Ulster: A Parish Atlas of the Diocese of Clogher* (Belfast, Institute of Irish Studies, Queen's University, in conjunction with Clogher Historical Society, 1993).

44. Terence Dooley, *The Murders at Wildgoose Lodge: Agrarian Crime and Punishment in Pre-Famine Ireland* (Dublin, Four Courts Press, 2007).

45. P. H. Gulliver and Marilyn Silverman, *Merchants and Shopkeepers, An Historical Anthropology of an Irish Market Town* (Toronto, University of Toronto Press, 1995); Marilyn Silverman, *An Irish Working Class, Explorations in Political Economy and Hegemony 1800–1950* (Toronto, University of Toronto Press, 2001); Cohen, *Linen, Family and Community in Tullylish*.

46. Articles appearing in the *Connaught Telegraph* in the recent past include 'Forgotten Man of History, James Daly, the *Telegraph's* Most Famous Editor'; 'Michael Davitt, Mayo's Most Famous Son'; 'Lord Frederick Cavendish, Champion of the Oppressed'. http//www.mayohistory.com/, 14 November 2005.

47. K. W. Nicholls, 'The Development of Lordship in County Cork 1300–600', in O'Flanagan and Buttimer, *Cork, History and Society*, pp. 157–212; Darren MacEiteagáin, 'The Renaissance Lordship of Tír Chonaill 1461–1555', in Nolan, Ronayne and Dunleavy, *Donegal, History and Society*, pp. 203–28; David Edwards, 'The MacGiolla Padraigs of Upper Ossary 1532–1641', in Padraig G. Lane and William Nolan (eds), *Laois, History and Society* (Dublin, Geography Publications, 1999), pp. 327–75; 'The Lordship of O'Connor Faly 1520–1570', in Timothy P. O'Neill and William Nolan (eds), *Offaly, History and Society* (Dublin, Geography Publications, 1998).

48. L. M. Cullen, 'The 1798 rebellion in Wexford, United Irishman Organisation, Membership, Leadership', in Whelan, *Wexford, History and Society*, pp. 248–95; Sean Cloney, 'The Cloney Families of County Wexford', in Whelan, *Wexford, History and Society*, pp. 316–41; Conor O'Brien, 'The Byrnes of Ballymanus', in Hannigan and Nolan (eds), *Wicklow, History and Society*, pp. 305–40; Ruan O'Donnell, 'The Rebellion of 1798 in County Wicklow', in Hannigan and Nolan, *Wicklow, History and Society*, pp. 341–78; Thomas Bartlett, '"Masters of the Mountain", The Insurgent Careers of Joseph Holt and Michael Dwyer in County Wicklow 1798–1803', in Hannigan and Nolan, *Wicklow, History and Society*, pp. 379–410.

49. Ciarán Ó Murchadha, *Sable Wings over the Land, Ennis, County Clare and its Wider Community During the Great Famine* (Ennis, CLASP Press, 1998); Daniel Grace, *The Great Famine in Nenagh Poor Law Union, Co. Tipperary* (Nenagh, Relay Books, 2000); Brian MacDonald, *A Time of Desolation, Clones Poor Law Union 1845–50* (Enniskillen, Clones Historical Society, 2001; James Grant, 'The Great Famine in County Tyrone', in Charles Dillon and H. A. Jeffries (eds) *Tyrone, History and Society* (Dublin, Geography Publications, 2000), pp. 587–615; Diarmaid Ferriter, *Cuimhnigh ar Luimneach: A History of Limerick*

County Council 1898–1998 (Limerick, Limerick County Council, 1998); Edward J. Marnane, *Cork County Council, the First Hundred Years* (Cork, Cork County Council, 1999).

50. Denis A. Cronin, *A Galway Gentleman in the Age of Improvement: Robert French of Monivea*, Maynooth Studies in Local History (Dublin, Irish Academic Press, 1995); John Joe Conwell, *A Galway Landlord and the Famine*, Maynooth Studies in Local History (Dublin, Four Courts Press, 2003); Dermot James, *John Hamilton of Donegal 1800–1884: This Recklessly Generous Landlord* (Dublin, Woodfield Press, 1998).

51. Terence Dooley, *The Decline of the Big House in Ireland. A Study of Irish Landed Families 1860–1960* (Dublin, Woolfhound Press, 2001); Olwen Purdue, *The MacGeough Bonds of the Argory: An Ulster Gentry Family, 1880–1950*, Maynooth Studies in Local History (Dublin, Four Courts, 2005).

52. Bob Cullen, *Thomas L. Synnott, The Career of a Dublin Catholic 1830–1870* Maynooth Studies in Local History (Dublin, Irish Academic Press, 1997); Fintan Lane, *In Search of Thomas Sheahan, Radical Politics in Cork 1824–1836*, Maynooth Studies in Local History (Dublin, Irish Academic Press, 2001).

53. Nuala McAllister, 'Contradiction and Diversity, the Musical Life of Derry in the 1830s', in O'Brien (ed.), *Derry and Londonderry, History and Society*, pp. 465–95.

54. Damhnait Nic Suibhne, 'Donegal Fiddling, the Donegal Fiddle Tradition' and Lillis Ó Laoire 'An Ceol Dúchais i dTír Conaill', in Nolan, Ronayne and Dunleavy, *Donegal, History and Society*, pp. 758–838; Dáibhí Ó Cróinín (ed.), *The Songs of Elizabeth Cronin, Irish Traditional Singer* (Dublin, Four Courts Press, 2000).

55. Liam Bane, 'John McEvilly and the Catholic Church in Galway, 1857–1902', in Gerard Moran (ed.), *Galway, History and Society* (Dublin, Geography Publications, 1996), pp. 421–44; Thomas McGrath, *Religious Renewal and Reform in the Pastoral Ministry of Bishop James Doyle of Kildare and Leighlin 1786–1834* (Dublin, Four Courts, 1999); *Politics, Interdenominational Relations and Education in the Public Ministry of Bishop James Doyle of Kildare and Leighlin 1786–1834* (Dublin, Four Courts, 1999); Evelyn Bolster, *History of the Diocese of Cork* (Ballincollig, Tower Books, 1993); James S. Donnelly, Jr, 'Lough Derg, the Making of the Modern Pilgrimage', in Nolan, Ronayne and Dunleavy, *Donegal, History and Society*, pp. 491–508; David Hempton and Myrtle Hill, *Evangelical Protestantism in Ulster Society 1740–1890* (London, Routledge, 1992); Stewart J. Brown, 'Presbyterian Communities, Transatlantic Visions, and the Ulster Revival of 1859', in J. P. Mackey (ed.), *The Cultures of Europe, the Irish Contribution* (Belfast, Institute of Irish Studies, Queen's University Belfast, 1994), pp. 103–14.

56. Margaret Urwin, *A County Wexford Family in the Land War, the O'Hanlon-Walshs of Knocktartan*, Maynooth Studies in Local History (Dublin, Four Courts, 2002); Rosaleen Fallon, *A County Roscommon 1892, the Marriage of John Hughes and Mary Gavin*, Maynooth Studies in Local History (Dublin, Four Courts, 2004).

57. Kevin O'Neill, *Family and Farm in Pre-Famine Ireland* (Wisconsin, University of Wisconsin Press, 1984, republished 2003).

58. Caroline Windrum, 'The Provision and Practice of Prison Reform in County Down 1745–1894', in Proudfoot, *Down, History and Society*, pp. 327–52.

59. Patrick Durnan, 'Aspects of Poor Law Administration and the Workhouse in Derry 1838–1948', in O'Brien, *Derry and Londonderry, History and Society*, pp. 537–73; Sinéad Collins, *Balrothery Poor Law Union, County Dublin, 1839–1851*, Maynooth Studies in Local History (Dublin, Four Courts Press, 2005); Christine Kenealy, 'The Workhouse System in County Waterford 1838–1923', in Nolan and Power, *Waterford, History and Society*, pp. 579–96.

60. Angela Bourke, *The Burning of Bridget Cleary, A True Story* (London, Pimlico, 1999); Frank Sweeney, *The Murder of Connell Boyle, County Donegal, 1898*, Maynooth Studies in Local History (Dublin, Four Courts Press, 2002).

61. Gerard O'Brien, 'Our Magee Problem, Stormont and the Second University', in O'Brien, *Derry and Londonderry, History and Society*, pp. 647–79.

62. William Nolan, *Tracing the Past* (Dublin, Geography Publications, 1982); William Nolan and Anngret Simms (eds), *Irish Towns, a Guide to Sources* (Dublin, Geography Publications, 1998); Peter Collins, *Pathways to Ulster's Past* (Belfast, Institute of Irish Studies, Queen's University, 1998); Gillespie and Hill, *Doing Irish Local History*; Terence Dooley, *Sources for the History of Landed Estates in Ireland* (Dublin, Irish Academic Press, 2000); Raymond Refaussé, *Church of Ireland Records* (Dublin, Irish Academic Press, 2000); Patrick J. Corish and David C. Sheehy, *Records of the Irish Catholic Church* (Dublin, Irish Academic Press, 2001); Philomena Connolly, *Medieval Record Sources* (Dublin, Four Courts Press, 2002; Brian Gurrin, *Pre-census Sources for Irish Demography* (Dublin, Four Courts Press, 2002); E. Margaret Crawford, *Counting the People: A Survey of the Irish Censuses, 1813–1911*(Dublin, Four Courts Press, 2003); Brian Hanley, *A Guide to Irish Military Heritage, 1813–1911* (Dublin, Four Courts Press, 2004); Jacinta Prunty, *Maps and Map-making in Local History* (Dublin, Four Courts Press, 2005; Brian Griffin, *Sources for the Study of Crime in Ireland* (Dublin, Four Courts Press, 2005); Toby Barnard, *A Guide to the Sources for Irish Material Culture, 1500–2000* (Dublin, Four Courts Press, 2005).

63. The objectives of the Offaly Historical Society include 'preserving, protecting the history of our families, workplaces and communities' (www.offalyhistory.com/), while the combination of past- and place-centred identity is clear in the title chosen by the West Limerick Heritage Group based in Newcastlewest – 'As Dúchas Dóchas' (Out of heritage [comes] hope), and Kevin Whelan's sense of pride in County Wexford is unashamed in his reference to 'my native county' in *Wexford, History and Society*, p. v.

64. Maura Cronin, '"Of One Mind"? O'Connellite Crowds in the 1830s and 1840s', in Peter Jupp and Eoin Magennis (eds), *Crowds in Ireland c. 1720–1920* (Basingstoke, Macmillan, 2000).

65. See, for example, John O'Connor, *On Shannon's Shore: A History of Mungret Parish* (Limerick, Pubblebrien Historical Society, 2003); Jack Mahon, *For Love of Town and Village* (Dublin, Blackwater Press, 1997); Cathy Birmingham, *The Cork Butter Exchange Band: A Living Tradition* (Cork, Cork Butter Exchange Band, 1996); Richard T. Cooke, *Cork's Barrack Street silver and Reed Band, Ireland's Oldest Amateur Musical Institution* (Cork, Cork Barrack Street Band, 19920; *'When brethren are met in their Order so grand'*, A Brief History of Orangeism and Orange Lodges in Larne District (Larne, Larne 1996 Committee, 1995).

66. J. G. Kohl, *Travels in Ireland* (London, Bruce and Wyld, 1844), p. 95.

67. John A. Murphy, 'Cork, Anatomy and Essence', in O'Flanagan and Buttimer, *Cork, History and Society*, p. 3.
68. Sean Dunne (ed.), *The Cork Anthology* (Cork, Cork University Press, 1993); Jim Kemmy (ed.) *The Limerick Anthology* (Dublin, Gill and Macmillan, 1996); Patricia Craig (ed.) *The Belfast Anthology* (Belfast, Blackstaff, 1999).
69. Frank McCourt, *Angela's Ashes: A Memoir* (London, Harper Collins, 1996); Other Limerick memoirs include Cristóir Ó Floinn, *There is an Isle* (Cork, Mercier Press, 1998); Denis O'Shaughnessy, *A Spot So Fair: Tales from St. Mary's* (Limerick, Margo Press, 1998); Patrick Galvin, *Song for a Poor Boy: A Cork Childhood* (Dublin, Raven Arts, 1990).
70. Charles Flynn, 'Dundalk 1900–1960, An Oral History', unpublished PhD Thesis, National University of Ireland, Maynooth, 2000; John McGrath, 'Social and Economic Identity in St Mary's Parish, Limerick, 1890–1960' (Unpublished M.A. thesis, Mary Immaculate College, University of Limerick, 2006); Daniel Grace, *Portrait of a Parish, Monsea and Killodernan, Co. Tipperary* (Nenagh, Relay Books, 1996); Maura Cronin's *Country, Class or Craft, the Politicisation of the Skilled Artisan in Nineteenth Century Cork* (Cork, Cork University Press, 1994) explores Cork artisans' multiple identity as Irishmen, craftsmen and Corkonians.
71. Dooley, *The Decline of the Big House in Ireland*, p. 256.
72. Related to me by an undergraduate history student at Mary Immaculate College, September 2005, regarding his attempted interview in March–April 2005.

7

institutionalisation in irish history and society

catherine cox

introduction

From 1750 to 1950, throughout Europe and elsewhere, institutions were identified as appropriate sites for the relief, segregation and containment of destitution, criminality, insanity, prostitution and disease. The period witnessed the rise and expansion of hospitals, prisons, workhouses, orphanages and other institutions. Ireland participated fully in this 'great confinement';[1] the rural and urban landscape provides testimony to the presence of a range of institutions in every county. By 1900 significant sections of society were familiar with the confines of a variety of institutions and this propensity to incarcerate has continued into the twenty-first century. International writings by historians, sociologists and other academics have focused on explanations for the emergence and operation of these institutions. Explanatory frameworks encompass, among others, Whiggish reformist zeal, theories surrounding social control, professional ambition and Victorian sensibilities. In the Irish context, institutions and their development have received less attention. Although the nineteenth century possibly marks the zenith of institutional construction and confinement, Laurence Geary and Margaret Kelleher's recent guide to nineteenth-century historiography bears witness to the limited research or perhaps interest in the area. Maria Luddy's chapter on 'Women's History' contains a section on institutions, while Marilyn Cohen and Joan Vincent's survey of anthropological and sociological studies briefly examines recent sociological studies of lunatic asylums and inebriate reformatories.[2] In the same volume, quite remarkably, Gary Owen's consideration of social history contains almost no mention of institutional care or confinement.[3] This neglect is by no means a recent phenomenon, as evidenced by the near

169

absence of any analysis of the role played by institutions in Irish society in the excellent *New History of Ireland V: Ireland under the Union I: 1801–1870*. The exceptions are Oliver MacDonagh's and R. B. McDowell's comprehensive consideration of the political dynamics informing the establishment of state institutions in nineteenth-century Ireland.[4]

This is not to suggest that analysis of the function of institutions in Irish society is absent. Some work has been completed. Fruitful avenues of interrogation have included examinations of individual sites (their construction and administration), assessments of the role of philanthropy and religious orders in this process and analyses of women's experiences of institutions. The first approach has provided fascinating institutional histories. Many of the hospital histories, which once dominated Irish medical history, provide the reader with a complex understanding of the policies and the personalities that influenced the development of individual hospitals in Ireland. However, as Greta Jones and Elizabeth Malcolm have noted in their consideration of medical institutions, 'one can almost be seduced into forgetting that hospitals function primarily for the care of patients'.[5] This imbalance has been addressed to a certain extent by historians who have attempted an assessment of the female experience of institutional care and administration. Women's involvement in institutions encompassed their roles as founders, administrators, carers and occupants. Research into the philanthropic and religious origins of various institutions have emphasised this female role, but also underlined the importance of non-state provision in the framing of institutional care and confinement.

As it is not possible to examine all institutions in this chapter I have selected institutions which are representative of different regimes of care and containment and of varying philanthropic, religious and state management. I have chosen not to include educational institutions. The chapter outlines the origins of the variety of institutions, considers the main trends within the historiography and proceeds to identify new opportunities of research. Due to the constraints of space, I have not attempted to review every institutional study, rather I have chosen studies which are representative of particular theoretical or historiographical frameworks.

legislative overview

The origins of hospitals, workhouses, prisons, asylums and other institutions are diverse, sometimes overlap and cover a broad chronological period. In Ireland, the vast majority of institutions have their roots in the eighteenth and nineteenth centuries, although some were founded prior to that date.[6] This institutional zeal was partly fuelled by philanthropic endeavour and partly by state initiatives, often a product of reformist lobbying. In international historiography of institutional innovation the development of the penal system has received concentrated attention.[7] Its emergence in Ireland has been rather neglected, although work has been completed on political imprisonment in Ireland[8] and on the innovations introduced by Sir Walter Crofton.[9] The policy of constructing prisons appears to have been introduced to Ireland by two statutes during the reign of Edward I.[10] Subsequent construction of bridewells and prisons has its antecedents in the seventeenth century. There had been a bridewell in Dublin since 1602/3, while provincial equivalents appeared in the 1650s.[11] The 1610 English penal act, introduced to Ireland during the Dublin parliament of 1634–5, obliged each county to construct a house of correction for 'rogues, vagabonds [and] sturdy beggars'.[12] These earlier institutions were principally places of confinement for convicts awaiting transportation to America, and debtors.[13] Until 1775, the policy of transportation ensured that the majority of felons were not imprisoned. This altered with the outbreak of the American War of Independence and consequently, under legislation introduced in 1777, prisoners sentenced to transportation were put to hard labour in existing prisons.

Thus after this date, felons were increasingly punished by confinement in prisons in both Britain and Ireland.[14] Although transportation to Australia provided an alternative from 1787 until the end of transportation in 1853,[15] it was not sufficient to contend with the expanding convict population. The tendency to confine felons in prisons led to the further construction of penal institutions in the form of debtor's prisons, county gaols and houses of correction/industry or bridewells. The management of, and conditions in, these institutions were portrayed as corrupt, unregulated and neglectful by prison campaigners such as John Howard, Elizabeth Fry, Sir Jeremiah Fitzpatrick and Jeremy Bentham.[16]

By the late eighteenth and early nineteenth centuries, the programme for the reform of existing prisons and the construction of new institutions was well underway. For example Newgate prison in Dublin was relocated from Thomas Street to a new building designed by Thomas Cooley on Little Green in 1780 while Kilmainham gaol, Dublin, was built in 1780s.[17] Legislation introduced in 1810 provided for a comprehensive series of reforms of conditions and administration in existing prisons although its success is debatable.[18] Possibly, the most important prison, Mountjoy, was opened in Dublin in 1850, and was modelled on the Pentonville system.[19] As Michael Ignatieff and others have convincingly argued these reforms should not be interpreted as purely altruistic endeavours.

The institutional confinement of the poor, in the form of houses of correction/industry, was closely related to the emergence of local prisons. The 1610 penal act also stipulated that 'vagabonds, [and] sturdy beggars' be confined within institutions.[20] However, houses of correction were slow to emerge, and the interest in them was relatively short-lived and intermittent. It was not until the eighteenth century that further legislation was enacted. Cities were the particular focus of this legislation. In 1703, the first direct provision for the relief of the poor in Dublin city was introduced resulting in the erection, over the next three years, of a workhouse at the cost of £9,000.[21] In 1728, the function of the workhouse was recast and the site became a repository for foundling children.[22] The Cork city workhouse was opened in 1747 but from the outset was exclusively concerned with the confinement of foundling children.[23] In Belfast a poor house had been opened by the Belfast Charitable Society in 1774. Legislation passed in 1772, facilitated the further establishment of workhouses and houses of industry. Though concerned with the relief of the destitute poor, they were essentially punitive in character. The establishment of houses of industry was not mandatory; the legislators intended that local communities should take the initiative while funding would be supplemented by parliamentary grants. In these circumstances most counties were slow to introduce such relief and a limited number of houses were established under the legislation, in Dublin (1773), Cork (1778), Limerick, Clare, Wexford and Waterford. Existing institutions at Belfast (1774), Coleraine (1776) and Lisburn, which had been constructed under alternative schemes, were brought under its remit.[24] Thus the absence of a poor law prior to 1838 did not result in a complete absence of an institutional response to vagrancy and poverty in Ireland.

The number of workhouses was expanded following the introduction of the poor law to Ireland in 1838. Historians of the Great Famine have ensured that the political origins and ideology informing the workhouse system in Ireland has received significant attention.[25] The prevalence of extreme poverty in Ireland provoked various parliamentary enquiries into its extent, nature and possible amelioration.[26] A variety of proposals emerged, culminating in the decision to transfer the 1834 amendment to the English Poor Law to Ireland.[27] As Gerard O'Brien has suggested the resistance to the Poor Law in Ireland differed significantly to the anti-poor law agitation experienced in the north of England.[28]

The 1838 act for the relief of the destitute poor stipulated that Ireland be divided into 130 Poor Law unions, each with a centrally located workhouse. The construction of the workhouses was pursued with relative speed and by 1845, the majority had admitted paupers.[29] This first wave of construction buckled under the burden of the Famine,[30] resulting in the construction of additional workhouses under the 1847 amendment to the poor law.[31]

Although the houses of industry and workhouses were not ostensibly concerned with the relief of the sick poor, necessity required them to provide for this category, and a number of medical institutions, closely connected with poor relief, emerged. In 1801, at the Dublin house of industry, the governors established two hospitals, the Hardwicke (1810) and the Whitworth (1817).[32] The governors were also provided with a grant from central government for the establishment of a separate hospital for lunatics, later known as the Richmond lunatic asylum. The fear that wandering mendicants and the poor would assist in the spread of disease prompted additional state intervention. Legislation for the establishment of fever hospitals (1807, 1818), county infirmaries (1765) and medical dispensaries (1805) resulted in the emergence of a series of medical institutions which were funded by the grand jury system and through local subscription.[33] Throughout the nineteenth century, particularly after the Great Famine, the state became increasingly involved in the provision of medical facilities for the poor and introduced a series of legislative initiatives which expanded and centralised institutional provision in Ireland. This era of reform and centralisation altered the nature and management of existing institutions and also assisted in their expansion. For example, in 1817, legislation introduced a mandatory county asylum system to Ireland. Each county was obliged to provide institutional provision for the insane by either constructing their own institution or by co-operating with other counties. By 1901 there were 24 county asylums in Ireland. These expanded upon the existing philanthropic provision for the insane such as St Patrick's Hospital (1757) and the Citadella (1799) in Cork.[34] Further impetus was given to the establishment of dispensaries by the 1851 Medical Charities Act. It divided Ireland into over 700 dispensary districts, each of which had its own medical officer and midwife, who were under the jurisdiction of the Poor Law guardians.[35] Hospital provision for the poor was significantly expanded in 1862, when the sick poor became eligible for admission to workhouse infirmaries.[36] State institutional provision did not confine itself to hospitals, workhouses and prisons. As the nineteenth century progressed, reformatory schools, industrial schools and inebriate homes were established. The control and management of some, such as the industrial schools, was assumed by the religious orders, while others remained under state control.

Philanthropic fervour is crucial to understanding the emergence of institutions in this period. In the eighteenth and nineteenth centuries, philanthropists founded medical institutions, magdalen asylums, orphanages, lock hospitals and refuges. General voluntary hospitals were opened in most cities; in Dublin, Dr. Steeven's Hospital (1733), Charitable Infirmary (1718) and Mercer's (1734) were founded, while in Cork the South and North Charitable Infirmaries were opened. In Belfast and Limerick, general voluntary hospitals were slower to emerge, opening in 1817 and 1831 respectively.[37] The period also witnessed the emergence of the specialist hospitals such as those catering for the insane, expectant mothers – the lying-in hospitals in Dublin (1745), Belfast (1793) and Cork (1798) – and sufferers of venereal disease – lock hospitals and penitentiaries. These specialist institutions were often established by medical practitioners, who catered for the categories of patients usually excluded from the general hospitals. These philanthropic institutions often sought treasury funding, to supplement or replace donations and subscriptions, with varying success. For example, the lock hospitals usually experienced difficulty in attracting subscribers; the Westmoreland Lock Hospital in Dublin was entirely funded by the state.[38] State and philanthropic initiatives were thus intertwined in eighteenth-century Ireland.

The majority of earlier voluntary hospitals, general and specialist were established and managed by members of the Protestant upper and middle classes.[39] In the early nineteenth century, this pattern changed somewhat, as the revival of the Catholic Church and the new emerging Catholic middle classes became involved in the voluntary hospital movement. Female religious orders were pivotal in this process in Ireland; hospitals were founded by the Sisters of Mercy and the Sisters of Charity, including St. Vincent's (1834) and Mater Miscericordiae (1861) in Dublin, the Mercy Hospital (1857) in Cork and the Mater Infirmorum (1883) in Belfast.[40] The full extent of their dominance became clear in the 1930s when the hospital commission attempted to extend the existing hospitals. The programme, under its various guises, was successfully resisted by the religious orders with the support of the Catholic hierarchy.[41] The religious orders did not confine themselves to the establishment of medical institutions. They became involved in the provision of magdalen asylums, industrial schools and orphanages. Teresa Mulally opened a poor school and orphanage for Catholic girls in St. Michan's parish in Dublin, while Nano Nagle was involved in a variety of charitable endeavours for poor Catholic women in Cork. The most recent historiography suggests that 'from the eighteenth century at least forty-one asylums or refuges were established to rescue or reclaim "fallen women"' in Ireland. These asylums were operated by lay and female religious orders.[42] In the nineteenth century, the magdalen asylums were ostensibly involved in the care of 'fallen women', which mainly included prostitutes and some unmarried mothers. In the twentieth century, in addition to the asylums, unmarried mothers were maintained by the local authorities in the county homes, or were accepted into other private institutions.[43] Other institutional foundations had non-Catholic roots. The first magdalen asylum, opened in Dublin in 1766 by Lady Arabella Denny, was not a Catholic organisation. The Female Orphan House, opened in Prussia Street, Dublin (1791), and the House of Refuge, Baggot Street, Dublin (1802), were both founded by members of Protestant faiths, and were established to offer shelter to unemployed young women who lacked familial support. There were also mendicity institutions in Dublin (1819) and Derry which provided relief and lodgings for the poor.

motivation

By the end of the nineteenth century there was a growing tendency to institutionalise in Irish society. This phenomenon has received varying treatments within the historiography. Older traditional institutional histories have tended to portray their establishment in idealised and progressive terms. Medical institutions were particularly prone to such a portrayal, as the establishment of hospitals, particularly specialist hospitals, was associated with medicine's 'march of progress'.[44] Religious and philanthropic involvement has been subject to a similar treatment. The houses of industry and workhouses have received a rather different treatment possibly due to their punitive character and association with the Great Famine. By the 1970s, the historiography generally focused on the period after the passage of the Act of Union, particularly on legislation responsible for the establishment of medical institutions, workhouses and other institutions. These were examined in conjunction with other legislative initiatives in public health, law and order, education and poor relief, with particular focus on the apparent precipitate interventionist nature of the policy.[45] In his work, Oliver MacDonagh placed these developments within a colonial framework, maintaining that the Act of Union between Britain and Ireland was not a union between equals.[46]

An examination of the introduction of national, highly centralised and regulated, regimes, such as the Royal Irish Constabulary or the board of health led W. L. Burn to contend that 'The most conventional of English men were willing to experiment in Ireland on lines which they were not prepared to contemplate or tolerate at home'.[47] MacDonagh developed this argument in *Ireland: Union and Its Aftermath* (1977).[48] For a time, this framing of the legislation was extremely influential in writings on British government policy in Ireland and debates surrounding the provision of institutional care. For example Mark Finnane's study, *Insanity and the Insane in Post-Famine Ireland* (1981), originally his thesis supervised by MacDonagh,[49] places the early introduction of public asylums in Ireland within a similar framework.[50] More recently, Carroll-Burke's book on the development of the Irish penal system similarly assumes that Ireland 'under the act of union was a "colony" in all but name'.[51] This interpretation has been recently revisited by a number of historians.[52]

The role of lay philanthropy in the provision of institutional facilities, medical and otherwise, cannot be ignored when attempting an assessment of the ideological motivation behind institutional foundation. The tendency to focus exclusively on state legislation in isolation from the variety of philanthropic provisions has its pitfalls as evidenced by Oliver MacDonagh's assessment of welfare provision in Ireland in his chapter 'Ideas and Institutions' in *New History of Ireland, V* (1989). In it he posits that the early state funding of fever hospitals and dispensaries suggests that in public health, '*formally*', Ireland was 'one of the most advanced' European countries.[53] This fails to take cognisance of the wide-ranging philanthropic provision, both lay and religious, of institutional care in Europe. For example, in Britain, philanthropic rather than state endeavours were particularly central to the development of medical institutions. This positivistic interpretation of state intervention and centralisation is rather problematic and provides a one-sided impression of the range of institutions. Philanthropic and charitable influence upon institutional development in Irish society was, nonetheless, extremely significant, if less pronounced then elsewhere; the eighteenth and nineteenth centuries 'witnessed the emergence and development of private charitable provision'.[54] The nature of this activity was comprehensive and often denominational. As Roy Porter has highlighted, although the gift relation had different meaning for Protestants and Catholics in the eighteenth and nineteenth centuries, it is central to the comprehension of philanthropic activity.[55] Rosemary Raughter, in her consideration of eighteenth-century female philanthropists, noted that 'religious feeling was unquestionably the most commonly advanced reason for action, and women of all confessions recorded the pivotal part which their faith played in their philanthropy'.[56] Protestant charitable activity was disproportionate to their presence in the population, bearing testimony to the position of members of the Church of Ireland in Irish society. For example the majority of voluntary hospitals were founded by members of protestant faiths.[57] However, as noted by Raughter, religious zeal, though important, was not the sole incentive; eighteenth-century philanthropists were also driven by perceived threats posed by lawlessness and moral degeneracy. The privileged classes, through the provision of charity, often in an institutional form, could act as the moral guardians of the poor.[58] However, it was not sufficient to facilitate co-operation across confessional divides.[59] Shifting away from an unquestioning acceptance of the altruistic utterances of founders, characteristic of many of the older histories of these medical and charitable institutions, Raughter also explores the influence of the motivation to proselytise. She interrogates the aims and ambitions of philanthropists, hints at the complexity of the question and thus implies some similarities with the English context. To this end, Hilary Marland has shown in her work on medical institutions in Huddersfield and Wakefield in the north of England that philanthropists were driven by a combination of motivations: civic pride, reformist zeal, self-interest and fear of contagion.[60] Laurence Geary's *Medicine and Charity in Ireland 1718–1851* (2004) suggests that the 'voluntary hospital movement was inspired by a combination of charity and utilitarianism'[61] – disappointingly he fails to pursue this question in any great depth – while Maria Luddy posits that 'charitable endeavour, which often found its impulse in Christian teaching, also had pragmatic aims; to maintain Protestant and British rule in Ireland'.[62]

A useful pathway into the nature of charitable activity has been the interrogation of the extent of women's involvement in the establishment of institutions. An interesting series of essays in volume five of the *Field Day Anthology of Irish Writing* (2002) highlights the extent of women's involvement in the foundation of a variety of institutions sometimes characterising it as successful interventions in the public sphere and expressions of female agency.[63] These essays are based on substantial contributions to the field by their authors. Articles by Elizabeth Malcolm, Maria Luddy and Rosemary Raughter, examine, among other issues, the role of women in the establishment of hospitals, orphanages and magdalen asylums. In her essay on hospitals, Malcolm stresses that although the rise of the hospital undoubtedly contributed to the decline of women's role as traditional healers, it is important to stress that women played a major part in the hospital's rise to prominence.[64] Female involvement in philanthropic activity often developed as a result of an expansion in female religious orders, particularly Catholic activity.[65] Luddy's work on the establishment of magdalen asylums emphasises the problem of prostitution in Ireland in the eighteenth and nineteenth centuries; 'The prostitute was considered to be the site of both physical and moral degeneration, and attempts to resolve this problem focused on confinement.'[66] Confinement often took place in the magdalen asylums.[67] The founders were concerned with the 'reform' of the penitents and removing them from public view. By the mid-nineteenth century, nuns were deemed the most appropriate group to cater for 'fallen women' and all Catholic asylums were handed over to them.[68] James M. Smith's *Ireland's Magdalen Laundries and the Nation's Architecture of Containment* (2007) traces the influence of Catholic social thought on magdalen asylums in the twentieth century. Female religious orders also dominated the development of the industrial school movement in Ireland. Jane Barnes has completed a groundbreaking study on the introduction of the industrial school system to Ireland in 1868. She explores the context in which the system was introduced and importantly differentiates between the industrial and reformatory schools.[69] The religious orders increasingly assumed responsibility for these schools. The limited historiography on the subject has focused almost exclusively on Catholic orders, though there were some institutions managed by Protestant orders. Subsequent work has been slow to emerge; studies of Salthill Industrial School and of the role played by the Sisters of Mercy have been completed, the latter focusing on education and literacy.[70]

'the patient's view'?

In response to calls for 'history from below' and subsequent concern for the 'patient's view',[71] there has been a growing trend in institutional histories to explore life within the institutions both for staff and inhabitants. Within this framework, the various types of institutions have received an assortment of treatments often depending on the available source material. Once again studies of women's experiences of institutional confinement have provided some useful insights. Real knowledge of life within the eighteenth-century houses of industry is yet to emerge, partially due to the paucity of available source material. Helen Burke does explore the conditions within the Dublin city workhouse before it was transformed

into a founding hospital.[72] However, the preponderance of analyses of
life within the workhouse system focus on the post-1838 institutions
with particular emphasis on the famine period. These include general
surveys of conditions, gleaned from administrative sources, which
provide descriptions of workhouse diets, accommodation and punishments; many of the local studies of workhouses and general survey
histories have adopted this approach and provide an excellent overview.[73] Gerard O'Brien's analysis of conditions in workhouses before
the Famine highlights the yawning gap between bureaucratic intention
and experienced 'realities'. The regional variations he identified under-
score the impact individual boards of guardians had upon the living
conditions of the paupers.[74] While O'Brien has attempted to remove the
'myth' of the 'cruel' poor law, such a conception of the poor law is resil-
ient as evidenced by some studies of individual workhouses. Case studies of workhouses have been highly critical of workhouse management,
identifying shortfalls in diet and food supplies.[75] They have focused on
the incompetence and parsimony of the boards of guardians and the
punitive conditions within the workhouse.[76]

On the other hand, Cormac Ó Gráda and Timothy Guinnane's analysis
suggests that the link between the quality of workhouse management,
conditions and mortality rates was extremely complex.[77] In an article
published in 2001, a particularly interesting discussion is centered on
the interaction between diseases and mortality rates. Efficient or sympathetic management did not automatically produce low workhouse
mortality rates. The willingness of boards of guardians to succumb to
pressure and admit paupers exhibiting symptoms of contagious diseases
contributed to high mortality rates as such admissions not only put
other inmates at risk, but deterred the healthy from seeking relief until
they were too weak and debilitated to recover.[78] Nor did high workhouse mortality rates correlate with inefficient management or poor
living conditions. While some paupers died of diseases contracted while
in the workhouses, thereby suggesting mismanagement, others entered
the workhouse expressly to die.[79] In these circumstances, the conditions within the institution had little impact upon the survival rates.
The experience of female paupers within workhouses has also been the
subject of a number of studies. Women and children were the main
recipients of poor relief in Ireland. This fact has been interpreted in a
variety of ways. Helen Burke has suggested that women and children
were 'particular victims of the poor law system'.[80] On the other hand,
Dympna McLoughlin's work highlights female agency and mobility in
seeking relief contending that the women were 'not ignorant about the

lay of the land'.[81] She also problematises the traditional concept of the family, and attitudes towards the children.[82] David Fitzpatrick's analysis of female experience of workhouses borrows from Amartya Sen's theories concerning 'exchange entitlement relations during famine, asserting that the allocation of official relief favored dependents, women and children, facilitating female advantage in terms of mortality'.[83]

Virginia Crossman's studies of women and the poor law highlight further complexities. Although the workhouse test was 'accepted as appropriate for men, its usefulness was questioned when applied to women'.[84] Crossman posits that female pauperism inside and outside the workhouse was viewed both as a moral and an economic problem. Women were regarded as 'problem' inmates. Contemporary concerns with the segregation of male and female paupers and 'respectable' from 'immoral' female paupers created difficulties for the workhouse administration and impacted upon conditions. For example, in 1887 attempts to segregate alleged prostitutes in New Ross workhouse culminated in a riot. Crossman's article also highlights the possible connections between the land war, nationalism and concepts of female respectability.[85] Anna Clarke similarly uses a riot in South Dublin Union workhouse in 1860 to explore the 'tensions inherent to the liberal imperial state in mid-nineteenth century Ireland'. Her article, which assumes rather than interrogates Ireland's colonial status, explores the debates between the Catholic Church and female philanthropists, concerning the suitability of workhouses for the care of children.[86] While her article is not as nuanced as Crossman's work, it does provide an interesting insight into a neglected debate within the administration of poor law relief.

The experiences of patients within other institutions are less well documented. Histories of some medical hospitals and asylums have attempted to explore the patients' understandings of their period of confinement. While the majority of hospital histories have ignored patients' experiences and the doctor–patient relationship, some histories of the lunatic asylums have attempted to uncover this aspect of institutional life. Elizabeth Malcolm's and Joseph Reynolds' monographs on two hospitals for the insane in Dublin, Swift's hospital and Grangegorman,[87] provide some insight into patient experiences. In particular, Malcolm's exposition of letters from relatives seeking the admission of private patients gives an understanding of the wide range of factors influencing the decision to commit a relative. Both monographs use general administrative and medical sources to outline the conditions within the asylums. The relationship this bore to patients' experiences or their own feelings concerning their committal remains, however, unexplored.

Insights into patients' experiences and attitudes in other hospitals are even rarer. Geary's monograph affords some impression of the rules and regulation which controlled the lives of patients in general voluntary hospitals. Accounts of conditions within institutions managed by the religious orders have proved controversial and at times contradictory. An early example is Mavis Arnold and Healther Laskey's account of St. Joseph's in Co. Cavan, an institution run by Poor Clares.[88] Mary Raftery's television exposé and subsequent monograph on conditions in industrial schools for boys and girls managed by male and female religious orders helped to bring the issue of maltreatment to public attention.[89] Her work has been embroiled in controversy, and has resulted a re-examination of the role of Fr. Edward Flanagan's alleged criticism of the industrial school system in Ireland.[90] Also, there have been a number of memoirs published by former occupants of these institutions, which provide insights into treatment and conditions.[91] Accounts of life within the magdalen asylums have also proved contentious. Luddy's work has highlighted the significant differences in the magdalen asylums of the eighteenth and nineteenth from 'places of incarceration they were later to become'.[92] She provides a nuanced account of the function of the asylums and the treatment of the 'penitents' by the religious. Vitally, she highlights the extent to which their function may have altered in the twentieth century.[93] Frances Finnegan's monograph is a less well-balanced account of the asylums managed by the Sisters of the Good Shepherd in Cork, Waterford, New Ross and Limerick. Though ostensibly focusing on the nineteenth century, she was obviously deeply influenced by the scandals associated with the asylums in Ireland since 1993 and adopts a teleological approach to the subject.[94]

conclusion

The high quality of the existing scholarship has ensured that key aspects of the area have been explored comprehensively. However, I would like to suggest some new opportunities for research. Traditionally, historiography has examined institutions in isolation from the communities they claimed to serve. This is problematic as each institution was deeply embedded in its locality, often drawing on the local community for its staff, supplies and, of course, the occupants. A focus on the local experience would allow a re-appraisal of the national picture and its historiography. For example, Oonagh Walsh's work on Connaught District Lunatic Asylum, at Ballinasloe, Co. Galway, highlights the extent to which the asylum was welcomed by the surrounding community, anticipating employment opportunities and economic benefits.[95] The institutions were embedded into the communities in other ways. The acceptance of institutions by the wider community as a remedy to a perceived medical and/or social need is central to understanding their proliferation and expansion. Expansion was often driven by demand. This demand could originate with the individuals who chose to enter institutions or with their family or friends, who placed relatives in institutional care. Research on nineteenth-century lunatic asylums indicate the extent to which the system expanded steadily as more and more patients were committed by friends and family.[96] This pattern was not unique to Ireland. Luddy's work suggests that the general acceptance of containment as a solution to prostitution and venereal disease by the police and lay and religious bodies in the nineteenth century assisted in the proliferation of magdalen asylums and lock hospitals. Referrals to magdalen asylums came from a variety of sources: the religious, medical officials and families.[97] Neither was this confined to the nineteenth century. Lindsey Earner-Byrne in her monograph suggests that relatives may have interpreted institutionalisation as the most acceptable option when faced with the possible rejection of an unmarried, expectant daughter.[98] Thus families and communities were explicitly engaged in the form of social control exercised by the establishment of institutions.

There has also been a tendency in the historiography to examine individual institutions or institutional systems in isolation. The relationships between the various institutions needs be explored in greater depth. The interrogation of theoretical frameworks, such as Foucault's conception of the various systems as a 'carceral archipelago' is generally lacking. This lacuna was noted by historians as early as 1987 and reiterated subsequently but to little affect.[99] In England, studies of the relationship between prisons, workhouses, lunatic asylums and hospitals at a local level have identified the extent of their interdependence.[100] Such a conceptualisation of the intermeshed nature of the different institutional systems can be rewarding in the Irish context. Shane Kilcommins et al. have attempted an interesting and provocative exploration of the Irish 'carceral society' through the prism of a general penal policy. However their work incorporates hospitals and asylums within 'penal policy' which is problematic.[101] The extent to which the institutions are intertwined at a local level, often through personnel, should also be interrogated. Male members of the boards of governors of philanthropic institutions were often poor law guardians, lunatic asylum governors and superintendents of local prisons. This resulted in a relatively small élite group within local communities influencing the 'itinerary of inmates' through institutions. This overlap in personnel was not confined to the governing bodies of the institutions. Medical practitioners, matrons, warders and nursing staff moved from institution to institution gaining experience and seeking promotion. Of course, there was variety in the extent to which institutions were integrated and some remained largely separate, maintaining their own spheres of influence.

Another productive area of research would be an interrogation of the relationship between national and local administrative bodies responsible for these institutions. As Mary E. Daly has identified in her consideration of the activities of the Local Government Board in the nineteenth century, 'Local communities often resented the ... intrusion into their affairs and the supervision exercised by inspectors and auditors frequently created tensions between the centre and the periphery'.[102] While William Feingold's work has explored the tensions caused by the nationalisation of the boards of guardians of poor law unions, this relationship requires further interrogation.[103] The different sources of financial support – state and philanthropic – could be a source of contention between the national and local administrators. The complex and overlapping funding mechanisms of these various institutions undoubtedly informed this relationship. Local philanthropists and national administrators, situated in Dublin Castle, often had different ambitions for, and expectations of, these institutions. As noted earlier, at times these expectations may have been mutually re-enforcing, but expectations could also be sources of confrontation. In particular, any role anticipated for institutions in harmonising confessional relationships or strengthening relationships between communities and the state would be a fruitful area of research.

Similarly, further research into the poor law in Ireland would prove a significant addition to the historiography of institutional care. As noted earlier, with some exceptions, research on the Irish poor law has focused on the period of the Great Famine. There is comparatively little work done on the period after the 1850s. Recently, Virginia Crossman has attempted to redress this imbalance in her two monographs.[104] She has also embarked on a significant research project exploring the administration of the poor law in the later half of the nineteenth century that will prove very useful. An exploration of the governance of the poor law would be vital in any assessment of the uniformity of provision within the various institutions that came under its remit. While some work has been completed on the dispensaries and the public health movement, there has been no systematic study of provision of care and the impact of the constant expansion of the duties of the poor law administrators on the ability to deliver services to communities.

The existing scholarship on institutional provision in Ireland has highlighted the extent to which asylums, prisons, workhouses, hospitals and industrial schools were an integral part of Irish society. Although some excellent and fascinating work has been completed to date, I have attempted to suggest that there is ample scope to extend the exploration even further. As part of this, it may be necessary to move outside the institutions and into the surrounding environments, thus situating them in broader social, political, economic and cultural frameworks.

notes

1. Michel Foucault, *Madness and Civilization: A History of Insanity in the Age of Reason* (London, Routledge, 1999), pp. 38–65.
2. Maria Luddy, 'Women's History', in Laurence M. Geary and Margaret Kelleher (eds), *Nineteenth Century Ireland. A Guide to Recent Research* (Dublin, University College Dublin Press, 2005), pp. 56–8; Marilyn Cohen and Joan Vincent, 'Anthropological and Sociological Studies', in Geary and Kelleher, *Nineteenth-Century Ireland*, pp. 113–4; George Bretherton, 'Irish inebriate reformatories, 1899–1920: A Small Experiment in Coercion', in Ian O'Donnell and Finbarr McAuley (eds), *Criminal Justice History: Themes and Controversies from Pre-Independence Ireland* (Dublin, Four Courts Press, 2003), pp. 214–32.
3. Gary Owens, 'Social History', in Geary and Kelleher, *Nineteenth-Century Ireland*, pp. 27–42.
4. Oliver MacDonagh, 'Ideas and Institutions, 1830–45', in William E. Vaughan (ed.), *A New History of Ireland, V, Ireland Under the Union, I, 1801–70* (Oxford, Clarendon Press, 1989), pp. 193–217; R. B. McDowell, 'Administration and the Public Services, 1800–70', in Vaughan, *A New History of Ireland, V*, pp. 538–61.
5. Elizabeth Malcolm and Greta Jones (eds), *Medicine, Disease and the State in Ireland, 1650–1940* (Cork, Cork University Press, 1999), p. 1.
6. David Dickson, 'In Search of the Old Irish Poor Law', in Rosalind Mitchison and Peter Roebuck (eds), *Economy and Society in Scotland and Ireland 1500–1939* (Edinburgh, John Donald, 1988), pp. 149–59.
7. For example Michael Ignatieff, *Just Measure of Pain: The Penitentiary in the Industrial Revolution 1750–1850* (London, Macmillan, 1978); Barton L. Ingram, *Political Crime in Europe: A Comparative Study of France, Germany and England* (Berkeley, University of California Press, 1979); Victor Bailey (ed.), *Policing and Punishment in Nineteenth-Century Britain* (London, Croom Helm, 1981); David Garland, *Punishment and Modern Society* (Oxford, Oxford University Press, 1990); Norval Morris and David J. Rothman (eds), *The Oxford History of the Prison* (Oxford, New York, Oxford University Press, 1995); Michel Foucault, *Discipline and Punish: The Birth of the Prison* (New York, Random House, 1979); Séan McConville, *A History of English Prison Administration* (London, Routledge, 1981).

8. Beverly A. Smith, 'The Irish Prison System, 1854–1914: Prisoners and Political Prisoners' (PhD thesis, Miami University, 1977); Oliver MacDonagh, *The Emancipist Daniel O'Connell 1830–47* (London, Weidenfeld and Nicolson, 1989); Patrick Carroll-Burke, *Colonial Discipline: The Making of the Irish Convict System* (Dublin, Four Courts Press, 2000); William Murphy, 'The Tower of Hunger: Political Imprisonment and the Irish, 1910–1921' (PhD thesis, University College Dublin, 2007).

9. Elizabeth Dooley, 'Sir Walter Crofton and the Irish or Intermediate System of Prison Discipline', in Ian O'Donnell and Finbarr McAuley (eds), *Criminal Justice History: Themes and Controversies from Pre-Independence Ireland* (Dublin, Four Courts Press, 2003), pp. 196–213.

10. J. P. Starr, 'The Enforcement of Law and Order in Eighteenth Century Ireland' (PhD thesis, Trinity College Dublin, 1968); John-Paul McCarthy, '"In hope and fear": the Victorian Prison in Perspective', *Irish History: A Research Yearbook,1*, (Dublin, Four Courts Press, 2002), pp. 119–30.

11. Dickson, 'In Search of the Old Irish Poor Law', p. 149.

12. Carroll-Burke, *Colonial Discipline*, p. 21.

13. Carroll-Burke, *The Making of the Irish Convict System*, p. 21; David Kelly, 'The Conditions of Debtors and Insolvents in Eighteenth Century Dublin', in David Dickson (ed.), *The Gorgeous Mask: Dublin 1700–1850* (Dublin, Trinity History Workshop, 1987), pp. 98–120; Bernadette Doorley, 'Newgate Prison', in *The Gorgeous Mask*, pp. 121–31.

14. Doorley, 'Newgate Prison', p. 121.

15. Rena Lohan, 'Mountjoy Female Prison and the Treatment of Irish Female Convicts in the Nineteenth Century', in Angela Bourke, et al. (eds), *The Field Day Anthology of Irish Writing, V, Irish Women's Writings and Traditions* (Cork, Cork University Press, 2002), pp. 752–4.

16. For a discussion of the different philosophies of these reformers see Ignatieff, *Just Measure of Pain*, pp. 44–79 and for Ireland see Carroll-Burke, *Colonial Discipline*, pp. 21–60.

17. Doorley, 'Newgate Prison', pp. 122–23.

18. 50 Geo. III, c.103 (1810); for an assessment of its impact see Carroll-Burke, *Colonial Discipline*, pp. 47–8.

19. Tim Carey, *Mountjoy: The Story of a Prison* (Cork, Cork University Press, 2000).

20. Dickson, 'In Search of the Old Irish Poor Law', p. 149.

21. Dickson, 'In Search of the Old Irish Poor Law', p. 150.

22. Dickson, 'In Search of the Old Irish Poor Law', p. 151; Joseph Robins, *Lost Children: A Study of Charity Children in Ireland, 1700–1900* (Dublin, Institute of Public Administration, 1980).

23. Robins, *The Lost Children*, pp. 55–9.

24. Dickson, 'In Search of the Old Irish Poor Law', p. 155; *Eighth Report of the Inspectors General on the General State of the Prisons of Ireland*, H. C. 1830 [48] xxiv, p. 80.

25. Mary E. Daly, *The Famine in Ireland* (Dundalk, Dundalgan Press [W. Tempest], 1986); James S. Donnelly, *The Great Irish Potato Famine* (Sutton, Shroud, 2001); Peter Gray, *The Irish Famine* (London, Thames and Hudson, 1995); Christine Kinealy, *This Great Calamity: The Irish Famine 1845–52* (Dublin, Gill and Macmillan, 1994); Cormac Ó Gráda,

Black '47 and Beyond. The Great Irish Famine in History, Economy and Memory (Princeton, Princeton University Press, 1999); Cathal Póirtéir (ed.), The Great Irish Famine (Dublin, Mercier Press, 1995).

26. First, Second, Third Report of the Royal Commission on the Conditions of the Poorer Classes in Ireland, H. C. 1835 (369) xxxii, 1836 (35) xxx, 1836 (36) xxxi, 1836 (37) xxxii, 1836 (38) xxxiii, 1836 (39) xxxiv, 1836 (40) xxxiv, 1836 (41) xxxiv, 1836 (42) xxxiv, 1837 (68) xxxi, 1836 (43) xxx; First, Second, Third Report by George Nicholls on Poor Laws, Ireland, 1837 (69) li, 1837–8 (104) xxxviii, 1837 (126) xxxviii.

27. Oliver MacDonagh, 'The Economy and Society, 1830–45', in Vaughan, A New History of Ireland, V, p. 227.

28. Felix Driver, Power and Pauperism: The Workhouse System 1834–1884 (Cambridge, Cambridge Studies in Historical Geography, 1993); Gerard O'Brien, 'A Question of Attitude: Responses to the New Poor Law in Ireland and Scotland', in Mitchison and Roebuck, Economy and Society in Scotland and Ireland 1500–1939, pp. 160–70.

29. First Annual Report of the Commissioners for Administering Laws for the Relief of the Poor in Ireland, appendix B, H.C. 1847–8 [963] xxxiii, p. 153. The exceptions were Cahirciveen (17 October 1846), Castlerea (30 May 1846), Clifden (8 March 1847), Glenties (24 July 1846), Milford (10 April 1846), Swineford (14 April 1846) and Tuam (4 May 1846).

30. There are several local and national studies of the Great Famine and of workhouses. It is not possible to list them all. See Virginia Crossman, The Poor Law in Ireland 1838–1948 (Dundalk, Dundalgen Press [W. Tempest], 2006).

31. Helen Burke, The People and the Poor Law in Nineteenth Century Ireland (West Sussex, Women's Education Bureau Press, 1987), pp.130–3.

32. J. D. H. Widdess, The Richmond, Whitworth and Hardwicke Hospitals: St Laurence's Dublin, 1772–1972 (Dublin, 1972).

33. T. P. O'Neill, 'Fever and Public Health in pre-Famine Ireland', Journal of the Royal Society of Antiquaries of Ireland, 103 (1973), pp. 1–34.

34. There were numerous smaller institutions founded by different denominations which catered for members of their own faiths. These included two Quaker asylums at Donnybrook and Hampton House and three asylums at Finglas, kept by Dr. Harty, Dr. Jackson and Mr. Gregory. Documentations of such institutions is scarce and it is difficult to track their histories. There were also some private profit-making institutions. However, to adopt William Parry-Jones' phrase, there was not a 'trade in lunacy'. William Parry-Jones, The Trade in Lunacy: A Study of Private madhouses in England in the Eighteenth Century (London, Routledge and Keegan Paul, 1972).

35. Ronald Drake Cassell, Medical Charities, Medical Politics: The Irish Dispensary System and the Poor Laws (Suffolk, The Boydell Press, 1997), p. 92.

36. Ruth Barrington, Health, Medicine and Politics in Ireland 1900–1970 (Dublin, Institute of Public Administration, 1987), pp. 1–23.

37. R. S. Allison, The Seeds of Time, Being a Short History of the Belfast General and Royal Hospital, 1850–1903 (Belfast, Brough, Cox and Dunn Ltd, 1972).

38. Laurence Geary, Medicine and Charity in Ireland 1718–1851 (Dublin, University College Dublin Press, 2004), pp. 26–8; Maria Luddy, Prostitution and Irish Society 1800–1940 (Cambridge, Cambridge University Press, 2007), p. 135.

39. Geary, *Medicine and Charity*, pp. 3–40.
40. Elizabeth Malcolm, 'Hospitals in Ireland', in Bourke, et al., *The Field Day Anthology of Irish Writing, V*, p. 706.
41. Mary E. Daly, '"An Atmosphere of Sturdy Independence" The State and the Dublin Hospitals in the 1930s', in Malcolm and Jones, *Medicine, Disease and the State*, pp. 234–52.
42. Luddy, *Prostitution and Irish Society 1800–1940*, p. 77; Maria Luddy, 'Magdalen Asylums, 1765–1992', in Bourke, et al., *The Field Day Anthology of Irish Writing, V*, p. 736.
43. Lindsey Earner-Byrne, 'The Boat to England: An Analysis of the Official Reactions to the Emigration of Single Expectant Irishwomen to Britain, 1922 to 1972', *Irish Economic and Social History*, 30, (2003), pp. 52–70.
44. For example see J. D. H. Widdess, *The Charitable Infirmary, Jervis Street 1718–1987* (Dublin, 1968); T. C. P. Kirkpatrick, *History of St Steeven's Hospital, 1720–1920* (Dublin, 1924).
45. Oliver MacDonagh, *Ireland: Union and Its Aftermath* (London, George Allen and Unwin, 1977); R. B. McDowell, *The Irish Administration* (London, Routledge, 1964).
46. David Fitzpatrick, 'Ireland and the Empire', in A. Porter (ed.), *The Oxford History of the British Empire*, 3 (Oxford, Oxford University Press, 1999), pp. 499–501.
47. W. L. Burn, 'Free Trade in Ireland: An Aspect of the Irish Question', cited in Oliver MacDonagh, *Ireland: Union and Its Aftermath*, p. 33.
48. Oliver MacDonagh, *Ireland: Union and Its Aftermath*, pp. 33–52.
49. Elizabeth Malcolm, 'Asylums and other "Total Institutions" in Ireland: Recent Studies', *Past and Present*, xxii (1987), pp. 151–60.
50. Mark Finnane, *Insanity and the Insane in Post-Famine Ireland* (London, Croom Helm, 1981), p. 20.
51. David Fitzpatrick, 'Review of Patrick Carroll-Burke, *Colonial Discipline, The Making of the Irish Convict System* (Dublin, 2000)', *Irish Historical Studies*, 33 (2002), pp. 120–2.
52. Keith Jeffery (ed.), *An Irish Empire? Aspects of Ireland and the British Empire* (Manchester, Manchester University Press, 1996); Terence McDonough (ed.), *Was Ireland a Colony? Economics, Politics, and Culture in Nineteenth-century Ireland* (Dublin, Irish Academic Press, 2005); Stephen Howe, *Ireland and Empire: Colonial Legacies in Irish History and Culture* (Oxford, Oxford University Press, 2000).
53. Oliver MacDonagh, 'Ideas and Institutions', in *New History of Ireland V*, pp. 193–217; Oliver MacDonagh, *States of Mind: A Study of Anglo-Irish Conflict, 1780–1980* (London, Allen and Unwin, 1983); R. B. McDowell, *The Irish Administration*.
54. Maria Luddy, 'Religion, Philanthropy and the State in Late Eighteenth and Early Nineteenth-century Ireland' in H. Cunningham and J. Innes (eds), *Charity, Philanthropy and Reform: From the 1690s to 1850* (Basingstoke and New York: Macmillan and St Martin's Press, 1998), pp. 148–67.
55. Roy Porter, 'The Gift Relation: Philanthropy and Provincial Hospitals in Eighteenth-century England', in L. Granshaw and Roy Porter (eds), *The Hospital in History* (London, Routledge, 1989), pp. 149–78.
56. Rosemary Raughter, 'Philanthropic Institutions of Eighteenth-Century Ireland', in Bourke et al., *The Field Day Anthology of Irish Writing, V*, p. 683.

57. Geary, *Medicine and Charity*, p. 31.
58. Raughter, 'Philanthropic Institutions of Eighteenth-Century Ireland', p. 683.
59. Raughter, 'Philanthropic Institutions of Eighteenth-Century Ireland', p. 683.
60. Hilary Marland, *Medicine and Society in Wakefield and Huddersfield, 1780–1870* (Cambridge, Cambridge University Press, 1987), pp. 123–59.
61. Geary, *Medicine and Charity*, p. 15.
62. Luddy, 'Religion, Philanthropy and the State', in Cunningham and Innes, *Charity, Philanthropy and Reform: From the 1690s to 1850*, pp. 148–67.
63. Bourke, et al., *The Field Day Anthology of Irish Writing*, V.
64. Elizabeth Malcolm, 'Hospitals in Ireland', in Bourke et al., *The Field Day Anthology of Irish Writing*, V, p. 705.
65. Luddy, 'Magdalen asylums', pp. 736–51.
66. Luddy, 'Magdalen asylums', p. 736.
67. Luddy, *Prostitution and Irish Society 1800–1940*, pp. 76–123; James M. Smith, *Ireland's Magdalen Laundries and the Nation's Architecture of Containment* (Manchester, Manchester University Press, 2007).
68. Luddy, 'Magdalen asylums', p. 737.
69. Jane Barnes, *Irish Industrial Schools 1868–1908. Origins and Development* (Dublin, Irish Academic Press, 1989).
70. Tony O'Regan, *The Salthill Industrial School* (Galway, Labour History Group, 1993); Sheila Lunney, 'Institutional Solution to a Social Problem: Industrial Schools in Ireland and the Sisters of Mercy, 1869–1950' (MA thesis, University College Dublin, 1995).
71. E. P. Thompson, *The Making of the English Working Classes* (London, Pantheon Books, 1963); Roy Porter, 'Doing Medical History from Below', *Theory and Society*, 14 (1985), pp. 175–98.
72. Burke, *The People and the Poor Law*, pp. 54–61.
73. A substantial number of local studies of poor law unions and workhouses have been completed in recent years. For some examples see Christine Kinealy, 'The Workhouse Systems in County Waterford, 1838–1923', in William Nolan, Thomas P. Power and Des Cowman (eds), *Waterford History and Society* (Dublin, Geography Publications, 1992), pp. 579–96; James Grant, 'The Great Famine in County Down', in Lindsay Proudfoot and William Nolan (eds), *Down History and Society* (Dublin, Geography Publications, 1997), pp. 370–5; Patrick Durnin, 'Aspects of Poor Law Administration and the Workhouse in Derry, 1838–1948', in Gerard O'Brien and William Nolan (eds), *Derry History and Society* (Dublin, Geography Publications, 1999), pp. 537–57.
74. Gerard O'Brien, 'Workhouse Management in Pre-Famine Ireland', *Proceedings of the Royal Irish Academy, Section c*, 86 (1986), pp. 3–134.
75. Gerard MacAtasney, 'The Famine in Lurgan and Portadown', *Ulster Local Studies*, 17 (2) (1995), pp. 75–87; Gerard MacAtasney, *'This Dreadful Visitation' The Famine in Lurgan/Portadown* (Belfast, Beyond the Pale Publications, 1997), pp. 47–68.
76. Christine Kinealy, *Death-Dealing Famine: The Great Hunger in Ireland* (London, Pluto Press, 1997); MacAtasney, *'This Dreadful Visitation'*.
77. Timothy W. Guinnane and Cormac Ó Gráda, 'Mortality in the North Dublin Union During the Great Famine', *Economic History Review*, lv, 3 (2002), pp. 487–506; 'The Workhouses and Irish Famine Mortality', in Timothy Dyson

and Cormac Ó Gráda (eds), *Famine Demography: An Introduction* (Oxford, Oxford University Press, 2001), pp. 44–64.

78. Ó Gráda and Guinnane, 'The Workhouses and Irish Famine Mortality', pp. 49–53.

79. Andrés Eiríksson, *Parsonstown Union and Workhouse During the Great Famine: A Statistical Report* (Dublin, National Famine Research Project, 1996).

80. Burke, *The People and the Poor Law.*

81. Dympna McLoughlin, 'Workhouses and Irish Female Paupers 1840–70', in Maria Luddy and Cliona Murphy (eds), *Women Surviving* (Dublin, Poolbeg, 1990), pp. 119–47.

82. McLoughlin, 'Workhouses and Irish Female Paupers 1840–70'; Dympna McLoughlin, 'Workhouses' in Bourke, et al., *The Field Day Anthology of Irish Writing, V*, pp. 722–35.

83. David Fitzpatrick, 'Women and the Great Famine', in Margaret Kelleher and James H. Murphy (eds), *Gender Perspectives in Nineteenth-Century Ireland* (Dublin, Irish Academic Press, 1997), pp. 50–69.

84. Virginia Crossman, 'Viewing Women, Family and Sexuality through the Prism of the Irish Poor Laws', *Women's History Review*, 15, 4 (September, 2006), pp. 541–50.

85. Crossman, 'Viewing Women, Family and Sexuality through the Prism of the Irish Poor Laws'; Crossman, 'The New Ross Workhouse Riot of 1887: Nationalism, Class and the Irish Poor Laws', *Past and Present*, 179 (2003), pp. 135–58.

86. Anna Clarke, 'Wild Workhouse Girls and the Liberal Imperial State in the Mid-nineteenth Century Ireland', *Journal of Social History*, 39 (2005), pp. 389–409.

87. Elizabeth Malcolm, *Swift's Hospital: A History of St Patrick's Hospital, Dublin, 1746–1989* (Dublin, Gill and MacMillan, 1989) and Joseph Reynolds, *Grangegorman: Psychiatric Care in Dublin since 1815* (Dublin, Dublin Institute of Public Administration, 1992).

88. Mavis Arnold and Heather Laskey, *Children of the Poor Clares: The Story of an Irish Orphanage* (Belfast, Appletree Press, 1985).

89. M. Raftery and E. O'Sullivan, *Suffer the Little Children: The Inside Study of Ireland's Industrial Schools* (Dublin, New Island Books, 1999).

90. Dáire Keogh, '"There is no such thing as a bad boy": Fr Flanagan's Visit to Ireland, 1946', *History Ireland*, 12 (2004), pp. 29–32.

91. Diarmaid Ferriter, 'Suffer Little Children? The Historical Validity of Memoirs of Irish Childhood', in Joseph Dunne and James Kelly (eds), *Childhood and its Discontents* (Dublin, Liffey Press, 2002), pp. 69–107.

92. Maria Luddy, 'Review of *Do Penance or Perish: A Study of Magdalen Asylums in Ireland* (Oxford, 2001)', *The American Historical Review*, 110 (2005), p. 557.

93. Luddy, *Prostitution and Irish Society 1800–1940*, p. 122.

94. Frances Finnegan, *Do Penance or Perish: A Study of Magdalen Asylum in Ireland* (Oxford, Oxford University Press, 2001).

95. Oonagh Walsh, 'Lunatic and Criminal Alliances in Nineteenth-Century Ireland', in Peter Bartlett and David Wright (eds), *Outside the Walls of the Asylum: The History of Care in the Community 1750–2000* (London, The Athlone Press, 1999), pp. 132–52.

96. Mark Finanne, 'Asylums, Families and the State', *History Workshop*, 20 (1985), pp. 134–47.
97. Maria Luddy, '"Abandoned Women and Bad Characters": Prostitution in Nineteenth-century Ireland', *Women's History Review*, 6, 4 (1997), pp. 485–502.
98. Lindsey Earner-Byrne, *Mother and Child: Maternity and Child Welfare in Ireland, 1920s–1960s* (Manchester, Manchester University Press, 2007).
99. Elizabeth Malcolm, 'Asylums and Other 'Total Institutions' in Ireland', pp. 151–60; Malcolm and Jones, *Medicine, Disease and the State*, p. 3.
100. Janet Saunders, 'Institutionalised Offenders: A Study of the Victorian Institution and its Inmates with Special Reference to late Nineteenth Century Warwickshire', (PhD thesis, University of Warwick, 1983).
101. Shane Kilcommins, et al. (eds), *Crime Punishment and the Search for Order in Ireland* (Dublin, Institute of Public Administration, 2005), pp. 74–89.
102. Mary E. Daly, *The Buffer State: The Historical Roots of the Department of the Environment* (Dublin, Institute of Public Administration, 1997), p. 44.
103. William Feingold, *The Revolt of the Tenantry Local Government, 1872–1886* (Boston, Northeastern University Press, 1984).
104. Virgina Crossman, *Politics, Pauperism and Power in Late Nineteenth-century Ireland* (Manchester, Manchester University Press 2006); Crossman, *The Poor Law in Ireland 1838–1948*.

8

irish histories: gender, women and sexualities

mary mcauliffe

History writing has always been central to public debate and discourse in Ireland; from earliest times revision and reinterpretation of the past have been an essential part of the political process. Until the early twentieth century an indirect consequence of this intertwining of politics with history was the exclusion of women from the historical debate.[1]

introduction

In 1992 Margaret MacCurtain, Mary O'Dowd and Maria Luddy collaborated on 'An Agenda for Women's History in Ireland 1500–1900' published in *Irish Historical Studies*.[2] In comparison to their counterparts elsewhere, launching an agenda in 1992 may seem late; the authors of the 'agenda' do acknowledge that the 20 years prior to 1992 had seen women's history emerge as 'a major field of scholarly inquiry ... in western Europe and North America'.[3] This begs the question of where women's history stood, in Ireland, in the two or three decades prior to 1992? Margaret MacCurtain notes that 'writing women into Irish history became a subversive activity ... the universities were not ready for an innovation which, in the opinion of the historical establishment, processed neither a sound methodology nor reliable sources'.[4] Until the 1990's many of the developments in Irish Women's History research and writing took place outside the academy. Mary Cullen has detailed the many organisations and groups which developed into a 'small but important community of historians of women'.[5] These included the Feminist History Forum set up in Dublin in 1987, the Society for the History of Women (SHOW) set up by postgraduate students in

University College Dublin (UCD) in 1988, with the Irish committee of the International Federation for Research in Women's History also set up in 1989. This led to the foundation of the Irish Association for Research in Women's History,[6] which has been renamed the Women's History Association of Ireland (WHAI) and which still plays a prominent and active role in the development of women's history in Ireland today. The aim of the WHAI is to promote research into the history of women in Ireland.[7] One of its achievements was The Women's History Project, which began work in September 1997 and completed its Directory of Sources in 1999. The aim of the Project was to survey, list and publish historical documents relating to women in Ireland.[8] Along with these developments came the establishment of Women's Studies centres in several Irish universities from the early 1990s, where the research and writing of women's history came to be an essential component.

Conferences and seminars organised by the WHAI, by academic history departments and the women's studies centres allowed platforms for the academics to begin working on Irish women's history, as well as spaces for the very important debates, on the various theoretical and methodological approaches being used, to begin. It is these debates, in the context of the ongoing debates on the writing of Irish history, in general, that continue to be very important to the development and acceptance of Irish women's history in the mainstream. Prior to the mid-nineties Irish women's history received little or no attention in the theoretical debates on mainstream political, social and economic history in Ireland. The main engagement for many Irish historians was revisionism. The launching of *Irish Historical Studies* (IHS) in the late 1930s and the emergence of a new generation of Irish historians, either trained in or influenced by a more professional, scientific approach to historical research, changed the nature of Irish academic history.[9] The main focus of these professional historians was the pursuit of, as T. W. Moody puts it, a 'mental war of liberation from servitude to the myth'[10] of Irish nationalist history. This demanded a history that was 'value-free', that had been purged of 'its myths and its nationalist bias'[11] and that demanded historians have a more professional approach to historical research. Those historians who failed to base their scholarly works on primary source documents and archival research, or who demonstrated nationalist or 'celtic revivalist' tendencies in their writing, were considered outmoded and their works dismissed as biased and 'populist'.[12] The empirical research of these new historians had a narrow focus. Many were biased against the use of Irish language sources, preferring English language documents and more official government sources; most were dismissive of oral histories and folklore and their training could 'lead Irish historians to consider women as historically insignificant'.[13]

Irish historical revisionism was not without its critics. Brendan Bradshaw states that the new professionalism in Irish historiography served to 'inhibit rather than to enhance'[14] Irish history and other critics felt that the Irish revisionist approach was essentially conservative, narrow and inward looking.[15] Many of the political and economic histories produced were detailed narratives based on a close study of archival sources and allowing little room for the development of more inclusive philosophical or theoretical frameworks or, indeed, the inclusion of subaltern groups in Irish society in those narratives. MacCurtain et al. have, convincingly, argued that the very nature of this new Irish historiography was

> not only unsympathetic to incorporating the history of women but by its very nature excludes women ... [as] ... the prevailing concerns of Irish historians has been with political history ... [which] ... can rarely be in a position to incorporate the history of women.[16]

The conservatism of Irish revisionism not only insulated Irish historical research from exciting developments in the new historiographies, but also, until fairly recently, from the growing interest in and theoretical development of the discipline of Irish Women's History.

irish women's history

Second wave feminism in Ireland has its roots in 1970s and 1980s' political, social and cultural activism, particularly activisms around, among other issues, women's reproductive rights, equal pay, social housing, rights for widows and single mothers and, more broadly, cultural and creative activisms dealing with the representations of women in Ireland's past. Irish women's history grew from a concern among second wave feminists for a 'herstory' of their own – a concern stemming from the invisibility of women in Irish history which was seen as a 'product of the sexist value system'.[17] However, while second wave feminism significantly influenced the development of women's history in Ireland, there was also as strong an influence on the historians of Irish women from the 'development of Irish history as an academic discipline'.[18] Mary E. Daly argues that the primacy given by revisionists to political history is mirrored by historians of Irish women, writing, fairly exclusively at times, on Irish women's involvement in suffrage and nationalist causes. The idea that Irish history is somehow exceptional is mirrored by

the belief in the Irish female experience being markedly different as compared [and, somehow, worse!] to elsewhere because of the interaction of
issues such as post-colonialism, Irish Catholicism and an inward-looking,
conservative Irish society.[19] This influencing of women's history, with its
long development outside of, and many years spent looking for acceptance in, the academy, by the very methodologies and debates coming
from within that academy, has been mirrored elsewhere.

While the acceptance of women's history as a discipline in its own
right is to be lauded, many feminist historians feel that, once in the
academy, historians may 'succumb to the pressures to produce studies
that are palatable to their non-feminist colleagues – studies that avoid
hard feminist questions and that are seemingly more "objective" than
"political"'.[20] With the supposed entrenching of women's history within
the mainstream there is a sense of a loss of the feminist ideologies and
theories that informed many of the earlier writings. For Judith Bennett,
writing on women's history in the US in 1987, there was a need for a
new call to arms 'for historians of women to our moral vision, our political nerve, our feminist indignation'.[21] Therefore, it does not seem surprising that, in 1992, MacCurtain et al. could argue that Irish women's
history should develop outside of the mainstream; that the narrowness
of the concerns of the Irish historical tradition would actually serve to
hold back the development of Women's History in Ireland.[22] While the
dominant discourses of Irish history have to an extent excluded [and
to some degree continue to exclude] women,[23] research and writing
over the last 30 years has gone some way in redressing that imbalance.
While 'gender as a tool of analysis in Irish history has much to offer',[24]
MacCurtain et al. also struck a cautionary note in the use of gender history,[25] which has, at times, been approached by Irish historians in its
narrowest sense.[26] While they called for the broadening of the historical
base to permit the inclusion of a more gendered history, there was concern that there could be a 'tendency to misuse "gender" as a synonym
for "women", a misuse which allows the essence of gender analysis, that
sex is a social construct to be bypassed and allows men as a group to
again elude the historians scrutiny'.[27]

Other historians regard the idea of moving on from women's history
to gender history as dangerous, as many histories of women – working
class women, women of colour, lesbian women, traveller women and
emigrant women – have yet to be adequately researched and written. In
recent Irish history writing there has been a tentative acceptance that
the 'blindness of historians to gender roles and to women's historical
experience has deprived both women and men of important elements

of their past'.[28] One of the main arguments for a gender history is that women, as a group, do not necessarily, fit into accepted historical definitions, chronologies and paradigms, and while the vital undertaking of writing women back into history was and is still urgent, it has to be done in a way which allows for histories of women, both of and between themselves and in relation to men. Problematising, or indeed revisioning, the social and power relations and hierarchies which existed, the constructions of masculinities and femininities as well the almost exclusive hetronormative understanding of sexualities serves to broaden our understanding of the histories of all Irish women and men. As stated by Marilyn Cohen and Nancy Curtin 'a comprehensive analysis of Irish scholarship reveals [its] limiting empiricism particularly in history ... [and] placing gender at the centre of the feminist agenda is essential to advancing ... feminist scholarship'.[29] While these debates continue to enliven Irish women's history in particular and Irish history in general, and indeed as Irish historians of women bring their own interpretations to these debates, there exists much hope for the development of more rounded, inclusive, valid Irish histories.

early modern women

While the majority of publications on Irish women's history have concentrated on the late nineteenth and twentieth centuries there has been solid work produced on women from early modern to the late eighteenth century. In the 1992 Agenda, broad themes of interest for those researching women in the seventeenth century – including the end of Gaelic society, religious conflict, plantation, the effects of endemic warfare and the subsequent land settlements – were suggested.[30] One of the first survey books published on Irish women, Margaret MacCurtain and Donncha Ó Corrain (eds) *Women in Irish Society: The Historical Dimension* (1978), includes a chapter on 'The Role of Women in Ireland Under the New English Order' by Gearoid Ó Tuathaigh,[31] which gives us a brief, but tantalising, overview of the possibilities for research in this period – aristocratic marriage alliances, women and salons, female education, women's private and public writings, women's work outside the home, women within the family – subjects which have begun to excite the interest of both early modern and modern historians of Irish women. Margaret MacCurtain and Mary O'Dowd, *Women in Early Modern Ireland* (1991) continued with a series of 21 essays under three headings – law, politics and war, religion and education and family household and health. In the introduction MacCurtain and O'Dowd outline the possibilities and challenges of a history of early modern women in Ireland. They call for historians to 'examine the story behind the sources: their silences and their negative attitude to women. The advantages as well as the problems associated with a feminist interpretation of history need also be analysed from an Irish point of view'.[32] The 21 essays introduce the many and varied areas of interest to those studying early modern Irish women: War, politics, the law, continuing religious conflict, changing and developing marriage customs and the mixed outcomes for the position of women in the transition from Gaelic to English law in the late sixteenth and seventeenth centuries as well as the limited impact of education on 'silent and invisible' women, where their 'ability to question the female destiny in the dominant culture of patriarchy faltered as the growth of the public and private spheres trapped them in domesticity'.[33] This edited collection details the position of Irish women in a changing political, socio-economic, religious and cultural climate and provides students of that era with many and varied topics for further research.

Research and writing on early modern Irish women has yet to reach the volume of work on modern Irish women. While these articles add to this field of study, all discuss the very real problems of researching early modern Ireland, and in particular, researching women. These problems centre on the paucity of records relating to women, incomplete sources, limited anecdotal evidence and the patriarchal understanding of, and attitude, to women and their roles which are often apparent in the official records. Many historians are overcoming these drawbacks by addressing the problems inherent in this research and showing how valid the use of these, even incomplete, sources is.[34] Indeed as Margaret MacCurtain points out in Mary O'Dowd and Sabine Wichert (1995), *Chattel, Servant or Citizen: Women's Status in Church, State and Society* 'research into women's history has led to new sources being discovered'[35] and known sources being reread. Commemorations of significant historical events have also helped to bring women's participation to light. For example, the editors of *The Women of 1798* (1998), Daire Keogh and Nicholas Furlong state 'no aspect of the 1798 rebellion had been so neglected as that of the women's role in the events of that year'.[36] Subsequent to the rebellion women were rarely depicted in the histories of 1798 and if they were it was often an idealised image; the loyalist women suffering for her belief in the union, the innocent, passive murder or rape victim, the keening mourner bewailing Ireland's lost, patriotic sons. *The Women of 1798* had a stated aim of redressing this imbalance, showing that women had a full and complex role in the events of that time 'not alone as symbol, victim and observer, but as activist and combatant'.[37] Sources used are often non-traditional, including private letters, diaries and writings of women such as Mary Shackleton Leadbeater, Matilda Tone, Mary Ann McCracken[38] while images, songs, ballads and folktales illuminate the names of others who were active in 1798. *The Women of 1798* demonstrates the use of these non-official primary sources (letters, diaries, commentaries, songs, tales and folklore) and the rereading of official sources. Thomas Bartlett writes of rereading official court martial records to show women, not as the subjects (men) of the trials but in other roles, as confirming alibis, as informants, as petitioners.[39]

Mary O'Dowd's *A History of Women in Ireland, 1500–1800* (2004) is the first general survey of Irish women in the early modern period, themed under four headings (Politics, the Economy, Religion, Education and Ideas) using a huge volume of original source material and archival data relating to early modern women accessed by O'Dowd. She argues that while the life of Irish women in the seventeenth and eighteenth centuries was primarily domestic they were not totally absent from the political and economic areas. Élite women were present in parliamentary politics as political patrons, as providers of hospitality and facilitators of kinship networks. Outside of the élite, women were found in the many anti-English secret societies, many using their position as consumer to, literally, wear their politics – an early modern buy-Irish campaign! This period also saw interesting developments in the role women had in religion. Catholic and non-establishment Protestant women are shown as central to the maintaining of their faith and that of their families and communities in time of oppression. As legal sanctions on religion waned, they stepped back into the role as educator of children, while men took over the leadership roles. Her final chapter on 'Ideas' provides a fascinating account of the principles, theology and medical views that shaped early modern Irish society's understanding of women. O'Dowd shows that early modern Irish women both fit in with the theories on and life patterns and histories of European women and also differ in distinctly Irish ways. In particular she looks at the colonial context of the early modern Irish women, which leads to a history somewhat at odds with that of their English and European counterparts. While the works mentioned above have expanded our understanding of early modern Irish history, this is an era which still has many unexplored territories for women.

modern irish women

Nineteenth- and twentieth-century Ireland presents a different set of possibilities and problems of the historian of women. As Luddy stated for women 'nineteenth century Ireland [has a] ... great wealth of

material which is available for study and research'[40] but there seemed to
be 'a basic indifference on the part of most academics to the role played
by women in Irish history'.[41] Many of the suggestions for research in
the 1992 'Agenda', which include religious women and lay women in
relation to the development of philanthropy, the establishment and
growth of the convents and the role of nuns in Irish society, the suffrage movement, the involvement of women in more general political
activism, women and nationalism, women and sexuality, women and
family, women and work, class relations, women and prostitution,
women and the law, poverty, famine, education and emigration,[42] are
the very areas on which there have been, over the last two decades,
many publications. Prior to that, in 1983 Margaret Ward produced
Unmanageable Revolutionaries: Women and Irish Nationalism, which
was one of the first extended studies of the significant contribution
made by women to the nineteenth and early twentieth feminist and
nationalist struggles, from the Ladies Land League[43] to Cumann na
mBan.[44] In the same year Rosemary Cullen Owens produced *Smashing
Times: The History of the Irish Suffrage Movement 1890–1922* (1983),
and by 1988 the activism of working class women was recognised
in the publication of Mary Jones' *Those Obstreperous Lassies: the Irish
Women's Workers Union*.

These books, along with several others,[45] had begun the process of
rewriting women back into the major issues of nineteenth- and twentieth-
century Ireland, nationalism, feminism and socialism as well as religion.
While many of these scholars and historians of Irish women differed in
their use of theory and methodology and some were self-consciously
non-feminist in their theoretical approach, all of their publications
contributed to the ongoing debate on women's contribution to Irish
history. Unlike later histories these early publications are, for the most
part, uncritical of the relationship between feminism and nationalism,
a relationship subsequently perceived as quite complex. As Ward states,
the advent of suffrage activism in Ireland meant that a new discourse
of nationhood began ... [encouraging] ... politically active women to
develop a sustained critique of the political repercussions of the public and private distinctions confining then to the domestic sphere.[46]
Maria Luddy in her *Women in Ireland 1800–1918: A Documentary History*
(1995), the first major survey of original documents relating to modern
Irish women's lives, organised the collection along five central themes
that have, broadly, dominated the research and writing of nineteenth-
and twentieth-century Irish women's history: private life, education,
religion, work and politics.[47]

religion, philanthropy and rescue work

Most historians would recognise the immense contribution that the growth in women's education, participation in philanthropy and the development of female religious orders in Ireland made in expanding the involvement of Irish women in public life. As Luddy writes 'religion not only defined and limited a women's place in society ... but also, ironically opened a door on the work of work for these women willing to form and join religious communities'.[48]

Recent research on nineteenth-century religious women has looked at why women joined convents, at the work of these religious communities, the social and class relationships that existed among nuns and the power relations between the nuns and the church hierarchy. Caitriona Clear in, *Nuns in Nineteenth-Century Ireland* (1987) investigated the motivations of women joining the new religious orders. While the participation of nuns in charitable works allowed them some influences Clear argues that their contribution to the modernisation of the Irish church has not been undervalued: because of their subordinate position within the church hierarchy, their contribution was modest. In *Women and Philanthropy in Nineteenth-Century Ireland* (1995) Luddy discusses the sectarianism that dominated the involvement of women in nineteenth-century philanthropy: unlike elsewhere in Europe, Irish Catholic women involved in philanthropy were mostly in religious orders, especially from the 1850s onwards, whereas non-Catholic philanthropy was conducted by lay women who were not under any specific clerical control. Many of the advances in legislative improvements effecting women came from the work of these non-conformist women, some of whom were later involved in suffrage activism. Luddy's publication is one of the first to show the wide range of sources which can be accessed by the historian of Irish women; she uses the reports and records of the many charitable organisations she studied as well as convent archives, diocesan records, private letters and journals, to detail the lives and work both of the nuns and female philanthropists and, also, those women whose lives, morals and 'disreputable' activities were the root cause of their work.

Continuing on the work of Clear, Luddy and others Mary Peckham Magray's *The Transforming Power of the Nuns: Women Religion and Cultural Change in Ireland, 1750–1900* (1998) argues that convent subordination to the church hierarchy did not occur until the latter half of the nineteenth century. Prior to this Peackham Magray writes, Irish nuns can be read as radical innovators of social change in Ireland; convents were initiated mainly by the women themselves and these convents had more autonomy from episcopal authority that previously thought; it was the succeeding generations of nuns who, in the later nineteenth century, lost their struggles for autonomy with the church hierarchy. By then as Luddy states, the

> nuns were at a double disadvantage, as females in a church which does not allow women any say in decisions about faith and morals ... and as women without votes in a society where parliamentary politics were becoming increasing popular.[49]

Research in this area has also shown how philanthropy was gendered, as women were often both the 'service' providers and those who accessed or were forced into 'using' these services, while the leadership roles on committees, the decisions on the rules and regulations, and decisions on the use of the monies were taken by men. Interestingly while the asylums, the lock hospitals and the workhouses were indeed grim, forbidding, severely moralistic and regulatory, Luddy, McLoughlin, Blair and others have shown that women could and did use the system to better their lives. Through the nineteenth century, women entered and left the asylums seemingly at will, sometimes when faced with unexpected pregnancies or at times of stress and trouble, while others used the emigration schemes organised by boards of guardians of workhouses to leave Ireland and find new, and hopefully, better lives for themselves in America, Canada and Australia.[50]

One of the other areas of interest to historians is that there is the intersection of lay and religious women, of the most 'pure and chaste' women in Irish society with those women considered the most sinful and 'fallen', which is in rescue work. Through the late eighteenth and into the nineteenth century the idea of institutional care to help, regulate or confine 'disreputable' women became accepted. Magdalen Asylums, the first of which was set up in 1766,[51] developed and proliferated over the next century. These institutions, run, initially, by lay women, but falling under the control of the female religious orders as the century progressed, were for 'fallen women'. They provided for the confinement and containment of these women, removing them from public view and rendering them invisible to an Irish society which considered the respectability and purity of women an essential component of its well-being. Recent publications in this area include Maria Luddy's authoritative study *Prostitution and Irish Society, 1800–1940* (2007). In the nineteenth and twentieth centuries female sexuality, particularly

unregulated female sexuality, was a threat to the state, to national
(Irish) identity, to the moral standing of women and indeed, a threat
to the health, mental, physical and spiritual, of men. Prostitutes were
'encouraged' to reform and repent. That naming (as prostitute) was, as
Luddy shows, used to an elastic degree, so much so as to often include
single, unregulated women, unmarried mothers and sometimes, suffragettes. Their repentance, in the Magdalen laundries, was through
silence, contemplation, prayer and hard work. How Irish society dealt
with and continues to deal with the existence of these 'fallen women'
and the Magdalen asylums is dealt with by James H. Smith's *Ireland's
Magdalen Laundries and the Nation's Architecture of Containment* (2008).
Because many of the religious orders who ran the laundries have not
opened their archives, Smith argues that the history of the asylums
cannot be as yet fully written. Our understanding of the women who
were incarcerated is refracted more through story, literature, film and
witness/survivor stories. The change in the ideology of the asylums in
the twentieth century, from reformative to punitive is however 'evidence that the church and state colluded in facilitating the confinement
of these women ... [and] generations of women were abandoned to
asylums that operated under a penitential regime of prayer silence and
self-effacement'.[52]

women and suffrage

Morality, containment and regulation, as well as educational advancement and, increasingly, public roles in rights campaigns and nationalism
(and indeed unionism) were elements of Irish women's involvement in
suffrage. As well as achieving the parliamentary franchise, issues which
engaged women in the nineteenth and early twentieth century were
access to education for girls, morality and temperance crusades, opposition to the Contagious Diseases Acts and the struggle for women's role
in local government. From the mid-nineteenth century to the foundation of the Irish Free State in 1922 women played vitals roles in cultural
and political nationalism, in trade unionism, in the literary revival as
well as in feminism. Much has been made of the tensions between
women's involvement in nationalism and feminism but this tends to
obscure the fact that many women were involved in both. As Ruth
Tallion found from her research[53] the fact that equality was promised
in the Proclamation of Independence, 1916,[54] came more from the visible involvement of women in public organisations like the IWWU, the
IWFL[55] and Cumann na mBan than from the fact that James Connolly

was a farsighted feminist. There have been several recent publications
which detail women's contribution to the social, cultural and political
landscape of the first decades of the twentieth century. In finding these
women and rewriting them back into the historical record, historians
continue to expand the sources used to give voice to these women: official records, military statements, court records, newspapers, including
newspapers produced by the women activists, *Bean na hÉireann* and *The
Irish Citizen*,[56] private letters and diaries, pamphlets, political writings,
autobiographies, oral histories, poetry and plays etc. These publications include historical surveys and edited collections such as Ward,
Unmanageable Revolutionaries (1987), Rosemary Cullen Owens, *Smashing
Times: A History of the Irish Women's Suffrage Movement, 1889–1922*
(1984), Sinead McCoole, *No Ordinary Women; Irish Female Activists in the
Revolutionary Years* (2003), Louise Ryan and Margaret Ward (eds), *Irish
Women and Nationalism; Soldiers, New Women and Wicked Hags* (2004),
Rosemary Cullen Owens, *A Social History of Women in Ireland* (2005),
Cal MacCarthy, *Cumann na mBan and the Irish Revolution* (2007), Karen
Steele, *Women, Press and Politics During the Irish Revival* (2007) as well
as the many biographies and autobiographies produced on or by the
women involved in this period. Previously unseen private correspond-
ence, diaries, letters and family records, interwoven by historians with
the social and political context in which these women operated, are
used to give historical agency to 'forgotten' women, such as in Hilary
Pyle's *Red-headed Rebel: Susan L. Mitchell; Poet and Mystic of the Irish
Cultural Renaissance* (1998) and her *Cesca's Diary 1913–1916: Where Art
and Nationalism Meet* (2006). Oral histories have also added much to
the record of women's involvement in Irish history, see John Cowell,
A Noontime Blazing; Brigid Lyons Thornton, Rebel, Soldier, Doctor (2005).
Cowell spent many hours interviewing Dr. Brigid Thornton (the only
women officer in the Free State Army) before, as she stated, she took her
story 'to the grave with me', as so many women have done before her,
because 'nobody'd be interested'.[57]

For the history of feminism in Ireland, Cliona Murphy's *The Women's
Suffrage Movement and Irish Society in the Early Twentieth Century* (1989)
is a good introduction and Louise Ryan's *Irish Feminism and the Vote: An
Anthology of the Irish Citizen Newspaper 1912–1920* (1996) is one of the
best collection of sources for the Irish suffrage movement. However,
as Carmel Quinlan's *Genteel Revolutionaries: Anna and Thomas Haslam
and the Irish Women's Movement* (2002) demonstrates, Irish suffrage has
a long nineteenth-century history as well, albeit one that was middle
class, urban and mostly Protestant. From the 1870s, Anna and Thomas

Haslam, a Quaker couple, had been active in campaigning for women's suffrage, publishing a series of pamphlets in 1874 entitled *The Women's' Advocate*. In 1876 Anna Haslem formed the Dublin Women's Suffrage Society, which after a number of name changes became the Irish Women's Suffrage and Local Government Association (IWSLGA) in 1901. These early organisations had some victories, most notably with the granting of the vote to women in local government elections under the Local Government Act of 1898. Many of these women also campaigned on other social issues including sexual morality, improvement of educational opportunities for girls, protection and reform for women involved in prostitution, right to involvement and protection in the workplace and involvement in political decision making, as well as access to financial independence. Louise Ryan and Margaret Wards (eds), *Irish Women and the Vote; Becoming Citizens* (2007), deals with many of the above issues as well as expands our knowledge of the Irish suffrage women. They demonstrate that the Irish suffragettes were not adverse to the use of humour in their campaigns, and could be as militant as their English sisters when they used the hunger strike as a weapon. As William Murphy points out James Connolly used the hunger strike during the 1913 Lockout because he [Connolly] 'insisted "What was good enough for the suffragettes to use … is good enough for us"'.[58] The contributors to *Irish Women and the Vote* present detailed analyses of the complexity of the suffrage movement in Ireland, moving away from the idea that enfranchisement was the sole purpose of suffrage. Ward and Ryan et al. demonstrate the layered and extensive feminist involvement in issues ranging from vegetarianism, trade unionism, literary and cultural revival, sexual morality, campaigns against sexual abuse and domestic violence to conflicting feminist viewpoints on involvement in the First World War and, of course, in nationalism.

irish women and nationalism

Irish women's involvement in nationalism, the Easter Rising (1916), the War of Independence (1981–21) and the Civil war (1921–2) are areas which have received quite a lot of attention from historians in the past two decades. From general surveys to biographies and autobiographies the history of women's involvement in this fascinating period is perhaps the fullest we have for any period of Irish history. By 1916 women had shown that they were more than capable of organising and leading political campaigns: from the Ladies Land League in 1881, to Inghinidhe na hÉireann, set up by Maud Gonne in 1900, and the IWFL

(1908), to the IWWU (1911) and on to Cumann na mBan founded in 1914. They were not involved in the central planning of the Easter Rising but, as Sinead McCoole writes in *No Ordinary Women* (2003) there were female participants in each one of the rebel outposts, except Boland's Mill where Eamon deValera did 'not want women untrained for soldiering'.[59] In *Female Activists: Irish Women and Change 1900–1960* (2001), edited by Mary Cullen and Maria Luddy, the lives and activities of seven women who campaigned on the most significant issues of twentieth-century Ireland, Louise Bennett, Helena Moloney, Mary Galway, Hannah Sheehy Skeffington, Kathleen Lynn, Rosamond Jacob and Margaret Cousins, are detailed. While these women differed in their approach to politics, some were militant, some nationalist, some more interested in literary pursuits, there was one salient commonality among them, besides their friendship. It was that their personal circumstances allowed their life-long activism as 'most were unencumbered with a husband and children'.[60]

Some of the women involved in 1916 have garnered multiple biographies, such is the controversy of their fame. Countess Markievicz, socialist, nationalist, feminist and Anglo-Irish aristocrat, remains a woman who seems to engender both deep affection and admiration or implacable hatred. Yeats labelled her 'shrill' and several historians have tended to agree with this label. Ruth Dudley Edwards in her contribution to the Radio series and subsequent book *Speaking Ill of the Dead* (2007) does a hatchet job on the countess whom, she says, was a snob, fraud, show-off, neglectful of her own child and a murderer of an unarmed police constable during the Rising; she may have been a beauty, but it was all style and no substance.[61] She is aided and abetted in the modern-day demonisation of the Countess by columnist Kevin Myers, whose occasional polemics on the murderous, cowardly nature of the Countess serve to keep the controversy alive. Her first biographer was Sean O'Faolain who penned *Constance Markievicz, or The Average Revolutionary* in 1934. He brought up the neglect of her child Maeve, when he wondered if it was fair to compare her

> love for all mankind in general (except, alas, the English), and her love for the Irish people in particular, with her ruinous personal relations with her own family, her husband and her only child, whom she virtually abandoned as a baby?[62]

These comparisons, he said, were not to demean the Countess but to give a broad picture of her character. She is later served by biographies from Anne Marreco, *The Rebel Countess: The* Life *and Times of Constance Markievicz* (1967), *Jacqueline* Van Voris, *Constance de Markievicz: Her Fight for the Liberation of Ireland and Women* (1972), Diana Norman, *Terrible Beauty: A Life of Constance Markievicz, 1868–1927* (1987), Anne Haverty, *Constance Markievicz: Irish Revolutionary* (1993) and Joe McGowan, *Constance Markievicz: The People's Countess* (2003). Haverty refutes the charge of murdering the constable and both Haverty and Norman produce sympathetic biographies of the Countess. With these multiple biographies is there anything new to add about Constance Markievicz? Both her supporters and detractors seem to think so, that there is in her participation in cultural nationalism, her copious writings, her nationalist plays, the problematic issue of her maternal nature, her militancy and the nature of her relationship with her pacifist sister Eva Gore-Booth among other issues a demand for further research and analysis of her life and activities.

With the elections of 1918 where Sinn Féin was triumphant due, in no small part, to the first-time women voters, six women were elected and Markievicz was appointed the Minister for Labour in the first Irish Dáil. Women's relationship with republicanism, with the fight for Irish freedom and with the state created by the Anglo-Irish Treaty is much more complex than most historians have yet analysed. One of the problematic issues is the insistence by many women, particularly those in Cumann na mBan, that the women had been auxiliaries, cheer leaders, fund raisers and healers rather than leaders. One female activist of the time, Jenny Wyse Power, understood that the men went to fight while the women cheered despite the fact that over 200 women were 'out' in 1916, functioning as messengers (Julia Grenan), nurses, leaders (Markievicz in the College of Surgeons and Kathleen Lynn in City Hall), negotiating the terms of surrender (Elizabeth O' Farrell) and sniping (Margaret Skinnider). During the War of Independence the participation of women in what was essentially a guerrilla war was different but, nevertheless, essential. Women provided the safe houses, hid and transported the guns, carried dispatches, spied on the RIC, the Black and Tans and the Auxiliaries. However, once the truce was declared and the Anglo-Irish Treaty negotiated (there were no women on the treaty delegation, a fact which did not bode well for the political future of Irish women), the public positioning of women was to change rapidly and radically.

The time between the treaty debates through the civil war to the firm establishment of the Irish Free State is a complex period in the envisioning of modern Irish women. Cumann na mBan members are often written as the most implacable foes of the treaty and the main cause of the Civil War. The women members of the Dáil are often represented as hysterical, fanatic and bitter. They were most often the voices who spoke for the dead patriots, a fact which allowed them little room to accept a treaty which gave a truncated 26-counry Free State, instead of a 32-county Republic for which their son, fathers and husbands had shed their blood and given their lives.[63] Jason Knirck's *Women of the Dáil: Gender, Republicanism and the Anglo-Irish Treaty* (2007) examines the arguments which deal with the positioning of women in politics in the new Irish Free State and the reasons why women were soon excluded from the centre of Irish politics, despite their immense contribution to the republican cause. Many of the women who were members of the Dáil were there because of their association with dead patriots. None of these women were really representative of those women who had been active in politics prior to 1922–3. The demands of the female government members for equality and full citizenship based on their contribution to the republican cause was not one the suffrage women had made, but now, at least, the republican women were looking for their own rights as women. However this proved to be an impossible task. Mary Cullen writes that many women were encouraged to continue in Cumann na mBan rather than join their local Sinn Féin cumann; Sinn Féin denied there was any sex bar, although Hanna Sheehy Skeffington 'acknowledged that sex antagonism was a factor. Sinn Féin did not welcome women'.[64] Ward argues that despite the valiant efforts of these women to 'claim agency.... mainstream nationalism.... [remained] as heavily gendered ... as prior to the First World War'.[65] Maryann Valiulis acknowledges that the positioning of women as 'a living vessel through which the dead may speak'[66] deprived them of any independence of though and action and allowed the masculinisation of Irish politics and the highly gendered nature of the Irish Free State to grow. On the other hand Knirck sees that the women of the early Dáil used their role as 'Speaker for the Dead' to carve out a legitimate revolutionary role for themselves. However as the pro-treaty politicians sought to undermine the claims of the Republicans, the conflation of women and extreme republicanism was ultimately to undermine the position of women at the centre of Irish politics; with 'these furies', as P. S. O' Hegarty called the political women, 'there would be no peace'.[67] Knirck's argument is that the women 'consistently positioned themselves as the very embodiment of the Irish republican tradition, both before and after the treaty'[68] which triggered a 'gendered' response from a hostile pro-treaty government and ultimately lead to the slow but steady removal of women from the centre of politics in Ireland in the 1920s and 1930s. This argument, while interesting, does remove agency from women, there is no sense from Knick's work that women wanted a society any different from that on offer. We see nothing of Markievicz's visioning of a socialist republic or the attempt by women to have the franchise issue (to give women between the ages of 21 and 30 the vote) resolved before the treaty debates. This was according to Knirck, an attempt by women to wreck the treaty rather than, as Ward suggests, an active attempt on the part of women to be allowed their full say in the future of the country, considering their full participation in the fight to achieve that country.[69]

women in ireland, 1922–72

This debate may continue but ultimately repeated legislation 'on the part of successive Free State governments [served] to define women out of politics'.[70] Women were most decidedly and successfully positioned in the home. The contributors to *Women and Irish History; Essays in Honour of Margaret MacCurtain* (1997) provide interesting analyses of the position of women in the post-1922 period. Valiulis focuses on the restrictions imposed on women serving on juries, despite feminist demands for full and equal citizenship which included the civil right of the citizen to be tried by a jury of his or *her* peers. However by using the argument of gender difference, whereby the unique abilities (of nurturing and caring) inherent in women were what would made their contribution to juries valuable, feminist 'weakened women's ability to withstand the onslaughts of the 1920s and 1930s'.[71] The focus for women changes quite dramatically in the 1920s and 1930s. Physical and spiritual exhaustion from the vicissitudes of the wars of the previous decades left many women unable and unwilling to continue the fight. However, as Caitriona Beaumont notes there were still issues around which women organised. While the Irish Free State was creating the identity of women as wives and mothers (or perhaps as nuns), women were, themselves, making some choices. Beaumont shows that, despite the culture of female domesticity, feminists consistently challenged the State's attempts to undermine full citizenship for women, and indeed, they scored some notable victories, including the amendment of the 1927 Juries Act. Organisations such as the Irish Housewives Association (IHA), set up in 1942, and the Irish Countrywomen's Association (ICA) (evolving from United Irishwomen set up in 1910), although ideologically non-feminist, campaigned for better conditions for women within the home. Mary E. Daly in her 1997 essay, '"Turn on the Tap": The State, Irish Women and Running Water', argues that the lack of government urgency to provide running water for the homes, compared with the urgent and well subsidised provision of electricity for businesses and farms, shows the distinct gendered nature of the Irish government's modernisation project.[72] Water was essential to the work of women at home, yet this work was invisible to state agencies, whereas electrical power was essential to modern businesses, which were men's work. This neglect amply demonstrates that State's lack of care for women, its ignoring of their contribution to the State by their work in the home and their important, but invisible, role in the modernisation of Ireland.

Joanna Bourke's *Husbandry to Housewifery: Women, Economic Change and Housework in Ireland 1890–1891* (1993) details the changes in women's work in Ireland and the effects statutory bodies such as Congested Districts Board, the Irish Agricultural Organisation Society founded in 1894 and later, the Department of Agriculture and Technical Instruction founded in 1899, had on the positioning of women in 'enforced housewifery', although as Ciara Breathnach states it 'was a combination of modernisation and the increasing opposition of the clergy to paid female employment that enforced housewifery on Irish females' rather than, solely, the combined efforts of the organisations above.[73] Bourke, however, does argue that a combination of government agencies, education, moral teaching and laws positioned women at the hearth in order to promote the ideal of the happy family, stem emigration and open employment solely for men. In *Women of the House; Women's Household Work in Ireland 1922–1961* (2000) Caitriona Clear uses traditional and non-traditional sources, including oral history, pamphlets, advice books, women's magazines and government records to analyse how Irish politicians, female activists and writers regarded the work of these housewives. She demonstrates how the IHA lobbied for a school lunch programme and were attacked in some quarters as being a communist front for doing so, while the ICA promoted education about better nutrition among its members. Most of these organisations campaigned for a recognition of the valuable contribution women made to Irish society, by recognising the importance of motherhood and demanding that women have full legal equality at home. The Marriage Bar was one of the pieces of legislation which defined the gendered nature of the State. Precedence and entitlement in the public sphere was given to men, and it was demanded, legally and morally, that women confine their duties to their homes. Their roles as wives, their reproductive capabilities, motherhood and child care were the duties which defined women in

Irish society. As Eileen Connolly writes, the gender regime of the pre-1970s' Irish State contained four key elements, 'a strong emphasis on gender difference; the hierarchical ranking of male and female; a clear division between the public sphere and the private/domestic sphere; and the subjugation of the individual rights within the family'.[74]

While the State firmly recognised, as least in spirit, the invaluable contribution of women to Ireland, successive governments discriminated against women in many and varied ways, to the point of denying the Irish woman the full and equal citizenship promised to her in the Proclamation of Independence of 1916. While the constitution may have promoted women's position and rights as wives and mothers (something members of the IHA and ICA supported) it undermined women's right to a visible presence in the workforce and the body politic. Many women's organisations[75] opposed these articles of the Constitution; Hanna Sheehy Skeffington called it a 'fascist model' and felt that its enactment would 'regulate women to permanent inferiority'.[76] Luddy notes that the inclusion of these articles in the Constitution directly affected the type of political activism women were involved in from the 1940s onwards, leading to an increased emphasis on the rights of wives and mothers, a situation which continued until the advent of second wave feminism in Ireland.

second wave feminism

The 1960s and 1970s mark a period of rapid social and economic change in Irish society, with more women entering the workforce; the stranglehold on Irish social mores by the Catholic Church was loosening, censorship was being scaled back and news from emigrant daughters, radio and television was opening women's minds to a new world. Linda Connolly's *The Irish Women's Movement: From Revolution to Devolution* (2003) details four clear periods in the history of Irish feminism from 1922 to the present: abeyance, advancement, reappraisal and new directions. Connolly does not see that there was any rupture between the feminism of the early twentieth century and the second wave of the 1970s, she argues that feminists were there, although in abeyance, working behind the scenes, leading on in time to the second wave. The second wave in the 1970s was the period of an advancement; a reappraisal (rather that a backlash) happened in the late 1980s and the new directions, adapting to new challenges (an Irish third wave!) allowed feminism to be part of future Irish society. Using social movement and postcolonial theory, history and a feminist lens, Connolly provides an understanding of a more continuous, embedded feminist history in the nineteenth and twentieth centuries. There was, she argues evidence that 'since the nineteenth century the women's movement in Ireland has always been sustained by a core cadre of highly motivated feminist activists, devising strategies appropriate to the socio-political environment.'[77]

In *Documenting Irish Feminisms: The Second Wave* (2005) Connolly and Tina O'Toole provide a detailed account of the development of second wave feminism in Ireland. This book was the end result of a research project entitled *The Irish Women's Movement*, which was established in the Sociology Department at University College Cork in 1999. Connolly and O'Toole look at the various social, political and cultural activisms of women in Ireland, ranging from contraception, abortion and reproductive rights, family law, social policy, feminism and the State, cultural feminism [which played its part in the development of Irish women's history], lesbian feminism, the rights of unmarried mothers, working class women and the growth of women's studies in the academy. The sources for research were the archives of the many socio-political groups which were active from the 1970s and earlier, from the archives of the ICA, to the papers of Hilda Tweedy, founder of the IHA, to the collections of the Irish Queer Archive and papers of individuals involved in second wave feminism. Also included are interesting case studies of the people or events which were markers of the 1970s–1990s in Ireland (for example, the teenage Ann Lovett dying while giving birth in a grotto in Granard, Joanne Hayes and 'The Kerry Babies' case), while the inclusion of the manifestoes and charters of many of the early feminist organisations makes for fascinating reading. The many struggles women faced are detailed here: the several referenda on abortion, on divorce, campaigns for the legalisation of contraceptives, campaigns for the rights of unmarried mothers, widows, deserted wives, adequate social housing, the right to full participation in the workplace, equal pay, better access to education, campaigns against violence against women, improvement in the laws around rape, domestic violence and sexual abuse.

There have been immense changes for women in Irish society in the last three decades. Women are now a slight majority in the workforce, the Irish government has enshrined into law one of the most enlightened equality legislations in Europe, contraception and divorce are available and legal, homosexuality has been decriminalised, social and affordable housing is seen as a right for all, the dominance of the Catholic Church over the bodies of women is much altered, the double standard in sexual morality has changed – and yet there are still gender inequalities in Irish society. Pat O'Connor (1998) *Emerging Voices: Women in Contemporary Irish Society* details both the huge changes for women and the battles which still need to be fought. Women may be in the workforce but many are at the lower levels of pay and responsibility, women still carry the main responsibility for childcare and housework, the issue of abortion remains highly emotive and abortion is unavailable in Ireland and the ideology of the family and women's place within it is still embedded in the Irish Constitution.[78] While she seems to regard that activism by feminists was essentially confined to urban, middle class women she does acknowledge that cultural feminism did have an impact on Irish society. Perhaps the history of the second wave feminist movement and its position as a significant player in social, political, economic and cultural change in modern Ireland still needs to be written. Ursula Barry (ed.) *Where are We Now? New Feminist Perspectives on Women in Contemporary Ireland* (2008) looks at the many, positive, changes which have been effected for women in Irish society and details, also, the inequalities in power, economic independence, social justice for minority women, childcare issues and safety and protection for all women which still need to be addressed.

women and sexuality

In 1992 Luddy states that 'we know very little about the sexual activity of Irishwomen'[79], and while that statement is somewhat untrue today, sexuality is still an area of invisibility, especially for women in Irish history. Tom Inglis notes that modern Ireland has brought an 'ongoing struggle between the taken for granted "traditions" and newly emerging ... system which had very different understanding of women and sex'.[80] The identities of the 'respectable' women and the sexually deviant 'bad' woman have been altered utterly. Perhaps the dying stings of the 'old, traditional' Ireland can be seen, as Inglis, shows in the demonisation of women like Joanne Hayes in 1984.[81] All charges of infanticide against Hayes were eventually dropped but the case galvanised the country for months. Once the body of a murdered baby was found in Kerry the local Gardaí[82] focused their investigation on any sexually transgressive women, those women outside of 'proper' relationships, women who had broken romances, those known to be having affairs, those who married because of pregnancy. The Tribunal Judge in his report declared that it was Joanne Hayes who was to blame for finding herself in trouble, her fault for having an affair with a married man, her fault for 'doing away with her baby', which he saw as all part of the moral decay happening in 'modern' Ireland.[83] For Inglis, the Kerry Babies case shows the close connection between morality and the law; this connection had been exercised over women's bodies for centuries in Ireland. Throughout modern Irish history, Irish women's sexuality has been an exercise in contradiction, the virgin/whore, the seductive temptress and the pure guardian of public and private morality. The church recommended the figure of the Virgin Mary as the role model for Irish women; she was the ideal woman/mother, passive, self-sacrificing, nurturing and wholly unconnected with sex or sexuality. Until the 1960s Ireland was constructed as socially conservative, traditional and rural. Women were idealised as desexualised married mothers or asexual nuns. Those who did not fit these ideals, the unmarried pregnant woman, the prostitute and the sexually deviant were punished and removed from society's view – as the unregulated diseased female was an immense danger to the moral fibre of men and women and needed to be excised. The culture of female sexual immorality and containment is a subject which has exercised the scholars of the twentieth century. The punitive punishments for heterosexual transgressions, the constant surveillance of female and, to an extent, male sexuality and the constraining of 'respectable' women to conform to appropriate ideal [non]sexual behaviours are well documented.[84] Other areas which are beginning to receive notice from scholars include censorship and sexuality, sex education, pregnancy, childbirth, sexualities within marriage, celibacy and the private and public realms of sexuality.[85]

For many in Ireland sexuality meant, simply, either heterosexual, procreative married sex, or transgressive heterosexual behaviours outside of marriage rendering all other sexualities invisible. Invisibility does not mean absence, however. One of the interesting aspects of Peckham Magray's *The Transforming Power of Nuns* (1998) is her chapter on the nature of 'particular friendships' among nuns, which she states were 'homosocial, intensely homoemotional and, at times, homoerotic relationships'.[86] Yvonne McKenna in her study of Irish nuns also deals with the issue; she writes that particular friendships 'were forbidden since nothing is more contrary to the chastity and union which must reign in a religious house'.[87] These rules tacitly acknowledged the existence of various female sexualities; as McKenna writes they 'offered a discourse of sexuality in which the existence ... of heterosexuality, lesbian sexuality, and autoeroticism were often referred to in veiled or less-veiled terminology'.[88]

Several publications in the recent decade have begun to redress the imbalance on the history of women and sexuality in Ireland. Maryann

Gialanella Valiulis and Anthony Bradley (eds) *Gender and Sexuality in Modern Ireland* (1997) began the process of integrating discussions of sexuality into the broader social historical analysis of modern Ireland. However one of the absences, which occurs again and again, in the few discourses on women's sexuality in Ireland is that of female same-sex desire. Eibhear Walshe's *Sex, Nation and Dissent in Irish Writing* (1997) explores the constructions of Irish identities from a lesbian and gay perspective. In the introduction Walshe touches on some of the problems of writing lesbian history in Ireland. He notes that biographers will sometime try [too hard] to defend their subjects against the charge of sexual abnormality.[89] He outlines the case of Gifford Lewis' double biography of Somerville and Ross and Victoria Glendinning's study of Elizabeth Bowen. Lewis, while accepting that Edith Somerville and Ross (Violet Martin) were 'lifelong friends', cannot see them as the life partners that they named themselves.[90] Glendinning has similar problems with the lesbian or bisexual experiences in the life of Elizabeth Bowen. Lewis also spent a long time in the Introduction to her double biography of Eva Gore-Booth and her lifelong companion Esther Roper establishing, what she considered, the non-sexual nature of their friendship.

More recently the suspect relationships of women, many of whom are now well known historical figures because of their involvement in feminism, nationalist or other activism have been either ignored or deliberately obscured. In her 2008 biography of Ella Young, Rose Murphy declares that Young's probable lesbianism is irrelevant and that she [Murphy] would not look 'her life through a contrived lesbian-feminist lens'[91] as if lesbian history can only be written through a lesbian-feminist lens. Twice more Murphy mentions Young's lesbianism: she writes that a lesbian 'lifestyle' would have been unacceptable in Victorian Ireland, and later she hints that while Young may have had an awareness of her sexual orientation, generally there is an 'unsurprising' silence 'given the time she lived in' about her sexual preferences.[92] Given the time she lived in (1867–1956) it is surprising that Murphy expected a mention about anything concerning Young's sexuality. Women, especially unmarried women, of Young's class were not supposed to be sexual in any way. Dismissing Young's lesbianism (and it is obvious that Murphy accepts Young was a lesbian), because it is not written of in any diaries or letters, is, unfortunately, something that happens too often when historians are themselves uncomfortable with their subjects' sexuality. The writing of the history of women's sexuality in Ireland is in its infancy. The methodologies, theoretical approaches, historical practices and new directions which have been debated among the historians of sexuality over the past 20 years need to be engaged with in the Irish context. Social history often includes the study of marginalised groups, and the 'twice marginal, twice invisible'[93] status of lesbian women in Ireland deserves serious redressing.

conclusion

This general overview of research and writing on women in Irish history has been surprising, in that more has been happening in this area of research than had been previously thought. In putting together a list of publications on women it was surprising to note that there are, now, upwards of a dozen books a year appearing which can be catalogued as Women's History or Gender history. Given the huge volume of publication on mainstream Irish history this may not seem like a lot, but it is certainly more than had been anticipated. Within these publications, there are themes which do receive most of the attention; the main focus is on the nineteenth and twentieth centuries, with the period 1850–1920 commanding a large portion of the energies of these scholars. The Suffrage Movement, women and Nationalism, the sexual repression and containment of women, religious women, philanthropic women, women and colonialism, women and imperialism, women and education, morality crusades and women activism around equality and civil rights are some of the areas which have been studied in close detail. All of these themes have added to our understanding of women in Irish history, but it is an uneven concentration and there are areas of women's lives and histories which still demand attention. One of the most outstanding is, sexuality or indeed the broader focus of sexualities. Historians also need to integrate issues such class, ethnicity, (more recently, race), region (urban/rural, north/south) into their studies. We also need to ask questions of received categories of historical experience, these, until now, have been based on the histories of men, how and where do women fit? Bennett would suggest that we create our own historiography, 'centred on the crucial question of the endurance of patriarchy', and make feminism central to women's history[94] while Cohen and Curtin suggest that we need a more gendered perspective, albeit one informed by feminist consciousness, to understand the 'constructions of masculinities and femininities as well as the transformative and transgressive dynamics within gendered systems of power and social organisation'.[95]

Theory and methodology are at a developmental phase in Irish women's history. Some practitioners outline their various theoretical frameworks – ranging from feminist, to gender analysis, to postcolonial, to sociological – but there has been no real interactive, ongoing, consistent discussion among those who work on women's or gender history. These debates would add immensely not only to the value of Irish women's history but also to its practice. Research and writing on Irish women has, without doubt, influenced history writing in Ireland. General history surveys such as Diarmuid Ferriter's (2004) *The Transformation of Ireland 1900–2000* explores the more traditional socio-political concerns of Irish history alongside previously marginalised subject areas, families, women, children, the rural poor and the socially marginalised. Roy Foster's (2007) *Luck and the Irish: A Brief history of Change 1970–2000* also deals with the changing position of women in Irish society. The use of non-traditional primary sources to find women's lives and voices is also an element of women's history that is becoming more acceptable within the academy. Mary Muldowney in *The Second World War and Irish Women: An Oral History* (2007) interviewed over 20 women and used their narratives to analyse the experiences of Irish women, in relation to class, religion, work and identity in 1940s' Britain. In using gender as an analytical tool, historians are bringing a feminist lens to the analyses of Irish histories and are beginning to contest traditional methods of research and reassess existing historical certainties. The project of writing women back into Irish history, in whatever form and despite its sometimes marginalised position in the academy, is here to stay and can only become more influential and more inclusive in the coming decades.

notes

1. Mary O'Dowd, 'Interpreting the Past: Women's History and Women Historians 1840–1945' *The Field Day Anthology of Irish Writing, Volume V: Irish Women's Writing and Traditions* Angela Bourke, Siobhan Kilfeather, Maria Luddy et al. (Cork, Cork University Press, 2002), p. 1102.
2. Mary O'Dowd, Margaret MacCurtain and Maria Luddy, 'An Agenda for Women's History in Ireland, 1500–1900', *Irish Historical Studies*, vol. XXVII, no. 109, May 1992 MacCurtain and O'Dowd dealt with 1500–1800 and Luddy with 1800–1900. Hereafter 'the 1992 Agenda'.
3. O'Dowd et al., 'An Agenda for Women's History in Ireland', p. 1.
4. Margaret MacCurtain, *Ariadne's Thread: Writing Women into Irish History* (Galway, Arlen House, 2008).
5. Mary Cullen, 'Women's History in Ireland', in Karen Offen, Ruth Roach-Pierson and Jane Rendall (eds), *Writing Women's History: International Perspectives* (London, Macmillan, 1991), p. 430.
6. Mary Cullen, 'Women's History in Ireland', pp. 430–1.

7. WHAI web site http://www.whai.ie accessed 03/05/08.
8. http://www.nationalarchives.ie/wh/whp.html accessed 03/02/08. The resulting *Directory of Sources for Women's History in Ireland* can be searched on the National Archives of Ireland website.
9. Two of the more influential Irish historians of the twentieth century Robin Dudley Edwards and T. W. Moody attended Institute of Historical research in London, 1929–32 and others were trained at Peterhouse College, Cambridge. For an overview of on Irish revisionism see Ciaran Brady (ed.), *Interpreting Irish History*
10. T. W. Moody, 'Irish History and Irish Mythology' *Hermanathea*, 124, Summer (1978), pp. 7–24.
11. Brendan Bradshaw, 'Revising Irish History', in O Ceallaigh, Daltun (ed.), *Reconsiderations of Irish History and Culture* (Dublin, Leirmheas, 1994), pp. 32–4.
12. While many women historians (among them Mary Hayden, Mary Donovan O'Sullivan, Constantia Maxwell) contributed to both the teaching and writing of Irish history up to the mid-twentieth century, most of their engagement was with social history, which, with the establishment of IHS and the ensuing bias in favour of political history meant that the style of history used by many women historians was regarded as old fashioned and populist, and, indeed, suspect in its methodology and use (or lack of use) of primary sources. See Mary O'Dowd (2002) (ed.), Interpreting the Past, pp. 1102–05.
13. O'Dowd et al. (1992), 'An Agenda for Women's History', p. 5.
14. Brendan Bradshaw, 'Nationalism and Historical Scholarship in Modern Ireland', *Irish Historical Studies*, 26, no. 104, November (1989), pp. 335–6.
15. Kevin Whelan, 'The Revisionist Debate in Ireland', *Boundary 2*, 31. 1, (2004) p. 185.
16. O'Dowd et al., 'An Agenda for Women's History', p. 4.
17. Mary Cullen, 'Women's History in Ireland', p. 422.
18. Mary E. Daly, '"Oh! Kathleen Ni Houlihan, Your Way's a Thorny Way!": The Condition of Women in 20th Century Ireland', in Anthony Bradley and Maryann Gialanella Vlaulis (eds), *Gender and Sexuality in Modern Ireland* (Amherst, University of Massachusetts Press, 1997), p. 103.
19. Mary E. Daly, '"Oh, Kathleen Ni Houlihan", pp. 103–05.
20. Judith M. Bennett, 'Feminism and History', in Sue Morgan (ed.), *The Feminist History Reader* (London, Routledge, 2006), p. 61.
21. Judith M. Bennett, 'Feminism and History'.
22. O'Dowd et al., 'An Agenda for Women's History', pp. 3–6.
23. O'Dowd et al., 'An Agenda for Women's History', p. 5.
24. O'Dowd et al., 'An Agenda for Women's History', p. 3.
25. Care has to be taken not to see gender history as simply a different name for women's history, or that gender history is a successor to women's history. The boundaries between women's history and gender history remain fluid, and the varying approaches and theoretical debates to either exclude the other. Each still has much to add to the continuing development of women's history and the ongoing investigation into the multifaceted relationships between the sexes.
26. See Margaret Kelleher and James H. Murphy, *Gender Perspectives in Nineteenth-century Ireland: Public and Private Sphere* (Dublin, Irish Academic Press, 1997) for a discussion on gender as a category of analysis in Irish history.

27. Mary Cullen, 'History Women and History Men: The Politics of Women's History', *History Ireland*, Summer (1994), p. 36.
28. Mary Cullen, ' Foreword', in Margaret Kelleher and James H. Murphy, *Gender Perspectives in Nineteenth-Century Ireland: Public and Private Sphere*, p. 7.
29. Marilyn Cohen and Nancy J. Curtin (eds), *Reclaiming Gender; Transgressive Identities in Modern Ireland* (London, Macmillan Press, 1999), p. 4.
30. O'Dowd et al., 'An Agenda for Women's History', p. 9–13.
31. Gearoid Ó Tuathaigh, 'The Role of Women in Ireland under the New English Order', in Margaret MacCurtain and Donncha Ó Corrain (eds), *Women in Irish Society: The Historical Dimension* (Dublin, Arlen House Press, 1978), pp. 26–36.
32. Margaret MacCurtain and Mary O'Dowd, *Women in Early Modern Ireland* (Dublin, Wolfhound, 1991), p. 14.
33. Margaret MacCurtain, 'Women, Education and Learning in Early Modern Ireland', in MacCurtain and O'Dowd, *Women in Early Modern Ireland*, p. 175.
34. Edited collections, many of which have originated as conference papers, often serve to address these research problems and contribute to the development of the methodological approaches of historians of the early modern period. See, for example, Bernadette Whelan (ed.), *Women and Paid Work in Ireland*, 1500–1930 (Dublin, Four Courts Press, 2000) which developed out of a 1998 WHAI conference. Also Mary O'Dowd and Sabine Wichert, *Chattel, Servant or Citizen: Women's Status in Church, State and Society* (Belfast, Institute of Irish Studies, 1995) which developed from the twenty-first Irish Conference of Historians, the theme of which was the history of women. A volume of essays, *Gender and Power in Irish History*, edited by Maryann Valiulis and forthcoming, Sept. 2008, from Irish Academic Press originated in papers delivered at the 2006 WHAI conference held at Trinity College, Dublin, will also include essays on the early modern period.
35. O'Dowd and Wichert, *Chattel, Servant or Citizen*, p. xi.
36. Daire Keogh and Nicholas Furlong (eds), *The Women of 1798* (Dublin, Four Courts Press, 1998), p. 7.
37. Keogh and Furlong (eds), *The Women of 1798*, p. 8.
38. Mary Shackleton Leadbeater, Quaker, b. 1758, the daughter of Richard Shackleton, the Master of Ballitore School, Co. Kildare. She married William Leadbeater in 1791 and was first postmistress in Ballitore village. Her Annals of Ballitore, began in 1766 and finished in 1824, recounts life and events in her own life and in Ballitore, including the 1798 rebellion. She died in 1826. Matilda (Martha) Tone, nee Witherington (1769–1849), was 16 when she eloped with Theobold Wolfe Tone. While Tone went about the 'manly' business of revolution she looked after their home and family in Ireland, America, France and Germany. After his death in 1798 she raised her children as republican and kept Tone's memory alive by editing and publishing his papers. She was the very epitome of the virtuous republican widow. Mary Ann McCracken (1770–1866) was the sister of executed rebel leader Henry Joy McCracken and a remarkable woman, social reformer and believer in rights for women.
39. Thomas Bartlett, 'Bearing Witness: Female Evidence in Courts Martial Convened to Suppress the 1798 Rebellion', in Keogh and Furlong (eds), *The Women of 1798*, pp. 64–86.

40. O'Dowd et al., 'An Agenda for Women's History', p. 19.
41. O'Dowd et al., 'An Agenda for Women's History', pp. 19–20.
42. O'Dowd et al., 'An Agenda for Women's History', pp. 19–37.
43. The Ladies Land League was set up in 1881, by Anna Parnell, in response to the British government's Coercion Act of 1881, which undermined the operations of the Land League and imprisoned its leaders, including Charles Steward Parnell (her brother) and Michael Davitt. The Ladies' organisation, unaffected by the Coercion Act, held public meetings and encouraged withholding of rent, resisting of evictions and boycotting of those who defied the Land League. By 1882 they had 500 branches and thousands of women members. Parnell was released from jail in May 1882 and the Ladies' Land League was to be brought firmly under male control, it was eventually dissolved that year leaving a legacy of resentment among the women. Anna Parnell wrote an angry account of her experience in *Tale of a Great Sham*, which was published posthumously in 1986. She never spoke to her brother after 1882 again and she died in 1913 in swimming accident in Cornwall.
44. Cumann na mBan was founded in 1914 as an women's auxiliary for the Irish Volunteers. Initially its main aim was to raise funds to arm and equip the Irish Volunteers. These aims were later amended to state the organisation aimed for the 'arming and equipping of the men and women of Ireland' and a commitment to 'follow the policy of the Republican Proclamation [of 1916] by seeing that women take up their proper position in the life of the nation'. Many members of Cumann na mBan took part in the Easter Rising, the War of Independence and the Civil War.
45. See also Cliona Murphy, *The Women's Suffrage Movement and Irish Society in the Early Twentieth Century* (New York, Harvester Wheatsheaf, 1989), as well as biographies of women involved in nationalism, feminism and socialism, including Leah Levenson and J. Naderstad, *Hannah Sheehy Skeffington: Irish Feminist* (New York, Syracus, 1986); Margaret Ward, *Hanna Sheehy Skeffington: A Life* (Cork, Attic Press, 1987); Charlotte Fallon, *Soul of Fire: A Biography of Mary MacSwiney* (Dublin, Mercier, 1986); Anna Parnell, *The Tale of the Great Sham*, Dana Hearne (ed.) (Dublin, Arlen House, 1986); Armanda Sebestyn, *Prison Letter of Countess Markievicz* (London, Virago, 1987), Andro Linklater, *An Unhusbanded Life: Charlott Despard, Suffragette, Socialist and Sinn Féiner* (London, Hutchinson, 1980); Margaret Mulivihill, *Charlotte Despard: A Biography* (London, Pandora, 1989); Marie O'Neill, *From Parnell to DeValera: A Biography of Jennie Wyse Power, 1858–1941* (Dublin, Blackwater Press, 1991); Helen Litton (ed.), *Kathleen Clarke 1878–1972: My Fight for Irelan''s Freedom* (Dublin, O'Brien Press, 1991); Jane Côté, *Fanny and Anna Parnell: Ireland's Patriot Sisters* (Dublin, Gill and Macmillan, 1991).
46. Margaret Ward, 'Gender: Gendering the Revolution', in Joost Augusteijn, *The Irish Revolution 1913–1923* (Basingstoke, Palgrave Macmillan, 2002), p. 170.
47. Maria Luddy, *Women in Ireland 1800–1918: A Documentary History* (Cork, Cork University Press, 1995), p. xxvi.
48. Maria Luddy, *Women in Ireland 1800–1918*, p. 10.
49. Maria Luddy and Cliona Murphy (eds), *Women Surviving; Studies in Irish Women's History in the 19th and 20th Centuries* (Dublin, Poolbeg Press, 1990), p. 45.

50. See Maria Luddy, *Women and Philanthropy in Nineteenth-Century Ireland* (New York, Cambridge University Press, 1995); Dympna McLoughlin, 'Superfluous and Unwanted Deadweight – the Necessary Emigration of Nineteenth Century Irishwomen', in Patrick O'Sullivan (ed.), *The Irish Worldwide: Heritage, History and Identity* (Leicester, October, 1994); Grainne Blair, '"Equal Sinner": Irish Women Utilising the Salvation Army Rescue Network', in Margaret Kelleher and James H. Murphy (eds), *Gender Perspectives on Nineteenth-Century Ireland* (Dublin, Irish Academic Press, 1997).
51. The first Magdalen Asylum was set up on Leeson St., Dublin, by Lady Arabella Denny. Maria Luddy in *Prostitution and Irish Society* (2007) shows that close to 40 Magdalen asylums existed in Ireland, 1765–1993.
52. James H. Smith, *Ireland's Magdalen Laundries and the Nation's Architecture of Containment* (Manchester, Manchester University Press, 2007), p. 82.
53. Ruth Tallion, *When History was Made; The Women of 1916* (Belfast, Beyond the Pale Publications, 1996).
54. This was a document issued by the Irish Volunteers and Irish Citizen Army in 1916 setting out the reasons for rebellion and the aims of the rebels. It was read by Padraig Pearse outside the GPO and this piece of revolutionary theatrics marked the beginning of the Rebellion of 1916. The seven signatories of the Irish Proclamation were Padraig Pearse, James Connolly, Thomas Clarke, Thomas MacDonagh, Sean MacDermott, Joseph Plunkett and Eamonn Ceannt and all were executed after the Rebellion.
55. IWWU is the Irish Women's Workers Union which was founded in 1911 and lead by Delia Larkin. The IWFL was the Irish women's Franchise League set up in 1908 to campaign for the enfranchisement of women on an equal basis with men.
56. *Bean na hÉireann* was founded by Inghinidhe na hÉireann in 1908 and was edited mainly by Helena Moloney. It was Ireland's first women's nationalist journal and included articles from many of the main female players in Irish feminism and nationalism until it ended in 1911. The women of the IWFL launched their own newspaper *The Irish Citizen* later in 1912 and this lasted until 1920.
57. John Cowell, *A Noontime Blazing; Brigid Lyons Thornton, Rebel, Soldier, Doctor* (Dublin, Currach Press, 2005), p. 12.
58. William Murphy, 'Suffragettes and the Transformation of Political Imprisonment in Ireland, 1912–1914', in Louise Ryan and Margaret Ward (eds), *Irish Women and the Vote; Becoming Citizens* (Dublin, Irish Academic Press, 2007), p. 128.
59. Sinead McCoole, *No Ordinary Women; Irish Female Activists in the Revolutionary Years* (Dublin, O'Brien Press, 2003), p. 38.
60. Mary Cullen and Maria Luddy (eds), *Female Activists; Irish Women and Change 1900–1960* (Dublin, The Woodfield Press, 2001), p. 3.
61. http://www.independent.ie/opinion/analysis/she-was-a-snob-fraud-showoff-and-murderer-136328.html accessed 05/03/08
62. Sean O'Faolain, *Constance Markievicz, or The Average Revolutionary* (London, Jonathan Cape, 1934), p. 7.
63. All the women elected to the second Dáil were, with the exception of Countess Markievicz, related to the dead patriots of the struggle for Irish

Independence. They stood firmly by their claim to speak for their martyred loved ones. The executive committee of Cumann na mBan rejected the Treaty by a wide margin of 24 to 2 as it offered a truncated, despised version of the Republic their men had fought and died for.

64. Margaret Ward, 'Gender; Gendering the Irish Revolution', in Joost Augusteijn, *The Irish Revolution 1913–1923*, p. 180.

65. Margaret Ward, 'Gender; Gendering the Irish Revolution' in Joost Augusteijn, *The Irish Revolution 1913–1923*, p. 183.

66. Maryann Gialanella Valiulis (1995), 'Neither Feminist nor Flapper: The Ecclesiastical Construction of the Ideal Irish Woman', in Mary O'Dowd and Sabine Wichert (eds), *Chattel, Servant or Citizen; Women's Status in Church, State and Society*, p. 170.

67. Margaret Ward, 'Gender; Gendering the Irish Revolution', in Joost Augusteijn, *The Irish Revolution 1913–1923*, p. 182.

68. Jason Knirck, *Women of the Dáil: Gender, Republicanism and the Anglo-Irish Treaty* (Dublin, Irish Academic Press, 2006), p. 18.

69. Margaret Ward, 'Gender; Gendering the Irish Revolution', in Joost Augusteijn, *The Irish Revolution 1913–1923*, p. 181.

70. Maryann Valiulis, '"Free women in a Free Nation"': Nationalist Feminist Expectations for Independence', in Brian Farrell (ed.), *The Creation of the Dáil* (Dublin, Gill and Macmillan, 1994), p. 86.

71. Maryann Gialanella Valiulis, 'Engendering Citizenship: Women's Relationship to the State in Ireland and the United States in the Post-Suffrage period', in Maryann Gialanella Valiulis and Mary O'Dowd (eds), *Women and Irish History: Essays in Honour of Margaret MacCurtain* (Dublin, The Wolfhound Press, 1997), p. 171.

72. Mary E. Daly, '"Turn on the Tap": The State, Irish Women and Running Water', in Maryann Gialanella Valiulis and Mary O'Dowd (eds), *Women and Irish History*. (Dublin, Wolfhound, 1997), pp. 206–19.

73. Ciara Breathnach, 'The Role of Women in the Economy of the West of Ireland, 1891–1923', in *New Hibernia Review*, 8.1 (2004), p. 92.

74. Eileen Connolly, 'Durability and Change on State Gender Systems: Ireland in the 1950's', in *The European Journal of Women's Studies*, vol. 10 (1), (2003), p. 80. Earlier the 1937 Constitution had placed women firmly at home and equated all women with motherhood. Article 41.2.1 holds that 'the State recognises that by her life within the home, woman gives to the State a support without which the common good cannot be achieved'.

75. These included the National University Women's Graduate Association (WGA), The Joint Committee of Women's Societies and Social Workers, The Irish Women's Workers Union and Old Cumann ma mBan.

76. Maria Luddy, 'Irish Women's Opposition to the 1937 Draft Constitution', in *Transactions of the RHS*, 15, (2005), p. 181.

77. Linda Connolly, *The Irish Women's Movement: From Revolution to Devolution* (London, Palgrave Macmillan, 2003), p. 223.

78. Pat O'Connor, *Emerging Voices: Women in Contemporary Irish Society* (Institute of Public Administration, Dublin, 1998).

79. O'Dowd et al., *'An Agenda for Women's History in Ireland*, p. 28.

80. Tom Inglis, 'Sexual Transgression and Scapegoats: A Case Study from Modern Ireland', in *Sexualities*, vol. 5, no. 1, (2002), p. 5.

81. In April 1984, the body of a baby boy, with multiple stab wounds to his body, was found on a beach in Caherciveen, Co. Kerry. Two weeks later Joanne Hayes from Abbeydorney Co Kerry (about 50 miles from Caherciveen) was questioned by Gardaí. Hayes had been pregnant and now was no longer so, but no baby was to be found. During a search, the body of a second baby boy was found at the Hayes farm. Hayes was accused of giving birth to both babies, killing them and dumping their bodies. A forensic upset appeared when the Caherciveen baby had a blood type (A) incompatible with that of Joanne Hayes (O) and her [married] lover (O), however the Gardaí decided that she had sex with two men, one with blood O – her lover and an unknown man with blood type A, within a short period of time, conceived babies with both and then disposed of both babies when they were born.

82. The Irish Police

83. Tom Inglis, 'Sexual Transgression and Scapegoats: A Case Study from Modern Ireland', p. 9–11.

84. See, for example, Maryann Gialanella Valiulis, 'Neither Feminist nor Flapper; The Ecclesiastical Construction of the Ideal Irish Woman', in Mary O'Dowd and Sabine Wichert (eds), *Chattel, Servant or Citizen*; Sandra L. McAvoy, 'The Regulation of Sexuality in the Irish Free State, 1929–1935', in Greta Jones and Elizabeth Malcolm (eds), *Medicine, Disease and the State, 1650–1940* (Cork, Cork University Press, 1999); James H. Smith, 'The Politics of Sexual Knowledge: The Origins of Ireland's Containment Culture and the Carrigan Report (1931), in *Journal of the History of Sexuality*, 13.2, (2004).

85. See Siobhan Kilfeather, 'Sexuality, 1685–2001', in Angela Bourke et al. (eds), *The Field Day Anthology of Irish Writing: Irish Women's Writing and Traditions*, vol. 4 (Cork, Cork University Press, 2002), pp. 755–1189, for an overview of the history of sexuality in Ireland, 1865–2001.

86. Mary Peckham Magray, *The Transforming Power of the Nuns: Women, Religion, and Cultural Change in Ireland, 1750–1900.* (New York, Oxford University Press, 1998), p. 63.

87. Yvonne McKenna, 'Embodied Ideals and Realities: Irish Nuns and Irish Womanhood, 1930s–1960s', in *Éire-Ireland*, 41.1, (2006), p. 54.

88. Yvonne McKenna, 'Embodied Ideals and Realities', p. 55.

89. Eibhear Walshe, *Sex, Nation and Dissent in Irish Writing*, (1997), p. 8.

90. Eibhear Walshe, *Sex, Nation and Dissent in Irish Writing*, p. 8.

91. Rose Murphy, *Ella Young; Irish Mystic and Rebel: From Literary Dublin to the American West* (Dublin, The Liffey Press, 2008), p. 6.

92. Rose Murphy, *Ella Young: Irish Mystic and Rebel*, p. 16, p. 53.

93. This term is borrowed from an essay by Jacqueline Murray, 'Twice Marginal and Twice Invisible: Lesbians in the Middle Ages', in Vern L. Bullough and James A. Brundage (eds), *Handbook of Medieval Sexuality*. (New York, Garland Publishing, 1996).

94. Judith Bennet, 'Feminism and History', in Sue Morgan (ed.), *The Feminist History Reader* (New York, Routledge, 2006), p. 70.

95. Marilyn Cohen and Nancy J. Curtin (eds), *Reclaiming Gender: Transgressive Identities in Modern Ireland* (New York: St. Martin's).

9

ireland: identities and cultural traditions

leeann lane

introduction

Brian Graham notes how identity is 'defined by a multiplicity of often conflicting and variable criteria'.[1] Class, gender, ethnicity and religion intersect in various degrees to establish identity. Such demarcations of identity are at times oppositional and/or shifting; 'an individual may at one moment be identified as being a Catholic, at another as a woman, elsewhere as middle class, sometimes as Irish, on occasion British and perhaps even European'.[2] In Ireland, however, the focus on national identity defined along sectarian lines worked to silence or absorb other signifiers of identity. Graham, drawing on Edward Said, further defines identity as being 'about discourses of inclusion and exclusion – who qualifies and who does not – and is generally articulated by its contradistinction to a (preferably) hostile Other'.[3] In *Inventing Ireland: The Literature of the Modern Irish Nation* (1996) Declan Kiberd discusses how, even to this day, Ireland's self identity is Gaelic and Catholic. Kiberd notes how pervasive this identity is despite the fact that few can honestly claim an intimate knowledge of the language and notwithstanding the manpower crisis in the Irish Catholic Church.[4] Indeed, teaching nineteenth-century Irish history I am always amazed at the ease with which some students seamlessly interchange the nomenclatures Irish and Catholic. Yet in the last three decades historians and literary critics have increasingly focused on exploring, in the words of Foster, 'varieties of Irishness'.[5] Work, for example, by Cormac Ó Grada and Dermot Keogh on Jews in Ireland has moved the focus away from the binary focus on Catholics and Protestants.[6] New texts on Irish culture and Irish identity appear annually, the most recent being Joe Cleary's *Outrageous Fortune Capital and Culture in Modern*

222

Ireland (2006). Cleary describes his text as 'an historical materialist work that diagnoses how socio-historical forces converge to shape particular aesthetic ideologies and forms, and how the latter in turn coalesce to mould conceptions of the histories that initially stimulated them'.[7] Colin Graham's *Deconstructing Ireland* (2001) examines the manner in which the idea of Ireland and national identities are constructed through, for example, literature and popular culture. Graham argues that 'at every turn the idea [of Ireland] unravels and reforms itself, always in anticipation of the next act of definition and criticism'.[8] This notion of the fluidity of Irish identities informs much of the debate. Brian Graham, in considering revisionism, writes of the 'deconstruction of Irishness into a multicultural and multivocal diversity'. He writes how Irish cultural geographers 'have addressed ostensibly modernistic concepts of post-colonialism – notably the idea of open-ended cultural hybridity and the possibility that popular conceptions of place provide a syncretic nexus that might transcend the sectarianism of official versions of Ireland'.[9] In *The Irish Story: Telling Tales and Making it Up in Ireland* (2002) Roy Foster notes how cultural critics and historians 'are all for alternative histories now'.[10] In many respects then what still exists when one comes to examine issues of Irish cultural identities is the gap between the popular view of the Irish historical experience and conceptions of Irishness and the history produced within the Academy, a gap identified by Brendan Bradshaw in his iconoclastic post-revisionist article, 'Nationalism and Historical Scholarship in Modern Ireland' first published in *Irish Historical Studies* in 1988–9.[11]

The rise of Irish Studies programmes in the universities and colleges of the United States in the later twentieth century and the growth of interest in an inter and multidisciplinary approach to Irish literature and history has increased interest in Irish cultural history.[12] Joe Cleary highlights how three 'scholarly formations' – feminism, revisionism and post-colonial studies – command Irish literary and cultural studies.[13] The revisionist debate in Irish historiography, a debate politicised by the outbreak of the Northern troubles in 1968, has led to a concern to move away from the narrow image of Irishness promoted by the Irish-Irelanders during the late nineteenth- early twentieth-century Irish cultural revival and adopted by the culturally homogenous Free State in 1922 and move towards a more complex understanding of notions of identity and culture; the articles in *Interpreting Irish History* (1994) edited by Ciaran Brady facilitate an understanding of the shifting parameters of the revisionist debate since the establishment of the

Moody and Edwards' school of Irish history in the 1930s.[14] Revisionist texts tend towards a concern to break up what is viewed as the reductive and seamless linear narratives of Ireland's struggle for independence and focus instead on plurality and the contradictions of and in the Irish past. Foster writes how alternative histories of Ireland can be arrived at through cultural history but also through individual, microscopic studies.[15] In this context Brian Graham comments on the importance of the Irish County History series under the auspices of Geography Publications in 'redressing official, monolithic histories and representations of place'.[16] S. J. Connolly's article, 'Culture, Identity and Tradition' offers an excellent overview of the manner of 'the fragile and contingent nature of the political and cultural identities that different groups have created for themselves'.[17]

Brian Graham states in his preface to the edited volume of essays entitled *In Search of Ireland. A Cultural Geography* (1996) that the 'rhetoric of nationalist Ireland and unionist Ulster was careless of class and gender distinction, concentrating instead upon a crude and masculine ethnic division, which conceals a plethora of finely detailed schisms within Ireland's societies'.[18] The influence of postcolonial theory and subaltern studies has placed an emphasis on, in the words of Niall Ó Ciosáin, 'histories and experiences which are said to be "hidden", "occluded" and "subaltern".[19] Work on popular culture, still an underdeveloped area, has permitted a move away from an examination of élite cultural traditions and towards an understanding of, in the words of Declan Kiberd, 'the inner experience of those caught up in the process'.[20] Ryder's review of Nineteenth Century Irish Literature in English Laurence M. Geary and Margaret Kelleher (eds), *Nineteenth-Century Ireland: A Guide to Recent Research* (2005) discusses the large gap in the field of popular culture. He notes how Joep Leerssen's, *Remembrance and Imagination* (1996) deals with the élite culture of nineteenth-century Ireland, that of historians and antiquarians, the writers of the middle and upper classes. In his groundbreaking work on the use of Irish literature as a primary source Tom Dunne similarly noted how literary texts allow an understanding of the 'ethos, if not of the whole society, at least that of its cultural and social elites'.[21] Ryder does note how, by contrast, David Lloyd's 'Adulteration and the Nation' in *Anomalous States* (1993) deals with street balladry, a different form of literary representation than the ballads produced in *The Nation*.[22] Work by Maura Cronin has also been highly important in this field.[23]

Kiberd states his belief in *Inventing Ireland* (1996) that 'literature and popular culture can help us to recover many voices drowned out by official regimes or by their appointed chroniclers'.[24] Of course, as Niall Ó Ciosáin argues, it is vital that in the process of the recovery of subaltern practices the same processes of marginalisation are not re-enforced. Ó Ciosáin refers to the manner in which issues relating to Irish language usage and sources have been marginalised in postcolonial works concerned with the subaltern voice.[25] In the context of recovering voices elided by official narratives, Angela Bourke's *The Burning of Bridget Cleary* (1999) is a landmark text. Bourke's work highlights the importance of the Irish voice/s that emerges/emerge through an examination of popular culture. Bourke's truly interdisciplinary study of the death of Bridget Cleary at the hands of her husband and family in 1895 is much more than the study of an individual tragedy. Bourke's text indicates how a worldview based on the oral tradition existed in parts of Ireland as late as the nineteenth century, side by side, and intersecting with a modernising culture based on the printed word. Indeed, it might be argued that Bourke's focus on the cultural landscape of those who adhered to the oral tradition acts as an example of what Brian Graham describes as 'the parallel existence of other – often elided – dimensions to identity, which help produce popular representations of place that contradict and subvert the official versions of state-imposed ideology'.[26] Further, by suggesting that Michael Cleary used the fairy machinery as a cover to commit an act of domestic violence against his wife, Bourke's study also underscores the patriarchal nature of late nineteenth-century Irish society. A woman like Bridget Cleary, childless, sexually confident and the dominant partner within her marriage was an anomaly in her society. By designating her as fairy changeling Michael Cleary hoped to show her and the wider community that he was in charge and in that way to re-establish the correct gender relationship within his home.[27] The development of women's history in Ireland since the late 1970s has facilitated an understanding of the manner in which gender intersects cultural identity, a point underscored in Bourke's study.[28] The growing interest in aspects of the Irish diaspora permits an understanding of how Irish migrants and their descendants have, as William Murphy remarks in this volume, 'created a multiplicity of new categories of Irishness'. The influx of large migrant populations into Ireland from the 1990s will, no doubt, force further and more radical work in the area of extending definitions and notions of what constitutes Irishness.

The evolution of the received image of Irishness adopted by the Free State and the historiographical trends in the later twentieth century to revise, extend and modify notions of Irishness are important aspects of this study. The developing interest in Irish cultural studies has created a counter to the enshrined notion of Irishness as Catholic and Gaelic, focusing on Irish peoples rather than the Irish people. This chapter aims to look at the manner in which received notions of Irish identity as Catholic and Gaelic were formed in the nineteenth century. In the process it will be shown how Irish identities shaped around religious affiliation mutated and changed from the seventeenth century. In the nineteenth century, for example, Irish Catholics, perspectives of class notwithstanding, shared a common sense of historical grievance. Thus the Catholic landlord, Daniel O'Connell, was able to form common ground with the Catholic lower classes in his campaign for Catholic Emancipation in the 1820s and Repeal of the Act of Union in the 1830s and early 1840s. By contrast, in the late sixteenth and in the first half of the seventeenth century it is necessary to distinguish between the different perspectives and aims of Old English Catholics and the Gaelic Irish Catholics. Until the middle of the seventeenth century the term Irish Catholic could not be used as generic or inclusive. Similarly, Irish Protestants were decried as the alien occupiers of Irish land in the nineteenth century and in general regarded as not Irish by their Catholic detractors. Yet it was among Irish Protestants that the first expressions of Irish political autonomy were voiced. Arguing against the subordination of the Irish, and by the eighteenth century wholly Protestant, Parliament under Poynings' Law (1494), the commitment of Irish Protestant patriots was, as Joep Leerson argues, focused on the Protestant community with no understanding of a wider concept of the Irish nation. However, the Protestant colonial nationalists of the eighteenth century were the first to develop the language and imagery that was to underpin the discourse of Irish nationalism in the nineteenth century and into the early twentieth century.[29]

received versions of irishness

No culture stands outside the political and social. However as Luke Gibbons states in the introduction to *Transformations in Irish Culture* (1996), the frontier myth linked to Ireland's colonised status has ensured that historically politics and culture in Ireland were inextricably combined. Representing Ireland as a wasteland, necessitous of the civilising effects of the coloniser, the frontier myth provided a justification for colonisation. In reaction, Irish cultural production was prevented from escape into the purely imaginary or aesthetic but instead was forced to engage with the realities, regularly divisive, of Irish social, economic and political life. 'To engage in cultural activity in circumstances where one's culture was being effaced or obliterated, or even to assert the existence of a civilisation prior to conquest was to make a political statement, if only by depriving the frontier myth of its power to act as an alibi for colonisation'.[30] The numerous assertions of Irish culture and cultural identity since the seventeenth century are thus, Gibbons argues, firmly rooted in the political. In the essays in *Transformations in Ireland* (1996) Gibbons is concerned with the transformative power of Irish culture. He notes the tension produced by the heavily politicised discourse of Irish culture when set against the notion of art for art's sake – the idea that culture can transcend the material realities of social, economic and political life.[31] The period of the late nineteenth-century literary revival exemplifies the pattern in the Irish past whereby culture was used by, in Gibbons' words, 'imperial subjects attempting to become citizens'.[32] The literary revival period also offers an iconic example of the tension Gibbon's identifies between aesthetic notions of culture and the wider political resonances of cultural discourse and production. The debate between art for art's sake and art as propaganda in the service of the national cause was, as Nicholas Grene shows in *The Politics of Irish Drama* (1999), played out in the theatre movement of the early twentieth century.[33] This theme is explored also in Lionel Pilkington's *Theatre and the State in Twentieth-Century Ireland* (2001), a text which examines theatre history in context of the politics of the British, Irish and Northern States.[34] P. J. Mathews' *Revival* (2003) similarly engages with the manner in which cultural forms, particularly theatre productions, were utilised in the decolonisation programme of Sinn Féin and other self-help groups in the early twentieth century.[35]

The politicisation of Irish culture, which reached its zenith in the Irish Ireland movement of the revival, ensured that a very specific and narrow image of what constituted Irishness was carried into the independent State established in 1922. Terence Brown's classic history of Irish culture and society in the twentieth century, the first edition published in 1981, testifies to the narrow conception of Irishness inherited by the Free State. Noting the homogenous nature of the Free State and the stultifying effect of a conservative Catholic hegemony on cultural production, Brown is concerned to investigate the counter cultural activities and utterances of lone intellectuals such as, for example, George Russell who promoted the values of integration and cultural diversity throughout the 1920s in the *Irish Statesman*.[36] The endemic equation of Irishness with Catholicism and Gaelicisation identified also by Kiberd in *Inventing Ireland* (1996) had been in the making since the nineteenth century and even earlier. In the eighteenth century, among the lower class Catholics in Ireland, a sense of their subjection to an oppressive regime based on the penal laws and their hope of deliverance through the restoration of the 'rightful' Stuart dynasty to the British throne was kept alive in poems and ballads, one of the themes of Éamonn Ó Ciardha's 2002 study of Irish Jacobitism in the eighteenth century. The penal laws which discriminated against Catholics in the areas of land rights, religious and educational freedom were implemented incrementally in the period immediately after the 1691 Treaty of Limerick which brought an end to the hopes of Irish Catholics under James II.

Ó Ciardha argues that perceptions of repression among Catholics under the penal laws must take precedence over the views of historians who argue that the impact of the penal laws has been exaggerated.[37] This is, of course, similar to Joep Leerssen's statement in *Mere Irish and Fíor Gael* that '[H]istory is not just an accumulation of events, but crucially also the human experience of those events', an argument advanced earlier by Oliver MacDonagh in his 1970 O'Donnell lecture on the nineteenth-century Irish novel and Irish social history.[38] Ó Ciardha's work then represents a post-revisionist perspective on self-perceptions and identities among Catholics in the penal era and modifies the work of historians such as Louis Cullen and Sean Connolly. Cullen, for example, argued that the 'actual application of law, and its interpretation from day to day, as opposed to the dead and abstract letter of the law is a subtle and complex issue not amenable to quick or easy conclusion'. He notes that landed Catholics could continue to wield a political influence as the 'immediate' landlords of protestant tenants.[39] Indeed, Tom Barlett's, *The Fall and Rise of the Irish Nation* (1992) moves the debate onwards arguing that there can be no measure of the success or otherwise of the penal laws as there was no agreement as to their purpose.[40]

While it is clear from the work of Cullen and Connolly that actual levels of Catholic oppression in the eighteenth century were less than popularly presented, on a macroscopic level, the Irish language and the Catholic religion were linked in a perception of oppression and struggle against an alien administration and the anglicising world of the settler communities introduced through a series of plantations since the mid-sixteenth century. This perception of religious and linguistic oppression was active at the level of popular discourse, as Ó Ciardha has shown, and was transmitted into the nineteenth century and early twentieth century shaping notions of Catholic self-identity. Ó Ciardha argues that Jacobite poetry was not a literary motif devoid of political resonance. This poetry 'became the medium whereby news of political and military events percolated down the social pyramid'. Ó Ciardha discusses how 'Irish Jacobite poets from Aogán Ó Rathaille to Eoghan Rua Ó Súilleabháin echoed [an] acute sense of grievance' at the state of Ireland consequent on the exile of the Stuart dynasty and Wild Geese, 'grievances which many historians have ignored when writing about the penal laws'.[41] Late sixteenth- and seventeenth-century Irish poets lamented the dismemberment of an aristocratic Gaelic world.

Poets of the period reflected on how the lack of patronage from the exiled or impoverished Gaelic chieftains impacted on their own position as poets or on the declining status of the bardic schools. Seán Ó Tuama and Thomas Kinsella's introduction to their edited collection, *An Duanaire 1600–1900* offers a succinct overview of the main themes while work by Tom Dunne, Michelle O'Riordan, Brendan Bradshaw and Marc Caball offer more comprehensive treatment of the debate on bardic poetry as a response to conquest and colonisation of the sixteenth and seventeenth centuries.[42] By the pre-famine period the notion of the death of a Gaelic aristocracy had given way to a perception that all Catholics had been dispossessed by and oppressed by an alien regime the iconic visibility of which was the figure of the Protestant landlord. Ó Ciardha's work traces how by the 1790s 'Irish popular political consciousness made the transition from Jacobite to Jacobin and 'Bony' (Bonaparte), and later Daniel O'Connell, replaced the 'Bonny Prince' as the darling of the popular political consciousness'.[43] The millenarian Pastorini prophecies that circulated in the early nineteenth century reflected the lower class Catholic belief that the elimination of Protestantism and Protestants from Ireland would result in the elevation of Catholics to their rightful land inheritance.[44]

In the nineteenth century, language, religion and nationalism became inextricably combined. A key work in this regard is Bartlett's *The Fall and Rise of the Irish Nation* (1992) already referred to. Bartlett discusses the rise of a Catholic nation as the penal laws were repealed in the second half of the eighteenth century. With the granting of Catholic emancipation in 1829 what remained was the need to create a 'Catholic state to reflect the interests and meet the needs of that Catholic nation which had emerged during the previous sixty years'.[45] The link between Catholicism and nationalism was decisively forged in Daniel O'Connell's campaign in the 1820s for Catholic Emancipation and in his later campaign for the repeal of the Act of Union, both crusades introducing the

Catholic priest as a central component of Irish politics as discussed by Sean Connolly in *Priests and People in Pre-Famine Ireland* (1982).[46] While Douglas Hyde in 'The Necessity for the De-Anglicisation of Ireland' (1892) indicted O'Connell for his failure to value Irish culture and the Irish language, the link between Gaelicisation and religion was to strengthen from the mid-nineteenth century, a good example evident in James Duffy's periodical, the *Irish Catholic*. Gaelicisation, of course, was a broader concept than a mere commitment to the Irish language, although as Ó Ciosáin notes, perceptions of the orality of later nineteenth-century popular Gaelic culture were exaggerated by the core emphasis on the primitive in the cultural revival.[47] Gaelicisation implied a commitment to what were often undefined or latently imagined national cultural values; the key notion was that to be national or Gaelic was to be Catholic.

Duffy's periodical appeared in February 1847 and was published monthly with 22 issues appearing in total. The article entitled 'a Catholic Literature for Ireland' in the first issue of the *Irish Catholic* anticipated, as W. J. McCormack argues, the blend of national and Catholic values that was to thrive in the later nineteenth century.[48] His periodical, Duffy wrote, was to be the forerunner of a Catholic literature in Ireland. Highlighting the refusal of Irish Catholics to jettison their faith despite the 'insults and mockeries' they had to endure, Duffy notes how one of the results of the penal laws was to 'burn into the heart of the Irish Catholic an intense devotion to his religion'. Duffy discusses the education received by Catholics in the eighteenth century: the gentleman abroad, the peasant in the hedge-schools of Ireland. The hedge-school masters, he argues, instilled a love of religion, blended with a fierce hatred of its oppressors; during the struggle against religious tyranny the idea of Catholicism became linked with the idea of liberty. This situation was, he claimed in 1847, changing. There was no longer the bond of persecution.

The intensity of the religious struggle had abated. However, the intellectual and spiritual future of Ireland was now the theme of present-day anxiety. Duffy likened Ireland's condition to that of a 'vigorous mind'. Because the country was too long cramped and restrained it was all the more concerned, when released from bondage, to seize the fruit of knowledge but was in danger of pernicious cultural influences. To counter alien influences Ireland needed a Catholic literature,

a literature religious to the core, which should reflect the majesty and eternal truth of our Faith and its beauty and poetry as well; Irish, too, to the core – thrilling with our Celtic nature, and colored by our wonderful history; such a literature, and its glorious associate, a high Catholic and national art.[49]

While Duffy recognised the cultural campaign of the Young Irelanders in the 1840s to unite the Irish regardless of religion by fostering a renewed interest in their shared cultural traditions, he effectively designated Davis and the Young Ireland project as not fully Irish by virtue of their lack of a Catholic ethos. In the pages of the *Nation* newspapers the Young Irelanders sought to elide religious and cultural division between the different traditions in Irish society by bringing Irishmen to an understanding of their shared heritage and their common enemy – the Saxon.

The Young Ireland emphasis on uniting men of different creeds through a shared appreciation of Irish culture and Irish history would be part of the programme of the early cultural revival at the end of the nineteenth century. F. S. L. Lyons's still thought-provoking *Culture and Anarchy in Ireland 1890–1939* (1979) discusses the manner by which a unity of culture was believed, for a brief period at the end of the nineteenth century, to have the power to transcend religious and political divisiveness.[50] However, such attempts at cultural inclusivity were sidelined by the dominant and increasingly hegemonic discourse in which, in the words of D. P. Moran, the true Catholic was the true Gael. This essentialist view of Irishness and Irish culture based on religion delineated by Duffy in the mid-nineteenth century was to reach its zenith during the debates of the cultural revival and can be found in writing by D. P. Moran, Daniel Corkery and Aodh de Blacam. Moran, Corkery and others distilled and honed sentiments expressed earlier by such as Duffy, producing a prescribed and narrow version of Irishness which designated Yeats, Synge and others of the Protestant Anglo-Irish caste as essentially un-Irish. In *Synge and Anglo-Irish Literature* published in 1931 Corkery posited an essentialist view of Irishness as Catholic, rural and nationalist. The 'three great forces' he wrote, 'which, working for long in the Irish national being, have made it so different from the English national being, are: (1) The Religious Consciousness of the People; (2) Irish Nationalism; and (3) The Land'.[51] D. P. Moran likewise created a fundamental link between Catholicism and Gaelic culture in *The Philosophy of Irish Ireland*, a collection of his writings in *New Ireland Review* between the years 1898 and 1900, sentiments he developed in his contributions to the *Leader*, a paper founded in 1900. The republication of *The Philosophy of Irish Ireland* (2006) under the

UCD Press series, Classics of Irish History, is useful for students and those teaching in the area.[52] Moran dismissed the notion of an Irish literature written in the English language in this way dismissing Yeats and Synge's literary contribution to the cultural revival as essentially un-Irish. Works already mentioned by Terence Brown, Roy Foster and Declan Kiberd, among others, discuss the manner in which the Irish-Ireland view of nationality and culture formed and established itself to become the dominant discourse of the newly independent Ireland.

The partition of Ireland by the 1920 Government of Ireland Act created a homogenous 26-county Irish State predicated on Catholic and rural values and committed to a programme of Gaelicisation through the education system. It was, as Terence Brown argues, the ideal of the virtuous countryman, Catholic and rural, that was adopted by the Irish Free State established in 1922; the emphasis on heroism during the cultural revival jettisoned in favour of an image that a culturally and politically insecure postcolonial State could cleave to. Two comprehensive recent works by Philip O'Leary treat of the literature and debates of the Irish-Ireland movement from 1881–1939.[53] O'Leary discusses among other matters the reflection of rural life in Gaelic literature and the relationship of Gaelic writers to the heroic tradition. If the new State adopted any version of heroism it was not that encapsulated in such plays as *An Baile Strand* by Yeats or in Standish O'Grady's *History of Ireland: The Heroic Period* (1878) or *History of Ireland: Cuculain and His Contemporaries* (1880).[54] Recent histories of the theatre in Ireland by Chris Morash and Robert Welch indicate how prevalent plays based on heroic legend were on the stages of the Abbey theatre in the early years of the twentieth century.[55] The new State, however, adopted a version of heroism which cleaved to a peculiarly Catholic notion of martydom symbolised by Patrick Pearse's blending of the values of the Catholic blood sacrifice with the bravery of Cuchlain who cared not if he lived another day as long as his deed was preserved for the historical record. Augustine Martin in his introduction to Prose Fiction in the period 1880–1945 in the *Field Day Anthology of Irish Writing* writes that for Daniel Corkery 'the Easter Rising had a sacramental efficacy: it had redeemed the land on which St. Finbarr walked'.[56] Corkery's volume of short stories, *A Munster Twilight* (1917), Martin argues, was written 'out of the heat of that conviction'.[57]

The descendants of the English in Ireland, and all Protestants, were denounced in the writings of men such as Moran and Corkery as anti-Irish and anti-national. They were defined by what they were not. The nineteenth-century Anglo-Irish novel offers a key means of accessing

Ascendancy identities. John Banim's *The Anglo-Irish of the Nineteenth Century* (1828) illustrates the Protestant siege mentality expressed through the constant threat in the novel of a Catholic uprising. The manner in which the Anglo-Irish were designated not quite the equal of their English contemporaries is also well portrayed in this text.[58] The Anglo-Irish crisis of identity depicted in Banim's novel is the focus of L. P. Curtis's article, 'The Anglo-Irish Predicament'.[59] Twentieth- and twenty-first-century studies on Anglo-Irish mentalities are prolific. Toby Barnard's *A New Anatomy of Ireland: The Irish Protestants, 1649–1770* (2003) and Clare O'Halloran's *Golden Ages and Barbarous Nations* (2004) are recent publications which focus on the eighteenth century.[60] Work on the nineteenth-century Anglo-Irish by Patrick Buckland, J. C. Beckett, Ian d'Alton and F. S. L. Lyons in the 1970s and early 1980s was followed in later decades in key studies by Tom Dunne and Roy Foster.[61]

The majority of those involved in the cultural revival in its early years belonged to the Anglo-Irish Ascendancy but in the words of John Wilson Foster in *Fictions of the Irish Literary Revival* (1987)

> they chose to rebel against their racial, class and religious heritage and to don the mask of another identity ... Their rebellion took the form of self recruitment to the ranks of Catholic Ireland but shed of Catholicism; we would do better to call it "native Irish", thereby evoking the Gaelic language, pagan belief, ancient literature in the native tongue and nationalism.[62]

Aware that the passage of the 1869 Disestablishment Act and of the various Land Acts since 1870 meant that the British connection could no longer be relied on, the Southern Protestant community was, Oliver MacDonagh argues in *States of Mind*, (1983) 'well on the way to an identity crisis'.[63] A rediscovery of Ireland's past on a cultural level seemed to offer them a means of reasserting their authority and leadership qualities in a fresh arena; as a cultural élite rather than one based on social, political and economic dominance. Recent work has emphasised the manner in which certain individuals amongst the Anglo-Irish at the end of the nineteenth century sought to re-establish themselves as, in the words of George Russell, 'an aristocracy of intellect and culture'. The huge interest in mysticism among many of the revivalists was, according to J. W. Foster,

> in part a withdrawal through unconscious pique into esotericism, in part – and this could be ventured, *mutatis mutandis* of the whole

Anglo-Irish revival – an attempt to regain leadership (intellectual and cultural where moral and social leadership had faltered) by concealing new symbols of power in cabalistic language and gesture.[64]

Seamus Deane in *A Short History of Irish Literature* (1986) similarly put the emphasis on Anglo-Irish perceptions of their own sense of superiority and their need to maintain it or re-establish it in alternative spheres given the political, social and economic changes of the late nineteenth century. Deane argues that a hankering to belong to a privileged group of people who would 'become the priesthood of a new spiritual revival' explains Yeats' predilection for organising cultural and spiritualist groups.[65] Our understanding of the mentality of the Anglo-Irish involved in the cultural revival has been enhanced by recent important biographies of Yeats and George Russell, among others.[66] The impact of cultural exclusion on Protestants living in the Free State and through the early years of the Republic was reflected in the writings of Hubert Butler and in the article by F. S. L. Lyons, written from the dual perspective of an academic and a member of that minority. Lyons, drawing on his own experiences, argues that the Protestant minority became an 'enervated' minority. The southern Protestant minority, Lyons argues, alternated between periods of total isolation and 'relative tranquility'. He argues that the minority was, or seemed to be, rendered feeble, by the almost repressive tolerance shown to it by the majority. It was taken for granted, Lyons argues, that the minority would keep to themselves socially.[67]

the other

In nationalist historiography, the lower class Catholic world within which the traditions of Gaelic Ireland were kept alive in the eighteenth century was considered a wholly distinct world from the Ireland of the Protestant ruling class. According to Daniel Corkery this was a hidden Ireland. In *The Hidden Ireland* published in 1925 Corkery characterised eighteenth-century Ireland as one dominated by unique cultural divisions between rulers and ruled, a binary very much premised on the 'them and us' – Catholics and Protestants – or 'them against us' – Catholics versus Protestants – notion of identity which has been so detrimental to this day to a full understanding of the complexities of Irishness.[68] Corkery's portrayal of the stark divisions between Gaelic and Anglo-Ireland in the eighteenth century has been questioned in recent decades, notably by Louis Cullen, in *The Hidden*

Ireland: Reassessment of a Concept (1988).[69] However, this polarised view of Irish historical identity was one of the dominant features of much of Irish historiography into the twentieth century. A number of arbitrary examples from the seventeenth century to the early twentieth century offer examples of this binary approach to Irish history and identity. Edmund Spenser's 1596 *A View of the Present State of Ireland* posited a dual view of Irish society; the civility of English cultural and social norms, agricultural practices and the Protestant religion of the new sixteenth-century English settlers was set against the barbarity, not just of the Gaelic Irish Catholics, but also of the descendants of the original Norman settlers who had degenerated through excessive interaction with their Gaelic neighbours. In this oppositional discourse, as Canny and Carpenter argue, geography and topography took on the values of civility or barbarity: 'Protestantism was symbolised by a tamed and domestic environment, while Catholicism was associated with wild forests and marshy places'.[70]

The notion of the west of Ireland as a contested site in the English-Ireland colonial struggle during the period of the late nineteenth and early twentieth century, was a later manifestation of this dichotomy whereby geographical space was imagined and constructed from a dual perspective. For late nineteenth-century Irish nationalists and the leaders of the cultural revival the west, as the area furthest from England, represented the soul of Ireland, pure and unpolluted; for the English it was the area furthest from English civilising values and consequently ridden with violence and subversion. Irish Ireland and the Anglo-Irish leaders of the revival clashed over the portrayal of the west. Nicholas Grene and Chris Morash discuss how much of the source of the riots against J. M. Synge's *The Playboy of the Western World* on its first staging in 1907 revolved around the manner in which the nationalist audience reacted to a view of the west on stage which they did not recognise.[71] Crucially many Irish Irelanders and nationalists attributed this 'false' view of the west to Synge's 'alien' religion, linking in this way Irish nationalist politics with a view of Irish culture as Catholic-centered. The real Ireland was sought by the literary revivalists in the glory of the pre-Norman past or in the picturesque community of the native population.

The location of the 'real' Ireland in the past or among the native peasantry with links to that past, was as Joep Leerssen argues, a denial of realism.[72] As Roy Foster states, what English administrators saw as an economic disaster area the Gaelic League and the poets and playwrights of the literary revival saw as containing the remnants of a Celtic

civilisation. As the myth of the west was being created, its population was leaving.[73] Indeed, the myth of the west was more than just the notion propagated by the Anglo-Irish leaders of the cultural revival of, in Foster's words, a 'spiritual empire far greater than England's tawdry industrialised hegemony'.[74] The creation of a peasantry in the literature of the revival has been discussed by Kiberd, Seamus Deane and Roy Foster.[75] This created peasant acted as a counter to the perceived bourgeois mores of the rising Catholic middle classes. George Russell wrote in *The Irish Homestead* in October 1905 that to have an Irish civilisation 'worthy of the name we must begin at the cottage'. Russell believed that if the future configuration of Irish society was not conceived from the perspective of the small rural dweller then Ireland was in danger of contamination by vulgar bourgeois materialistic values.[76] Sean Ryder argues that it was Yeats's construction of the canon of nineteenth-century Irish literature which prevailed into the late twentieth century. In Yeats' nineteenth-century schema Ireland was divided between an aristocratic Protestant Ireland epitomised by Parnell and a demagogic Catholic Ireland characterised by O'Connell. Ryder argues that up until recent years the 'bulk of nineteenth-century Irish writing remained unexamined by critics' citing Yeats' construction of the nineteenth century, the nationalist canon of cultural criticism epitomised by Corkery and the influence of international modernism on literary criticism with its concern for detachment.[77]

'varities of irishness'

The 1641 rebellion was, as Raymond Gillespie discusses, one of three stages. Gaelic Irish landowners in Ulster staged a limited rebellion in October 1641 concerned to establish a position of strength from which to negotiate issues around land and religion with Charles I. This limited revolt, however, was quickly followed by a spontaneous revolt of the Catholic tenantry, many the victims of the Ulster Plantation of 1609, leading to attacks and counterattacks by both natives and settlers. Finally in 1641 the Old English Catholics believed that they had no alternative but to join the rebellion if they were to retain their religious and ethnic identities.[78] The rebellion then indicates the divisions among Irish Catholics that existed in the first half of the seventeenth century. These divisions, based on ethnicity and class were elided from a nationalist historiography premised on a simplistic sectarian binary. To some extent this was due to the official representation of the rebellion in Protestant discourse; near contemporary accounts such as that by John Temple in 1646 pegged the rebellion as a premeditated assault by all Catholics on all Protestants.[79] Temple's work republished throughout the seventeenth and eighteenth centuries and into the next century, acted as constant reminder to the Protestant population in Ireland of, as Canny and Carpenter discuss, the 'menace of catholicism'.[80] Nicholas Canny discusses how as Temple's account became the official version of events, 'the Protestant explanation of 1641 stood alone'.[81] Such Protestant historiography paved the way for the confiscation of all Catholic land under the Cromwellian Plantation of 1652; since Catholics were collectively responsible for the 'massacre' the way was open for collective punishment. Seeking money from the English parliament to continue his military campaign in Ireland Cromwell could write in the aftermath of the Drogheda massacre that revenge had been taken for 1641; in his words he had executed 'a righteous Judgement of God upon these Barbarous wretches, who have imbrued their hands in so much innocent blood'.[82]

If contemporaries such as Temple and Cromwell designated the rebellion a Catholic rebellion with no distinction between Old English and Gaelic Irish Catholics or between the upper and lower class Gaelic Irish involved in the events, by contrast twentieth- and twenty-first-century scholars of early seventeenth-century Ireland have isolated the divisions among Irish Catholics. While the members of the English colony in Ireland acknowledged the Protestantism of Henry VIII they refused to conform to it; they stressed that loyalism was perfectly compatible with Catholicism and engaged in a number of loyal rebellions including 1641 in a bid to preserve both their religious and ethnic heritage. They stressed their Englishness and their English political heritage. This should have given them a prime position as mediators between the King's government and the Gaelic Irish subjects. However, the growing stress on Protestantism as the State religion, beginning in the reign of Elizabeth I (1558–1603) and gaining momentum under James I (1603–25), increased the alienation of the Old English from the English monarch. As the sixteenth century drew to a close, the English identity of the Old English was lessened in the eyes of the Crown and they were relegated to the fringes of political power. This process was made overt during the reign of the first Stuart King, James I (1603–25) and particularly during the reign of Charles I (1625–49), as Aidan Clark shows in *The Old English in Ireland*, a seminal work first published in 1966 and republished in 2000 by Four Courts Press in the History Classics series.[83] Although the government of James I was concerned to proceed against Catholics and protestantise Ireland this did not mean that the Old English turned for support to their co-religionists, the Gaelic Irish. Later work by Sean Connolly, notably *Religion, Law and Power: The Making of Protestant Ireland 1660–1760* (1992) discusses how the term Old English was a title which allowed a distinction to be made between Catholics in Ireland. Certainly, the history of the seventeenth century would show how ultimately, the two groupings, the Old English and the Gaelic Irish, merged under the common title Catholics. However, as Sean Connolly has noted, the division was not so watertight prior to this point as the Old English community comprised members of Old Irish families absorbed into the English colony.[84] The New English were themselves divided by adherence to the different strains of Protestantism, the Ulster plantation of 1609–10 facilitating the arrival of large numbers of planters from Presbyterian Scotland.

The aim of most Irish historians and academics working in the field of Irish Studies, as the above examples illustrate for the history of the seventeenth century, has been to replace the old story of holy Ireland versus treacherous, deceitful and disloyal England with a less simplistic and sentimental account.[85] The traditional 'story' of Ireland, as Roy Foster discusses in *The Irish Story*, (2003) designated all things Irish as worthy and all English cultural and other influences as negative, hostile and corrupting, a binary opposition reflected notably in the debates generated by the 1929 Censorship of Publications Act and discussed by Michael Adams in *Censorship, The Irish Experience* (1968) and more recently by Terence Brown, Senia Paseta and Peter Martin.[86] The fact that the Republic proclaimed in 1916 was not that established in reality in 1922 created insecurity and unease which exacerbated anxieties of a new postcolonial state. Moreover, there was a fear that although Ireland may have gained a degree of political autonomy, the country was culturally enslaved to British values and norms. Political insecurity merged with cultural angst to aggressively promote the notion of a distinctly Catholic and Gaelic nation which had to be preserved from alien and immoral cultural influences.

How Irish history was conceived and written in traditional accounts is the theme of Roy Foster's *The Irish Story* (2003). A. M. Sullivan, a Cork politician and journalist, whose *The Story of Ireland* came out in 1867, described England's narrative as a 'history of falsehood, rapine and cruelty' by contrast with Ireland's history of 'faithfulness, noble endurance and morality'.[87] Nationalist and Unionist narratives were heavily dependent on the construction of the stereotypical image of the 'Other'. Irish nationalist identity has been shaped by a belief in a hostile and evil Britain. Unionist identity is shaped by reference to a belief in the negative traits of Catholic Republicanism as Other. Therefore the definition of unionism revolves round what it is not rather than what it is – it is not Catholic or Republican. Similarly, the descendants of the English in Ireland, and all Protestants, were denounced as anti-Irish and anti-national. They were, according to the narrow definition of identity in the fore from the mid-nineteenth century, defined by what they were not. Contemporary practitioners in the field of Irish Studies and Irish history are concerned to arrive at a more ecumenical and inclusive definition of Irishness which reflects the different traditions in Ireland. Kiberd, drawing on postcolonial literary theory, is concerned in *Inventing Ireland* with literary texts which transcend binary polarisation. Wilde's creation of manly women and womanly men in *The Importance of Being Earnest* offers a paradigm to escape the creation of the self in opposition to the 'other'. Thus Kiberd is interested to examine literary texts which illuminate the concept of a fusion of identities, English and Irish, male and female, tradition and modernity.[88]

The publication of the, initially three, and by 2002, five volumes of *The Field Day Anthology of Irish Writing* have allowed easy access to voices of the different cultural groupings in Ireland. Indeed, arguably one of the more important features of the volumes is that different voices are juxtaposed, indicating the complexity of notions of Irishness and the manner in which identities were historically determined. The Field Day Monographs were also hugely influential in promoting innovative research on aspects of Irish culture and Irish cultural categories in this way adding to work already published on literature and culture in the *New History of Ireland*.[89] The publication of *The Cambridge History of Irish Literature* in 2006 has added to this corpus of work; Diarmaid Ferriter's *The Transformation of Ireland 1900–2000* (2004) indicates the willingness of historians to integrate issues of cultural history, gender and popular history into mainstream narrative accounts. While Foster's *Modern Ireland 1600–1972* (1990) stands out as a text which illuminates issues of culture and tradition, Ferriter's inclusion of details of popular cultural pursuits and impetuses establishes *The Transformation of Ireland* as a milestone text. His willingness to engage with the concept of gender history, among other issues, marks the text out from others in the genre of survey history, notably J. J. Lee's *Ireland 1912–1985* (1989).[90]

In 1979 F. S. L. Lyons published *Culture and Anarchy*, stressing the notion of Irish cultural traditions as divisive and combative. Lyons viewed the period of the cultural revival at the end of turn of the twentieth century in terms of a battle of civilisations. Yeats, Synge, Lady

Gregory, George Moore and the other leading figures of the Anglo-Irish literary revival were viewed in opposition to the 'Irish-Ireland' school of Arthur Griffith and D. P. Moran.[91] A decade later, Roy Foster noted how *Culture and Anarchy* 'fits tightly into the Yeatsian scheme of things ... it is also over-determined and reductionist'. Instead of a 'battle of two civilisations' Foster calls for the 'seeking out the interactions, paradoxes and subcultures'.[92] The Irish–Catholic landlord, linked both to the lower classes by religion and to the ruling classes by virtue of social status, represents one such subculture much neglected although Oliver MacDonagh's biography of O'Connell is a notable exception.[93] In 1868 Father Patrick Lavelle depicted the nationalist politician, George Henry Moore, as the antidote to Cromwell. This description placed the Catholic landlord in direct opposition to his family history.[94] The Moores, as descendants of a Protestant officer in William III's army were associated with a settlement which upheld the Cromewellian confiscations. Moore's son, George, reacted against contemporary perceptions of his father's politics as Catholic, nationalist and inimical to landlord interests and in *Hail and Farewell* attempted to rewrite his family history. His fiction and autobiographical writings in that way reflect the tensions inherent in the role of the Irish Catholic landlord.[95]

In *Before the Revolution* (1999) Senia Paseta highlights a further example of such a subgroup, noting the tension experienced by many Catholic students in the period of the cultural revival, a tension which exemplifies the reductive tendencies of *Culture and Anarchy* referred to by Foster: 'they were to become the future leaders of a Home Rule Ireland, while at the same time they were parodied and criticised for their intrusion into English strongholds including the professions and élite social circles. This dichotomy, complicated by the increasing influence of cultural nationalism which stressed 'Irishness' above all else, reflected the deepening tendency of educated Irish nationalists to become entwined in a British middle-class culture which stressed the virtues of respectability, professional advancement and social refinement'.[96] Paseta, indeed, notes how Irish Irelanders remained a fringe group in the period. She offers the example of the civil service boarder in the residence of J. J. Horgan 'whose allegiance hovered between Kipling and *Kathleen ni Houlihan*'.

'The attraction of the past had to compete with the realities of the present, and while a knowledge of Irish history and culture might have strengthened one's nationalist credentials, it did not aid one's advancement in the professions, or for that matter, in the world of high politics. The majority strain of Irish culture during the period was that of 'respectable, provincial Victorian Ireland'. Irish-Ireland enthusiasts remained a fringe group; the fact that Moran found it necessary to criticise middle-class Catholics for failing to attend the Gaelic League's Irish language classes exemplifies the marginal *and* provisional dedication to the Irish revival'.[97]

This is similar to the complexity McCormack stresses as central to the intellectual revival of the 1830s and 1840s. McCormack cautions a narrow definition of the intellectual production and discourse as the output of a protestant revival; 'to see the period in terms of a rigid division and conflict between two politicised denominations would be a gross oversimplification. There was a body of opinion among Catholics who favoured their own advancement within Britain and whose intellectual energies were directed into such channels as the *Dublin Review* (founded in 1836)'.[98] The notion that all Catholics in Ireland unquestioningly espoused the values of Irish Ireland is the cultural equivalent of the determinist view of Irish political history discussed by Foster in the various essays in *The Irish Story* (2003). The traditional picture is of Ireland as, in the words of Declan Kiberd, 'a seamless garment'; increasingly this picture has given way to the notion of Ireland as 'a quilt of many patches and colors, all beautiful, all distinct, yet all connected. No one element should subordinate or assimilate the others: Irish or English, rural or urban, Gaelic or Anglo, each has its part in the pattern'. What remains to be seen is to what extent the focus of the Academy on Irish peoples percolates the popular consciousness and allows for a real and lasting cultural assimilation of the new immigrants groups into Irish society.

notes

1. Brian Graham, 'Ireland and Irishness. Place, Culture and Identity', in Brian Graham (ed.), *In Search of Ireland. A Cultural Geography* (London, Routledge, 1997), p. 7.
2. Brian Graham, 'Ireland and Irishness, p. 2.
3. Brian Graham, 'Ireland and Irishness, p. 5, p. 13.
4. Declan Kiberd, *Inventing Ireland. The Literature of the Modern Irish Nation* (London, Vintage, 1996), p. 648.
5. Roy Foster, *Modern Ireland 1600–1972* (London, Penguin, 1988), p. 3.
6. Cormac Ó Grada, *Jewish Ireland in the Age of Joyce, A Socioeconomic History* (Princeton, Princeton University Press, 2006); Dermot Keogh, *Jews in Twentieth-Century Ireland* (Cork, Cork University Press, 1998).
7. Joe Cleary, *Outrageous Fortune. Capital and Culture in Modern Ireland* (Dublin, Field Day Publications 2007), p. 1.

8. Colin Graham, *Deconstructing Ireland: Identity, Theory, Culture* (Edinburgh, Edinburgh University Press, 2001), p. x.

9. Graham, 'Ireland and Irishness', p. 9, p. 11.

10. Roy Foster, *The Irish Story. Telling Tales and Making it Up in Ireland* (London, Penguin, 2001), p. xiii.

11. Brendan Bradshaw, 'Nationalism and Historical Scholarship in Modern Ireland', in Ciaran Brady (ed.), *Interpreting Irish History. The Debate on Historical Revisionism* (Dublin, Irish Academic Press, 1994), p. 215.

12. Boston College's Irish Studies programme was established in 1978 by Professor Kevin O'Neill and Professor Adele Dalsimer. The Keogh Institute for Irish Studies in Notre Dame was founded in 1993 under the directorship of Professor Seamus Deane. Both of these universities have premises in Dublin. Since the early twenty-first century a number of Irish universities and third level institutions have offered programmes in Irish Studies.

13. Cleary, *Outrageous Fortune*, p. 2.

14. Brady (ed.), *Interpreting Irish History*. Joe Cleary notes how there has been no revisionist study in the area of the arts and literary and cultural criticism in Ireland. Cleary, *Outrageous Fortune*, p. 3, note 3.

15. Foster, *The Irish Story*, pp. xiii–xiv.

16. Graham, 'Ireland and Irishness', p. 11.

17. S. J. Connolly, 'Culture, Identity and Tradition. Changing Definitions of Irishness', in Graham (ed.), *In Search of Ireland*, p. 44.

18. Graham (ed.), *In Search of Ireland*, p. xii.

19. Niall Ó Ciosáin, 'Gaelic Culture and Language Shift', in Laurence M. Geary and Margaret Kelleher (eds), *Nineteenth-Century Ireland A Guide to Recent Research* (Dublin, UCD Press, 2005), p. 137.

20. Kiberd, *Inventing Ireland*, p. 646.

21. Tom Dunne, *Maria Edgeworth and the Colonial Mind* (Dublin, National University of Ireland, 1984). See also Tom Dunne, 'A Polemical introduction, literature, literary theory and the historian', in Tom Dunne (ed.), *The Writer as Witness, Literature as Historical Evidence* (Cork, Cork University Press, 1987).

22. Sean Ryder, 'Literature in English', in Geary and Kelleher (eds), *Nineteenth-Century Ireland*, p. 127.

23. Maura Murphy, 'The Ballad Singer and the Role of the Seditious Ballad in Nineteenth-Century Ireland, Dublin Castle's View', *Ulster Folk Life*, vol. 25 (1979); Maura Cronin, 'Revolution from the Bottom Up, Street Balladry and Memory', in Laurence M. Geary (ed.), *Rebellion and Remembrance in Modern Ireland* (Dublin, Four Courts, 2001). See also G.D. Zimmerman, *Songs of Irish Rebellion Political Street Ballads and Rebel Songs 1780–1900* (Dublin, Allen Figgis, 1967).

24. Kiberd, *Inventing Ireland*, p. 646.

25. Ó Ciosáin, 'Gaelic Culture and Language Shift', p. 137.

26. Graham, 'Ireland and Irishness', p. 12.

27. Angela Bourke, *The Burning of Bridget Cleary. A True Story* (London, Pimlico, 1999). For another, although less nuanced, account of the murder of Bridget Cleary see Joan Hoff and Marian Yeates, *The Cooper's Wife is Missing, The Trials of Bridget Cleary* (New York, Basic Books, 2000).

28. For the development of women's history in Ireland see Maria Luddy, 'Women's History', in Geary and Kelleher (eds), *Nineteenth-Century Ireland*.

29. Joep Leerssen, *Mere Irish and Fíor-Ghael: Studies in the Idea of Irish Nationality, its Development and Literary Expression prior to the Nineteenth Century* (Cork, Cork University Press, 1988).
30. Luke Gibbons, *Transformations in Irish Culture* (Cork, Cork University Press, 1996), p. 8.
31. Gibbons, *Transformations in Irish Culture*, pp. 8–9.
32. Gibbons, *Transformations in Irish Culture*, p. 9.
33. Nicolas Grene, *The Politics of Irish Drama. Plays in Context from Boucicault to Friel* (Cambridge, Cambridge University Press, 1999).
34. Lionel Pilkington, *Theatre and the State in Twentieth-Century Ireland, Cultivating the People* (London, Routledge, 2001).
35. P. J. Mathews, *Revival. The Abbey Theatre, Sinn Féin, The Gaelic League and the Co-operative Movement* (Cork, Cork University Press, 2003).
36. Terence Brown, *Ireland: A Social and Cultural History, 1922–2002* (London, Harper Perennial, 2004).
37. Éamonn Ó Ciardha, *Ireland and the Jacobite Cause 1685–1766: A Fatal Attachment* (Dublin, Four Courts Press, 2002), pp. 28–9.
38. Leerssen, *Mere Irish and Fíor-Ghael*, p. 4; Oliver MacDonagh, *The Nineteenth Century Novel and Irish Social History, Some Aspects* (Dublin, National University of Ireland, 1970), p. 8. MacDonagh wrote, 'One part of the historical reality is the actor's interpretation. Whatever, say, a modern economist's conception of the agrarian "facts" of 1800 might be, what men thought they were, helps to explain their conduct, as it also helped to shape the new facts of tomorrow'.
39. Louis Cullen, 'Catholics under the Penal Laws', *Eighteenth-Century Ireland*, vol. i (1986) p. 23, pp. 26–7. Sean Connolly also argues that 'the Catholic share of landed property should not be seen solely in terms of the five per cent of outright ownership suggested by Arthur Young' but rather one has to take account of property in the form of leasehold and livestock held by Catholics. S. J. Connolly, *Priests and People in Pre-Famine Ireland* (Dublin, Gill & Macmillan, 1982), pp. 26–7.
40. Tom Bartlett, *The Fall and Rise of the Irish Nation, the Catholic Question 1690–1830* (Dublin, Gill and Macmillan, 1992).
41. Ó Ciardha, *Ireland and the Jacobite Cause*, p. 47, p. 80, p. 151, p. 156.
42. Seán Ó Tuama and Thomas Kinsella (eds), *An Duanaire 1600–1900, Poems of the Dispossessed* (Laois, Dolmen Press, 1990); Tom Dunne, 'The Gaelic Response to Conquest and Colonisation, The Evidence of the Poetry,' *Studia Hibernica*, 20 (1980); Michelle O'Riordan, *The Gaelic Mind and the Collapse of The Gaelic World* (Cork, Cork Univ. Press, 1990); Marc Caball, 'Bardic Poetry and the Analysis of Gaelic Mentalities,' *History of Ireland*, 2 (1994); Breandán Ó Buachalla, *Aisling Ghéar, Na Stíobhartaigh Agus An tAos Léinn, 1603–1788* (Baile Átha Cliath, An Clóchomhar Tta, 1996). Michelle O' Riordan's recent work by contrast to the earlier focus on historical context explores bardic poetry as a literary form in its own right. Michelle O' Riordan, *Irish Bardic Poetry and Rhetorical Reality* (Cork, Cork University Press, 2007).
43. Ó Ciardha, *Ireland and the Jacobite Cause*, p. 51.
44. On an aspect of the pastorini prophecies see James S. Donnelly, 'Pastorini and Captain Rock: Millenarianism and Sectarianism in the Rockite Movement of 1821–4', in Samuel Clarke and James S. Donnelly (eds), *Irish Peasants,*

Violence and Political Unrest 1780–1914 (Madison, University of Wisconsin, 1983).

45. Bartlett, *The Fall and Rise of the Irish Nation*, p. 343.
46. Connolly, *Priests and People in Pre-Famine Ireland*.
47. Ó Ciosáin, 'Gaelic Culture and Language Shift', p. 145.
48. W. J. McCormack, 'The Intellectual Revival (1830–50)', in Seamus Deane (ed.), *The Field Day Anthology of Irish Literature*, vol. i, (Derry, Field Day, 1991) p. 1292.
49. James Duffy, 'A Catholic Literature for Ireland', in Deane (ed.), *The Field Day Anthology of Irish Literature*, vol. i.
50. F. S. L. Lyons, *Culture and Anarchy in Ireland 1890–1939* (Oxford, Oxford University Press, 1979).
51. Daniel Corkery, *Synge and Anglo-Irish Literature* (Cork, Cork University Press, 1931), p. 19.
52. Patrick Maume (ed.), D. P Moran, *The Philosophy of Irish Ireland* (Dublin, UCD Press, 2006).
53. Philip O'Leary, *Prose Literature of the Gaelic Revival 1881–1921* (Pennsylvania: Pennsylvania State University Press). *Ideology and Innovation*; Philip O'Leary, *Gaelic Prose in the Irish Free State 1922–1939* (Dublin, UCD Press, 2004).
54. See Michael McAteer, *Standish O'Grady, AE and Yeats, History, Politics, Culture* (Dublin, Irish Academic Press, 2002).
55. Chris Morash, *A History of the Irish Theatre 1601–2000* (Cambridge, Cambridge University Press, 2002); Robert Welch, *The Abbey Theatre: Form and Pressure* (Oxford, Oxford University Press, 2003).
56. Augustine Martin, 'Prose Fiction 1880–1945', in Deane (ed.), *The Field Day Anthology of Irish Writing*, vol. ii, p. 1024.
57. Augustine Martin, 'Prose Fiction 1880–1945', p. 1024.
58. John Banim, *The Anglo-Irish of the Nineteenth Century* (London, Henry Colburn, 1828).
59. L. P. Curtis, 'The Anglo-Irish Predicament', *Twentieth-Century Studies*, iv (November 1970).
60. Toby Barnard, *A New Anatomy of Ireland. The Irish Protestants, 1649–1770* (New Haven, Yale University Press, 2003); Clare O'Halloran, *Golden Ages and Barbarous Nations. Antiquarian Debate and Cultural Politics in Ireland c. 1750–1800* (Cork, Cork University Press, 2004).
61. J. C. Beckett, *The Anglo-Irish Tradition* (London, Faber and Faber, 1976); Patrick Buckland, *Irish Unionism One, The Anglo-Irish and the New Ireland 1885–1922* (Dublin, Gill and Macmillan, 1972); Ian d'Alton, *Protestant Society and Politics in Cork 1812–1844* (Cork, Cork University Press, 1980); Lyons, *Culture and Anarchy*; Roy Foster, *Paddy and Mr. Punch, Connections in Irish and English History* (London, Allen lane, 1993); Tom Dunne, 'Fiction as "the best history of nations", Lady Morgan's Irish Novels', in Dunne (ed.), *The Writer as Witness*; Tom Dunne, '"A gentleman's estate should be a moral school": Edgeworth in Fact and Fiction, 1760–1840', R. Gillespie and G. Moran (eds), *Longford, Essays in County History* (Dublin, Lilliput, 1991).
62. John Wilson Foster, *Fictions of the Irish Literary Revival. A Changeling Art* (Syracuse, Syracuse University Press, 1987), p 60, p. xviii.
63. Oliver MacDonagh, *States of Mind. A Study of Anglo-Irish Conflict* (Boston, George Allen and Unwin, 1983), p. 106.

64. Foster, *Fictions of the Irish Literary Revival*, p. 60.
65. Seamus Deane, *A Short History of Irish Literature* (Notre Dame, Notre Dame Press, 1986), p. 148.
66. R. F. Foster, *W. B. Yeats, A Life I, The Apprentice Mage 1865–1914* (Oxford, Oxford University Press, 1987); R. F. Foster, *W. B. Yeats, A Life II, The Arch-Poet 1915–1939* (Oxford, Oxford University Press, 2003); Terence Brown, *The Life of W. B. Yeats, A Critical Biography* (Dublin, Gill and Macmillan, 1999); Nicholas Allen, *George Russell (AE) and the New Ireland, 1905–30* (Dublin, Four Courts Press, 2003).
67. See, for example, Hubert Butler, 'The Minority Voice', in Hubert Butler, *In the Land of Nod* (Dublin, Lilliput, 1996) first published 1955; F. S. L. Lyons, 'The Minority Problem in the 26 counties', in Francis MacManus (ed.), *The Years of the Great Test* (Cork, Mercier Press, 1967).
68. Daniel Corkery, *The Hidden Ireland: A Study of Gaelic Munster in the Eighteenth Century* (Dublin, Gill & Macmillan, 1983).
69. Louis Cullen, *The Hidden Ireland, Reassessment of a Concept* (Mullingar, Lilliput, 1988).
70. Nicolas Canny and Andrew Carpenter (eds), 'The Early Planters, Spenser and his Contemporaries', in Deane (ed.), *The Field Day Anthology of Irish Writing*, vol. i, pp. 171–2.
71. Grene, *The Politics of Irish Drama*; Chris Morash, 'All Playboys Now, The Audience and the Riot', in Nicholas Grene (ed.), *Interpreting Synge, Essays From the Synge Summer School 1991–2000* (Dublin, Lilliput, 2000).
72. J. Leerssen, *Remembrance and Imagination* (Cork, Cork University Press, 1996), p. 11, p. 225.
73. Foster, *Modern Ireland*, p. 448–9.
74. Foster, *Modern Ireland*, p. 448.
75. Declan Kiberd, *Irish Classics* (London, Granta, 2000) particularly the chapter on Synge, *The Aran Islands*; Seamus Deane, *Celtic Revivals, Essays in Modern Irish Literature, 1880–1980* (London, Faber and Faber, 1987); R. F. Foster, 'Protestant Magic, W. B. Yeats and the Spell of Irish History', Foster, *Paddy and Mr. Punch*.
76. Leeann Lane, '"It is in the Cottages and Farmers' Houses that the Nation is Born", AE's *Irish Homestead* and the Cultural Revival', *Irish University Review* 33, 1 (Spring–Summer 2003), p. 167.
77. Ryder, 'Literature in English', pp. 118–121.
78. Raymond Gillespie, 'Destabilizing Ulster, 1641–2', in Brian MacCuarta (ed.), *Ulster 1641: Aspects of the Rising* (Belfast, Institute of Irish Studies, 1993).
79. John Temple, *The Irish Rebellion*, first published in London in 1646. See Deane (ed.), *The Field Day Anthology of Irish Writing*, vol. i, pp. 221–5.
80. Nicholas Canny and Andrew Carpenter (eds), 'The Early Planters, Spenser and his Contemporaries', in Deane (ed.), *The Field Day Anthology of Irish Writing*, vol. i, p. 221.
81. Nicholas Canny, 'What Really Happened in 1641?', in Jane H. Ohlmeyer (ed.), *Ireland from Independence to Occupation 1641–1660* (Cambridge, Cambridge University Press, 1995), p. 25.
82. Oliver Cromwell, 'Letters from Ireland' (1649) in Deane (ed.), *The Field Day Anthology of Irish Writing*, vol. i, p. 859.
83. Aidan Clarke, *The Old English in Ireland, 1625–1642* (Dublin, Four Courts, 2000).

84. Connolly, 'Culture, Identity and Tradition', p. 45. See also Sean Connolly, *Divided Kingdom: Ireland, 1630–1800* (Oxford: Oxford University Press, 2008).
85. Kiberd, *Inventing Ireland*, p. 642.
86. Michael Adams, *Censorship, the Irish Experience* (Alabama, University of Alabama Press, 1968); Brown, *Ireland, A Social and Cultural History*; Senia Paseta, 'Censorship and its Critics in the Irish Free State, 1922–1932', *Past and Present* (2003); Peter Martin, *Censorship in the Two Irelands 1922–1939* (Dublin, Irish Academic Press, 2006).
87. Foster, *The Irish Story*, p. 8.
88. Ryder, 'Literature in English', p. 125.
89. See, for example, Brian Ó Cuív, 'Irish Language and Literature 1691–1845', in T. W. Moody and W. E. Vaughan (eds), *A New History of Ireland*, iv, *Eighteenth-Century Ireland* (Oxford, Clarendon, 1986); Brian Ó Cuív, 'Irish Language and Literature 1845–1921', in W. E. Vaughan (ed.), *A New History of Ireland*, vi, *Ireland under the Union, II* (Oxford, Clarendon, 1996).
90. J. J. Lee, *Ireland, 1912–1985, Politics and Society* (Cambridge, Cambridge University Press, 1989).
91. Lyons, *Culture and Anarchy*, p. 57.
92. R. F. Foster, 'Varieties of Irishness', in Maurna Crozier (ed.), *Cultural Traditions in Northern Ireland* (Belfast, 1989), p. 7, p. 18.
93. Oliver MacDonagh, *The Hereditary Bondsman, Daniel O'Connell 1775–1829* (London, Weidenfeld and Nicolson, 1988); Oliver MacDonagh, The *Emancipist, Daniel O'Connell 1830–47* (London, Weidenfeld and Nicolson, 1988).
94. Lavelle stated how Cromwell, standing on the top of Slieve-na-Mon in County Tipperary, pointed to his soldiers the 'country worth fighting for'. George Henry Moore: 'standing to-day on this platform, and pointing all round to you, his soldiers – the fields fertilised by the sweat of your brow, on which the worse than Cromwellian landlords, merely tolerate your existence, exclaims – "Behold your lands brave lads well worth fighting for"'. *Mayo Examiner*, 12 October 1868, G. H. Moore, Ms 899, National Library of Ireland.
95. George Moore, *Hail and Farewell Hail and Farewell, A Trilogy* (London, Heinemann, 1911–1914). For a recent biography of Moore see Adrian Frazier, *George Moore 1852–1933* (New Haven, Yale University Press, 2000). See also Leeann Lane, 'The Moores of Moore Hall, Political and Literary Responses to the Dilemma of the Irish Catholic Landlord', unpublished MA thesis, University College Cork (1992).
96. Senia Paseta, *Before the Revolution Nationalism, Social Change and Ireland's Catholic Elite, 1879–1922* (Cork, Cork University Press, 1999), p. 3.
97. Paseta, *Before the Revolution*, p. 67.
98. McCormack (ed.), 'The Intellectual Revival (1830–1850)', in Seamus Deane (ed.), *The Field Day Anthology of Irish Writing* (Derry, Field Day Publications, 1991), pp. 1174–5.

10
visualising irish history
vera kreilkamp

introduction

Ireland's visual tradition long had been the academic stepchild of Irish Studies, an interdisciplinary field generally anchored in departments of history and English literature. Neglected or largely excluded until the last few decades of the twentieth century, Irish art has only recently been drawn into the mainstream of interdisciplinary study. The publication of several historically contextualised collections about the popular or fine arts in the 1990s,[1] in addition to the exhibition catalogues, monographs, and essays discussed in this chapter, demonstrate how scholars from a range of disciplinary backgrounds are now exploring the role visual representation plays in illuminating Ireland's social, political, and cultural history. The inclusion of visual imagery in Irish Studies responds both to a shifting political climate and to new methodologies for describing and assessing Ireland's fine arts tradition. The revision of a narrowly nationalist historiography that was hostile to cultural forms largely associated with a colonial élite, as well as the recognition of broad European, not just British sources, for Ireland's art,[2] has generated an increasingly outward-looking nation's interest in its arts inventory. Through the application of postcolonial and feminist theories, a new generation of critics has drawn both the popular and fine arts traditions centrally into cultural studies scholarship. In addition, the availability of funding for a costly cultural activity in a post-nationalist Ireland firmly connected to the European Union, and with ties to an increasingly supportive Irish American Diaspora, encourages the global visibility of Irish art. In a recent overview of nineteenth-century Irish art and its historiography, Fintan Cullen noted the attainment of 'something resembling a level playing field with other areas

247

in cultural studies, most especially literature'.[3] In some cases academic institutions themselves have committed themselves to integrating Irish art into interdisciplinary projects. Boston College's McMullen Museum, for example, has presented five major exhibitions of Irish art since 1993, each accompanied by interdisciplinary publications, with recent exhibitions and their catalogues serving as focal points for Irish Studies courses organised around them.[4]

Although this chapter focuses on efforts to integrate the fine arts tradition into readings of Irish social and political history, scholars from several disciplines have successfully investigated a far broader range of visual imagery and artefacts for that purpose: country furniture,[5] maps and mappings,[6] newspaper caricature[7] and illustration,[8] tourist post cards,[9] photography,[10] imperial poster art,[11] public sculpture,[12] commercial reproductions of archaeological treasures,[13] even Daniel O'Connell's distinctive apparel.[14] Much of the recent examination of imagery from popular culture takes its cue from Perry Curtis's seminal analyses of nineteenth-century British stereotyping of the Irish in the British press. Curtis's research draws not only on the lore of physiognomy, the Darwinian debate over evolution, and the science of physical anthropology, but also on his considerable knowledge of the history of caricature as a visual form.[15] The lively controversy stemming from his conclusions has itself done much to engage historians in debates about popular visual material.[16] More recently, Curtis's detailed retrieval and analysis of visual images of Ireland as woman in the nineteenth-century press led him to challenge feminist readings of 'Mother Ireland' as an abject or submissive figure.[17] Focusing on representations of Ireland in a more recent period, Bill Rolstan has photographed and contextualised Northern Ireland's century-old mural tradition, providing a permanent record of a politically important but transient art form.[18] In *Mirrors: William III and Mother Ireland*, Brenda Loftus reveals a three-century old tradition of popular political iconography by examining the insistent reappearances of 'King Billy' and 'Mother Ireland' on, for example, murals, banners, flags, emblems, calendars, costumes, and medals.[19] Greater ease of accessing and reproducing images undoubtedly will encourage further interest, not only in the study of post-medieval Irish art in art history programmes, but also by Irish Studies instructors teaching courses within literature and history departments. In the past the small visual component of these curricula tended to focus on imagery drawn from the popular press; but with the growing publications of copiously illustrated history texts, the increased accessibility of visual material on the Web, and the development of specialised sites such as

ArtStore, the deployment not only of popular but of fine arts imagery will become increasing routine. Inevitably, with such accessibility comes concerns about its proper uses in interdisciplinary undertakings.

art as mere illustration

Using Ireland's art inventory as *illustration* in history texts is becoming a commonplace, inevitably more successfully in some instances than in others. Recently one art historian objected to the use of Irish art as illustrative material by outsiders to the discipline — charging that historians and literary critics too often reproduce images without knowledge of or interest in the formal traditions of art history.[20] Such a position represents a fair warning; genuine interdisciplinary work should engage with the literature, theory, and principles of analysis of more than one field. Yet these strictures can appear redolent of a territoriality that long hampered cross-disciplinary work in the academy. On the one hand, we need informed use of fine art, but on the other, we need to recognise the many functions of visual images, illustration being one of them. In his Preface to the *Oxford Illustrated History of Ireland*, editor Roy Foster makes a case for what we might call 'mere illustration'.

> In demonstrating … differences as well as the persistence of certain themes in an island whose terrain is nearly as complex as its historical inheritance, visual illustration is essential. Maps of one kind or another are a beginning. What this book has attempted to assemble is far more ambitious. An illumination in the margin of a charter, the achievements of medieval artists or Georgian architects, the panoply of a seventeenth-century countess's funeral procession, the iconography of 'No Surrender' or 'Erin Go Brágh', the romantic portraits of national heroes and heroines on a banner or a banknote, provide a vivid synthesis of rich traditions.[21]

But how should such illustration, offering a 'vivid synthesis' of traditions through visual material, be undertaken? To what extent must the historian or literary scholar, perhaps without formal training in the protocols of art history, contextualise such illustration in that discipline's scholarship? In a recent review essay, Fintan Cullen criticises Peter Gray's *The Irish Famine*, one of a series of texts giving relatively short, informed, and accessible introductions to a range of subjects.[22] In Gray's Thames and Hudson edition, the illustrations from Famine-era newspapers, illustrated texts, and fine arts sources are, as the art historian complains, unanalysed and often unidentified except by means of a condensed list of photo credits appearing at the end of the book.[23] Nevertheless, for the purposes of a mass-market series directed at general readers, the editors have succeeded admirably: a gifted historian has written a sharply focused introduction to a complex period. His edition is packaged with compelling visual material that illuminates the text and draws an increasingly image-based contemporary reader into the historical narrative. Although it does not provide an analytic framework for its many images, *The Irish Famine*, nevertheless, exposes its readers to a rich sampling of Ireland's visual culture.

In *Visual Politics: The Representation of Ireland, 1750–1930*,[24] Cullen urges a far more thoroughgoing interdisciplinary use of visual material. His suggestions outline a methodology for interdisciplinary study that, were it to be adopted by scholars addressing such imagery, would undoubtedly generate valuable new work. To clarify his argument, I contrast the deployment of a single image in *Visual Politics*, with the use of the same image by Gray in *The Irish Famine* and by James Donnelly Jr. in *The Great Irish Potato Famine* (2001) – another richly illustrated historical text.[25] All three authors reproduce George Frederic Watts's *The Irish Famine* (1849–50), a familiar British painting depicting a suffering family: the central figure, an anguished mother, holds her dying infant; the young father gases bleakly forward with clenched fist; beside him another female figure bends over with grief. The barren background made up of stone and an otherwise empty land and horizon is so unlocalised as to evoke universal desolation rather than a particular historical moment or locale. Gray and Donnelly offer Watts's painting as illustration in their history texts, Gray without commentary in a section on famine recurrence in 1848, Donnelly with a long caption noting how '[w]itnesses to the horrors of the Famine struggled to find the appropriate words or images to convey what they had seen'. In this caption, Donnelly includes a passage from an English midshipman's letter home describing the 'ghastly nightmare' of seeing lifeless babies on the road and a dead woman whose starving child had bitten through her nipple striving to find nourishment.[26] That the English painter Watts was a stranger to Ireland until a year after he created *The Irish Famine* is unmentioned by either historian — although Donnelly's use of the midshipman's commentary signals an outsider's response to a traumatic period in Irish history.

Cullen examines Watts's image to demonstrate how Ireland was frequently represented by outsiders; *The Irish Famine* supports his central thesis that familiar evocations of the country by, for example, the

visiting Scottish genre artist David Wilkie or a sympathetic English
painter like Watts, often presented inaccurate or unlocalised imagery
to depict Ireland, drawing on traditional conventions of European
art. The effect of such practices was to make the 'unseemly tolerable'
or, alternatively, picturesque.[27] Cullen reminds us that scholarship on
Watts's painting by art historians emphasises how its compositional
model emerges from a 'Renaissance Holy-Family' compact triangle,
wherein the Virgin and Child sit surrounded by Joseph and St Anne.[28]
Access to such information helps the viewer comprehend the image,
whose monumental, suffering heroic figures have so little to do with the
harrowing and abject specificity of dead and dying bodies evoked, for
example, by Donnelly's caption. Finding an illustration such as Watts's
The Irish Famine in a historical study raises key issues about representation facing the artist whose audience would almost certainly recoil
from the harrowing imagery relayed by the young English midshipman
in his private letter. Thus Watts's painting might indeed most usefully
be offered by the historian were it to be contextualised not only in the
trauma of the Famine, but also within the protocols of the art traditions
from which it emerges: as a symbolic plea for sympathy by a foreign
artist painting for upper middle-class and élite audiences familiar with
traditional Christian conventions of Western art, rather than as 'illustration' of actual Famine victims or conditions in Ireland.

Using visual imagery as a resource in a genuinely interdisciplinary Irish
Studies warrants attention to the nationality of the artist, his patron, and
the would-be customers who made up the audience that his imagery
was intended to reach – information essential in revealing the uses that
representation served. In the relatively small inventory of paintings
taking the Irish peasantry as subject matter from the late eighteenth
century through the Famine, the canvases generally depict an economically comfortable population, conditions at odds with those described
by contemporary visitors to Ireland or by later nationalist historians.
When country people appeared on canvases destined for middle- or
upper-class homes, these paintings ordinarily portrayed prosperous Irish
farmers rather than the precariously situated rural western tenants who
were soon to be swept away by death or emigration. Predictably, imagery
of comfortable pre-Famine Irish countrymen in Irish genre paintings has
been deployed to serve a revisionist historical narrative. In the few pages
devoted to the Famine and its aftermath in the *Oxford Illustrated History of
Ireland*, Roy Foster, whose chapter seeks to revise a nationalist historiography, includes a depiction of the prosperous country kitchen interior of
a 'strong farmer's' home; in his caption, Foster explicitly declares that he

offers the illustration 'as an antidote to the prevailing image of western cottier's cabins retailed by foreign travellers'.[29]

The increasing poverty, overpopulation, and the worsening economic conditions of vast numbers of rural Irish men and women in the early nineteenth century, while of growing concern to contemporary visitors writing about Ireland, were, until the appearance of illustrated news reporting in the popular press during the Famine,[30] generally thought to be absent from the artist's canvas.[31] In their depictions of a native Irish peasantry, artists typically followed the tradition of Dutch genre painting and avoided painting the conditions of the very poor. One surviving 1783 painting by Nathaniel Grogan (1740–1807), for example, pictures a preacher fruitlessly gesticulating while his bored and well-fed congregation laughs, sleeps, and talks (*The Itinerant Preacher*); in another, children play games and adults gossip around a laid-out corpse (*The Wake*). Stereotypical imagery of the rural Irish in the fine arts inventory was produced by the visiting Scottish artist Erskine Nicol, many of whose Victorian genre paintings of a sly or bumptious Paddy were converted into less expensive prints for middle-class homes. The image Foster reproduces in the pages of the *Oxford Illustrated History of Ireland*, John George Mulvany's *Cottage Interior* (1828), reflects a prosperous rural economy that was already under pressure for millions of Irish men and women by the end of the 1820s. But even paintings of a prosperous rural farming or middle class are proportionately rare in the Irish art tradition; thus James O'Connor's *Westport Quays* (1818), depicting a rising middle class engaged in the work of a small provincial port in the west, represents an unlikely (and never repeated) subject for an Irish artist struggling to sell his paintings. Like so many talented Irish artists of the nineteenth century, O'Connor would be forced to make his career in London, not in Ireland, responding to élite English patrons, customers, and tastes.

In recent years, however, two volumes have begun to redress the focus on élite subject matter – as well as the relative neglect of Irish genre painting by the fine arts establishment. This new scholarship turns primarily to paintings depicting the lives of ordinary people, a tradition developed, in part, to please the tastes of a developing middle-class audience for art in Ireland, England, and the United States. *Whipping The Herring: Survival And Celebration In Nineteenth-Century Irish Art*,[32] the catalogue for a 2006 exhibition at Cork's Crawford Art Gallery, draws together over 70 paintings that portray fairs, pilgrimages, festivals, marriages and wakes, as well as other occasions of everyday town and rural life by both local and visiting artists. In *Irish Rural Interiors in Art*,

Claudia Kinmonth, who contributed an essay to the Cork exhibition catalogue, traces 250 images for what they tell about 'how people lived rather than for the quality of their artistic achievement'.[33] Her book reveals the lives of ordinary rural men and women who developed ingenuous domestic arrangements and aesthetically interesting objects to feed and clothe their families, arrangements and objects that were often misunderstood by outsiders writing about rural Ireland. Drawing its images primarily from paintings, but also from postcards, photographs, and newspapers, Kinmonth's volume is an important work of visual archaeology. It provides new material for social historians by tracking, illustrating, and shedding light on the use of ephemeral objects that characterised Irish rural lives — from, for example, settle beds, chairs, and dressers to wicker basketry, clothing, and kitchen and workshop implements. Both *Whipping The Herring and Irish Rural Interiors in Art* reveal how genre paintings can, when carefully analysed, add rich detail to our understanding of both the visual and material culture of nineteenth-century Ireland. Kinmonth's concentration on a form of imagery that she describes as 'still unfathomed and unfashionable', often buried in private collections, suggests that more works in this Irish realist tradition await discovery and analysis by art historians and social historians.[34]

nationalist or imperial imagery?

Writing in *The Nation* in 1843, Thomas Davis envisioned an Irish art that would, like great poems, histories, or the winning of great battles, ennoble a people and express their aspirations.[35] His call for a national school of art arose in a period of exodus to London by many Irish writers and artists, a movement from the Irish periphery to the metropolitan centre that was to continue for more than a century and a half. The geographical exodus of post-Union painters, even more than literary figures, to receive instruction, find customers, and participate in new aesthetic developments has a long history and had major consequences for the nation's art. Because lack of support drove so many major Irish artists from their native country, a self consciously indigenous or 'local' Irish movement appears only in the revivalist period. Even in 1885, on the eve of the Revival, students at the Royal Hibernian Academy were urged to

[b]ear in mind that your chances of success, as long as you remain here, are poor indeed [...]. If you can be content with local reputation and satisfied with the paltry reward you can at best secure, you may

give up further study, indulge in relaxed discipline and [work] for an apathetic public. But if you have higher aspirations ... bend all your energies to arm yourself for the great artistic arena – the capital of the British Empire.[36]

Well over a century after Davis's call for a national art, the curator of a 1971 exhibition of nineteenth-century art,[37] Cyril Barrett, warned against seeking for evidence of Irish nationalism in the country's fine arts inventory.[38] Barrett instead noted the striking *absence* of a visual tradition reflecting the goals that Davis had advocated in *The Nation*. From the early decades of growing Catholic activity surrounding Daniel O'Connell's emancipation and repeal campaigns until the Literary Revival at the century's end, Barrett asserted, Ireland's meagre audiences for visual art showed no particular interest in nationalist imagery – and therefore very little of it was produced. Not only were Ascendancy patrons generally hostile to nationalism, but middle-class visitors to the National Gallery each year, were content, he maintained, with illustrations of the classics and with genre and history paintings depicting, for the most part, non-Irish subject matter. Barrett's repudiation of efforts to impose a nationalist lens on nineteenth-century Irish art has recently been revived by Fintan Cullen. Although acknowledging the persistence of national themes in late eighteenth- and nineteenth-century visual inventory, Cullen argues that the rare instances of such art are overwhelmed by a propagandistic mass imagery cheaply produced and disseminated by an imperial ruling class. He calls for a 'revisionist realignment' in the study of Irish art to correct the misrepresentation he identifies.[39]

Barrett's and Cullen's assessments of the paucity of an art reflecting the nationalist pressures shaping nineteenth-century Ireland suggest at least one explanation for the historian's disinclination to turn to such an inventory for evidence. But perhaps, as Kevin O'Neill has proposed, this resistance to using visual art reflects not the absence of relevant material or any intrinsic incompatibility between the historian's goals and the revelations offered by Ireland's art, but the lack of a sufficiently developed interdisciplinary (as opposed to formalist) vocabulary for its analysis: for O'Neill, this 'has left a major area of human expression largely unexplored by social historians, which in turn means that social historians have not yet made an adequate contribution to our understanding of the meaning of art itself'.[40] Although he encourages historians to locate and integrate visual material from popular culture into their repertoires, O'Neill also turns, in his essay, to evidence from the fine art tradition, specifically to images of Dublin's classical Ascendancy buildings and to largely depopulated street scenes produced by artists Francis Wheatley, Samuel Frederick Brocas, William H. Bartlett, and Michael Angelo Hayes. To some extent, O'Neill's conclusions suggest that those viewers seeking to integrate Irish art into social history must respond to absences at least as much to presences, to those aspects of the human landscape that are elided (or neutralised) from an image created for middle-class or élite audiences.

Geographer P. J. Duffy, in 'The Changing Rural Landscape 1750–1850: Pictorial Evidence',[41] offers information about the kinds of paintings of the Irish countryside that were being created in Ireland preceding and during the first half of the nineteenth century. In addition to a rich inventory of portraits of individual landowners and political figures,[42] Irish artists produced a substantial archive of estate portraits – landscape paintings that proprietors had begun to commission in the eighteenth century to celebrate the houses and parks they were building in the countryside. Increasingly, painters created images to fulfill the imaginative needs of their patrons – from early map-like 'prospects' to romantic views of expansive landscape parks and elaborate big houses.[43] Compared to their English counterparts, these artists created proportionately more images of houses and demesnes — a 'preferred' or 'valued' landscape subject in Irish art until about 1820.[44] Occupying their estates under colonial land settlements and often surrounded by native families whom they had dispossessed, eighteenth- and early nineteenth-century Irish landlords welcomed such cultural assertions of ownership. Such houses and pleasure grounds had long been ripe subjects for portraiture, and in commissioned paintings throughout the eighteenth- and early-nineteenth centuries, artists celebrated their patrons' taste in transforming a wild and uncivil landscape.

Like the cultural topography of Rome or Greece, Irish landscape was to become incorporated into late eighteenth- and nineteenth-century travel itineraries – attracting visitors as diverse in their interests as Arthur Young, John Carr, Thomas Carlyle, William Thackeray, or Chevalier de Latocnaye. Influenced by Edmund Burke's *A Philosophical Inquiry into the Origins of Our Ideas on the Sublime and Beautiful* (1757), a major text for eighteenth-century landscape aesthetics, tourists and artists followed well-travelled routes to the spectacular natural settings of Wicklow, Killarney, the Boyne Valley, northern Antrim, and Connemara;[45] they turned as well to ruined castles and abbeys and other markers of decay, thus seemingly drawing Ireland into the generalised decay-of-empire discourse of Romanticism. The bleak and marginal conditions of life in these landscapes were aestheticised, emptied of their economic and political realities. Such imagery, invoked both in painting and literature, was related to the mouldering castles, glowering weather, and precipitous cliffs of a European Gothic and later Romantic tradition.

Typically, most nineteenth-century Irish art produced to grace the drawing rooms of Anglo-Irish or English homes followed popular and saleable versions of Romantic conventions. The deployment of sublime settings to invoke historical loss and a doomed resistance to imperialism by literary figures like Sydney Owenson or Charles Maturin, who helped initiate the form of the national tale in the early nineteenth century, differs from the far more depoliticised landscape tradition typically found in Irish visual art. Eighteenth-century artists such as George Barret, Senior or Thomas Roberts, who responded to British taste for awe-inspiring scenery, created craggy mountains, waterfalls, and cliffs alluding to a Burkean sublime without ever invoking the resistance to imperialism that Owenson's and Maturin's later fiction identified with the Irish landscape. For example, Barret's famous views of a popular tourist site on a Wicklow demesne – as in *A View of Powerscourt Waterfall* (1764) – introduce an early Romantic tradition, to be developed by William Ashford and Thomas Roberts, whereby natural scenes were depicted within the controlled prospects of the Ascendancy demesnes. Such imagery evidences little development of any politicised visual tradition in a country with few customers for the nationalist artist.[46]

But the Irish topographical tradition, with origins in map-making and detailed depictions of real places, could lead not only to country house portraits invoking pride of possession or to romantically sublime paintings, but, as in the literary tradition, to memories of imperial dispossession and national loss in a colonised country. Such imagery dominates the major landscapes of George Petrie, one of Ireland's polymath figures.[47] Identifying Petrie with nationalism is, or course, fraught with contradictions, for neither his class background nor his loyalist political leaning identify him as the artist whom Davis had called for in *The Nation*. An Anglo-Irishman, Petrie was nevertheless, according to his biographer, 'a liberal in politics ... at once a loyalist and a patriot'.[48] His many watercolours of the Irish landscape, combining romantic and topographical styles, respond to and subtly develop the insights of late eighteenth-century patriotic antiquarianism. Like Owenson and Maturin, Petrie sought in Ireland's Celtic ruins and surviving indigenous literature and music the lifeblood for an economically and culturally depressed post-Union country.

In Petrie's imagery, as in the national tale, the Irish ruin endures as emotive text attesting not just to romantic melancholy or Gothic terror, but also to the effects of imperial depredation. The painter's depictions of abandoned monastic settlements, forts, and castles in the Irish country-side replace the idealised classical ruins characteristic of Nicolas Poussin or Claude Lorrain, his European predecessors in landscape art. Some of Petrie's many early images of Ireland's ruin-filled landscape were com-mercial works produced for nineteenth-century Irish tourist guides, but others arguably transformed his personal responses to a romantically conceived landscape – influenced by his readings of Wordsworth – into charged evocations of national loss. The potential of such a 'cultivation of remembrance' (to use Joep Leerssen's term) cannot be separated from an evolving nationalism. Tom Dunne argues that Petrie's two versions of *The Last Circuit of Pilgrims at Clonmacnoise*, paintings that draw the Irish peasantry into the iconography of Ireland's monastic ruins and thereby into the imagery of the country's rich cultural past, should be viewed as national, if not overtly political art.[49] In such paintings Petrie invokes a native Irish-speaking population as the bearer of and living heir to a rich Gaelic culture – rather than as an imperial discourse would have it, as made up of boorish rustics or dangerous insurgents.

Cultural historians generally place the construction of 'the West' – authentic, uncorrupted, and Celtic – in the period of the late nineteenth-century Literary Revival. Peter Murray, however, argues that early in the nineteenth century, Petrie's antiquarian subject matter was already establishing the stereotypical imagery of a 'Celtic Twilight', complete with round towers and dramatic sunsets, that was to dominate Irish history and culture for the following century.[50] This notion of an aristo-cratic Celtic locale, fixed in its ancient traditions, was to be revived and developed later in the century by figures such as Ernest Renan, Matthew Arnold, John Millington Synge, and W. B. Yeats — and by painters such as Paul Henry, Charles Lamb, and Seán Keating in the early decades of the Irish Free State.

Whereas Barrett and Cullen warn against exaggerating the extent of a nationalist imagery before the twentieth century, recent interdiscipli-nary readings of Irish art explore anti-imperial impulses appearing far earlier. Although such imagery far from dominates the art inventory of a country economically and socially under London's sway, it suggests a persistent strain of resistance to imperial hegemony. Luke Gibbons, for example, demonstrates how the London-based eighteenth-century Irish artist James Barry created – in what the critic terms a 'simple and auda-cious move' – a new kind of history painting in which Catholic Ireland, not England, was 'the true repository of the kind of freedom and virtue enshrined in republican discourse'.[51] Cullen's recent monograph *The Irish Face* notes a body of portraiture of republican political figures by Hugh Douglas Hamilton: most famously a painting of Lord Edward Fitzgerald and a striking portrait of Arthur O'Connor in a declamatory pose, dressed in a red cloak redolent of French revolutionary radicalism.[52] But only rarely, as with Daniel Maclise's staging of his image *The Installation of Captain Rock* (1834) in an abbey destroyed by Cromwell, did Irish visual artists gesture towards or explicitly engage with contemporary political matter.[53]

More typically, as in William McEvoy's panoramic 1862 landscape of one of post-Famine Ireland's most scenic tourist routes, *Glengariffe From the Kenmare Road, Evening*, artists avoided the politics of landscape. McEvoy's depiction of the Beare Peninsula in County Kerry that witnessed some of the worst suffering during the Famine suggests merely the emptiness of a newly accessible tourist route, a sublime landscape conveniently cleared for visitors by the effects of social trauma. Those searching for national themes in Irish art will, with this landscape painting and many more, need to examine, as Kevin O'Neill suggests, significant absences as well as presences. Painting for élite audiences in a developing market economy, the most successful nineteenth-century Irish artists generally avoided those particularised exposures of empire's depredations that figure so prominently in the national tale. Nevertheless, working in Ireland or the imperial centre of empire, artists such as Barry, Petrie, or Maclise, indicated directions that were to assert themselves in Irish art by the early decades of the twentieth century.

revivalist ireland and after

By the late nineteenth century, nationalist themes appeared more frequently in Irish paintings. The British painter Lady Butler's *Evicted* (1890), in which a majestic peasant woman stands before her destroyed cabin in a sublime Wicklow landscape, or Aloysius O'Kelly's *Mass in a Connemara Cabin* (1883), an early record of Western Catholic piety, make clear that Erskine Nicol's condescending mid-century depictions of Irish peasants were being challenged by new sorts of images. In her catalogue on the painter and news illustrator Aloysius O'Kelly, Niamh O'Sullivan describes his depiction of a rural celebration of the sacraments as invoking the seamless transition 'from socialising to politicising'.[54] And certainly by the early twentieth-century Revivalist and Free-State periods, the analysis of nationalist sentiment in Irish culture must take visual as well as literary evidence into account. What is generally termed the Irish Literary Revival is a partial misnomer, for Irish artists participated in, and substantially contributed to, the cultural shifts accompanying and following independence. The Revival's transformation of Ireland's high culture is more typically associated with the literary work of Douglas Hyde, William Butler Yeats, and John Millington Synge than with the contributions of Free-State painters such as Jack Yeats, Sean Keating, Paul Henry, Maurice McGonigal, or Charles Lamb. But developing and extending the literary revival's brief to move the centre of cultural life from London back to Ireland – in essence to transform the periphery into a center – these painters provided imagery for a new nation. Urban revivalist or post-revivalist artists, several influenced by their reading of Synge's *The Aran Island*, visited the west to paint an isolated landscape; in doing so they portrayed a rural Gaelic nation and hardy country people that was to feed directly into the needs of an emerging nationalist culture. Their unabashedly political focus on the west — the region viewed as most Irish because least anglicised — and in the case of Keating or McGonigal, on the heroic countryman residing there, provided Eamon de Valera's inward-looking and patriarchal Free State with powerful visual icons.

Many among the nation's art establishment, however, have been reluctant to accept such explicitly political iconography. In *The Discovery of Ireland's Past: The Celtic Revival 1830–1930,* Jeanne Sheehy argues that real success in establishing a distinctive national art was attained in architecture and the applied arts, not in the fine arts, where, she suggests, nationality expressed itself in subject matter rather than innovative style.[55] Major art historians have long championed the European-centred Irish modernists like Mainie Jellett at the expense of an artist like Keating – who has been dismissed by leading disciplinary authorities for his 'almost propagandist subject matter' that was 'adopted by the independence movement to straightjacket Irish art into nationalist terms'.[56] For the more historically inclined interpreter, however, such imagery was creating new archetypal images of a rural landscape and participating in the task of rebuilding national confidence and identity during the process of decolonisation. Among the group of painters who remained in Ireland, Jack Yeats has persistently retained support and popularity among all camps: his expressionist technique, Republican sympathies, and steadfastly Irish subject matter appear successfully to have synthesised both the 'inward-looking' and 'outward-looking' directions of early twentieth-century Irish art.

The uneasiness with Free-State iconography in the art establishment is by no means universal, as the political focus of early twentieth-century Irish art has been increasingly explored by both historians and art historians. In the catalogue of Éire/Land, an exhibition exploring eight centuries of Irish landscape imagery in an explicitly political context, Síghle Bhreathnach-Lynch and Rob Savage examine the ideological contexts for the Free-State painters.[57] Bhreathnach-Lynch's dissatisfactions with a formalist art criticism looking primarily at style are developed in *Ireland's Art Ireland's History Representing Ireland, 1845 to Present*, a useful introduction for those seeking to incorporate visual imagery into an interdisciplinary Irish Studies classroom.[58] In *Visual Politics*, Fintan Cullen's 'case for realism' – juxtaposing Keating's figurative painting about the Irish nation with the French abstraction that Maime Jellett sought to introduce – mounts an economically and politically grounded rebuttal of the art historian's uneasiness with a didactic, conservative, and figurative art.[59] Such interventions provide an alternative to the interpretation of figures such as Keating, McGonigal, or even (although to a lesser extent) Paul Henry, as clichéd agents of de Valera's vision of Ireland.[60]

The provincialism of a colonial arts community drove many late nineteenth- and early twentieth-century artists to study in France and Belgium. A disproportionate number of them, including several important women painters, emerged from economically secure, Protestant backgrounds that made such travel to the centres of European artistic innovation available.[61] Terry Eagleton's analysis of Anglo-Irish 'mandarin modernism' as strikingly conservative, essentially as an ahistorical aesthetic substitute for a newly dispossessed ruling class's social rootlessness in the early twentieth century, provides a political and social context for this turn from realistic to modernist forms.[62] Certainly the famous controversy surrounding Hugh Lane's attempt to establish a gallery of modern art in Dublin – an episode that led W. B. Yeats to write one of his notorious attacks on Irish Catholic 'paudeens' – rests as much on a Catholic nationalist class's uneasiness with Lane's relationship to the often arrogant Anglo-Irish leaders of the Literary Revival as on a nationalist rejection of modern art.[63]

The exodus from Ireland of artists as well as writers persisted well into the second half of the twentieth century. Although friction between international modernists and more figurative traditionalists associated with Free-State ideology remained a source of tension, significant changes emerged in the last three decades of the century. In these years, contemporary conceptual artists and curators began to perceive their work through an explicitly historicising lens: as Dorothy Walker puts it in *Modern Art in Ireland*, 'Irish history, far from being embalmed in books, is a living jumble of ideas and images.'[64] Increasingly, through interdisciplinary attempts to merge aesthetic and historical readings of images, journalists, historians, and literary and cultural critics, as well as art historians, contributed their perspectives to catalogues.[65] A growing number of innovative exhibitions explored the intimate connections between the national and global contexts for modern Irish society; in these installations, artists negotiated productive relationships between tradition and change, the local and the global, the margin and the centre. Because these exhibitions have themselves become major interpretative texts, I conclude by analysing several of those mounted in the 1990s – reading them as key historical interventions in the cultural discourse about identity in contemporary Irish society.

nationalism

In 1991 Dublin became the 'European Capital of Culture', and one year later Ireland assumed the presidency of the European Community. *In a State: An Exhibition in Kilmainham Goal on National Identity* explored the shadow cast by British colonial rule and the implications of nineteenth-century nationalism for Ireland's recently conceived European identity.[66] The appositely titled exhibition of work by 21 artists from both the north and south occurred at the major shrine and museum of local republican martyrdom. It was situated in a building associated with imperial state supremacy, but ironically, once recognised for its modernity – as an enlightenment example of utopian prison architecture. By 1991 Ireland was on it way to becoming one of the most globalised societies in the world; it remained, however, in Fintan O' Toole's words, a 'sedimentary' culture, 'with layers of experience and emotion folded on top of each other'.[67] The artists exhibiting in Kilmainham's cells explored their relationships with what is arguably one of the nation's most troubled sites of memory – where leaders of the Easter Rising were executed and where members of the Free State Army shot four young Republican prisoners in 1922. Dorothy Cross, working with popular colonial stereotypes, displayed a foetal pig, curled up in a bed of straw, ironically revealing, as Robin Lydenberg observes, 'not the heroic version of the museum's narrative, but the degrading cartoon image of the Irish as they appeared in the British press'.[68] Robert Ballagh exhibited *The New Revised History of Ireland*, in which 'two peasants [in 1847] debate the benefits of a low starch diet', and well dressed matrons, '[t]o encourage social mobility', teach English to starving peasants.

Alice Maher's installation, *Cell*, was a giant ball constructed of a tangle of thorn-covered brambles that connoted suffering and grew inward rather than outward towards the light. In effect, the participants of In a State transformed national heritage into a symbolic language of art – into the culture of an Irish society that was ironically renegotiating its historical identity and sense of itself as imprisoned, colonised victim.

feminism

Re/Dressing Cathleen, organised by Boston College's MacMullen Museum in 1997, explicitly intervened in the emerging discourse about women's roles in Irish society.[69] Irish feminist activism was galvanised in the 1980s not only by the Kerry Baby tribunal and the fate of 15-year-old Ann Lovett, who died alone with her new born infant next to a statue of the Virgin Mary, but also by the Abortion Referendum (1983) and Divorce Referendum (1986). Visitors to *Re/Dressing Cathleen* in the next decade confronted subversive, often witty engagements with the nation's constructions of gender. Through appropriations of male imagery or destabilisations of long-established female icons, 13 women artists 'redressed' Mother Ireland/Cathleen Ni Houlihan/Hibernia/Dark Rosaleen – all traditional representations of Irish womanhood. Rita Duffy's surreal image of the Irish mother in *Becoming* appeared to drain her boiled dead child in a chalice/colander, while in *Body Maps*, Kathy Prendergast depicted the female body as a mapped and exploited colonised space. In Pauline Cummings and Louise Walsh's video installation *Sounding the Depths*, open mouths projected on women's headless torsos (traditionally, mute objects of the male gaze) laughed and shouted, announcing that Irish women were silent no more.

postnationalism

In 1998, 94 per cent of voters in the Republic and 71 per cent in Northern Ireland approved of the Northern Ireland peace agreement, thereby abandoning nationalism's major demand that Northern Ireland rejoin the Irish state. For some, this vote signalled that an older Irish nationalism was dead.[70] Only one year after that seemingly seismic shift, the Irish Museum of Modern Art organised the travelling exhibition, *Irish Art Now: From the Poetic to the Political*. Declan McGonagle described its artists as contemporary witnesses and beneficiaries, but also contributors to the process of renegotiation of identity and acknowledgement of change occurring in Irish society.[71] Two photographs by Derry-based

Willie Doherty gesture towards the complexity of such renegotiations. Menacingly captioned *Incident* and *Border Incident*, the photographs present images of burnt-out cars on a rural road. Because of our knowledge of Doherty's Northern Ireland nationality and of his country's troubled history, depending on our position on the political/sectarian divide, we seek to invest the images with violent meanings, with associations of hijackings, guerrilla attack, or state killings. In fact only one 'incident' was connected with political violence; the other car, the catalogue essay tells us, was simply burnt out in the process of disposing of it. Writing about Doherty's photographers in a postnational Ireland, curator Declan McGonagle suggests that they tell us that 'there are at least two, if not more sides to every story'.[72]

migration

Many contemporary Irish artists view themselves as part of a larger global community, participating in centuries-old patterns of migration. But by the end of the twentieth century, migration trends in the nation were radically changing; increasingly emigrants came not just from the traditional groups of skilled and semi-skilled labourers, but from a transnational professional class. And as a buoyant economy encouraged pattern of reverse migration, for the first time in the 60 years following independence Ireland ended an average yearly loss of 0.5 percent of its population through emigration.[73] With a title referring to the telephone dial code between England and Ireland, *0044* displayed the work of 13 Irish artists living in Britain.[74] At a time of major change in Ireland's identity as a nation of emigrants, the exhibition explored conceptual borders, interrogating received notions of the relationship between the periphery and the centre, the nature of borderline territory between one nation and another, the interaction between a former colony and the metropolitan centre. Participants, all involved in London's international arts community, conveyed not a settled sense of Irish ethnicity, but a distrust of nationalism and acceptance of hybridity and mobility. For example, Paul Seawright, photographing borders between Protestant and Catholic communities in Belfast, viewed such desolate 'non-space' or no-man's land as 'a metaphor for where we are now politically right now, which is somewhere between the past of Ireland and an uncertain and unknown future'.[75] Choosing to reimagine Ireland from the perspective of native-born outsiders, contributors to *0044* conveyed not a sense of their exile but of a chosen dislocation and marginality. Migration now represented a source of artistic vision.

The above projects represent a mere selection from among many innovative late twentieth-century exhibitions, each accompanied by interdisciplinary catalogues exploring the role of the visual arts and the creative imagination in the narrative of Irish history. Such installations explicitly take on the role of cultural criticism as well as aesthetic display; they suggest how contemporary Irish artists and curators have become increasingly aware of their roles as shapers and interpreters of national identity. Practitioners of Irish history might take notice.

notes

1. Adele Dalsimer (ed.), *Visualising Ireland: National Identity and the Pictorial Tradition* (Boston, Faber and Faber, 1993); Raymond Gillespie and Brian Kennedy, (eds) *Ireland Art into History* (Town House, Dublin, 1994); Lawrence McBride (ed.), *Images, Icons and the Irish Nationalist Imagination* (Dublin, Four Courts Press, 1999). For an encyclopaedic study of Irish painting from the perspective of art historians, organised around biography and stylistic relationships rather than historical context, see Ann Crookshank and the Knight of Glin, *Ireland's Painters 1600–1940* (New Haven, Yale University Press, 2002). For artists' biographies see Strickland, Walter, *A Dictionary of Irish Artists*, 2 vols (Dublin and London, Maunsel, 1913) facsimile edn, (Shannon, Irish University Press, 1969).
2. See Aidan Dunne, 'Introduction', *Irish Art: The European Dimension* (Dublin. RHA Gallagher Gallery, 1990), p. 10; Julian Campbell, *The Irish Expressionists: Irish Artists in France and Belgium 1850–1914* (Dublin, National Gallery of Ireland, 1984).
3. Fintan Cullen, 'Art History', in Laurence Geary and Margaret Kelleher (eds), *New Perspectives on Nineteenth-Century Ireland: A Guide to Recent Research,* (Dublin, UCD Press, 2005), p. 154.
4. To accompany a visiting exhibition of drawings and watercolours from the National Gallery of Ireland, Adele Dalsimer edited *Visualising Ireland: National Identity and the Pictorial Tradition* (Boston, Faber and Faber, 1993). In subsequent years the museum itself published the following catalogues to accompany exhibitions: Adele M. Dalsimer and Vera Kreilkamp (eds), *America's Eye: Irish Paintings from the Collection of Brian P. Burns* (Boston, Boston College Museum of Art, 1996); Jennifer Grinnel and Alston Conley (eds), *Re/Dressing Cathleen: Contemporary Works from Irish Women Artists* (Boston, McMullen Museum of Art); Vera Kreilkamp (ed.), *Eire/Land* (Boston, McMullen Museum of Art, 2003); Robin Lydenberg, *[GONE]: Site-specific Works by Dorothy Cross* (Boston, McMullen Museum, 2005).
5. Claudia Kinmonth, *Irish Country Furniture, 1700–1950* (New Haven, Yale University Press, 1993).
6. See, for example, Catherine Nash, 'Remapping the Body/Land: New Cartographies of Identity, Gender and Landscape in Ireland', in Alison Blunt and Gillian Rose (eds), *Writing Women and Space: Colonial and Postcolonial Geographies,* (New York, Guilford, 1994), pp. 227–50; and the 'Mapping' sections of *Éire/Land*, pp. 27–45; 141–50.

7. Perry Curtis, *Anglo-Saxons and Celts: A Study of Anti-Irish Prejudice in Victorian England* (Bridgeport, CT, Conference of British Studies, 1968) and *Apes and Angels: The Irishman in Victorian Caricature* (Newton Abbot, David and Charles, 1971); rev. edn Washington and London, Smithsonian Institution Press, 1997.

8. See, for example, Niamh O'Sullivan, *Aloysius O'Kelly* (Dublin, Hugh Lane Municipal Gallery of Modern Art, 1999); N. O'Sullivan, 'Lines of Resistance: The O'Kelly Brothers in the Sudan', *Éire-Ireland: An Interdisciplinary Journal of Irish Studies* (Special Issue: the Visual Arts), xxxiii & xxxiv (1998/1999), pp. 131–56; N. O'Sullivan, 'Imaging the Land War', *Éire-Ireland*, 39 (2004), pp. 59–80. Also see essays by Gerard Moran, Joel Hollander, Lawrence McBride and Ben Novick in Lawrence McBride (ed.), *Images, Icons and the Irish Nationalist Imagination*.

9. *Hindesight, John Hinde Photographs and Postcards* (Dublin, Irish Museum of Modern Art/ Orchard Gallery/Cornerhouse, 1993).

10. Spurgeon Thompson, 'The Politics of Photography: Travel Writing and the Irish Countryside, 1900–1914', *Images, Icons and the Irish Nationalist Imagination*, pp. 113–29.

11. Michael Cronin, 'Selling Irish Bacon: The Empire Marketing Boards and Artists of the Free State', *Éire-Ireland*, 39: 3 & 4 (2004), pp. 81–109.

12. See, for example, Síghle Bhreathnach-Lynch, 'Commemorating the Hero in Newly Independent Ireland: Expressions of Nationhood in Bronze and Stone,' *Images, Icons and the Irish Nationalist Imagination*, pp. 148–65; Judith Hill, *Irish Public Sculpture* (Dublin, Four Courts Press, 1998).

13. See Nancy Netzer, 'Art/Full Ground: Unearthing National Identify and an Early Medieval "Golden Age"', in *Éire/Land*, pp. 49–56.

14. Gary Owens, 'Visualising the Liberator: Self-Fashioning, Dramaturgy, and the Construction of Daniel O'Connell', *Éire-Ireland*, xxxiii & xxxiv (1998/1999), pp. 103–30.

15. Curtis, *Anglo-Saxons and Celts: A Study of Anti-Irish Prejudice in Victorian England*, and *Apes and Angels: The Irishman in Victorian Caricature*.

16. The two key arguments against Curtis's thesis – that the 'white' Irish were objects of religious, not racial prejudice (Sheridan Gilley, 'English Attitudes to the Irish in England 1780–1900', in Colin Holmes (ed.), *Immigrants and Minorities in British Society* [London, George Allen and Unwin, 1978], pp. 81–110) and that the cartoons are far less virulent in intention than Curtis assumes (Roy Foster, *Paddy and Mr. Punch* [London, Penguin, 1993], pp. 171–94) – are vigorously contested in the new edition of *Apes and Angels* through the deployment of substantial new visual evidence.

17. See Perry Curtis Jr., 'The Four Erins: Feminist Images of Ireland, 1780–1900', *Éire- Ireland*, xxxiii & xxxiv (1998/1999), pp. 70–102; Perry Curtis Jr., *Images of Erin in the Age of Parnell*, (Dublin, National Library of Ireland, 2000).

18. Bill Rolston, *Drawing Support: Murals in the North of Ireland* (Belfast, Beyond the Pale Publications. 1992); *Drawing Support 2: Murals of War and Peace* (Belfast, Beyond the Pale Publications, 1995).

19. Brenda Loftus, *Mirrors: William III and Mother Ireland* (Dundrum, Co Down, Picture Press, 1990).

20. Fintan Cullen, 'Art History', p. 159.

21. R. F. Foster, 'Preface', in R. F Foster (ed.), *The Oxford Illustrated History of Ireland* (Oxford, Oxford University Press, 1989), p. vii.

22. Peter Gray, *The Irish Famine* (London, Thames and Hudson, 1995).
23. Fintan Cullen, 'Art History', p. 160.
24. Fintan Cullen, *Visual Politics: The Representation of Ireland, 1750–1930* (Cork, Cork University Press, 1997).
25. James S. Donnelly, Jr., *The Great Irish Potato Famine* (Thrupp, Gloucestershire, Sutton, 2001).
26. Donnelly, plate in *The Great Irish Potato Famine*.
27. Cullen, *Visual Politics*, p. 130.
28. Cullen, *Visual Politics*, p. 144.
29. Roy Foster, 'Ireland after the Famine', in *The Oxford Illustrated History of Ireland*, p. 205.
30. For an analysis of contemporary famine illustration in *The Illustrated London News*, see Margaret Crawford, 'The Great Irish Famine 1845–9: Image versus Reality', *(Ireland Art into History)*, pp. 75–88.
31. See Sighle Bhreathnach-Lynch's 'Framing the Irish: Victorian Paintings of the Irish Peasant', *Journal of Victorian Culture*, 2: 2 (1997), pp. 245–64. Claudia Kinmonth, however, includes reproductions illustrating the homes of the very poor in *Irish Rural Interiors in Art* (New Haven, Yale University Press, 2006). See, among other examples, reproductions of Alfred Downing Fripp's *The Poacher Alarmed*, p. 81; George Jones, *Interior of an Irish Cottage*, p. 84; George Washington Brownlow's wood engraving for *The Illustrated London News, The West of Ireland in 1862*, p. 137. In *Whipping the Herring: Survival and Celebration in Nineteenth-Century Irish Art*, (ed.), Peter Murray (Cork, Crawford Art Gallery, 2006), see the reproduction of Brownlow's *The Welcome Return*, p. 40, for a rare painting of a house of the poorest rural class, one built entirely of stone and turf and lacking any visible windows.
32. Peter Murray (ed.), *Whipping the Herring: Survival and Celebration in Nineteenth-Century Irish Art*.
33. Kinmonth, *Irish Rural Interiors in Art*, p. 1.
34. Kinmonth, *Irish Rural Interiors in Art*, p. 4.
35. Thomas Davis, *The Nation*, Review of Royal Hibernian Academy Exhibition, 1843, in D. J. O'Donoghue (ed.), *Essays Literary and Historical by Thomas Davis* (Dundalk, Dundalgan Press, 1914), pp. 119–23. Reprinted in Fintan Cullen's *Sources in Irish Art* (Cork, Cork University Press, 2000), pp. 65–70.
36. Quoted in Paula Murphy, 'Observations for an Artist's Century', in *Artists' Century: Irish Self-Portraits and Selected Works, 1900–2000* (Oysterhaven, Kinsale, Gandan Editions, 2000), p. 12.
37. Cyril Barrett, *Irish Art in the Nineteenth Century*, Crawford Municipal School of Art (Cork. 1971).
38. Cycil Barrett, 'Irish Nationalism and Art 1800–1921', *Studies*, LXIV: pp. 256, 392–407. An edited version is reprinted in Fintan Cullen's *Sources in Irish Art*, pp. 273–81.
39. Fintan Cullen, 'The Visual Arts in Ireland', *The Cambridge Companion to Modern Irish Culture* (Cambridge, Cambridge University Press, 2005), p. 307.
40. Kevin O'Neill, 'Looking at the Pictures: Art and Artfulness in Colonial Ireland', in *Visualising Ireland: National Identity and the Pictorial Tradition*, p. 55.
41. P. J. Duffy, 'The Changing Rural Landscape 1750–1850: Pictorial Evidence', in *Ireland Art into History*, pp. 26–42.
42. See Fintan Cullen, *The Irish Face* (Dublin, National Portrait Gallery, 2004).

43. The term 'big house' is an ambivalently derisive term for the country house that is unique to colonial and postcolonial Ireland. In England the equivalent term is 'great house'.
44. Duffy, p. 38.
45. Duffy, pp. 30–1.
46. Fintan Cullen, *Visual Politics*, p. 41.
47. Petrie's work as an antiquarian, ethnographer, scholar, musician, and artist has recently been celebrated in a comprehensive exhibition of his work and explored by Joep Leerssen in a major interdisciplinary volume of cultural criticism. See Peter Murray, *George Petrie (1790–1866): The Rediscovery of Ireland's Past*. (Cork, Crawford Municipal Art Gallery 2004); Joep Leerssen, *Remembrance and Imagination: Patterns in the Historical and Literary Representation of Ireland in the Nineteenth Century* (Cork, Cork University Press, 1996). Also see Joep Leerssen, 'Petrie: Polymath and Innovator', Introduction to *George Petrie (1790–1866): The Rediscovery of Ireland's Past*, pp. 6–11.
48. William Stokes, *The Life and Labour in Art and Archeology of George Petrie L.L.D. M.R I.A.* (London, Longman Green & Co., 1868), p. 394; quoted by Tom Dunne, 'Towards a National Art? George Petrie's Two Versions of *The Last Circuit of Pilgrims of Clonmacnoise*', in *George Petrie (1790–1866): The Rediscovery of Ireland's Past*, p. 128.
49. Tom Dunne, pp. 126–36.
50. Peter Murray, *George Petrie (1790–1866): The Rediscovery of Ireland's Past*, p. 51.
51. Gibbons, Luke, '"A Shadowy Narrator": History, Art and Romantic Nationalism in Ireland 1750–1850', *Ideology and the Historians* (ed.), Ciaran Brady (Dublin, Lilliput, 1991), p. 110.
52. Fintan Cullen, *The Irish Face*, p. 158; p. 171.
53. See Luke Gibbons, '"Between Captain Rock and a Hard Place": Art and Agrarian Insurgency', in Tadhg Foley and Seán Ryder (eds), *Ideology and Ireland in the Nineteenth Century* (Dublin, 1998), pp. 23–44.
54. Niamh O'Sullivan, *Aloysius O'Kelly*, p. 17.
55. Jeanne Sheehy, *The Discovery of Ireland's Past: The Celtic Revival 1830–1930* (London, Thames and Hudson, 1980), p. 188.
56. Ann Crookshank and the Knight of Glin, *Ireland's Painters 1600–1940*, p. 281. See also S. B. Kennedy, *Irish Art and Modernism 1880–1950* (Belfast, Hugh Lane/Institute of Irish Studies, 1991). The major 1984 exhibit *The Irish Impressionists* documented the many Irish artists who, from the mid-nineteenth century, travelled to France and Belgium to study. Despite the exhibition's popularity, the catalogue author, Julian Campbell, concluded by warning that no successful Irish impressionist school ever existed (115).
57. Síghle Bhreathnach-Lynch, 'Painting the West: The Role of Landscape in Irish Identity', *Éire/Land*, pp. 99–104; Rob Savage, '"The Soil of Ireland for the People of Ireland": the Politics of Land in Irish Visual Imagery, 1850–1936', in *Éire/Land*, pp. 93–8.
58. Síghle Bhreathnach-Lynch, *Ireland's Art Ireland's History Representing Ireland, 1845 to Present* (Omaha, NE, Creighton University Press, 2007).
59. Fintan Cullen, *Visual Politics*, pp. 162–72.
60. For an exploration of the changing uses of a figurative tradition, see *When Time Began to Rant and Rage: Figurative Painting from Twentieth-Century Ireland* (ed.), James Christen Steward (London, Merrell Holberton, 1998).

61. See *Irish Women Artists From the Eighteenth Century to the Present Day* (Dublin, The National Gallery of Ireland and the Douglas Hyde Gallery, 1987).
62. Terry Eagleton, *Heathcliff and the Great Hunger*, (London, Verso, 1995) pp. 299–300.
63. William Butler Yeats, 'September 1913'. In The *Discovery of Ireland's Past: The Celtic Revival 1830–1930*, pp. 107–19, Jeanne Sheehy provides a useful summary of the affair. R. F. Foster's version of Lane and Yeats's aggressive role in events leading to the rejection of Lane's proposed gift suggests some of the dangers of reading the episode as a simple example of Irish philistinism. See R. F. Foster, *W. B. Yeats: A Life I: The Apprentice Mage* (Oxford, Oxford University Press, 1997), pp. 478–83.
64. Dorothy Walker, *Modern Art in Ireland*, (Dublin, Lilliput Press, 1997), p. 188.
65. See, for example, *Re/Dressing Cathleen; Eire/Land; George Petrie (1790–1866): The Rediscovery of Ireland's Past*; Fintan Cullen and R. F. Foster, *'Conquering England': Ireland in Victorian London* (London, National Portrait Gallery, 2005).
66. *In a State: An Exhibition in Kilmainham Goal on National Identity* (ed.), John Graeve (Dublin, Project Press, 1991).
67. Fintan O'Toole, 'Ireland', in *Irish Art Now: From the Poetic to the Political* (London, Merrell Holberton, 1999), p. 23.
68. Robin Lydenberg, 'Contemporary Irish Art on the Move: At Home and Abroad with Dorothy Cross', *Éire-Ireland*, 39: 3 & 4 (2004), p. 149. See also, Lydenberg, *[Gone]: Site-specific Works by Dorothy Cross*, pp. 21–5.
69. *Re/Dressing Cathleen: Contemporary Works from Irish Women Artists*.
70. O'Toole, 'Ireland', p. 23.
71. Declan McGonagle, 'From the Poetic to the Political', *Éire Ireland*, xxxiii & xxxiv (1998/1999), p. 189.
72. Declan McGonagle, 'Renegotiating the Given', in *Irish Art Now From the Poetic to the Political*, p. 12.
73. Mary P. Corcoran, 'The Process of Migration and the Reinvention of the Self: The Experience of Returning Irish Emigrants', *Éire-Ireland*: XXXVII (2002), pp. 175–76.
74. *0044*, Peter Murray, ed. (Cork, Crawford Municipal Art Gallery, 1999).
75. 'Paul Seawright', Interview by Claire Schneider, p. 136.

appendix: chronology of irish history 1590–2006

1595–1603	Rebellion of Hugh O'Neill, Earl of Tyrone.
September 1601	Spanish army lands at Kinsale.
December 1601	Tyrone and 'Red Hugh' O'Donnell defeated at the Battle of Kinsale.
March 1603	Surrender of Tyrone at Mellifont.
September 1607	Flight of the Earls (including Tyrone and Tyrconnell) from Lough Swilly.
January 1621	Patents granted from plantations in Leitrim, King's County (Offaly), Queen's County (Laois) and Westmeath.
August 1632	Compilation of the Annals of the Four Masters completed.
October 1641	Outbreak of rebellion in Ulster.
1642–9	Confederation of Kilkenny: government of Catholic Confederates.
August 1649	Oliver Cromwell arrives in Dublin as civil and military Governor of Ireland.
September 1649	Massacre at Drogheda.
October 1649	Massacre at Waterford.
May 1650	Cromwell returns to England.
August 1652	Act for the settlement of Ireland.
1652–3	Cromwellian land confiscations.
1660–5	Restoration land settlement.
March 1669	James II lands in Ireland.
April 1689	Siege of Derry begins.
July 1690	Battle of the Boyne. The forces of James II defeated by those of William of Orange.
October 1691	Treaty of Limerick.
1691–1703	Williamite land confiscations.
September 1695	Beginning of the Penal Laws; acts restricting the rights of Catholics to religious freedom, to education, to bear arms etc.

April 1720	Declaratory Act defines right of English parliament to legislate for Ireland. Winter 1740–Spring 1741 'Bliadhain an Áir' ('The year of the Slaughter'): large-scale famine, with a mortality estimated at over 200,000 in a population of 2 million.
1745	Foundation of the Rotunda Hospital, the first 'lying-in' maternity hospital in Europe.
October 1761	Beginnings of the Whiteboy movement in Munster.
1766	First Magdalen Asylum in Dublin, founded by Lady Arabella Denny.
March 1778	Beginning of Volunteer Movement, first company enrolled in Belfast.
April 1783	British Renunciation Act acknowledges exclusive right of the Irish parliament to legislate for Ireland (inaugurates 'Grattan's Parliament).
October 1791	Foundation of the Society of United Irishmen in Belfast. April 1792 and April 1793 Catholic Relief Acts allow Catholics to practise law and give parliamentary franchise.
September 1795	Foundation of the Orange Order.
1798	Rebellion of the United Irishmen which begins in Leinster (May); outbreaks in Ulster (June), French Forces land in Killaha (August) and surrender (September).
August 1800	Act of Union dissolves Irish parliament and declares legislative union.
January 1801	Act of Union takes effect.
July 1803	Robert Emmett's rebellion in Dublin; Emmett is executed in September.
Autumn 1816	Failure of the potato crop leads to a major famine, the first since 1742.
May 1823	The Foundation of the Catholic Association by Daniel O' Connell.
1825	William Thompson and Anna Doyle Wheeler publish *'Appeal of One Half of the Human Race, Women, Against the Pretensions of the Other, Men'*.
July 1828	Daniel O'Connell elected MP for Clare.

April 1829	Catholic Emancipation Act enables Catholics to enter parliament and to hold civil and military offices.
September 1831	State system of National education introduced.
June 1837	Accession of Victoria.
April 1840	Repeal association founded.
June 1841	Census of Ireland: population of island 8,175,124.
1842	'The Nation' newspaper founded by Thomas Davis.
1844	Queen's University founded, with colleges in Belfast, Dublin, Cork and Galway.
September 1845	Arrival of the potato blight is first noted.
June 1846	Repeal of the Corn Laws.
August 1846	Recurrence of the potato blight, large mortality in the winter of 1846–7.
May 1847	Death of Daniel O'Connell.
July 1848	Abortive rising by William Smith O'Brien in Ballingarry, Co. Tipperary. Beginning of the short-lived Young Ireland rebellion.
March 1851	Census of Ireland: population is 6,552,385.
March 1858	James Stephens founds Irish Republican Brotherhood (IRB) in Dublin.
April 1859	Fenian Brotherhood established in America.
1867	Fenian Rising in Ireland. Execution of the Fenian 'Manchester Martyrs' in November.
July 1869	Irish church Act disestablished the Church of Ireland.
May 1870	Issac Butt founds the Home Government association; beginning of the Home Rule Movement.
August 1870	Gladstone's first Land Act.
1871	Isabella Tod founds the Northern Society for Women's Suffrage.
1872	Anna and Thomas Haslam found the Dublin Women's Suffrage Association.
1876	Society for the Preservation of the Irish Language founded.
August 1876	Charles Stuart Parnell elected President of the Home Rule Confederation of Great Britain.

1877	National Library of Ireland established.
1879	Royal University Act allows women into Higher Education.
August 1879	Foundation of the National Land League of Mayo by Michael Davitt.
October 1879	Foundation of Irish National Land League by Davitt and Parnell.
May 1880	Parnell elected chairman of Irish Parliamentary Party (IPP).
October 1880	Foundation of the Ladies' Land League in New York.
August 1881	Gladstone's second Land Act.
May 1882	'Phoenix Park' murders of Lord Frederick Cavendish and Thomas Burke.
November 1884	Foundation of the Gaelic Athletic Association (GAA).
June 1886	Gladstone's Home Rule Bill defeated.
October 1886	Announcement of 'Plan of Campaign' to withhold rents on certain estates.
October 1891	Death of Parnell.
July 1893	Foundation of the Gaelic League (Conradh na Gaeilge).
September 1893	Second Home Rule Bill passed by the House of Commons but defeated in the House of Lords.
1896	Women can be elected as Poor Law Guardians.
August 1899	Irish Local Government Act.
May 1899	First production by Irish Literary Theatre.
1900	Visit of Queen Victoria to Ireland. Foundation of Inghínidhe na hÉireann led by Maud Gonne.
September 1900	Foundation of Cumann na nGaedheal led by Arthur Griffith.
March 1901	Census of Ireland: population 4,458,775.
August 1903	Wyndham Land Act.
1904	Trinity College, Dublin opens all its degrees to women.
December 1904	Opening of the Abbey Theatre.
April 1907	Cumann na nGaedheal and Dungannon Clubs become Sinn Féin League.
December 1908	Foundation of the Irish Transport Workers Union (later ITGWU).

1908	Bean na hÉireann, Ireland's first women's newspaper, published by Inghínidhe na hÉireann.
May 1908	Foundation of the Irishwomen's Franchise League.
1911	Founding of Women Workers Union.
April 1911	Census of Ireland: population 4, 381,951.
April 1912	Third Home Rule Bill passed by House of Commons; twice defeated in the Lords (January and July 1913).
September 1912	Solemn League and Covenant signed in Ulster.
January 1913	Foundation of Ulster Volunteer Force.
August 1913	Beginning of ITGWU strike in Dublin, becomes a general lockout.
November 1913	Formation of Irish Citizen Army and Irish Volunteers.
March 1914	'Curragh mutiny': resignation by 60 cavalry officers in British army at Kildare.
April 1914	Ulster Volunteer Force gunrunning.
April 1914	Foundation of Cumann na mBan.
May 1914	Home Rule Bill passes again in the Commons.
July 1914	Howth gunrunning by Irish Volunteers.
August 1914	Outbreak of World War I.
September 1914	Home Rule Bill suspended; John Redmond calls on Irish Volunteer to support British war effort; movement splits into National (pro-Redmond) and Irish (anti-Redmond) Volunteers.
April 1916	Easter Rising.
May 1916	Execution of rebel leaders.
December 1918	General election called; women over 30 have the vote. Sinn Féin victory in election. Countess Markievicz is first woman elected to the British Parliament but she does not take her seat.
January 1919	First meeting of Dáil Éireann at Mansion House with Eamon De Valera elected president.
1919	Irish Volunteer organisation increasingly known as Irish republican Army (IRA).
1919–21	Irish War of Independence/Anglo-Irish War.
January 1920	First recruits of British ex-soldiers ('Black and Tans') join the Royal; Irish Constabulary.

December 1920	Government of Ireland Act provides for creation of separate parliaments in Dublin and Belfast.
June 1921	George V opens Northern Irish parliament.
July 1921	Truce between IRA and British Army.
December 1921	Anglo-Irish Treaty signed.
January 1922	Treaty approval by Dáil Éireann (64 to 57); Cumann na mBan among the groups which reject the Treaty. Establishment of Irish Free State.
June 1922	Beginning of Irish Civil War between pro-Treaty (Free State) and anti-Treaty (Republican) forces.
April 1923	Cumann na nGaedheal (political party) founded as first new post-independent party.
April 1923	Suspension of Republican campaign.
July 1923	Censorship of Films Act.
September 1923	Irish free State enters League of Nations
1923	W. B. Yeats is awarded the Nobel Prize for Literature.
1925	George Bernard Shaw awarded Nobel Prize for Literature.
November 1925	Findings of Boundary commission leaked.
April 1926	Census of Ireland: population of Irish Free State: 2,971,992; population of Northern Ireland: 1,256,561.
May 1926	Foundation of Fianna Fáil.
1928	Irish Manuscripts Commission founded.
July 1929	Censorship of Publications Act.
1930	Ireland elected to the Council of the league of Nations.
February 1932	Fianna Fáil win general election.
June 1932	Thirty-first International Eucharistic Congress held in Dublin.
September 1933	Foundation of Fine Gael (replaces Cumann na Ngaedheal).
June 1936	IRA declared illegal.
June 1937	De Valer's new constitution (Bunreacht na hÉireann) approved; Éire declared official name of state.
June 1938	Douglas Hyde becomes first president of Ireland.
September 1939	Éire's policy of neutrality announced.

1939–45	'Emergency' years.
April and May 1941	Air raids on Belfast.
1947	Beginning of the Rural Electrification Scheme.
February 1948	Fianna Fáil loses overall majority; replaced by Coalition government under John A. Costello.
December 1948	Republic of Ireland Act under which Éire becomes Republic of Ireland and leaves Commonwealth.
April 1951	Catholic hierarchy condemns 'Mother and Child' Scheme; resignation of Dr. Noël Browne as Minster of Health.
December 1955	Republic of Ireland joins United Nations.
December 1956	IRA begins campaign on Northern Border.
1957	Ban on married women national teachers lifted.
June 1959	De Valera elected president.
December 1961	RTÉ (Radio Telefís Éireann) begins television service.
March 1963	Terence O'Neill becomes prime minister of Northern Ireland.
1965	Succession Act – widows entitled to the family home and one half of the estate where there are no children, otherwise entitled to one third of the estate.
1966	Ulster Volunteer Force (UVF), loyalist paramilitary group founded.
January 1967	Foundation of Northern Ireland Civil Rights Association.
August–October 1968	Civil rights marches in Northern Ireland; clashes between marchers and police in Derry mark beginning of 'the Troubles'.
1969	Samuel Beckett awarded Nobel Prize for Literature.
January 1970	IRA Splits into Official IRA and Provisional IRA.
1970	First Commission on the Status of Women set up; Women's Liberation Movement founded.
August 1970	Foundation of the Social democratic and Labour Party (SDLP) in Northern Ireland.
August 1971	Internment introduced in Northern Ireland.
October 1971	Ian Paisley founds Democratic Unionist Party (DUP).

30 January 1972	'Bloody Sunday': 14 civilians killed and 12 wounded in Derry by British army
March 1972	Stormont parliament in Belfast suspended; direct rule from London introduced.
21 July 1972	'Bloody Friday': 22 bombs set off in Belfast by IRA; nine people killed and about 130 wounded.
January 1973	Republic of Ireland joins European Economic Community (EEC).
1973	Marriage Bar lifted; married women in Public service no longer lose their jobs.
May 1974	Ulster Worker's Council declares general strike.
1974	Anti-discrimination Pay Act.
December 1975	Suspension of internment without trial in Northern Ireland.
1977	Employment Equality Act passed; Employment Equality Agency is set up.
September 1979	Pope John Paul II visits Ireland.
October–December 1980	Hunger strikes in Maze and Armagh jails.
May–August 1981	Ten IRA and Irish National Liberation Army (INLA) hunger-strikers die, including Bobby Sands (elected MP, April 1980).
1982	First Minister of State for Women's Affairs.
September 1983	Amendment to constitution passed by referendum, seeking to prevent any possible legalisation of abortion.
May 1884	Report of New Ireland Forum is published.
November 1985	Anglo-Irish Agreement signed by Garret Fitzgerald and Margaret Thatcher.
June 1986	Referendum upholds constitutional ban on divorce.
May 1987	Referendum approves Single European Act.
November 1990	Mary Robinson elected president of Ireland.
November 1992	Referendum held on three abortion related issues; the right to travel and the right to information supported.
December 1993	Downing Street Declaration signed by Albert Reynolds and John Major.
August and October 1994	IRA and Loyalist paramilitaries declare ceasefires (later suspended and restored).

October 1995	Seamus Heaney awarded Nobel Prize for Literature.
November 1995	Referendum allowing divorce is carried.
October 1997	Mary McAleese is elected president of Ireland.
April 1998	Good Friday agreement is negotiated and endorsed in referendums in Republic of Ireland and Northern Ireland (May).
December 1999	Northern Irish Assembly meets.
2001	Census of population of Northern Ireland: 1,685,267.
June 2001	Irish voters reject the Treaty of Nice designed to pave the way for 12 new members of the EU.
November 2001	The Police Service of Northern Ireland (PSNI) established, replacing the RUC (Royal Ulster Constabulary).
March 2002	Abortion referendum seeking a total ban on abortion in the Republic is defeated.
April 2002	Census of population of Republic of Ireland: 3,917,203.
May 2002	Fianna Fáil are returned to power in a general election.
July 2002	IRA issues an apology for the hundreds of civilian deaths over the last 30 years.
October 2002	Second referendum on the Treaty of Nice is successful.
March 2004	The Republic of Ireland bans smoking in all enclosed workplaces, which included restaurants, pubs and bars.
June 2004	Irish voters overwhelmingly approve a constitutional amendment to tighten the citizenship laws.
November 2004	Mary McAleese is inaugurated for a second seven-year term as President of Ireland.
December 2004	In Northern Ireland, armed robbers steal over £22 million from the headquarters of the Northern Bank. Unionists and the PSNI hold the IRA responsible, stalling the peace process.
October 2005	Irish author John Banville wins the prestigious Booker Prize for fiction with his 14th novel, *The Sea*.

July 2006   A government report says Ireland's population
                          has surged this year to a modern high of more
                          than 4.2 million people, largely because of
                          immigrants from the newest EU nations.

This chronology is based, in part, on chronologies in *The Cambridge
History of Irish Literature* (Cambridge, Cambridge University Press, 2006),
Margaret Kelleher and Philip O'Leary (eds), and in *A New History of
Ireland*, vol. VIII: *A Chronology of Irish History to 1976* (Oxford, Oxford
University Press, 1983), T. W. Moody, F. X. Martin and F. J. Byrne (eds).

contributors

Catherine Cox is a Lecturer in the School of History and Archives, University College Dublin (UCD), a Director of the Centre for the History of Medicine in Ireland and Director of Research, School of History and Archives. Her research interests include the history of mental illness and the spread of 'medical knowledge' in eighteenth- and nineteenth-century society and she has published widely in these areas. Her book *Managing Insanity in Nineteenth-Century Ireland* (2008) is forthcoming from Manchester University Press.

Maura Cronin is a Senior Lecturer, History Department and Co-ordinator of the Oral History Centre, Mary Immaculate College, Limerick. Author of *Country, Class or Craft: The Politicisation of the Skilled Artisan in Nineteenth-Century Cork* (Cork University Press 1994) and numerous articles on nineteenth- and twentieth-century social history.

Nancy J. Curtin is Professor of History and Director of the Institute of Irish Studies at Fordham University in New York City. She is the author of *The United Irishmen: Popular Politics in Belfast and Dublin 1791–98* (Oxford, 1994) and co-author with Marilyn Cohen of *Reclaiming Gender: Transgressive Identities in Modern Ireland* (New York, 1999) as well as many book chapters and articles on political culture. A former president of the American Conference for Irish Studies, she has also served from 1996 to 2001 as co-editor of *Éire-Ireland: An Interdisciplinary Journal of Irish Studies*.

Margaret Kelleher is Director of An Foras Feasa: The Institute for Research in Irish Historical and Cultural Traditions, NUI Maynooth. She is the author of *The Feminization of Famine* (Cork UP and Duke UP, 2007) and co-editor, with Philip O'Leary, of *The Cambridge History of Irish Literature* (Cambridge UP, 2006). She has published extensively in the area of famine studies, Irish literary history, and women's writings.

Vera Kreilkamp is Professor of English at Pine Manor College, Visiting Professor with the Irish Studies Program at Boston College and

Co-editor (for literature and the arts) of *Éire-Ireland: an Interdisciplinary Journal of Irish Studies*. Her research and publishing are in the areas of nineteenth- and twentieth-century Irish fiction, as well as Ireland's visual arts.

Leeann Lane is a graduate of University College Cork (UCC) and Boston College. She is co-ordinator of Irish Studies at Mater Dei Institute of Education Dublin City University (DCU). She is completing a biography of Rosamond Jacob and working on the children's novelist Patricia Lynch.

Mary McAuliffe is a graduate of the School of History, Trinity College Dublin (TCD). She lectures on Women in Irish history on the Women's Studies Programme, School of Social Justice, UCD. Her research interests include medieval Irish women and power, female representations and identities in Irish History, feminist and gender historiography and Irish feminist histories. She is secretary of the Women's History Association of Ireland (WHAI).

Patrick Maume has lectured on politics (Queens University Belfast (QUB) 1995–2001) and modern Irish history (UCD 1994–5, QUB 2001–3). He is currently a researcher on the Royal Irish Academy's Dictionary of Irish Biography. His publications include biographies of *Daniel Corkery* (1993) and *D. P. Moran* (1995), and he has edited ten texts in the UCD Press Classics of Irish History reprint series. His particular interests include print culture and media history, nationalism and unionism, the Home Rule era and the history of the Irish diaspora.

William Murphy is a lecturer in Irish Studies at Mater Dei Institute of Education, Dublin City University. His research interests include the Irish revolution, prison history, sports history and the Irish diaspora.

Katherine O'Donnell is a Senior Lecturer, Women's Studies, School of Social Justice in University College Dublin. She has published widely on Irish literature and the history of sexuality.

Michelle O'Riordan is an Assistant Professor in the School of Celtic Studies, Dublin Institute for Advanced Studies. She is author of *Irish Bardic Poetry and Rhetorical Reality* (Cork University Press, 2007); *The Gaelic Mind and the Collapse of the Gaelic World* (Cork University Press, 1990); and co-editor of *Celtica 22* (1991), and *Celtica 23* (1999).

Niamh Puirséil lectures in the School of History and Archives, UCD. Her research focuses on politics and society in independent Ireland and Irish labour and radical movements. Her publications include *The Irish Labour Party, 1922–73* (UCD Press, 2007) and *Essays in Irish Labour History, A Festscrift for Elizabeth and John W. Boyle* (Irish Academic Press, 2008) (jointly edited with Francis Devine and Fintan Lane). She is joint editor of *Saothar*, the journal of the Irish Labour History Society.

index